"This is a wonderful introduction to the history of Christianity. It pays the most attention to the rise and spread of the Christian faith in the ancient near east and the medieval and modern west. But it also tells the story of this faith's rapid shift to the global south and far east during the past 100 years – and does so with the kind of clear and compelling English prose that will be recognized as vintage McGrath by experts in the field. I strongly recommend it, and look forward to using it frequently with students and other readers."

—*Douglas A. Sweeney, Trinity Evangelical Divinity School*

"As Christianity expands around the globe, this intelligent introduction introduces key figures, ideas, and developments in Christian history, balancing illuminating generalizations with engaging detailed examples. The mutual interactions of churches and cultures are highlighted, and theological developments are clearly articulated. McGrath succeeds in whetting the reader's appetite for further study."

—*Anne T. Thayer, Lancaster Theological Seminary*

"It is difficult to write a comprehensive text on Christian history in this day and age. There are deeply rutted roads in scholarship that lead the conventional historian to focus on the twilight of Christianity in the west and the inevitability of secularization. These developments, while all too true, distort both the present vitality of Christian faith and its future. McGrath avoids these pitfalls. While firmly rooted in the essentials of the Christian story, he also has a clear sense of the new paths Christian faith is taking in global evangelical outreach."

—*Walter Sundberg, Luther Seminary*

Also by Alister E. McGrath from Wiley-Blackwell

Historical Theology: An Introduction to the History of Christian Thought, Second Edition (2012)
Reformation Thought: An Introduction, Fourth Edition (2012)
Theology: The Basic Readings, Second Edition (edited, 2012)
Theology: The Basics, Third Edition (2012)
Luther's Theology of the Cross: Martin Luther's Theological Breakthrough, Second Edition (2011)
Darwinism and the Divine: Evolutionary Thought and Natural Theology (2011)
The Christian Theology Reader, Fourth Edition (edited, 2011)
Christian Theology: An Introduction, Fifth Edition (2011)
Science and Religion: A New Introduction, Second Edition (2009)
The Open Secret: A New Vision for Natural Theology (2008)
The Order of Things: Explorations in Scientific Theology (2006)
Christianity: An Introduction, Second Edition (2006)
Dawkins' God: Genes, Memes, and the Meaning of Life (2004)
The Intellectual Origins of the European Reformation, Second Edition (2003)
Christian Literature: An Anthology (edited, 2003)*
A Brief History of Heaven (2003)
The Blackwell Companion to Protestantism (edited with Darren C. Marks, 2003)
The Future of Christianity (2002)
Reformation Thought: An Introduction, Third Edition (2000)
Christian Spirituality: An Introduction (1999)
Historical Theology: An Introduction (1998)
The Foundations of Dialogue in Science and Religion (1998)
The Blackwell Encyclopedia of Modern Christian Thought (edited, 1995)
A Life of John Calvin (1990)

* out of print

CHRISTIAN HISTORY

AN INTRODUCTION

ALISTER E. MCGRATH

A John Wiley & Sons, Ltd., Publication

This edition first published 2013
© 2013 John Wiley & Sons, Ltd

Wiley-Blackwell is an imprint of John Wiley & Sons, formed by the merger of Wiley's global
Scientific, Technical and Medical business with Blackwell Publishing.

Registered Office
John Wiley & Sons Ltd, The Atrium, Southern Gate, Chichester, West Sussex, PO19 8SQ, UK

Editorial Offices
350 Main Street, Malden, MA 02148-5020, USA
9600 Garsington Road, Oxford, OX4 2DQ, UK
The Atrium, Southern Gate, Chichester, West Sussex, PO19 8SQ, UK

For details of our global editorial offices, for customer services, and for information about how to
apply for permission to reuse the copyright material in this book please see our website at
www.wiley.com/wiley-blackwell.

The right of Alister E. McGrath to be identified as the author of this work has been asserted in
accordance with the UK Copyright, Designs and Patents Act 1988.

Library of Congress Cataloging-in-Publication Data is available

HB: 9781118337790
PB: 9781118337806

A catalogue record for this book is available from the British Library.

Cover image: Cathedral of Brasilia at night, architect Oscar Niemeyer. © imagebroker.net /
SuperStock
Cover design by Nicki Averill

Set in 10/13 pt Minion by Toppan Best-set Premedia Limited
Printed in Singapore by Ho Printing Singapore Pte Ltd

1   2013

Brief Contents

Full Contents

Maps and Illustrations

Maps

Illustrations

How to Use This Book

This book is designed to be an accessible, interesting, and reliable introduction to two thousand years of Christian history. It has been written on the assumption that you know little about the history of Christianity, and aims to make studying it as easy as possible. Every technical term and key theological debate is introduced and explained. You should be able to use this book on your own, without needing any help, although it will work best when used as part of a taught course.

It's not easy to provide a survey of two thousand years of Christian history in such a short book. A lot of thought has been given about how to pack as much useful information as possible into so small a space, and break it down into manageable sections. You will get the most out of this book by bearing five key points in mind:

1. This book is about Christian history, not just church history.
2. The material has been broken down into historical periods which link up with many college and university courses.
3. The principle of "selective attention" has been used to manage the amount of historical material presented.
4. The text is grounded in the best recent scholarly literature, which often corrects older literature on points of detail, and occasionally forces us to see things in quite different ways.
5. This book is deliberately designed as an introduction, and does not aim to be comprehensive or detailed.

Each of these points needs a little more explanation.

First, this book is about *Christian* history. It's not another history of the *church*, which tend to be preoccupied with the institutional history of denominations. This book is about the development of Christianity, and its impact on culture. We'll make sure that we cover all the key themes in church history, but will go beyond these, considering such matters as the interaction of Christianity with the arts, literature, and science. We will consider both the importance of the Second Vatican Council for the shaping of Catholicism in the late twentieth century, and the importance of C. S. Lewis for more personal approaches to Christianity in the same period.

Second, we need to remember that all division of history into "ages" or "eras" is a little arbitrary. The great Cambridge historian George Macauley Trevelyan (1876–1962) made this point well two generations ago.

> Unlike dates, periods are not facts. They are retrospective conceptions that we form about past events, useful to focus discussion, but very often leading historical thought astray.

Trevelyan's point is well taken. Furthermore, there is a healthy debate over the points of detail of any attempt to divide history into periods. For example, just when did the Middle Ages begin? Or end? Does it really matter?

Nevertheless, we still need to try and organize the material into workable blocks or sections, rather than rambling aimlessly through the centuries. In practice, there is widespread agreement over the broad division of the history of Christianity for teaching purposes. If you're using this book alongside a taught course, you ought to be able to work out how to get the most from it very easily. This work divides the history of Christianity into five broad sections, corresponding to courses taught at many colleges, seminaries, and universities.

1. The period of the early church, sometimes still referred to as the "patristic period," during which the Christian faith began to gain a significant following throughout the Mediterranean world.
2. The "Middle Ages," a period of Christian history in western Europe which witnessed significant cultural and intellectual development. The movement generally known as the "Renaissance" is included in this period.
3. The age of Reformation in western Europe, which witnessed the birth of Protestantism, and the consolidation of Catholicism, eventually leading to the Wars of Religion.
4. The Modern Age. This chapter looks at the development of Christianity in the eighteenth and nineteenth centuries. Although the scope of our discussion is global, we focus particularly on developments in western Europe and North America, culminating in the outbreak of the Great War of 1914–18.
5. The Twentieth Century. This final chapter looks at the dramatic changes in the shape of global Christianity in the century following the end of the Great War, including discussion of important developments in Africa, South America, and Asia.

Third, you need to appreciate that this work is based on the principle of *selective attention*. It recognizes that it is impossible to do justice to everything that happened in two thousand years of history. It sets out to try and see beyond a mass of historical detail, and identify broader historical patterns. As a result, this work tries to help you track some of the significant changes in Christian history, illustrating these wherever possible with interesting examples or important episodes.

The work thus aims to be *representative* in its coverage, rather than *comprehensive*, allowing you to build on the basic structure it provides. Each of its 160 sections is roughly the same length (about 1000 words), designed to be read in ten minutes, and assimilated in twenty.

The object is to help you work out what is really going on, rather than bombarding you with facts. This means that you will get to hear about all the landmarks of Christian history – the major figures and events that everyone (rightly) talks about. And while we'll explore a few interesting byways off the main tourist routes, the main object of this textbook is to hit the high points and make sure you've seen what everyone expects you to have seen. Once you've got a good idea of what's on the map, you can explore things further in your own time.

Fourth, this book is based on the best recent literature, most of it published within the last two decades. This research often forces correction of material found in older textbooks – sometimes over points of detail, and sometimes over larger issues. Some of the global assertions that were common in older works – such as the "decline of late medieval religion" – have been discarded or radically modified by recent research. This book brings you up to speed, aiming to give you a reliable overview of the present state of scholarship.

Fifth, and finally: this book is an *introduction*. It's a sketch map of a fascinating landscape. It's like a tourist guide to a strange country or a new city. It can't tell you everything about the place – but it will help you find your way around, make sense of what you see and hear, and (hopefully) make you want to explore more on your own. There are lots of excellent more advanced studies that will be well within your reach, once you've worked your way through this textbook.

You will get the most out of this book by reading it right the way through in the order in which it is written. Yet each chapter has been designed to stand on its own. This means that you will be able to start your reading anywhere. Each chapter opens by setting the context for the material it contains. It gives you the background material you need to make sense of what follows. Sometimes, you'll need to go back to an earlier chapter, to refresh your memory over exactly who someone like Augustine of Hippo was (as you'll discover, he's an early church writer who is important for the religious history of the Middle Ages and the Reformation period). And we'll explain terms that you need to know and use – like "patristic."

That's all you need to know to get the most out of this book. We're ready to start.

Alister E. McGrath
King's College London
July 2012

Source of Quotation

p. xvi: G. M. Trevelyan, *English Social History: A Survey of Six Centuries from Chaucer to Queen Victoria*. London: Longman, 1944, 92.

For Further Reading

The following are recommended as excellent overall accounts of the development of Christian history. Those with marked with one asterisk (*) are especially recommended as interesting and up-to-date accounts of Christian history. Those marked with two asterisks (**) focus particularly on the development of Christian thought.

Chidester, David. *Christianity: A Global History*. San Francisco: HarperSanFrancisco, 2000.

Ferguson, Everett. *Church History*. Grand Rapids, MI: Zondervan, 2005.

*González, Justo L. *The Story of Christianity*. 2 vols. San Francisco: HarperOne, 2010.

Hastings, Adrian. *A World History of Christianity*. Grand Rapids, MI: Eerdmans, 1999.

Hill, Jonathan. *Handbook to the History of Christianity*. Oxford: Lion Hudson, 2009.

*MacCulloch, Diarmaid. *Christianity: The First Three Thousand Years*. New York: Viking, 2010.

**McGrath, Alister E. *Christian Theology: An Introduction*. Oxford: Wiley-Blackwell, 2011.

McManners, John, ed. *The Oxford History of Christianity*. Oxford: Oxford University Press, 2002.

Noll, Mark A. *Turning Points: Decisive Moments in the History of Christianity*. Grand Rapids, MI: Baker Books, 2000.

Nystrom, Bradley P., and David P. Nystrom. *The History of Christianity: An Introduction*. Boston: McGraw-Hill, 2004.

**Pelikan, Jaroslav. *The Christian Tradition: A History of the Development of Doctrine*. 5 vols. Chicago: University of Chicago Press, 1989.

Shelley, Bruce L. *Church History in Plain Language*. Dallas, TX: Thomas Nelson, 2008.

Vidmar, John. *The Catholic Church through the Ages: A History*. New York: Paulist Press, 2005.

1

The Early Church, 100–500

At some point around the year 60, the Roman authorities began to realize there was some kind of new secret society in the heart of their city, which was rapidly gaining recruits. The reports that filtered back spoke of a sect based on some mysterious and dark figure called "Chrestus" or "Christus," whose origins lay in one of the more obscure and backward parts of the Roman Empire. But who was he? And what was this new religion all about? Was it something they should be worried about, or could they safely ignore it?

It soon became clear that this new religious movement might have the potential to cause real trouble. The great fire which swept through Rome during the reign of the Emperor Nero in 64 was conveniently blamed on this new religious group. Nobody liked them much, and they were an obvious scapegoat for the failings of the Roman authorities to deal with the fire and its aftermath. The Roman historian Tacitus (56–117) gave a full account of this event just over fifty years later. He identified this new religious group as "the Christians," a group who took their name from someone called "Christus," who had been executed by Pontius Pilate back in the reign of Tiberius. This "pernicious superstition" had found its way to Rome, where it was gaining a large following.

As a result, Nero pinned the guilt (and inflicted highly refined tortures) on a class hated for their abominations, called "Christians" by the people. Christus, from whom they derived their name, suffered the extreme penalty during the reign of Tiberius at the hands of one of our procurators, Pontius Pilatus. Yet this pernicious superstition, though checked for the moment, broke out again not only in Judaea, the primary source of the evil, but even in Rome, where everything that is repulsive and shameful from every part of the world converges and becomes popular. Accordingly, all who pleaded guilty were arrested. Their information led to the conviction of an immense multitude, not so much for the crime of setting the city on fire, as for hating humanity.

Christian History: An Introduction, First Edition. Alister E. McGrath.
© 2013 John Wiley & Sons, Ltd. Published 2013 by John Wiley & Sons, Ltd.

Yet, muddled and confused though the official Roman accounts of this movement may be, they were clear that they centered on the shadowy figure of "Christus." It was not regarded as being of any permanent significance, being seen as little more than a passing minor irritation. At worst, it posed a threat to the cult of emperor worship. Yet less than three hundred years later, this new religious movement had become the official religion of the Roman Empire. So how did this happen? In this chapter, we shall tell the story of the emergence of this new religion during its first five hundred years, and track its growth from a fringe movement on the margins of imperial society to the dominant religion of the Roman Empire.

1.1.   Setting the Context: The Origins of Christianity

Christianity began as a reform movement within the context of Judaism (1.1.7), which gradually clarified its identity as it grew, and began to take definite shape in the world of the first-century Roman Empire. There are no historical grounds for believing that the term "Christian" originated from Jesus of Nazareth himself. Early Christians tended to refer to each other as "disciples" or "saints," as the letters of the New Testament make clear. Yet others used alternative names to refer to this new movement. The New Testament suggests that the term "Christians" (Greek: *Christianoi*) was first used by outsiders to refer to the followers of Jesus of Nazareth. "It was in Antioch that the disciples were first called 'Christians'" (Acts 17:26). It was a term imposed upon them, not chosen by them. Yet it seems to have caught on.

However, we must be careful not to assume that the use of the single term "Christian" implies that this new religious movement was uniform and well-organized. As we shall see, the early history of Christianity suggests that it was quite diverse, without well-defined authority structures or carefully formulated sets of beliefs (1.1.4). These began to crystallize during the first few centuries of Christian history. This first chapter sets out to explain how this process took place, and explore some of its results. It focuses on the highly significant period between the death of the last apostle (c. 100) and the Council of Chalcedon (451).

The first major era of Christian history (c. 100–451), during which Christianity began to expand rapidly throughout the Mediterranean world and beyond, is sometimes called the "patristic period." The unusual term "patristic" comes from the Greek word *patēr* ("father"), referring to the "fathers of the church," such as Athanasius of Alexandria or Augustine of Hippo.

It is difficult to make sense of the historical development of Christianity without a good grasp of this formative period, particularly its great theological debates. Yet it is also impossible to understand the development of Christianity without knowing something about its historical origins. We shall therefore begin our discussion of early Christianity by reflecting on its emergence within Judaism, and its rapid transformation into a faith which refused to recognize ethnic or social boundaries.

1.1.1.   The Crucible: The History of Israel

From its outset, Christianity saw itself as continuous with Judaism. Christians were clear that the God that they followed and worshipped was the same God worshipped by the

Israelite patriarchs Abraham, Isaac, and Jacob. The New Testament sees the great hope of the coming of a "messiah" to the people of Israel as having been fulfilled in Jesus of Nazareth (1.1.3). Indeed, the New Testament use of the title "Christ" is an explicit reference to this belief. (The Hebrew term "Messiah" literally means "the anointed One," an idea translated by the Greek term *Christos*.) Although most western readers assume that "Jesus Christ" is a name similar to "John Smith," it is really a statement of identity: "Jesus who is the Christ."

The continuity between Judaism and Christianity is obvious at many points. Judaism placed particular emphasis on the Law (Hebrew: *Torah*), through which the will of God was made known in the form of commands, and the Prophets, who made known the will of God in certain definite historical situations. The New Testament gospels report that Jesus of Nazareth emphasized that he had "not come to abolish the Law or the Prophets, but to fulfil them" (Matthew 5:17). The same point is made by Paul in his New Testament letters. Jesus is "the goal of the Law" (Romans 10:4, using the Greek word *telos*, which means "end" or "objective"). Paul also stresses the continuity between the faith of Abraham and that of Christians (Romans 4:1–25). The Letter to the Hebrews points out both the continuity of the relationship between Moses and Jesus (Hebrews 3:1–6), and between Christians and the great figures of faith of ancient Israel (Hebrews 11:1–12:2).

Throughout the New Testament, the same theme recurs: Christianity is continuous with Judaism, and brings to completion what Judaism was pointing towards. This has several major consequences, of which the following are the most important. First, both Christians and Jews regard more or less the same collection of writings – known by Jews as "Law, Prophets, and Writings" and by Christians as "the Old Testament" – as having religious authority. Although there have always been more radical thinkers within Christianity – such as the second-century writer Marcion of Sinope (1.2.3) – who argued for the removal of any historical or theological link with Judaism, the majority opinion has always been that it is important to affirm and value the link between the Christian church and Israel. A body of writings which Jews regard as complete in itself is seen by Christians as pointing forward to something which will bring it to completion. Although Christians and Jews both regard the same set of texts as important, they use different names to refer to them, and interpret them in different ways.

Second, New Testament writers often laid emphasis on the manner in which Old Testament prophecies were understood to be fulfilled or realized in the life and death of Jesus Christ. By doing this, they drew attention to two important beliefs – that Christianity is continuous with Judaism, and that Christianity brings Judaism to its true fulfillment. This is particularly important for some early Christian writings – such as Paul's letters and the gospel of Matthew – which often seem to have a particular concern to explore the importance of Christianity for Jews. For example, at twelve points the gospel of Matthew notes how events in the life of Jesus can be seen as fulfilling Old Testament prophecy.

Yet the continuity between Christianity and Judaism also helps us understand some of the conflicts in early Christian history, especially in the region of Palestine. The New Testament suggests that at least some Christians initially continued to worship in Jewish synagogues, before controversy made this problematic. The letters of Paul help us understand at least some of those controversies. Two questions were of particular importance, and were keenly debated in the first century.

First, should Christian converts be required to be circumcised? Those who emphasized the continuity between Christianity and Judaism believed they should be. Yet the view which ultimately prevailed was that Christians were no longer subject to the cultic laws of Judaism – such as the requirement to be circumcised, or observe strict food laws.

Second, were non-Jewish converts to Christianity to be treated as Jews? (The Jewish term "Gentile," meaning "someone who is not a Jew," was widely used in this discussion, and is often encountered in the New Testament references to this issue.) Again, those who emphasized the continuity between Judaism and Christianity argued that Gentile believers should be treated as Jews. For this reason, they demanded the circumcision of male Gentile converts. Yet the majority view was quite different: to be a Christian was not about reinforcing a Jewish ethnic or cultural identity, but about entering a new way of living and thinking that was open to everyone. By the late first century, Christians largely saw themselves as a new religious movement, originating within Judaism, but not limited by its cultic and ethnic traditions. We shall consider this point in more detail later (1.1.7).

Yet despite Christianity having its origins within Judaism, which was viewed as a "legal religion" (Latin: *religio licita*) by the Roman authorities, early Christian communities were not considered to be entitled to imperial legal protection. These communities thus lived under the shadow of possible persecution, forcing them to maintain a low public profile. They had no access to power or social influence, and were often the object of oppression by the secular authorities.

One of the factors that helped crystallize a growing sense of religious identity within the churches was the rapid growth of Christianity outside Palestine, as it gained a growing following within the Greek-speaking world of the eastern Mediterranean. We shall explore this further in the following section.

1.1.2.   A Wider Context: The Pagan Quest for Wisdom

Although its historical origins lay within Palestine, Christianity rapidly gained a following in the Greek-speaking world, especially within the cities of the Roman Empire. The missionary journeys of Paul of Tarsus, described in the New Testament, are of importance here. Paul was a Jewish religious leader who converted to Christianity, changing his name from "Saul" to "Paul." His missionary expeditions took him to many cities and regions throughout the northeastern Mediterranean area – including Europe. As Christianity began to gain a foothold on the European mainland, the question of how it was to be preached in a non-Jewish context began to become of increasing importance.

Early Christian preaching to Jewish audiences, especially in Palestine, tended to focus on demonstrating that Jesus of Nazareth represented the fulfillment of the hopes of Israel. Peter's sermon to Jews in Jerusalem (Acts 2) follows this pattern. Peter here argues that Jesus represents the culmination of Israel's destiny. God has declared him to be both "Lord and Christ" – highly significant terms, which Peter's Jewish audience would have understood and appreciated. But what were Christians to do when preaching to Greek audiences, who knew nothing of the Old Testament, and had no connection with the history of Israel?

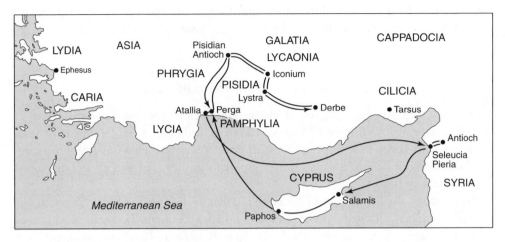

Map 1.1   Paul's first missionary journey

An approach that came to be particularly significant in the early Christian world can be found in Paul's sermon, preached at the Areopagus in the Greek city of Athens at an unknown date, possibly around 55. Paul here makes no reference to the ideas and hopes of Judaism. Instead, he presents Jesus of Nazareth as someone who revealed a god who the Athenians knew about, but had yet to encounter definitively. "What therefore you worship as unknown, this I proclaim to you" (Acts 17:23). Paul declared that the god who was made known through Jesus of Nazareth was the same god who had created the world and humanity – the god in whom, as the Athenian poet Aratus declared, "we live and move and have our being" (Acts 17:28).

Where early Christian preaching to Jewish audiences presented Jesus as the fulfillment of the hopes of Israel, Paul presented the Christian faith as the fulfillment of the deepest longings of the human heart and the most profound intuitions of human reason. This was easily adapted to make use of some of the core themes of classic Greek philosophy, such as the idea of the "word" (Greek: *logos*) – the fundamental rational principle of the universe, according to popular Platonic philosophy of the first century (1.3.3). This theme is developed in the opening chapter of the gospel of John, which presents Jesus of Nazareth as the "word" by which the universe was originally created, and which entered into the world to illuminate and redeem it. "And the Word became flesh and lived among us, and we have seen his glory" (John 1:14).

This was not necessarily seen as displacing Christianity's historical and theological roots in Judaism. Rather, it was seen as a way of setting out the universal appeal of the Christian faith, which was held to transcend all ethnic, racial, and cultural barriers. The universal validity of the Christian gospel was held to imply that it could be proclaimed in ways that would resonate with every human culture. As we shall see, this approach to the appeal of Christianity would be of immense significance throughout its history, especially in missionary contexts.

Yet we have already assumed too much knowledge about the identity and significance of Jesus of Nazareth. We need to consider this central figure of the Christian faith in more detail.

1.1.3. The Turning Point: Jesus of Nazareth

Christianity is an historical religion, which came into being in response to a specific set of events – above all, the history of Jesus of Nazareth. Although a full treatment of Jesus of Nazareth lies beyond the scope of this short work, it is nevertheless important to appreciate something of its fundamental themes, especially as they are taken up and developed within Christian history.

Traditionally, the life of Jesus of Nazareth is dated to the opening of the Christian era, with his death being located at some point around 30–3. Yet virtually nothing is known of Jesus of Nazareth from sources outside the New Testament. The New Testament itself provides two groups of quite distinct sources of information about Jesus: the four gospels, and the letters. Although the parallels are not exact, there are clear similarities between the gospels and the classical "lives" written by leading Roman historians of the age – such as Suetonius's *Lives of the Caesars*, or Lucian's *Life of Demorax*.

The gospels mingle historical recollection with theological reflection, reflecting both on the identity and the significance of Jesus of Nazareth. The four gospels have their own distinct identities and concerns. For example, the gospel of Matthew seems especially concerned with establishing the significance of Jesus for a Jewish readership, where the gospel of Luke seems more concerned with explaining his importance to a Greek-speaking community. Establishing the identity of Jesus is just as important as recording what he said and did. The gospel writers can be thought of as trying to locate Jesus of Nazareth on a map, so that his relationship with humanity, history, and God can be understood and appreciated. This leads them to focus on three particular themes.

1. What Jesus taught, particularly the celebrated "parables of the Kingdom." The teaching of Jesus was seen as important in helping believers to live out an authentic Christian life, which was a central theme of Christian discipleship – most notably, in relation to cultivating attitudes of humility towards others and obedience towards God.
2. What Jesus did – especially his ministry of healing, which was seen as important in establishing his identity, but also in shaping the values of the Christian community itself. For example, most medieval monasteries established hospitals, as a means of continuing Christ's ministry in this respect.
3. What was said about Jesus by those who witnessed his teaching and actions. The gospel of Luke, for example, records Simeon's declaration that the infant Jesus was the "consolation of Israel," as well as the Roman centurion's assertion that Jesus was innocent of the charges brought against him. These can be seen as constituting public recognition of the identity of Jesus.

The letters of the New Testament – sometimes still referred to as "epistles" (Greek: *epistolē*, "a letter") – are addressed to individuals and churches, and often focus on issues of conduct and belief. These letters are important in helping us make sense of the emerging under-standings of the significance of Jesus of Nazareth within the Christian community. The example of Jesus is regularly invoked to emphasize the importance of imitating his attitudes – for example, treating others better than yourself (Philippians 2). Although the letters make virtually no direct reference to the teachings of Jesus, certain patterns of behavior are clearly regarded as being grounded in those teachings – such as humility, or a willingness to accept suffering.

The letters also emphasize the importance of certain patterns of behavior – such as repeating the actions of the Last Supper, using bread and wine as a way of recalling and celebrating the death and resurrection of Christ. The sacraments of both baptism and the eucharist are clearly anticipated in the New Testament, and are traced back to the ministry of Jesus himself.

Yet perhaps more importantly, the letters also reveal the understandings of the identity and significance of Jesus of Nazareth which were becoming characteristic of Christian communities. The most important of these themes are:

1. Jesus of Nazareth is understood to be the means by which the invisible God can be known and seen. Jesus is the "image of the invisible God" (Greek: *eikōn;* Colossians 1:15), or the "exact representation" (Greek: *charaktēr*) of God (Hebrews 1:3).
2. Jesus is the one who makes salvation possible, and whose life reflects the themes char-acteristic of redeemed human existence. The use of the term "savior" (Greek: *sōtēr*) is highly significant in this respect.
3. The core Christian belief in the resurrection of Jesus of Nazareth is seen as a vindication of his innocence, a confirmation of his divine identity, and the grounds of hope for believers. Through faith, believers are understood to be united with Christ, sharing in his sufferings at present, while also sharing in the hope of his resurrection.

Each of these themes would be further developed as the Christian community reflected on their significance, and relevance for the life and thought of believers. The letters of Paul were of particular importance in setting out both the beliefs of Christianity and shaping its early social and cultural attitudes. We shall consider how early Christian thinkers devel-oped these ideas later in this chapter.

1.1.4.   The Early Spread of Christianity

The historical evidence suggests that Christianity spread very rapidly during the first and early second centuries. This naturally raises two questions. First, what were the mechanisms by which the movement spread? And second, what was it about the movement that proved attractive to people at the time? Unlike early Islam, Christianity was not spread by force; if anything, force was used against it by the imperial authorities. Since Christianity was not recognized as a legal religious movement until the fourth century, converts clearly believed there was something about the new religion that made it worth risking penalization or persecution. But what?

Figure 1.1   Rome was seen as especially important by early Christians, as it was believed that both the apostles Peter and Paul were martyred there. *The Martyrdom of St. Peter*, by P. Brancacci and F. Lippi. Church of St. Mary of Carmine, Florence. Photo: akg-images/De Agostini Picture Library

Earlier historians suggested that one of the primary mechanisms for the spread of Christianity was public preaching, noting the importance of Paul's missionary journeys, described in the Acts of the Apostles. Yet there are relatively few historical accounts of the public preaching of the Christian faith, probably reflecting the fact that these would have been suppressed by the imperial authorities. Paul's speech at Athens is a rare example of such public preaching; his preferred method was preaching in synagogues to Jewish audiences.

More recently, historians have noted the importance of networks in spreading the Christian faith. These loose organizations, often based around professions or specific localities, avoided meeting in public. Interested outsiders would be invited along to what were essentially secret meetings, often by Christians whose social or professional connections brought them into contact with such people. Early Christian gatherings or assemblies (Greek: *ekklēsia*) usually took place in private households, creating a strong sense of belonging and identity, given further weight by "sacred oaths" (Latin: *sacramenta*) of loyalty.

There is considerable evidence for the importance of commerce and trade in spreading Christianity, with itinerant preachers and teachers attending house churches in cities in which they had business. At this early stage, there was no centralized religious authority, no standard model of community organization at the local level, and no dedicated church buildings or cathedrals. It was only after the conversion of the emperor Constantine that bishops from throughout the Christian movement would be able to meet together, and begin to resolve debates over Christian beliefs and provide official statements of faith.

So what was the appeal of Christianity? Why did so many convert to Christianity, despite the dangers this entailed? It is clear that this appeal was multi-layered, and not easy to characterize. At the social level, Christianity offered a new sense of identity and status. The growing realization of the importance of networks in spreading Christianity throughout the Roman Empire clearly points to the importance of a sense of belonging – of achieving significance and meaning. Roman society was strongly hierarchical; Christianity, in contrast, minimized the importance of socially constructed values. The Pauline letters, for example, declare that "in Christ there is neither Jew nor Greek, neither male nor female, neither slave nor free" (Galatians 3:28). Christian communities developed a value system that enabled those who would otherwise be at the base of the social hierarchy to develop an elevated sense of personal worth and value. The appeal of early Christianity to women (1.3.6), slaves, and other socially marginalized groups clearly reflects this perception.

Yet this emphasis on the importance of all members of the community of faith was supplemented by practical support. Early Christian communities seem to have regarded social outreach and support as being integral to their identity, raising funds to allow them to care for the poor, sick, and needy. A good example of this was the church's care for widows, a social group which tended to be treated as insignificant in Roman society. Contemporary documents suggest that the Roman churches supported large numbers of widows, many of whom otherwise would have been without any perceived social value or personal means of survival.

Contemporary accounts suggest that many were drawn to consider the ideas of Christianity through the impact that it had upon their lives. It is no accident that the early church used medical models and imagery when referring both to Christian bishops and rites. The first-century bishop Ignatius of Antioch, for example, famously described the eucharistic bread and wine as the "medicine of immortality." This vision of Christianity as a religion and community of healing resonated strongly with many, particularly at times of uncertainty and instability.

The theme of resurrection played an important role in early Christian outreach, not least in encouraging an attitude of contempt towards death. Accounts of the martyrdoms of early Christian leaders frequently emphasize their lack of fear of death, and the impact this had on pagan audiences. This remarkable absence of fear in the face of death – widely noted by cultural commentators of the age – was not due to any Stoic notion of indifference, but to the firm belief in immortality that was characteristic of Christianity.

Finally, we must give due weight to the powerful ideology that was implicit within the early Christian proclamation. Early Christian apologists emphasized the ability of their faith to make sense of the deep moral structure of the universe. It enabled them to cope with the enigmas of evil and suffering, by offering a fundamental reassurance that justice would ultimately triumph over deceit and oppression. Christianity proclaimed a wise and righteous governor of the universe, to be contrasted with the moral decadence of secular imperial institutions of power. Christianity offered an alternative vision of reality, which seemed to many to be preferable to what they experienced around them.

The appeal of Christianity to the world of late antiquity was thus complex and multileveled, capable of connecting with multiple aspects of the culture of this age.

1.1.5.   The Apostolic Age

The first major period in Christian history is generally known as the "apostolic age." The term "apostle" derives from the Greek verb *apostelein*, "to send," and is often used to designate those commissioned by Jesus of Nazareth to continue and extend his ministry. Traditionally, this is defined in terms of the period during which the apostles were still alive, thus ensuring historical continuity between the church and the original community of faith which gathered around Jesus of Nazareth. We know frustratingly little about this period, even though it is clearly of immense historical importance. However, we can begin to sketch some of its aspects, providing an important transition to the better-understood history of the early church.

As we noted earlier, at the heart of the Christian movement lay a series of reports and interpretations of the words and deeds of Jesus of Nazareth. His significance was presented in terms of both his identity and his function, using a rich range of Christological titles and images of salvation, often drawn from the Jewish roots of Christianity. Initially, Christian groups appear to have been established in leading urban centers, such as Jerusalem, by individuals who had personally known Jesus of Nazareth, or who were familiar with his immediate circle.

Other Christian communities were established by others with more complex associations with the Jerusalem church, most notably Paul of Tarsus. According to the New Testament itself, Paul was responsible for establishing Christian churches in many parts of the Mediterranean world. At first Christianity would almost certainly have been seen simply as one more sect or group within a Judaism that was already accustomed to considerable diversity in religious expression. As recent historical studies of this period have made clear, Judaism was far from being monolithic at this time.

These Christian communities were scattered throughout the Roman Empire, each facing its own distinctive local challenges and opportunities. This raises two significant historical questions, neither of which can be answered with any degree of certainty. First, how did these individual Christian communities maintain their identity with regard to their local cultural context? It is clear, for example, that early Christian worship served to emphasize the distinctiveness of Christian communities, helping to forge a sense of shared identity over and against society in general.

Second, how did these individual communities understand themselves as relating to a larger universal community, increasingly referred to as "the church" in the later writings of the New Testament? There is evidence that these communities maintained contact with each other through correspondence and traveling teachers who visited clusters of churches, and especially through the sharing of foundational documents, some (but not all) of which were later incorporated into the canon of the New Testament.

It is widely thought that these concerns underlie some of the themes explored in the Pastoral Epistles – three later New Testament letters (1 Timothy; 2 Timothy; Titus), possibly dating from the final decades of the first century, which show a particular concern for the specifics of church order, and the importance of transmitting the key themes of faith to a later generation. Where earlier Pauline letters see faith primarily as trust in God, the Pastoral Epistles tend to treat faith more as a body of teaching, to be passed faithfully from one generation to another (1.5.8). The letters are an important witness to the increasing institutionalization of faith, and the exploration of the forms of ecclesiastical structure best suited for the future needs of the Christian faith.

There is no doubt that the early Christian communities believed that they shared a common faith, which was in the process of spreading throughout the civilized world. Individual churches or congregations saw themselves as local representatives or embodiments of something greater – the church. While it is possible to argue that early second-century Christianity possessed a fundamental theological unity, based on its worship of Christ as the risen Lord, the early Christians expressed and enacted their faith in a diversity of manners.

While some historians still speak of early Christianity as a single tradition, it is probably better thought of as a complex network of groups and individuals, who existed in different social, cultural, and linguistic contexts. All Christians might worship Jesus; this did not, however, lead to any kind of monolithic – or even uniform – Christian culture. These groups sought to relate their faith to those contexts, and express it in terms which made sense within those contexts. While it is potentially misleading to speak of these groups as "competing," it is certainly fair to suggest that they possessed more autonomy at this early stage than is often appreciated. Early Christianity, as we shall emphasize later, did not possess any authority structures which allowed for the imposition of any kind of uniformity. Indeed, many intellectual historians value the sheer intellectual excitement of the era, evident in the way in which the early Christians explored and expressed their faith.

However, this historical observation does not imply that there was no core unifying strand in early Christianity. The sociological diversity of early Christianity was not matched by anything even remotely approaching theological anarchy. It is possible to identify a pattern derived from the apostolic witness and maintained across time as the "deposit of faith" (Latin: *depositum fidei*), referred to in the New Testament as "the faith once delivered to the saints" (Jude 3). This pattern is embedded, like some kind of genetic code, in both the texts of the New Testament and the writings and worship of the early church. Yet despite this core "pattern of truth" which united them, early Christian communities clearly show diversity as well as unity. Although some scholars speak of the "emergence of diversity" within Christianity as if this was a later development, the evidence suggests that such diversity was there from the outset, even if later developments caused it to become more noticeable in certain situations.

1.1.6. Women in Apostolic Christianity

Women played an important role in Christianity during the apostolic age. As we have noted, Christianity emerged from Palestinian Judaism, which often adopted strongly negative attitudes towards women (1.3.6). It is for this reason that the gospels note that Jesus of Nazareth's encounters with women occasionally provoked hostility and criticism from the official representatives of Judaism. It is clear from the gospel accounts of the ministry of Jesus that women were an integral part of the group of people who gathered round him. They were affirmed by him, often to the dismay of the Pharisees and other religious traditionalists. The gospel of Luke emphasizes the significant role of women in the spreading of the gospel. We are told that "many women" (Luke 8:2–3) were involved in early evangelistic endeavors.

Our most important source for the history of apostolic Christianity is the Acts of the Apostles, written by the same Luke who compiled the third of the four gospels. Acts emphasizes the important role of women in providing hospitality for early Christian missionaries to Europe, with women converts such as Lydia making their homes available as house churches and staging-posts for missionaries. Luke appears to be concerned to bring out clearly the important historical point that the early church attracted significant numbers of prominent women within cultures which gave them a much greater social role than in Judaism, and offered them a significant role in the overall evangelistic and pastoral ministry of the early church.

In particular, Luke singles out Priscilla and Aquila as a husband-and-wife team who were engaged in an evangelistic and teaching ministry (Acts 18:1–3, 24–6). Paul commends to the Roman church "our sister Phoebe, a servant of the church at Cenchrea" (Romans 16:1), commenting on how helpful she had been to him. Other passages in the New Testament letters (such as 1 Timothy 3:11 and 5:9–10) clearly point to women exercising a recognized and authorized ministry of some form within the church. Amid the large number of folk whom Paul lists as sending greetings in his Epistle to the Romans are Prisca, a "fellow-worker"; and Tryphaena and Tryphosa, "workers in the Lord" – descriptions that Paul also applies to men in the same passage.

Paul's extended list of greetings in his letter to the Romans also includes Junia, who is named, along with Andronicus, as "prominent among the apostles" (Romans 16:7). Andronicus is a male name; Junia, a female name. (One early manuscript reads "Julia," rather than "Junia.") Early Christian writers regularly identified Andronicus's partner as a woman. John Chrysostom (347–407), widely regarded as one of the greatest preachers of the eastern church, commented on this text as follows.

> "Greet Andronicus and Junia who are outstanding among the apostles." To be an apostle is something excellent. Yet to be "outstanding among the apostles" is a wonderful song of praise. They were outstanding on the basis of their works and virtuous actions. Indeed, how great the wisdom of this woman must have been, since she was deemed worthy of the title of apostle.

Later copyists of the thirteenth and fourteenth centuries, when female leadership within the church was frowned upon, appear to have found it difficult to believe or accept that Junia could have been an apostle. In producing their manuscript copies of the text, they therefore altered this female name to the masculine form of "Junius." In the thirteenth century, Giles of Rome came up with an alternative approach, declaring that while "Junia" was the correct form of the name, this actually referred to a man. Yet the textual evidence does not support these interpretations.

Alongside this clear evidence of women playing an important role in the life of early Christian communities, we find early Christians reflecting on the theoretical aspects of this ministry. The New Testament affirms the theoretical equality among Christians. Differences of racial origin, gender, or class are seen in a new way on account of the new order that is understood to have arisen through Jesus of Nazareth. Spiritual gifts, Paul insists, are not bestowed on the basis of gender, race, or class.

This attitude is expressed in one of Paul's earliest statements. "There is neither Jew nor Greek, slave nor free, male nor female, for you are all one in Christ Jesus" (Galatians 3:28). This verse stands as the foundation of Paul's approach to differences of gender, class, or race. Paul affirms that being "in Christ" transcends all social, ethnic, and sexual barriers. Perhaps this vigorous and unambiguous statement was provoked by the local situation in Galatia, in which "Judaizers" (that is, people who wished Christians to retain the traditions of Judaism; see 1.1.7) were attempting to maintain customs or beliefs which encouraged or justified such distinctions. Paul does not mean that people should cease being Jews or Greeks, or male and female, as a result of their conversions. His point is that, while these distinctions may have importance in the social contexts within which the church was taking root, in the sight of God, and within the Christian community, they are transcended by the union between Christ and the believer.

Paul's affirmation potentially has two major consequences. Firstly, it declares that there are no barriers of gender, race, or social status to the gospel. The gospel is universal in its scope. Secondly, it clearly implies that, while Christian faith does not abolish the particularities of one's existence, they are to be used to glorify and serve God in whatever situation Christians might find themselves.

So how did these new ideas work out in practice? The new status that the early Christian movement accorded to slaves and women did not sit easily with traditional Roman or Jewish attitudes. It is therefore not surprising that the New Testament letters comment on some practical issues that arose at the time within church life and Christian families.

One issue that Paul engages is whether women should cover their heads during public worship (1 Corinthians 11:2–16). This passage is difficult to interpret, because we do not know enough about the Corinthian church, or local Corinthian culture, to be sure that we have understood Paul's point properly. One suggestion is that a woman with an uncovered head might have been mistaken for a prostitute. In that Corinth was noted as a center of prostitution, partly on account of the fact that it was a major commercial port, it is possible that this explanation would make sense of Paul's recommendation. However, there is not enough evidence to support this contention.

Historians suggest that Christianity laid the foundations for the undermining of traditional Roman and Jewish attitudes towards both women and slaves at two levels:

1. It asserted that all were one "in Christ" – whether Jew or Gentile, whether male or female, whether master or slave. Differences of race, gender, or social position were declared to place no obstacles between all believers sharing the same common faith.
2. It declared that all peoples – whether Jew or Gentile, whether male or female, whether master or slave – were members of the same Christian fellowship, and ought therefore to worship and pray together. Society might force each of these groups to behave in different manners, but within the Christian community, all were to be regarded as brothers and sisters in Christ.

Yet, as we shall see, these early ideals were imperfectly realized. Paul's letter to Philemon presupposes that Christian masters continue to employ slaves. Paul urges Philemon to receive back a runaway slave, and treat him compassionately. There is no call for the abolition of slavery, but a plea to Philemon to receive Onesimus back "no longer as a slave" (Philemon 16) – that is to say, either to make him a free man, or to treat him in such a way that he would no longer be treated as if he were a slave.

The same pattern is observed in attitudes towards women. Traditional cultural attitudes towards social hierarchies and gender roles proved difficult to ignore, particularly when Christianity became the official religion of the Roman Empire in the fourth century. Perhaps this was most obvious in Christian worship, where after a period of fluidity concerning attitudes towards women, traditional gender roles came to the fore once more. Even in the late first century, writers such as Polycarp and Ignatius of Antioch indicate that public worship was led only by men. Whatever activities women might have had in the apostolic age begin to become curtailed through the rise of a clerical hierarchy of bishops, presbyters, and deacons, with women tending to be excluded as either bishops or priests.

1.1.7.   Christianity and Judaism: A Complex Relationship

Early Christianity developed within Judaism, and most of the first converts to the movement were Jews. The New Testament frequently mentions Christians preaching in local synagogues. So similar were the two movements that outside observers, such as the Roman authorities, tended to treat Christianity as a sect within Judaism, rather than as a new movement with a distinct identity.

Although Christianity emerged from within Judaism, it rapidly developed its own distinctive identity. One of the most striking differences between the two faiths, evident by the early second century, is that Judaism tended to define itself by correct practice, where Christianity tended to appeal to correct doctrines. Historians of this age thus often speak of Jewish *orthopraxy*, and Christian *orthodoxy*.

While Christians declined to adopt the cultic rituals of Judaism (such as food laws, Sabbath observance, and circumcision) which served to identify Jews within a Gentile community, Marcion of Sinope's radical proposal in the second century that Christianity should be declared utterly distinct from Judaism failed to gain widespread support (1.2.3).

Christian self-definition was initially directed towards clarification of the relationship of Christianity and Judaism, centering upon the identity of Jesus, and subsequently upon the role of the Old Testament Law. It is thus perfectly reasonable to suggest that the Pauline doctrine of justification by faith represents a theoretical basis for the separation of Gentile Christian communities from Judaism.

This relationship between the Christian church and Israel was often expressed in terms of two "covenants" or "testaments." This terminology is used in the New Testament, especially the Letter to the Hebrews, and became normative within Christian thought over the following centuries. The phrase the "Old Covenant" is used by Christian writers to refer to God's dealings with Israel, as seen in Judaism; the phrase "New Covenant" is used by Christians to refer to God's dealings with humanity as a whole, as this is revealed in the teaching and person of Jesus of Nazareth. The Christian belief that the coming of Christ inaugurates something *new* expresses itself in a distinctive attitude towards the Old Testament, which could basically be summarized thus: *religious principles and ideas* (such as the notion of a sovereign God who is active in human history) are appropriated; religious *practices* (such as dietary laws and sacrificial routines) are not.

This recognition of a continuity between Christianity and Judaism raised a number of serious difficulties for the early Christians, especially during the first century. What was the role of the Jewish Law in the Christian life? Did the traditional rites and customs of Judaism have any continuing place in the Christian church? There is evidence that this issue was of particular importance during the 40s and 50s, when non-Jewish converts to Christianity came under pressure from Jewish Christians to maintain such rites and customs.

The issue of circumcision was particularly sensitive, with Gentile converts to Christianity often being pressed to become circumcised, in accord with the Law. This controversy is recorded in the Acts of the Apostles, which notes how, in the late 40s, a section of the church argued that it was essential that male Christians should be circumcised. Unless males were circumcised, they could not be saved (Acts 15:1). In effect, this group – often referred to as "Judaizers" – seemed to regard Christianity as an affirmation of every aspect of contemporary Judaism, with the addition of one further (and highly significant) belief – that Jesus of Nazareth was the long-awaited messiah.

The New Testament gives an account of how this issue was resolved during the apostolic period. The first General Council of the Christian church – the Council of Jerusalem in 49 (Acts 15:2–29) – met to consider the complex relationship between Christianity and Judaism. The debate is initially dominated by converted Pharisees, who insisted on the need to uphold the law of Moses, including the circumcision requirements. Yet Paul's account of the growing impact of the Christian gospel among the Gentiles caused the wisdom of this approach to be questioned. If so many Gentiles were becoming Christians, why should anything unnecessary be put in their way? Paul conceded the need to avoid food which had been sacrificed to idols – an issue which features elsewhere in his letters (1 Corinthians 8:7–13). But there was, he insisted, no need for circumcision. This position won widespread support, and was summarized in a letter which was circulated at Antioch (Acts 15:30–5).

Yet although the issue was resolved at the theoretical level, it would remain a live issue for many churches in the future. Paul's letter to the church at Galatia, probably written around 53, deals explicitly with this question, which had clearly become a contentious issue in the region. Paul notes the emergence of a Judaizing party in the region – that is, a group within the church which insisted that Gentile believers should obey every aspect of the law of Moses, including the need to be circumcised. According to Paul, the leading force behind this party was James – not the apostle James, who is thought to have died around 44, but the brother of Jesus of Nazareth who was influential in calling the Council of Jerusalem, and wrote the New Testament letter known by his name.

For Paul, this trend was highly dangerous. If Christians could only gain salvation by the rigorous observance of the law, what purpose did the death of Christ serve? It is faith in Christ, not the scrupulous and religious keeping of the law of Moses, which is the basis of salvation. Nobody can be justified (that is, put in a right relationship with God) through keeping the law. The righteousness on which our salvation depends is not available through the law, but only through faith in Christ. Aware of the importance and sensitivity of this issue, Paul then explores this question in some detail (see Galatians 3:1–23). The Galatians have fallen into the trap of believing that salvation came by doing works of the law, or by human achievement. So what has happened to faith? Did the gift of the Holy Spirit ever come through keeping the law?

Paul argues that the great Jewish patriarch Abraham was "justified" (that is, put in a right relationship with God) through his faith (Galatians 3:6–18). The great patriarch was not put in a right relationship with God through circumcision; that came later. That relationship with God was established through Abraham's faith in God's promise to him (Genesis 15:6). Circumcision was simply the external sign of that faith. It did not establish that faith, but confirmed something that was already there. Nor does the law, or any aspect of it, abolish the promises which God had already made. The promise to Abraham and his descendants – which includes Christians, as well as Jews – remains valid, even after the introduction of the law. Gentiles could share Abraham's faith in the promises of God – and all the benefits that result from this faith – without the need to be circumcised, or be bound to the fine details of the law of Moses.

This controversy is important for several reasons. It casts light on tensions within the early church; it also raises the question of whether Jewish Christians enjoyed special privileges or status in relation to Gentile Christians. The final outcome of the debate was that Jews and Gentiles were to be given equal status and acceptance within the church. The chronological priority of Israel over the church did not entail the privileging of Jews over Gentiles within the Christian community. While the theological and ethical teaching of the Old Testament was to be honored and accepted by Christians, they were under no obligation to obey the ceremonial or cultic aspects of the Law, including circumcision or sacrifice. Those were both fulfilled superseded by the coming of Jesus Christ. For many early Christians, the fact that Jesus of Nazareth had himself been circumcised removed any need for them to undergo the same painful process.

The position of Jewish Christianity within an increasingly Gentile church became more difficult with the passage of time. Gentile Christians regarded themselves as liberated from cultic rules concerning circumcision, food laws, or the observation of the Sabbath, and cited Paul in support of their position. Although some accounts of the development of Christianity suggest that these issues were essentially resolved in favor of the Gentiles by the end of the first century, there is evidence that they lingered on well into the second century. For example, Justin Martyr's *Dialogue with Trypho*, written in Rome around the year 150, explicitly refers to such tensions. As we shall see later, the issue became contentious in Rome at this time, due to the teachings of Marcion of Sinope (1.2.3).

1.2. Early Christianity and the Roman Empire

It is impossible to understand the development of early Christianity without a good understanding of the Roman Empire, which many historians regard as having reached its zenith during the reign of the emperor Trajan, who ruled from 98 to 117. Christianity had its origins in the Roman province of Judaea, a relatively obscure and politically insignificant region, and would expand rapidly within the empire, eventually becoming its official reli-

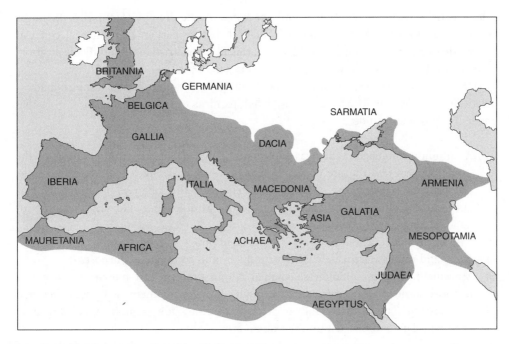

Map 1.2   The Roman Empire under Trajan, c. 117

gion. In view of the importance of the Roman imperial context to the rise and shaping of Christianity, we shall look at this context in more detail.

1.2.1.   The Roman Empire, c. 100

The expansion of Roman influence began during the period when Rome was a republic. However, political weaknesses led to power being centralized in a single figure of authority – the emperor (Latin: *imperator,* "one who gives orders"). For political reasons, this supreme ruler was not referred to as "king," as this term was regarded as no longer being acceptable because of associated abuses of power in the pre-republican era. The term "emperor" was devised as a name for Rome's supreme ruler, mainly because it avoided using language which linked it to discredited periods in Roman history. It was during the reign of the first emperor, Caesar Augustus, that the gospel of Luke places the birth of Jesus of Nazareth.

A significant degree of Roman territorial expansion took place during the reign of Augustus, especially in Egypt and northern Europe. The imperial province of Egypt became of particular importance, providing substantial grain imports to feed the Roman population. Yet Augustus's successor Tiberius, who reigned from 14–37, proved an ineffective emperor, preferring to live in seclusion on the island of Capri. Under Trajan, however, the stability of the empire was initially restored, followed by a period of further territorial expansion. A major program of public building in Rome itself enriched the city, emphasizing its status as the center of the greatest empire the world had then known.

A form of "civil religion" began to emerge at this time, linked with worship of the Roman emperor as an expression of allegiance to the Roman state and empire. A dead emperor who was held worthy of the honor could be voted a state divinity (Latin: *divus*), and be incorporated into the Roman pantheon. Refusal to take part in this imperial cult was regarded as an act of treason. As we shall see, this placed Christians in a difficult position, as many of them refused to worship anyone other than the God of Jesus Christ.

The administrative and commercial links established by the Roman Empire made it relatively easy for new ideas – especially religious ideas – to be spread. The factors that made this possible include:

1. A common language. Latin was the official language of the empire, although the Romans permitted the use of local languages – such as Greek – wherever possible. The virtually universal use of Latin ultimately led to this language becoming the language of the church and academy during the Middle Ages, allowing the limits of national languages to be transcended.
2. Ease of transport. The Roman navy suppressed piracy, making travel by sea relatively safe. Land routes were widely used for military and commercial purposes.
3. Movement of people. Soldiers, colonial administrators, and merchants were free to move around the empire, often bringing home with them new ideas they had encountered. The Mithraic cult, or "cult of Mithras," for example, appears to have been especially popular within the Roman army.
4. Immigration from the colonies to Rome. During the first century, the population of Rome expanded, with large numbers of immigrants from the colonies settling in the city, bringing their religious beliefs and traditions with them. While all were expected to conform to Roman civil religion, there was a substantial expansion of variety of personal religious beliefs and practices. Christianity easily fits into this general pattern of Roman religious diversification in this period.

In view of the importance of religion within the Roman Empire of this period, we shall consider the phenomenon of Roman religion in more detail. First-century Roman religion tended to draw a distinction between a state cult which gave Roman society stability and cohesion, and the private views of individuals. The Latin term *religio* derives from a root meaning "to bind together." In many ways, this is a useful summary of the role of the state cult: to give the city and empire a stable sacred foundation. Religion was primarily understood in terms of "devotion" (Latin: *pietas*) – a social activity and attitude that promoted unity and loyalty to the state.

Roman citizens were free to adopt other religious practices and beliefs in private, so long as they did not conflict with this "official" civil religion. These private religions would take place in the household, with the head of the family (Latin: *paterfamilias*) taking charge of domestic prayers and ceremonial rites in much the same way as the public representatives of the people performed the state ceremonial rites. During the first century, these private religions often took the form of mystery cults, originating in Greece or Asia, brought back to Rome by soldiers and merchants. The best known of these was the cult of Mithras, which is thought to have originated in Persia.

Christianity would easily have fitted into this pattern of Roman religious diversity at this time. Yet Christians found it difficult to accept the distinction between public and private religious beliefs, holding that their allegiance to the one God prevented them from taking part in the official Roman cult. This became increasingly problematic through the rise of the "imperial cult" in the late first century, which we shall consider in the following section.

1.2.2. Christianity and the Imperial Cult

The political background against which the early Roman suspicion of Christianity is to be set is dominated by the "imperial cult." This is probably best understood as a highly elevated view of the Roman emperor, which resulted from the remarkable achievements of Augustus. It was no longer possible to regard Augustus simply as an outstanding ruler; he was widely regarded as a *divus*, being invested with some form of supernatural or transcendent significance. It was not regarded as necessary for imperial figures to be dead before they were accorded some form of divine status; there is ample evidence to indicate that at least some members of the imperial family (such as Julius Caesar) were treated as divine during their lifetimes.

The cult appears to have become especially significant in the two or three decades before the birth of Christ; by the second half of the first century – at which time Christianity was becoming a significant presence in the eastern regions of the empire – it had become firmly established as a routine aspect of Roman colonial life.

The cult seems to have taken different forms in the various regions of the empire. A distinction was drawn between the forms of the cult appropriate to Roman citizens and those who were not. In the east, the cult of "Rome and Julius" was prescribed for Roman citizens; others were required to take part in the cult of "Rome and Augustus."

The cult appears to have been especially strong in those regions of the eastern empire in which Christianity would take root, such as the city of Corinth and the region of Galatia, both landmarks in the ministry of Paul of Tarsus. Imperial festivals became an important part of the life of Corinth during the first half of the first century. The figure of Julius Caesar was of particular importance to this cult, not least on account of his having given Corinth the status of a Roman colony shortly before his death. In Galatia, the imperial cult had become firmly established by the first decade of the century.

The imperial cult was so deeply rooted in the major cities of the eastern Roman Empire that it was inevitable that some form of confrontation between Christianity and the state authorities would take place. One of the most frequently cited pieces of evidence here is the famous letter of Pliny the Younger to Trajan, dating from about 112 (1.4.1). In this letter, Pliny asked advice as to how to deal with the growing number of Christians who refused to worship the image of the Roman emperor. It is quite clear from Pliny's letter that Christianity was suspect on account of its refusal to worship the emperor, which suggested that it was bent on overthrowing the existing social order.

The refusal of Christians to conform to the imperial cult helps us understand one of the more puzzling developments of this age – the tendency of Roman critics of Christianity to ridicule it as a form of "atheism." This makes no sense if "atheism" is understood in the modern sense of the term – namely, rejection of belief in God. Yet the term "atheism" was widely used in classical culture to refer to a rejection of the official state religion. The classical Greek philosopher Socrates was forced to commit suicide four centuries before the apostolic age for "atheism" – that is, rejecting the Athenian state religion. Socrates, of course, was no atheist in the modern sense of the word.

The relation between Christianity and the imperial authorities is one of the most important themes in the history of early Christianity. Yet other themes also emerged as important. The complex relationship between Christianity and Judaism, often the subject of discussion within the New Testament, became the topic of heated debate at Rome in the second century, leading to the emergence of a growing consensus that Christianity should not, and could not, abandon its Jewish heritage. We shall consider this debate in the next section.

1.2.3.   Christianity and Judaism: Marcion of Sinope

Christianity's relationship with Judaism remained a matter of debate in the late first and early second centuries (1.1.7). One group known as the "Ebionites" echoed Jewish ideas at a number of points, especially in their understanding of the identity of Jesus of Nazareth. The term "Ebionite" is thought to derive from the Hebrew word *Ebyonim* ("the Poor"), perhaps originally applied to early Christians because they came from lower social groups and tended to be socially deprived. Ebionitism was an attempt to use ideas that were inherited from the Jewish context within which early Christianity emerged, and use these to explore and express the significance of Jesus of Nazareth.

The origins of such a trend can be seen inside the New Testament itself, in that the gospels record attempts to make sense of Jesus which are drawn from contemporary Judaism – such as interpreting Jesus of Nazareth as a second Elijah, a new Jewish prophet, or a High Priest of Israel. On this approach, Jesus of Nazareth was a human being who was singled out for divine favor by being possessed by the Holy Spirit, in a manner similar to, yet more intensive than, the calling of a Hebrew prophet. In the end, Christians discarded this approach as inadequate. Yet it remains an important early witness to the existence of Christian communities that saw Judaism as having continuing utility and significance for the church.

Precisely the opposite approach was advocated in the middle of the second century by Marcion of Sinope (c. 110–60), a wealthy Christian in Rome. By this time, Christianity had gained a significant following in the imperial capital. Marcion wanted to bring about a fundamental change to the way in which the church positioned itself in relation to Judaism. Christianity ought to sever all its links with Judaism, and should have nothing to do with its God, beliefs, or rituals. A clean break was necessary. The god of the Old Testament was a war-god, who had nothing to do with the Christian god.

What Marcion was proposing represented a radical break with both the established tradition of the church, and the writings of the New Testament. The majority position within the church, at Rome and elsewhere, was that Christianity represented the fulfillment of the covenant between God and Abraham, not its rejection or abrogation. The God whom Christians worshipped was the same as that worshipped by Abraham, Isaac, and Jacob, and whose will was disclosed through the law and the prophets. In marked contrast, Marcion proposed severing links with Judaism completely, seeing Christianity as a new faith in a new God.

Marcion's core argument was that the "God" of the Old Testament was not the same as that of the New Testament. The Old Testament God was to be seen as inferior, even defective, in the light of the Christian conception of God. There was no connection whatsoever between these deities. For Marcion, the gospel comes from nowhere, without any historical context. There is no sense of it being the climax and fulfillment of God's engagement with humanity, which began with the call of Abraham.

Marcion proposed that Jesus of Nazareth had no direct relation to the Jewish creator god, and that he was not to be thought of as the "messiah" sent by this Jewish God. Rather, Jesus was sent from a previously unknown, strange God, characterized by love rather than the jealousy and aggression which Marcion regarded as hallmarks of the God of the Old Testament. The second-century theologian Irenaeus of Lyons observed that Marcion took the view that the Jewish God "is the creator of evil things, takes delight in wars, is fickle, and behaves inconsistently." The third-century theologian Tertullian points to Marcion's core belief in two quite different gods, "of unequal rank, the one a stern and warlike judge, the other gentle and mild, kind, and supremely good."

Yet Marcion was not prepared to rest content with affirming the radical difference between the God of the Jews and the God of Jesus of Nazareth. Many of the documents that were being widely accepted as authoritative by early Christians – which would later be canonically gathered together as the New Testament – made extensive reference to the Jewish scriptures. Marcion thus developed his own authorized collection of Christian documents, which excluded works which he regarded as contaminated by Jewish ideas and associations (1.5.2).

Needless to say, Marcion's biblical canon excluded the Old Testament altogether. It also omitted any New Testament works which seemed sympathetic towards Judaism, such as the gospel of Matthew. Marcion's Bible consisted simply of ten of Paul's letters, along with the gospel of Luke. Yet Marcion was obliged to edit even these works, in order to remove contaminating influences which suggested that there was some connection between Jesus and Judaism. Marcion thus removed the narratives of the annunciation and the nativity, Christ's baptism, temptation, and genealogy, and all references to Bethlehem and Nazareth from his version of Luke's gospel. Paul's letters also required some editorial work, to remove their associations with Judaism.

In the end, the church rejected Marcion's views. The model that began to gain the ascendancy in early Christianity was that of the fulfillment of the hopes of both pagans and Jews in Christ. As we shall see in the following section, writers such as Justin Martyr were adamant that the story of Jesus of Nazareth could not to be told in isolation from its Jewish context. To understand the identity and significance of Jesus, it was necessary to tell other stories, and explore how they interlocked and interrelated. One of those stories concerns God's creation of the world; another tells of God's calling of Israel; a third tells the age-old human quest for meaning and significance. For Justin Martyr, the story of Jesus intersects all three, ultimately to provide their fulfillment. Jesus is the focal point from which all other stories are to be seen, and on whom all finally and decisively converge.

1.2.4.   Christianity and Pagan Culture: Justin Martyr

One of the most important debates in the early church concerned the extent to which Christians could appropriate the immense cultural legacy of the classical world – such as its poetry, philosophy, and literature. How could Christians make use of classical philosophy in communicating or commending their faith? In what way could Christian writers use classical modes of writing – such as poetry – to expound and communicate the gospel? Or was the use of such ideas and literature impossible for Christians, because they had been tainted by their pagan associations? It was a debate of considerable cultural and intellectual importance, as it raised the question of whether Christianity would turn its back on the classical heritage, or appropriate it in a modified form.

One early and influential answer to this important question was given by Justin Martyr (103–65), a second-century writer with a particular concern to make use of the parallels between Christianity and Platonism as a means of communicating the gospel. Justin was born to pagan parents in the Roman province of Judaea, in the city of Flavia Neapolis (modern Nablus). He converted to Christianity as a young man, possibly at the great Asian city of Ephesus, partly through his admiration for the courage of Christians facing execution for their faith, and partly because of his fascination with the Old Testament prophecies that were fulfilled through the coming of Christ. Justin later recalled that, "While pondering on [Christ's] words, I discovered that his was the only sure and useful philosophy."

It is important to note that Justin speaks of Christianity as a "philosophy." At the time, this term meant more than simply a set of ideas. A philosophy was as much about a way of living as a way of thinking. After his conversion, Justin became one of the many itinerant teachers of this age, wearing the distinctive cloak of a philosopher. He eventually made his way to Rome, where he lived in a small room "above Myrtinus's baths." He is now remembered for three works: the *First Apology* and the *Second Apology,* and the *Dialogue with Trypho the Jew*. Justin was eventually betrayed to the Roman authorities, and executed in 165.

For Justin, Christianity brought the quest of the ancient world for wisdom to fulfillment. Both the Jewish law and the Platonic *logos* are fulfilled in Christ. God has sown the seeds of divine wisdom throughout the world, which meant that Christians could and should expect to find aspects of the gospel reflected outside the church. Justin developed a Christianized version of the Stoic idea of the "seed-bearing word" (Greek: *logos spermatikos*), which originates from God, and is divinely planted in the human mind. Justin's version of the *logos spermatikos* is best understood as an attempt to translate Paul's ideas about natural revelation, found in his letter to the Romans and the Athens address (Acts 17), into the language of contemporary philosophy. "All right principles that philosophers and lawgivers have discovered and expressed they owe to whatever of the Word they have found and contemplated in part. The reason why they have contradicted each other is that they have not known the entire Word, which is Christ." For Justin, Christians were therefore free to draw on the riches of classical culture, in that whatever "has been said well" ultimately draws upon divine wisdom and insight.

Justin commended the study of Greek philosophy for two reasons. First, it allowed Christians to be able to communicate effectively with secular culture, using language and

Figure 1.2 Justin Martyr and others in the early church encouraged a dialogue between Christianity and classical philosophy, such as Plato and Aristotle. Detail of Plato and Aristotle, from *The School of Athens*, by Raphael (1483–1520). Fresco. Stanza della Segnatura, Vatican City. © 2012. Photo: Scala, Florence

ideas that were already familiar to its cultural elite. Christians could express the core themes of their faith using Platonic terms, and adapting these as necessary. Yet perhaps just as importantly, engaging with secular Greek philosophy forced Christianity to try and give a more coherent and intelligent account of its ideas than might otherwise be the case.

Important though Justin's arguments may have been, they received a somewhat frosty reception in many sections of the Christian church. The main difficulty was that it was seen to virtually equate Christianity with classical culture, apparently suggesting that Christian theology and Platonism were simply different ways of viewing the same divine realities. The most severe criticism of this kind of approach was to be found in the writings of Tertullian, a third-century Roman lawyer who converted to Christianity. What, he asked pointedly, has Athens to do with Jerusalem? What relevance has the Platonic academy for the church? Christianity must maintain its distinctive identity, he argued, by avoiding such secular influences.

1.2.5.   Early Christian Worship and Life

Lacking official religious recognition and protection, Christianity could not be a public religion in the Roman Empire (1.4.1). There were no buildings dedicated to public

Christian worship. It is easy to see why the secrecy surrounding Christian gatherings and worship roused suspicions. Rumors rapidly developed that Christians indulged in orgies and cannibalism. It is easy to understand how this took place. There is much evidence that early Christian gatherings included a "love-feast" (Greek: *agapē*), which could easily be misunderstood in sexual terms. Equally, it is not difficult to see how the practice of consuming bread and wine as symbols of the body and blood of Christ could be misinterpreted by outsiders as some kind of cannibalism.

We possess several important witnesses to early Christian worship. One is a manual of church order and Christian living, dating from the late first or early second century, known as the *Didache* (a Greek word meaning "Teaching"). This work describes how Christians gathered together on the Lord's Day – in other words, Sunday – "to break bread and give thanks." The service is clearly understood to take place in a private home, not a public place.

Justin Martyr composed his *First Apology* in Rome in about 155. In this work, Justin describes two early Christian worship services. First, he provides an account of the baptism of new converts. Following their baptism, the new believers are led into the assembly of Christian believers. After prayers for the community and for the new convert, the worshippers greet one another with a kiss. Bread, wine, and water are then brought to the president, who offers a eucharistic prayer ascribing glory to the Father in the name of the Son and Spirit, and gives thanks that the gathered worshippers have been counted as worthy to receive the bread and wine. Justin does not use the term "priest" to refer to the president of this thanksgiving (Greek: *eucharistia*), presumably because this term had associations with Roman civil religion, which was then strongly hostile towards Christianity.

The second event that Justin describes is a regular Sunday gathering of the community of faith. Why meet on a Sunday, rather than the Jewish Sabbath? Justin explains that the community gathers on Sunday, or the first day of the week, both because it was the day of creation and because this was the day on which Jesus rose from the dead. Only those who have been baptized are permitted to attend this service. The service begins with some readings from the "memoirs of the apostles" (almost certainly a reference to the Gospels) or the writings of the prophets, followed by a sermon based on these texts. This is followed by prayers and the celebration of the eucharist, along the lines just described. At the end of the service, those with sufficient means are invited to bring gifts to the president, who will distribute them to those in need. Justin's description merits close reading.

> On Sunday we have a common assembly of all our members, whether they live in the city or the outlying districts. The memoirs of the apostles or the writings of the prophets are read, as long as there is time. When the reader has finished, the president of the assembly speaks to us. He urges everyone to imitate the examples of virtue that we have heard in the readings. Then we all stand up together and pray. When we have finished praying, bread and wine and water are brought forward. The president offers prayers and gives thanks to the best of his ability, and the people show their assent by saying, "Amen." The eucharist is distributed, everyone present communicates, and the deacons take it to those who are absent.

Funeral rites were also important for early Christians. Romans tended to cremate their dead, and place their ashes in carved urns. Christians insisted on burial, seeing this as

Figure 1.3   Fear of persecution drove early Roman Christians underground. The illustration shows the third-century Catacombs of Calixtus, with an underground passage with niches or wall-graves on either side. Photo: akg-images/Erich Lessing

resting on the precedent of the burial of Christ. From the beginning of the second century, Christians constructed vast underground burial sites by digging into the soft porous pumice rock underneath the city of Rome and its neighborhood. This network – known as "the Catacombs" – consisted of passages and tunnels, with niches carved into the walls in which bodies could be placed, to await the resurrection. The catacombs of St. Callixtus, constructed in the middle of the second century, are among the most important of the Roman catacombs. With the legalization of Christianity in the fourth century, the catacombs gradually fell into disuse, as Christians were able to provide funeral rites for their dead openly, without fear of persecution.

Early Christianity was not well organized, even in Rome, partly on account of difficulties in coordination while the Christian movement remained illegal. Although the movement possessed leaders, they were unable to offer any kind of centralized control. The Greek terms *episcopos* (bishop), *diakonos* (deacon), and *presbyteros* (elder) were all used to refer to leaders of the Christian community. It is significant that all three of these words were widely used in secular culture to refer to administrative positions within large households of the day. An *episcopos* was a domestic supervisor, a *diakonos* a servant, and a *presbyteros* a senior member of the household. Christianity appears to have taken over familiar secular words here, and invested them with specifically Christian meanings, referring to the "household of faith."

At this early stage, there is no suggestion that a bishop had oversight of a group of churches, or an ecclesiastical region. This development took place later, when Christianity became the official religion of the Roman Empire, even if anticipations of these developments can be found earlier. At this early stage, a "bishop" was often simply the leader of a single Christian community. The Roman churches in the second century are perhaps best compared to secular Roman clubs or societies (Latin: *collegium*), or to Jewish synagogues – essentially independent associations with no centralized control.

1.3.   Early Christianity and the Hellenistic World

The military campaigns of the Macedonian ruler Alexander the Great in the fourth century before Christ led to a massive expansion of Greek cultural and political influence in the eastern Mediterranean region, and far beyond. Tutored as a boy by the philosopher Aristotle, Alexander was proclaimed king of Macedon at the age of twenty, following the assassination of his father, Philip of Macedon. Alexander launched a massive military campaign against the Persian Empire, bringing vast areas of territory from Egypt to India under Macedonian control. After his sudden death, widely suspected to have been an assassination, Alexander's body was transported to the Egyptian city of Alexandria, where it was buried in an ornate tomb.

The phrase "Hellenistic world" is generally used to refer to the new political and cultural order which resulted from Alexander's conquests, especially in Egypt and the Levant. Jewish culture now found itself having to engage with Greek ideas, literature, and cultural norms. As Christianity began to take root in this area, it found itself engaging with the ideas and norms of this culture, which bore little relation to the Palestinian context from which it had emerged. In this section, we shall consider some aspects of this engagement.

1.3.1.   The Greek-Speaking World, c. 200

One of the most important outcomes of the engagement between Judaism and Hellenistic culture was the translation of the Hebrew Bible into Greek. This process, which is known to have begun three centuries before Christ, led to the Greek translation widely known as the "Septuagint," traditionally held to have been produced by seventy scholars (Latin: *septuaginta*, "seventy"). This translation, completed in the first century before Christ, was widely used by early Christian writers, and can be seen in use at several points in the New Testament.

The impact of this process of Hellenization on Jewish thought is best seen from the writings of Philo, a Jewish writer based in Alexandria in the early years of the first century. Philo is generally regarded as having attempted to achieve a synthesis of Jewish religious and Greek philosophical thought, based primarily on use of allegorical interpretations of the Old Testament and an appeal to the Platonic notion of the *logos*, noted earlier. Philo's doctrine of creation strongly resembles that set out by Plato in his dialogue *Timaeus*. However, it is important to note that Philo refused to accept Greek ideas which he held to be incompatible with Judaism – such as the Aristotelian doctrine of the eternity and indestructibility of the world. Philo's basic approach is that of the accommodation of Jewish ideas to Greek philosophy, not the rejection of distinctively Jewish ideas.

Philo's method of biblical interpretation is essentially allegorical, appealing to deeper meanings beneath the literal and historical senses of a passage. Philo considered allegorical ways of interpreting the book of Genesis to be a legitimate and appropriate way of bridging the gap between divine revelation (which primarily took the form of events) and Platonic philosophy (which primarily concerned abstract ideas). Rather than concentrating on the historical or literal sense of a passage, Philo argues that there is a deeper meaning concealed within the imagery of the text, which the skilled exegete can identify and explore. Philo does not want to depreciate or abolish the literal or the historical senses of the Bible, but to develop deeper meanings which are closer to the themes of secular wisdom. This kind of approach to biblical interpretation would be developed by early Alexandrian Christian writers, such as Clement of Alexandria (c. 150–c. 215) and Origen (184–253).

As Christianity expanded from its original heartlands of Palestine into the great Greek-speaking cities of Alexandria and Antioch, it was inevitable that it would be influenced by the ideas and methods of Hellenistic philosophy. Although theirs was still an illegal religion, Christian writers did not hold back from debating their ideas with secular and religious writers of the age. Yet Christian writers and thinkers could not engage with the culture around them without using at least some aspects of its language and concepts. This observation raises one of the most important questions which is raised by the development of early Christian theology. Did Christian writers absorb more Hellenistic thought that they realized through interacting with their culture?

One of the most influential discussions of this theme was due to the great German Protestant church historian Adolf von Harnack (1851–1930). Harnack argued that the expansion of Christianity from its original Jewish context to the great Greek-speaking cities of Egypt and Asia led to the progressive Hellenization of Christianity. This change, Harnack argued, was most obvious in the development of metaphysical theological views about God and Christ – such as the doctrine of the Trinity, or the doctrine of the "two natures" of Christ. These developments, he declared, were the "work of the Greek spirit on the soil of the gospel." The Christian faith came to be dependent on the categories of Greek metaphysics, distancing the church from its connections with the historical figure of Jesus of Nazareth.

More recent scholarship has questioned Harnack's judgment, concluding that he overstated his case for the "Hellenization" of the Christian faith. Yet there is equal agreement that some such process seems to have taken place, even if its extent and importance is open to debate. In any case, there is a problem with Harnack's implied suggestion that any such influence amounts to "corruption" or "distortion." It is difficult to see how Christian theology can avoid being influenced and shaped by a variety of cultural and philosophical sources.

Nevertheless, Harnack's concern is to be taken seriously. For example, consider this theological question: can God suffer? Many writers within the Hellenistic tradition worked with an essentially philosophical notion of God, which emphasized perfection as a core divine characteristic. How could a perfect being suffer? Suffering was a mark of imperfection – of decay or change, characteristics of the material world, but not of the unchangeable divine nature. Many Christian theologians in the Greek-speaking world seem to have accepted this judgment, despite the difficulties that this caused for them. If Jesus Christ suffered on the cross, and if Jesus Christ was God, surely a case could be made for God suffering in some sense of the word? Early Christian writers developed sophisticated ways of affirming the former but not the latter, wishing to ensure that they caused minimal intellectual offense to educated pagans at this point.

Yet the Hellenistic world was shaped by intellectual and cultural movements other than classical Greek philosophy. One of the movements that came to gain considerable influence in parts of Egypt and Asia was known as Gnosticism. As we shall see, this movement had considerable impact on the development of the Christian church's understanding of the identity of its core ideas, and how these could best be preserved.

1.3.2.   The Challenge of Gnosticism: Irenaeus of Lyons

Older historical textbooks often speak of "Gnosticism" as if it were a relatively well-defined coherent movement. There is now a growing consensus that the use of the single term "Gnosticism" is misleading, in that it gathers together a number of quite different unrelated groups, and presents them as if they represented a single religious belief system. Perhaps Gnosticism is best understood as a family of religious doctrines and myths that flourished in late classical antiquity with three shared beliefs:

1.   The cosmos is a result of the activity of an evil or ignorant creator, often referred to as the "Demiurge" (Greek: *dēmiourgos*, "craftsman" or "artisan");
2.   Humanity is trapped within this physical realm;
3.   Salvation is a process in which believers receive the knowledge (Greek: *gnōsis*) of their divine origin, allowing them to break free from their imprisonment on earth.

The idea of an inferior creator god – the "Demiurge" – is found in classical Greek philosophy, and plays a significant role in Plato's dialogue *Timaeus*. Gnosticism held that this demiurge created the physical world without any knowledge of the "true God," falsely believing that he was the only God. Since the demiurge acted in ignorance of the true God, his creation had to be considered as imperfect, or even evil. Most forms of Gnosticism believed there was a radical gulf between the visible world of experience and the spiritual world of the true God.

So what of the place of humanity within this created order? A core belief for many Gnostic thinkers was that the human body was a prison for the spirit, which was actively seeking its liberation. The Greek slogan *sōma sēma* ("the body is a tomb") was often used by such writers to express this idea of spiritual bondage. Most Gnostic teachers held that, while the human body was created by the demiurge, it nevertheless contains a divine spirit which had the potential to establish a connection with the highest God. Yet this divine spark can be awoken if and when a divine messenger awakes individuals from their dream of forgetfulness, allowing humanity to reconnect with its divine origins. For many forms of Gnosticism – especially Valentinism, the form of Gnosticism associated with Valentinus (c. 100–c. 160) and his circle at Rome in the second century – Christ was this redeemer-figure, who awakened the divine spark within humanity, enabling it to find its way back to its true home.

In responding to Valentinus, the second-century theologian Irenaeus of Lyons developed the idea of the "economy of salvation." The entire work of salvation, from creation through to its final consummation, was carried out by one and the same God. The creator God was no demiurge, nor was the redeemer some mere emissary from the heavenly realms. Irenaeus highlights the importance of the emerging doctrine of the Trinity as a means of articulating divine continuity throughout the history of the world on the one hand, and as safeguarding the essential unity of Scripture on the other. Matter is not intrinsically evil; it is God's good creation, which has fallen, and is susceptible to restoration and renewal. For Irenaeus, the doctrine of the incarnation and the Christian use of sacraments represent explicit denials of any Gnostic notion of an intrinsically evil matter. Did not God choose to become incarnate? Does not the church use water, wine, and bread as symbols of divine grace and presence? Matter is something that God chose to use, not to reject.

Irenaeus's main concern at this point was to place clear blue water between the church and its Gnostic alternatives. Yet underlying these differences of substance was a deeper concern about issues of method – above all, the interpretation of Scripture. As he reflected on Valentinus's interpretation of sacred texts, Irenaeus appears to have come to the conclusion that the Gnostics had hijacked the foundational documents of Christianity, and interpreted its core terms according to their own taste. The outcome, in Irenaeus's view, was that Valentinus turned Christianity into Gnosticism.

Irenaeus's response to this development is widely regarded as marking a landmark in early Christian thought. Heretics, he argued, interpreted the Bible according to their own prejudices. Orthodox believers, in contrast, interpreted the Bible in ways that their apostolic authors would have endorsed (1.5.7). Irenaeus declared that the apostles had handed down to the church not merely the biblical texts themselves, but a certain way of reading and understanding those texts. A continuous stream of Christian teaching, life, and interpretation could be traced from the time of the apostles to Ireneaus's own age. The church was able to point to those who have maintained the teaching of the church, and to certain public standard creeds which set out the main lines of Christian belief.

Irenaeus thus saw tradition as a way of ensuring faithfulness to the original apostolic teaching, a safeguard against Gnostic innovations and misrepresentations of biblical texts. The New Testament represents the teaching of the apostles, which is to be interpreted as the apostles themselves wished. The church, Irenaeus insisted, safeguarded both this text and its correct interpretation, passing both on to future generations.

This development is of major importance, as it underlies the emergence of "creeds" – public, authoritative statements of the basic points of the Christian faith. There was a need to have public standards by which such doctrines could be judged. We shall consider the importance of both tradition and creeds later in this chapter (1.5.7; 1.5.8).

1.3.3. The Challenge of Platonism: Clement of Alexandria and Origen

Christianity expanded rapidly in the Hellenistic world. This does not appear to have been the result of a deliberate strategy on the part of Christian leaders. On the whole, Christian leaders and communities tended to keep a low profile, aware of their vulnerable position on account of their lack of legal status. One factor in this expansion in the eastern Mediterranean area was the willingness of some Christian leaders to adapt the vocabulary and concepts of the Christian faith to chime in with the ideas and issues of classical Greek philosophy – especially the forms of Platonism dominant in the region at this time, often known as "Middle Platonism."

One of the most important centers of Christian engagement with Platonism was the great Egyptian city of Alexandria, founded by Alexander the Great. As we noted earlier (1.3.1), the Jewish writer Philo of Alexandria had developed approaches to Judaism which emphasized its compatibility with Platonism. Some Christian writers in Alexandria took the building blocks used by Philo, and developed ways of thinking about the Christian faith which made it particularly attractive to Platonists.

Why would they want to do this? One obvious reason is that it allowed them to translate Christianity into a way of speaking and thinking that was more adapted to Hellenistic culture. Writers such as Titus Flavius Clemens (c. 150–c. 215), better known as Clement of Alexandria, who was head of one of Alexandria's "catechetical schools" during the 190s, realized that the Hebraic ways of thought characteristic of apostolic Christianity did not make much sense to Greeks. Clement proposed that Christianity should be reformulated using concepts borrowed from Platonism and other classic Greek philosophical schools – such as Stoicism – which enhanced their appeal to this important audience.

Yet such a process of theological translation was risky. Using Platonic categories to communicate Christian ideas could lead to those ideas being distorted or misunderstood. Clement's critics were never entirely sure whether he was Christianizing Platonism or Platonizing Christianity. Clement himself was clear that he was prepared to take such risks, because of their obvious benefits. So was Origen (184–253), who emerged as head of another Alexandrian "catechetical school" in the first decade of the third century. Both believed that Hellenistic philosophical systems owed their origins to divine revelation, and thus held that they were justified in reclaiming them in the service of theology. Yet some other writers of this period – such as Tertullian – held that this move was corrupting, opening the door to heresy and the dilution of Christian truth.

So how did this increased use of Platonism show up in the theology of the early church? One obvious outcome of this approach was an increased use of allegorical biblical interpretation. Where the Hebrew mind saw truth expressed in history, most Greek minds saw it expressed in timeless ideas. As Philo of Alexandria had shown earlier (1.3.1), allegorical biblical interpretation allowed the biblical exegete to strip away the historical shell of the Bible, and uncover its philosophical core.

Origen adopted this approach to biblical interpretation, and took it a stage further. He drew a somewhat controversial distinction between uneducated Christians, who tended to read the Bible literally and historically, and their more sophisticated counterparts, who were able to go beneath the outward appearance of the text, and discover its hidden deeper "spiritual" meanings using allegorical methods of interpretation.

Yet the Platonism of Clement and Origen is more clearly seen in their specifically theological doctrines, rather than the means by which they arrived at these ideas. Both regarded the Platonic or Stoic notion of the *logos* as critically important for a proper Christology – that is, for an understanding of the identity of Jesus of Nazareth. Building on the gospel of John's declaration that the "word (Greek: *logos*) became flesh" in Jesus of Nazareth (John 1:14), Clement and Origen argued that Jesus of Nazareth was to be understood as the "word incarnate." This allowed them to emphasize that Jesus of Nazareth was the mediator between God and the creation. For Clement, the Logos "had come to us from heaven," in that God has "entered into" or "become attached to" human flesh, thus allowing God to become visible and tangible to humanity.

Origen also used Platonic ideas to resolve other more speculative theological questions – such as the shape of the resurrection body. What shape would human beings take after they had been raised from the dead? Origen's reply shows how he drew on Platonic norms in occasionally surprising ways. The resurrection body, he argued, would have to be a perfect shape. But according to Plato's dialogue *Timaeus*, a perfect body is spherical. Therefore, Origen concluded, the resurrection body would be a sphere.

The debate about the merits of the approaches adopted by Clement and Origen continues today. What can be said, however, is that their approach seems to have secured a hearing for Christianity in the more intellectually sophisticated quarters of Hellenistic culture, and given Christian theology the beginnings of a secure intellectual foundation. More work would need to be done (and, in some cases, existing ideas would need to be undone). But an important step had been taken in ensuring that Christianity would be taken seriously by the Hellenistic world of the third century.

1.3.4.   Christianity and the Cities: Alexandria and Antioch

Early Christianity established itself primarily in cities – such as the Greek-speaking port cities on the Asian coastline, including Ephesus and Pergamon – rather than in remote rural areas. Cities, especially ports, were centers of commerce and trade, one of the classical means by which new religious and philosophical ideas were spread in the ancient world. The cities also offered a greater degree of anonymity than was possible in the countryside, allowing Christians to conceal themselves during an age that was generally hostile to their beliefs and practices. Christian communities were able to meet in secret, celebrate their beliefs, and begin to share their vision with outsiders.

The link between Christianity and the cities of the Roman Empire became so significant that the Latin term for a "country-dweller" (Latin: *paganus*) later began to be used in western Christian circles to refer to someone who retained older Roman religious beliefs, at a time when the empire had adopted Christianity as its official religion. A Latin term that originally lacked any religious associations of any kind thus came to refer to someone who practiced traditional forms of religion.

As Christianity became more deeply embedded in the imperial cities, a number of significant institutional developments began to take place. One was the rise of the "metropolitan bishop" – that is, a bishop who was seen as the titular leader of all the churches in a city, rather than of one specific Christian community. The most important of these were the bishops of Alexandria, Antioch, Constantinople, Jerusalem, and Rome. After the legalization of Christianity, these metropolitan bishops began to wield considerable political power – especially the bishop of Rome, who was seen as having a symbolic authority linked with the imperial authority of the city of Rome itself.

The two intellectual centers of Hellenistic Christianity were the cities of Alexandria and Antioch. Like Alexandria, Antioch had been founded by Alexander the Great. Located on the banks of the Orontes River in modern-day Turkey, this city came to be one of the great population centers of the Hellenistic world. (A smaller city of the same name is referred to as "Pisidian Antioch.") By the middle of the fourth century, these two cities were firmly established as the leading intellectual and administrative centers of Hellenistic Christianity.

While it is important not to inflate the differences between them, two quite distinct approaches to the Christian faith became associated with each city during the early fourth century. One point of difference concerned their preferred ways of interpreting the Bible. Alexandria remained a center where allegorical exegesis was seen as particularly important; Antioch, however, preferred a more literal or historical approach.

Yet the more important difference was Christological, concerning the way in which the identity of Jesus of Nazareth was understood. The "catechetical schools" of both great cities were agreed that Jesus was to be understood as fully divine and fully human – a view set out by the Council of Nicaea in 325. Yet they understood this basic belief in quite distinct manners. During the fourth century, two different traditions began to crystallize.

The Alexandrian school insisted that, if human nature is to be deified, it must be united with the divine nature. God must therefore become united with human nature in such a manner that the latter is enabled to share in the life of God. This was what had happened in and through the incarnation of the Son of God in Jesus Christ. The Second Person of the Trinity assumed human nature, and by doing so, ensured its divinization. God became human, in order that humanity might become divine. Alexandrian writers thus placed considerable emphasis upon the New Testament text John 1:14 ("the Word became flesh"), which came to embody the fundamental insights of the school, and the liturgical celebration of Christmas. To celebrate the birth of Christ was to celebrate the coming of the *Logos* to the world, and its taking human nature upon itself in order to redeem it.

Antiochene theologians tended to place their emphasis at a different point. If redemption is to take place, it must be on the basis of a new obedience on the part of humanity. In that humanity is unable to break free from the bonds of sin, God is obliged to intervene. This leads to the coming of the redeemer as one who unites humanity and divinity, and thus to the reestablishment of an obedient people of God. Jesus Christ is at one and the same time both God and a real individual human being. There is a "perfect conjunction" between the human and divine natures in Christ.

This may seem a somewhat technical debate, of little relevance to the wider life of the church. Nevertheless, it is an important marker of the growing importance of these two cities, both as centers of theological reflection and ecclesiastical leadership. By the end of the fourth century, when Christianity had gained imperial recognition and privilege, the bishops of these two cities were significant players in debates about the location of spiritual authority within the church. Did power lie with the bishop of Rome, the capital city of the empire? Or was it dispersed among the bishops of the great cities of the empire, each of which was autonomous? These debates began to become increasingly important as the western empire came under threat, and political power began to shift to the eastern city of Constantinople (1.4.7).

1.3.5.   Monasticism: A Reaction against the Cities

The growing presence of Christianity in the cities of the Roman Empire was seen by many Christians as a positive development. Not only was it an important witness to the increasing influence of the Christian faith; it was a means by which Christianity could begin to work for the transformation of urban culture and society. Christianity, some argued, was like yeast in bread dough – a small presence, which would gradually grow, and eventually change things for the better.

Other Christians, however, were not so sure that this development was quite such a positive thing. While they did not rule out the possibility that urban expansion of the Christian faith might bring about a moral and spiritual transformation of the degeneracy of the imperial cities, it was quite possible that the reverse might happen. Might the immorality and debauchery of the cities – a frequent topic of concern in early Christian sermons – end up contaminating and corrupting the church?

One of the most important developments to take place within early Christianity was the rise of monasticism. (The terms "monk" and "monasticism" both come from the Greek word *monachos*, meaning "solitary" or "alone.") The origins of the monastic movement are generally thought to lie in remote hilly areas of Egypt and parts of eastern Syria. Significant numbers of Christians began to make their homes in these regions, in order to get away from the population centers, with all the distractions that these offered. Anthony of Egypt, who left his parents' home in 273 to seek out a life of discipline and solitude in the desert, is an excellent representative of this growing trend.

The theme of withdrawal from a sinful and distracting world became of central importance to these communities. Yet it soon became clear that there were two quite different ways of withdrawing from the world. On the one hand, there were those who saw monasticism in terms of a solitary and ascetic life (a form of monasticism often referred to as "eremitic"). On the other, there were those who saw monasticism in communal terms ("cenobitic" monasticism). The more communal approach began to gain the upper hand in the fifth century. Solitary monks (often referred to as "hermits") faced considerable difficulties. How would they find food? Or participate in the common prayer that was expected of all Christians?

While some lone figures continued to insist on the need for individual isolation, the concept of a communal life in isolation from the world gained the ascendancy. One important early monastery was established by Pachomius (c. 292–348), generally recognized as the founder of this communal form of monasticism, during the years 320–5. This monastery developed an ethos which would become normative in later monasticism. Members of the community agreed to submit themselves to a common life which was regulated by a Rule, under the direction of a superior. The physical structure of the monastery played an important role in reinforcing its spiritual values. The monastery complex was surrounded by a wall, highlighting the idea of separation and withdrawal from the world.

Figure 1.4   The Benedictine monastery at Montecassino (or "Monte Cassino"), Italy. © Witold Skrypczak/Alamy

The Greek word *koinōnia* (often translated as "fellowship"), frequently used in the New Testament, now came to refer to the idea of a common corporate life, characterized by common clothing, meals, furnishing of cells (as the monks' rooms were known), and manual labor for the good of the community. Monastic communities were increasingly seen as being more spiritually beneficial than solitary forms of the Christian life, in that communal charity could more easily be practiced and experienced.

The monastic ideal proved to have a deep attraction for many. By the fourth century, monasteries had been established in many locations in the Christian east, especially in the regions of Syria and Asia Minor. It was not long before the movement was taken up in the western church. By the fifth century, monastic communities had come into existence in Italy (especially along the western coastline), Spain, and Gaul. Augustine of Hippo, one of the leading figures of the western church at this time, established two monasteries in North Africa at some point during the period 400–25. For Augustine, the common life (now designated by the Latin phrase *vita communis*) was essential to the realization of the Christian ideal of love. Furthermore, intellectual study and spiritual reflection were best done together with other believers, rather than in solitary isolation. The monastery, Augustine argued, was thus the basis for the kind of study and reflection that would enrich both personal devotion and the life of the church.

Pachomius insisted that monks should not be ordained, so that they could not become involved in struggles for ecclesiastical preferment. Monks, Pachomius believed, should not make themselves vulnerable to temptation through ambition for promotion. Yet this view was not universally held. The Cappadocian writer Basil the Great held that monks could become priests, seeing this as a means by which the church as a whole could be enriched by monastic wisdom.

This development was consolidated after the fall of the Roman Empire. During the sixth century, the number of monasteries in the region grew considerably. It was during this period that one of the most comprehensive monastic "Rules" – the "Rule of Benedict" – made its appearance. Benedict of Nursia (c. 480–c. 550) established his monastery at Monte Cassino at some point around 525. The Benedictine community followed a rule which was dominated by the notion of the unconditional following of Christ, sustained by regular corporate and private prayer, and the reading of Scripture. Many argue that such monasteries acted as the agents of transmission of Christian theology and spirituality following the collapse of the Roman Empire, preparing the way for the theological and spiritual renaissance of the Middle Ages.

1.3.6.   The Cult of Thecla: Women and the Churches

As noted earlier, women played an important role in the apostolic church (1.1.6). Yet, for reasons that are not fully understood, the churches began to adopt more traditional, culturally accommodated approaches to headship and hierarchy. In the Greco-Roman world, the ideal woman was portrayed as self-effacing, industrious, and loyal to her family. Funerary monuments provide some of the clearest expressions of these cultural norms, celebrating a deceased woman's conformity to what was expected of her. This inscription on a first-century Roman tombstone illustrates how these virtues were embodied and commended.

> Here lies Amymone, wife of Marcus, best and most beautiful of women. She made wool, she was devoted to the gods and her family. She was modest, careful with money, and chaste. She stayed at home.

Inevitably, assimilation of such cultural norms led to the exclusion of women from positions of communal and liturgical leadership, even if they may have exercised considerable social and political influence behind the scenes. There were three orders of ministry within the early church: bishops, priests, and deacons. Although women rapidly found themselves excluded from the former two roles, they remained active as deaconesses. This form of ministry is recorded from the second century onwards, and played a significant role in the pastoral life of the churches.

The "Didascalia of the Apostles" (Latin: *Didascalia Apostolorum*), thought to date from the first half of the third century, suggests that male deacons should be compared to Christ, and deaconesses to the Holy Spirit. In practical terms, it seems that deacons undertook pastoral ministry to men, and deaconesses to women. The Council of Chalcedon (451) ruled that women should not be allowed to be ordained as deaconesses until they were forty. This regularization of this ministerial order is generally held to point to its importance in the life of the church at the time.

Figure 1.5   Ruins of the historic north African city of Carthage. © Silvestro Castelli/istockphoto. com

Martyrdom remained one of the most significant areas in which women played a leading role. Two of the most celebrated women martyrs of the early church in the west were Perpetua and Felicitas, who were martyred together in Carthage in the first decade of the third century. The traditional account of their martyrdom offers some insights into the social dynamics of the churches at this time. Perpetua, a Roman noblewoman, was a nursing mother; Felicitas, her pregnant slave. Perpetua had been baptized against the explicit wishes of her father, indicating that she was prepared to break with familial traditions and loyalties on account of her faith. The fact that both a noblewoman and her slave were martyred together reflects a growing tendency for martyrdom to become a means of self-empowerment for women at this time, when imperial hostility to Christianity often led to sporadic harassment and occasionally to systematic persecution.

One of the most remarkable witnesses to the aspirations of women in the early church is found in the cult of Thecla of Iconium. This is thought to have originated in the second half of the second century, and is described in a document of this period known as *The Acts of Paul and Thecla*. The document describes a noblewoman, Thecla, who was a traditional "stay at home" aristocrat. One day, she overheard the preaching of the apostle Paul through an open window. Enthralled by what she heard, she left behind her fiancé and her home to follow Paul, and eventually to travel and proclaim the gospel herself.

One of the core themes of this intriguing work is the rejection of the social role assigned to women of noble birth at this time in imperial Roman culture – especially the traditional bonds of familial loyalty, the expectation that they will marry, and their dedication to their home – as a result of the counter-cultural values and beliefs of the Christian faith. At one point, Thecla was condemned to death by the Roman authorities at the instigation of her mother, who was outraged by her rejection of traditional cultural norms. Yet Thecla eventually prevailed.

The importance of the story of Thecla lies in its affirmation of the role of women in carrying out church responsibilities that were increasingly allotted to male agents – such as public leadership and evangelism. Thecla was prepared to dress as a man in order to be able to carry out this role. As early as 190, the Latin theological Tertullian expressed concern that some were using the story of Thecla to justify the public ministry of women in churches, especially in baptizing and preaching – something to which Tertullian was opposed.

Yet Christian women were now playing a significant role outside the mainstream of church life. The Montanist movement of the mid-second century, for example, centered on three charismatic individuals in the province of Phrygia – Montanus himself, and two women colleagues: Prisca (sometimes called Priscilla) and Maximilla. Montanism is perhaps best understood as a religious renewal movement, similar in some ways to modern Pentecostalism. Contemporary sources suggest that Prisca and Maximilla achieved greater status than Montanus himself amongst the movement's followers. Although Montanism had considerable influence within the churches, especially in Africa, it is best seen as a movement operating outside the administrative and power structures of the church. This allowed women to assume charismatic leadership roles that were becoming problematic within church structures, which were increasingly conforming to Roman social norms.

The same is true of the monastic movement, which often arose as a response to concerns about the morality and spirituality of mainline Christian communities, especially in the cities (1.3.5). The *amma* (Aramaic: "mother") became a recognized female figure of spiritual wisdom and discernment in the monastic spirituality of the deserts of Egypt, Palestine, and Syria, especially during the fourth and fifth centuries. Syncletica of Alexandria (died c. 350) is one of a number of female spiritual writers whose sayings are included in the collection traditionally known as the "Sayings of the Desert Fathers."

If space permitted, other women of importance in early Christianity could be noted – such as Monica, the mother of Augustine of Hippo. Despite the increasing limitations placed on women within the churches, many found ways to subvert these, and exercise a significant public ministry. The "cult of Thecla of Iconium" is important both for the narrative of evangelical aspiration associated with Thecla herself, but also for the influence that this story came to have on many women in the early church.

1.4. The Imperial Religion: The Conversion of Constantine

Although Christianity was born into a culture in which there was little sympathy for its ideas or values, the new faith spread rapidly in both the western and eastern regions of the Roman Empire. This rise in influence can be thought of as a "bottom up" development, which took place without imperial intervention or support, or the use of violence or force by the early Christians. It is difficult to identify the "tipping point" – the moment at which the numerical strength of Christianity forced a change in the attitude of the Roman authorities towards its presence. As we shall see, one of the most significant turning points in the history of the Christian church took place in the early fourth century, with the conversion of the emperor Constantine (1.4.2). In this section, we shall consider the changing status of Christianity, and its implications for Christian identity within an imperial culture.

1.4.1. Roman Persecution of Christianity

Even in the New Testament, there are clear signs of awareness of antagonism on the part of the Roman authorities towards Christianity. The Roman historian Tacitus (56–117) provides some evidence of his popular resentment in the aftermath of the Great Fire of Rome (64), when he spoke of Christians as "a class hated for their abominations." The Revelation of St. John, the final work in the New Testament canon, is widely regarded as reflecting active hostility towards Christian groups in the late first century. It is thought to reflect the situation during the final years of the reign of the Roman emperor Domitian, particularly around 95. Yet although Domitian was a strong supporter of traditional Roman religion, there are no historical records of any official persecution of Christianity at this time. Cultural hostility may have been supplemented by local vendettas of one sort or another. But this was not centrally organized or authorized.

Cultural suspicion towards Christianity was aroused for a number of reasons. Christians refused to take part in games and other public ceremonies, because of their quasi-religious nature. This led to Christians being seen as hostile to their fellow citizens. They were also widely regarded as "atheists" on account of their refusal to acknowledge the official state religion, regarding their loyalty to God as preventing them from swearing allegiance to any other deities or figures – such as the emperor. Many Romans believed that proper devotion to the traditional gods was necessary for the well-being of cities and populations, and believed that Christianity's refusal to endorse such ceremonies was dangerous. The proverb "no rain, because of the Christians" was well-established by the fourth century.

Yet many popular criticisms of the early Christians arose from ignorance and misunderstanding of their practices. The eucharist, for example, was widely understood to involve cannibalism, incest, child murder, and orgies. In part, these rumors gained credence because of the secrecy of early Christian meetings (1.2.5). Nobody really knew what was happening. And in the absence of hard information, defamatory rumors abounded.

The absence of any official imperial policy towards Christianity is suggested by a letter written by Pliny the Younger, governor of the province of Bithnyia, around the year 112 to the emperor Trajan. Pliny asked for guidance on how to deal with Christians. The rise of Christianity in the region was causing some resentment – for example, from traders who specialized in votive offerings at temples. Pliny needed a ruling on whether Christianity itself was illegal, or whether it was certain actions which were associated with, or arose from, Christianity that merited prosecution.

The fact that Pliny had to seek clarification on this matter suggests that there was no legislation on the status of Christianity from either the Roman Senate or emperor. There were a number of general grounds on which Christians might face prosecution. One of the most significant was membership of a *collegium illicitum* – an illegal society, which might be considered to pose a threat to public order or imperial security. Such societies existed in Rome, Pompeii, and Ostia, and had caused problems for the magistrates. A second ground for prosecution was *coercitio* – the magistrates' right to enforce their rulings. A failure to comply was regarded as a disobedience of public authority. The third ground was the *lex maiestatis*, which made it treasonable to support enemies of the state. None of these were specific to Christianity; each, however, could be adapted to deal with at least some aspects of Christian behavior – for example, the refusal to take part in the imperial cult.

Pliny himself was puzzled about the legal basis for the prosecution of Christianity, as he indicated that his own investigations had uncovered nothing to suggest that the movement was seditious or dangerous. As far as he could establish, Christianity seemed to be about:

> coming to a meeting on a given day before dawn, and singing a hymn to Christ as to God, swearing with a sacred oath not to commit any crime, never to steal or commit robbery, commit adultery, dishonour a sworn agreement, or refuse to return a sum left in trust. When all this was finished, it was their custom to go their separate ways, and later to gather again to take food of an ordinary and simple kind.

There is no doubt that individual Christians and Christian groups were subjected to persecution at various points in the first three centuries. These, however, were often sporadic rather than systematic, local rather than global. There are also indications that popular demands for repression of Christianity were resisted by the imperial authorities at various points. One such persecution, however, merits closer attention: the Decian persecution in the middle of the third century.

During his brief reign (249–51), the emperor Decius ordered a general reversion to the religion of the classic Roman age, believing that this would safeguard the future of the empire. Decius's views were shaped by the fact that his reign marked the millennium of the city of Rome, whose founding was traditionally dated to 752 BC. Every inhabitant of the empire was required to offer a sacrifice to the gods, and receive a certificate of compliance (Latin: *libellus*) from the local magistrate.

Decius clearly hoped that a return to traditional Roman *pietas* would restore the fortunes of the empire, at a time when it faced increasing challenges from threats to its borders from potential invaders on the one hand, and from various oriental cults and superstitions on the other. The rise of these cults, it seemed to Decius, robbed the empire of its religious unity. The survival of the empire depended upon the "peace of the gods" (Latin: *pax deorum*), which was only guaranteed by observing the traditional cult.

The Decian persecution ended in June 251, when Decius was killed on a military expedition. Many Christians lapsed or abandoned their faith in the face of persecution. Division arose immediately within the church over how these individuals should be treated: did such a lapse mark the end of their faith, or could they be reconciled to the church by penance? Opinions differed sharply, and serious disagreement and tension resulted. Very different views were promoted by Cyprian of Carthage and Novatian. Both of these writers were martyred during the persecution instigated by the emperor Valerian in 257–8. Christians were now forbidden to visit their cemeteries. One early victim of this new persecution was Pope Sixtus II, who was beheaded in 258, and had to be buried in the safety of the underground catacombs.

One of the most severe outbursts of persecution came about in February 303, during the reign of the emperor Diocletian (284–313). An edict was issued ordering the destruction of all Christian places of worship, the surrender and destruction of all their books, and the cessation of all acts of Christian worship. Christian civil servants were to lose all privileges of rank or status and be reduced to the status of slaves. Prominent Christians were forced to offer sacrifice according to traditional Roman practices. It is an indication of how influential Christianity had become that Diocletian forced both his own wife and daughter, who were known to be Christians, to comply with this order. The persecution continued under successive emperors, including Galerius, who ruled the eastern region of the empire.

In 311, Galerius ordered the cessation of the persecution. It had been a failure, and had merely hardened Christians in their resolve to resist the reimposition of classical Roman pagan religion. Galerius issued an edict which permitted Christians to live normally again and "hold their religious assemblies, provided that they do nothing which would disturb public order." The edict explicitly identified Christianity as a religion, and offered it the full protection of the law. The legal status of Christianity, which had been ambiguous up to this point, was now resolved. The church no longer existed under a siege mentality.

Following the end of its persecution in 311, Christianity was now recognized as a legal religion; it was, however, merely one among many such religions. The conversion of the emperor Constantine changed this irreversibly, and brought about a complete change in the situation of Christianity throughout the Roman Empire. We shall consider this tipping point in the next section.

1.4.2.   The First Christian Emperor: Constantine

Flavius Valerius Aurelius Constantinus Augustus (272–337) – better known simply as "Constantine" – became emperor during a complex and difficult period in Roman imperial history, regarded by many historians as marking the transition between classical antiquity and late antiquity. A series of crises in the late third century (235–84) came close to bringing the Roman Empire to collapse through the threat of invasion, a damaging civil war, outbreaks of the plague, and serious economic depression. Finally, a compromise solution was devised in which absolute power was shared by four rulers. This arrangement, known as the "Tetrarchy," was a pragmatic response to a situation in which no individual commanded enough support to rule the entire empire. Each was allocated charge of a specific region. Although Rome remained the symbolic capital of the empire, the four "tetrarchs" established their bases close to the frontiers of the empire, in order to be able to deal with the threat of invasion from the north and east.

By the end of the first decade of the fourth century, however, the threats of invasion had receded. The Tetrarchy now began to break down, as difficulties arose concerning the succession. Between 309 and 313 most of the claimants to the imperial office were eliminated. Constantine forced Maximian's suicide in 310. Galerius, who had declared

Christianity to be legal, died of natural causes in 311. Following Maxentius's seizure of power in Italy and North Africa, Constantine led a body of troops from western Europe in an attempt to establish his authority in the region. Maxentius was defeated by Constantine at the Battle of the Milvian Bridge in 312 and subsequently killed. Maximinus committed suicide at Tarsus in 313 after being defeated in battle by Licinius. This left only two claimants for the title of emperor: Constantine in the west and Licinius in the east. It was not until 324 that Constantine finally defeated Licinius, and proclaimed himself the sole emperor of a reunited Roman Empire.

Constantine showed no particular attraction to Christianity in his early period. He declared himself to be a Christian shortly after his decisive victory at the Milvian Bridge, to the north of Rome, on October 28, 312, after which he was proclaimed emperor. This point is affirmed by both Christian and pagan writers. What is not clear is precisely why or when this conversion took place.

Some Christian writers (such as Lactantius and Eusebius) suggest that the conversion may have taken place before the decisive battle, with Constantine seeing a heavenly vision ordering him to place the sign of the cross on his soldier's shields. "In this sign you shall conquer" (Latin: *in hoc signo vinces*). Whatever the reasons for the conversion, and whether it dates from before or after the battle of the Milvian Bridge, the reality and consequences of this conversion are not in doubt.

Figure 1.6　Constantine I, the Great, the first Christian Roman Emperor, c. 280–337. Marble bust, 312–25. Museo del Prado. Photo: akg-images

The first change in imperial attitudes towards Christianity took place in 313, when Constantine and Licinius issued the Edict of Milan, proclaiming freedom of religion in both the western and eastern parts of the Roman Empire. This did not give Christianity any privileges; nevertheless, it opened the way to it playing a significant role in Roman society, allowing Christians to emerge from the shadows and margins, and assume major social roles. In the years that followed, Rome gradually became Christianized.

Yet Constantine proceeded cautiously. Initially, he retained traditional Roman pagan symbolism, anxious not to create popular discontent against his program of religious reform. The triumphal arch constructed in 315 to mark Constantine's victory in the Battle of the Milvian Bridge makes use of no Christian symbolism, but shows sacrifices being made to gods such as Apollo, Diana, and Hercules. In the late 310s, Constantine often made moves that could be interpreted as a reaffirmation of traditional paganism as much as of Christianity.

An important turning point took place in 321, when Constantine decreed that Christians and non-Christians should worship on the "day of the Sun." While this clearly reflected the Christian practice of meeting and worshipping on Sunday, it could also be presented as a reaffirmation of the sun-cult favored by earlier emperors, such as Aurelian. The Roman mints continued for some time to produce coins showing figures of traditional Roman deities, reassuring the population that traditional Roman paganism was still being taken seriously. Constantine proved to be an able diplomat, moving Rome towards Christianity while publicly retaining traditional religious symbols.

Yet alongside these traditional pagan images, Christian symbols now began to appear on Roman coins. Furthermore, Constantine stipulated that his statue erected in the Forum should depict him bearing a cross – "the sign of suffering that brought salvation," according to the inscription provided by the emperor himself. Christianity was now more than just legitimate; it was on its way to becoming the established religion of the empire.

A critical step in this process took place in 324–5, when Constantine led an army against the eastern emperor Licinius. The immediate cause of this campaign was religious: Licinius had reneged on the Edict of Milan, and had introduced policies which discriminated against Christians. Licinius was finally defeated at the Battle of Chrysopolis, near Chalcedon, on September 18, 324, and executed the following year. This victory made Constantine sole emperor over the entire Roman Empire. Christianity would now be tolerated throughout the empire. The city of Constantinople (from the Greek *Kōnstantinoupolis*, meaning "the city of Constantine") was established as a "new Rome," and would become the administrative center of the empire.

Apart from a brief period of uncertainty during the reign of Julian the Apostate (361–3), the church could now count upon the support of the state. Theology thus emerged from the hidden world of secret church meetings, to become a matter of public interest and concern throughout the Roman Empire. Increasingly, doctrinal debates became a matter of both political and theological importance. Constantine wished to have a united church throughout his empire, and was thus concerned that doctrinal differences should be debated and settled as a matter of priority. This led to the emperor summoning the Council of Nicaea in 325, to settle doctrinal disputes within the church and allow Christianity to function in a way that Constantine believed was appropriate for the religion of the empire.

1.4.3.   The Christianization of the Roman Empire

The conversion of Constantine and his victory over Licinius in 324 removed any remaining barriers to Christians openly practicing their faith throughout the Roman Empire. Christianity was given the same legal protection as that offered to other religions, and Christians were given freedom to worship as and where they pleased. The most immediate result of this was that Christians felt confident enough to worship in public, no longing needing to meet secretly in private houses. The way was now clear for Christians to construct and own their own purpose-built churches.

It is important not to overstate the importance of these developments. After all, even in the early days of Christianity, house churches in the imperial cities were difficult to conceal. Neighbors were generally aware that these were Christian meeting places, and often chose to say nothing about it. Many Christians began to adopt names that were distinctively Christian, marking them out from their pagan neighbors. Yet there was a difference. Now, these things could be done with impunity, without fear of official sanctions, discrimination, or persecution.

This new benign attitude on the part of the imperial authorities helped the consolidation of Christianity throughout the empire. Yet other factors must be acknowledged as well. The crisis of the late third century seemed to many to mark the end of an era, and the need for change. Might the pagan religion of classical Rome have had its day? Might it be time for something new? Cults from Egypt were gaining adherents, and loosening the hold of the older religious system. The rise of Christianity contributed still further to the sense that classical paganism was on the wane. In the view of some scholars, the greatest rival to Christianity at Rome in the third century may not have been traditional Roman paganism, but the Egyptian cult of Isis.

Yet perhaps most importantly, the withdrawal of state sanction and support for paganism left it exposed and vulnerable. Its future now depended on its capacity to attract adherents, rather than the traditional sponsorship of the state. The evidence suggests that it was not up to this challenge. In the past, emperors and wealthy citizens had endowed temples dedicated to the traditional Roman gods. They now began to endow Christian churches instead. Constantine was responsible for the building of large basilicas in many European cities, giving Christianity a public presence in the cities. Imperial financial support for pagan temples was discontinued. Private individuals followed their emperor's lead, switching their financial support from paganism to Christianity. Lacking the means to raise funds, pagan temples quickly fell into disuse, often being converted to Christian churches.

Within a generation, Christianity had moved from being a persecuted movement on the fringes of imperial culture to becoming its establishment. The Christian church was simply not prepared for this radical transition. Its bishops were once merely leaders of congregations; they now became pillars of Roman society, with power and influence. Its churches were once private homes; they were now massive dedicated buildings, publicly affirming the important place of Christianity in imperial culture. The simple forms of early worship were replaced by ceremonies and processions of increased complexity, adapted to the splendor of the great basilicas now springing up in the imperial cities.

There were setbacks – most notably, the curious reign of Julian the Apostate from 361–3, notable mainly for its unsuccessful attempts to reestablish a fading and tarnished paganism as the official imperial religion. A later source reports that Julian's final words were "You have won, O Galilean" (Latin: *Vicisti, Galilaee*). Yet Julian's abortive attempt to restore the fortunes of paganism merely proved to be an interlude in the inexorable rise of the political, social, and intellectual influence of Christianity. His successor, Jovian, rescinded Julian's legal measures directed against Christianity. Theodosius the Great, who reigned as emperor from 379 to 395, finally issued a series of measures that made Christianity the official religion of the Roman Empire, bringing to a conclusion the slow process of Christianization initiated by Constantine.

Yet many scholars argue that this process of establishment caused Christianity to change its character. In the next section, we shall consider the reasons for this concern.

1.4.4.   The Imperialization of Christianity

As we noted in the previous section, Constantine initiated the extended process which would eventually lead to Christianity becoming the official religion of the Roman Empire. Yet this involved more than Christianity being given prominence and privilege in Roman society. The social roles and norms of traditional Roman religion were now transferred to Christianity. And, as events made clear, this led to significant changes in the ethos and outlook of Christianity, which changed its public face.

So what expectations were imposed on Christianity in making it the imperial religion? One of the core roles of traditional Roman religion was the maintenance of social cohesion. The primary function of religion was to unite the people in a sense of sacred solidarity. Each city had its own patron deities, ensuring its cohesion and giving it a distinct identity. Family religious rituals were carefully observed, especially funeral rites. The Roman military regarded religion as especially important, linking proper religious observance with success in battle. Securing the "peace of the gods" (Latin: *pax deorum*) was seen as essential to Rome's continuing prosperity and expansion.

The Latin term *religio* means "binding together," thus highlighting its role in ensuring the social and political cohesion of Roman society and culture. The Roman authorities were content for individuals to follow their own private religious beliefs, provided these did not come into open conflict with the state religion. Those who openly flouted it were branded "atheists" (1.4.1). The terms "superstition" and "cult" were often used to denigrate religions that were considered to be subversive of traditional Roman values.

Yet Roman religion was primarily about practice and binding duties, rather than an official "theology" or set of beliefs. To use technical terms, it was more about orthopraxis than orthodoxy. While Roman intellectuals often had misgivings about aspects of the state religion, they nevertheless regarded it as a valuable traditional resource that was important in maintaining cultural identity and stability.

An official Roman religion, therefore, was about creating civic unity, social coherence, and political solidarity. These obligations and expectations were now increasingly imposed upon Christianity. Having only just emerged from the margins of Roman society through being recognized as a legitimate religion, Christianity now found itself propelled to the forefront of Roman civic life. It simply did not have time to acclimatize to being a legitimate faith before it became the religion of the imperial establishment.

As a result, it was relatively easy for Constantine to exploit the church as an instrument of imperial policy, impose his imperial ideology upon it, and deprive it of much of the independence which it had previously enjoyed. Christianity did not look much like a "religion" before Constantine. Yet Constantine's demand for it to take on the role of an imperial unifying religion led to it assuming some of the religious functions and trappings that had been inherited from classical paganism. Christianity began to change. Some welcomed its new power and influence; others were anxious that its new status would compromise its beliefs and above all its values.

As we have emphasized, Roman religion was about ensuring social unity and cohesion. To his dismay, Constantine soon realized that there was a lack of unity within the church, potentially compromising its crucial religious role as a unifying imperial influence. Events in the province of Africa in the early fourth century caused an immediate headache for Constantine. The "Donatist" controversy, which simmered for years (1.5.5), had its origins in tensions that arose in Africa between two rival groups of Christians, who took very different attitudes towards those who had lapsed in the Diocletian persecution. In the end, Constantine declined to resolve the matter personally, appointing a synod of bishops to deal with the matter. The ill-feeling arising from the Donatist crisis simmered on throughout the fourth century, and erupted again in the late fourth century. We shall consider the theological issues arising from this controversy later.

Yet the main point to note here is how Constantine became drawn into ecclesiastical disputes. The new imperial status of Christianity meant that its unity and polity were now matters of significance to the state. Up to this point, heresy and orthodoxy had been concepts of importance within the Christian communities alone. They now became imperial political concerns, with important legal implications. If Christianity was to be the religion of Rome, it would have to function as Romans expected it to.

A similar issue arose later with the Arian controversy, in which the topic under discussion was the divinity of Christ (1.5.3). For Constantine, this was a dangerous debate, in that it threatened the unity of the church – and hence of the state. It was inevitable that this theological debate would be politicized. Constantine demanded resolution of the issue, for the sake of imperial unity. As the church itself possessed multiple centers of authority in rivalry with one another, it seemed to Constantine that it was unable to achieve such a resolution. Constantine therefore determined to resolve the matter in a way that would achieve political expediency and efficiency, while at the same time respecting theological integrity. The evidence suggests that Constantine was quite clear about his role in this matter. He would be an independent facilitator, who would allow the church itself to decide which was right, and thus bring the dispute to an end. Constantine wanted clarity on this matter, so that religious division and dispute could be avoided.

Constantine's method of conflict resolution was without precedence in post-biblical Christianity. Never before had the bishops of the Christian church met together. Constantine summoned all the bishops of the church to a Council in Nicaea in Bithynia (now İznik in modern Turkey) in May 325. This was the first ever gathering of Christian leaders from across the empire, reflected in the title that is often given to this event: "the first ecumenical Council." The fact that the emperor had summoned the council made it quite clear that ultimate authority lay with the emperor within imperial Christianity. This was reinforced by Constantine's decision to model the proceedings of the council on those of the Roman Senate. The structures of the church were subtly being aligned with those of the state. We shall consider the theological outcome of this council later. Yet our concern here is to note how the church was being forced to resolve issues for the sake of the wellbeing of the empire. Establishment might well have its privileges; it also had its obligations.

Culturally, the imperialization of Christianity led to the absorption of a number of Roman customs into Christian practice, where they were given a new interpretation. Perhaps the most interesting of these is the development of the "cult of the saints." Traditional Roman religion honored the dead with ceremonial meals at the site of their tombs. This practice soon became absorbed into Christianity. Christians would gather at the tombs of prominent saints or martyrs, celebrating a eucharist in their honor. Though this practice was relatively easily accommodated theologically, it is important to note that its origins did not lie in the New Testament. Its development ultimately reflected the need for a Christian equivalent to a traditional Roman practice.

1.4.5.   Augustine of Hippo: The Two Cities

By the end of the fourth century, Christianity had displaced its religious rivals, and become the official religion of the Roman Empire. Yet by that time, it was clear that Rome was in difficulty. Its northern frontiers were vulnerable to invaders. Even the "eternal city" itself seemed in danger. As a precautionary measure, the seat of government of the western empire was moved from Rome – initially to the northern city of Milan, and then in 402 to the northeastern city of Ravenna, which was regarded as easier to defend.

For there was no longer any doubt that Rome was vulnerable. In 387, a Gallic tribal army overwhelmed Rome's defenses and briefly took control of the city. Yet the tipping point in the decline of Rome took place in 408, when a Visigoth army led by Alaric laid siege to Rome. In August 410, Alaric led his armies into the city, and pillaged it. This invasion was only a temporary development, lasting a few days. Yet before they withdrew from the city, the Alaric's army burned many parts of Rome, shaking the confidence of an entire civilization. The "eternal city" was in danger of being overthrown, if not completely destroyed.

Yet the sack of Rome did not mark the end of the Roman Empire. The administration of the empire was increasingly located in the east, at the new imperial city of Constantinople. As a result of earlier decisions, made with this possibility in mind, Rome was no longer even the capital city of the western empire. The government of the western empire continued without interruption for another generation. Most historians regard the western Roman Empire as coming to an end sometime around the year 476; the eastern empire, based at the great city of Constantinople, continued to exist for the best part of a thousand years. Yet the symbolic importance of the sack of Rome was massive. The era of the "eternal city" seemed to be coming to an end.

The shock waves of this event were felt especially in Roman North Africa, where Augustine (358–430), bishop of the city of Hippo Regius, had established a reputation as one of the greatest Christian thinkers. After sacking Rome, Alaric led his armies south, with the intention of occupying Sicily and North Africa. However, Alaric's fleet was destroyed during a storm. Shortly afterwards, Alaric died. The Visigoth armies headed north instead, and finally settled in Aquitaine, in the southwest of France. Although an immediate threat had receded, Italy was nevertheless left in a state of chaos.

Refugees from Rome and southern Italy began flooding North Africa, bringing with them the burning question of the moment. Why had Rome been sacked? Was this not a confirmation of the fears of pagan philosophers, who had declared the rise of Christianity as breaking the *pax deorum*? Pagans had no doubt who was to blame for the international humiliation of Rome. Christianity had violated the sacred roots of Roman culture. The gods had responded by abandoning Rome to its enemies.

Augustine could not fail to appreciate the importance of these criticisms. He began to write his massive work *The City of God* in 412, shortly after the sacking of Rome. In the end, the work took him fifteen years to complete. His concern was first to rebut pagan criticisms of Christianity, and then to reassure Christians who were bewildered by the events taking place around them. Against the pagans, he pointed out that the history of Rome was full of calamities and disasters long before the coming of Christianity. The pagan gods seemed incapable of offering Rome protection in the past. Why would anyone think that their reintroduction at this time of crisis might cause them to do so now?

Yet Augustine's deeper concern is to make some sense of the unsettling historical context, especially the deep sense of insecurity and instability which had taken root in Roman colonial circles following the seizure of the city of Rome. In one sense, Augustine does not provide an explanation for the fall of Rome. His concern is to offer a Christian reading of history, and thus help believers to understand how they fit into the unsettling and disturbing events taking place around them. Augustine's fundamental point is made with reference to the image of "two cities" – the earthly city, and the heavenly city. They are not to be confused. Augustine here has in mind the theology developed by an earlier writer, Eusebius of Caesarea, who tended to think of the Christianized Roman Empire as a divinely ordained instrument to rule the civilized world.

Augustine set out a very different position, avoiding any suggestion that any human political system or structure was to be regarded as possessing divine sanction or ultimate authority. Christians, he declared, may live in this world, but they are not of this world. They are to think of themselves as strangers who are passing through a foreign country. While they may enjoy the blessings that this world has to offer, they must always be ready to move on. They are sojourners on earth, not citizens. The "eternal city" was not Rome, but the New Jerusalem. Heaven is the true home and ultimate destiny of Christians, and that was where their ultimate affections and loyalties must lie.

According to Augustine, believers live in an "intermediate period," separating the incarnation of Christ from his final return in glory. The church is to be seen as in exile in the "city of the world." It is *in* the world, yet not *of* the world. There is therefore a tension between the present situation of believers, in which the church is exiled in the world, and somehow obliged to maintain its distinctive ethos while surrounded by disbelief, and their future hope, in which the church will be delivered from the world, and finally allowed to share in the glory of God.

The slow passing of the Roman Empire, for Augustine, is thus to be set against the backdrop of the rise and fall of other human empires. The Christian church is not to be identified with any human empire or city, but is to see itself as a Christian colony on earth, whose true homeland (Latin: *patria*) is in heaven. The fall of the Roman Empire was not to be understood as a sign of divine disfavor or divine abandonment. Rather, it was a reminder of the frailty and transiency of all human institutions – Rome included.

1.4.6.   The Decline of the Western Empire

In the end, the Roman Empire continued to prosper, and even expand, in the east for a thousand years, for reasons we shall explore presently (1.4.7). In the west, however, Roman imperial power was widely recognized to be in terminal decline. Historians are unable to agree on a precise date for the fall of the western empire, nor on the ultimate cause of this event. For our purposes, we shall suggest that this event could be seen as taking place on September 4, 476, when Romulus Augustus, the last western emperor, was overthrown by the German military ruler Odoacer (433–93), who was declared king of Italy. The administrative changes Odoacer put in place within Italy effectively ended any idea of a "Roman Empire." A nominal imperial center was maintained at the city of Ravenna for some time, but it never had the symbolic or actual power of Rome.

So why did Rome fall? In his *Decline and Fall of the Roman Empire* (1776–88), the British historian Edward Gibbon (1737–94) firmly – and not a little simplistically – identified the cause of Rome's collapse as a loss of any sense of civic virtue among the Roman ruling class. Yet most recent historians have dissented from this somewhat superficial judgment.

Some identify other single causes – such as civil wars sapping the strength of the army, or military discipline and loyalty being eroded through the increasing use of mercenaries. Others, however, suggest that the "fall of the Roman Empire" is better seen as an extended and complex process, with numerous landmarks along the way, and having multiple – rather than single – causes.

Indeed, some have argued that it is misleading to speak of a "fall" of the western Roman Empire, in that it gradually transformed into something else. Peter Brown, the noted historian of late classical antiquity, thus argues for the gradual transformation of the western Roman Empire into what we now know as the Middle Ages.

So what were the implications of this change for Christianity? What happened to an imperial faith when the empire began to crumble and fall apart? One immediate threat was the religious faith of Odoacer, who was an Arian – someone who understood the identity of Jesus of Nazareth in a way that diverged from the Council of Nicaea in 325 (1.5.3). Yet this theological inconvenience does not appear to have led to the difficulties that might be anticipated, possibly because Odoacer was distracted from the finer points of theology by the somewhat more pressing demands of the military and political crises he faced in his new kingdom of Italy.

The real importance of the decline of imperial power for the Christian church is best seen from the standpoint of the Middle Ages. Looking back at the period of the break-up of the Roman Empire, it becomes clear that many of the characteristic features of the church of the Middle Ages began to emerge as a result of this imperial decline (2.1.1). Three developments are of particular interest.

First, the erosion of Roman political and military power created a vacuum that was never really satisfactorily filled by the successors to the emperors. These rulers tended to see themselves as exercising local, rather than international, authority. Furthermore, such rulers often did not survive long enough to establish the traditions and institutions that would secure social and political stability. Gradually, the institution of the church began to emerge as a focus of constancy and continuity. Gregory the Great, who was pope from 590 to his death in 604, brought about reform and renewal of the church, and set in place missionary undertakings in northern Europe which led to the further expansion of Christian influence within the territories of the former Roman Empire.

Second, the rise of the monasteries created centers of learning, local administration, and leadership which were independent of national or international agencies (2.1.5). Although clearly affected to some extent by political and economic developments, the monasteries were able to offer intellectual and spiritual continuity during times of uncertainty and turbulence.

Third, the church continued to use Latin in its liturgy, preaching, administration, and works of theology. The language of the Roman Empire had a long history of use in political, philosophical, and theological contexts, and proved highly adapted to the needs of the western church. The emergence of Latin as an international language helped hold the western church together, enhancing its sense of being a coherent community. As academic communities gradually emerged from religious contexts – such as the great monastic cathedral schools – it was inevitable that Latin would emerge as the language of the academy in the Middle Ages.

These developments are all of major importance for an understanding of the history of Christianity in the west during the Middle Ages, which we shall consider in the next chapter. Yet it is important to understand that Christianity remained at the heart of a "new Rome" and a new empire for a thousand years. We need to turn to consider the rise of Constantinople as an imperial hub in the east, and the implications of this for the history of Christianity in this region.

1.4.7.   The "New Rome": Byzantium and the Eastern Empire

Having secured control of both the western and eastern regions of the Roman Empire through his defeat of Licinius in 325 (1.4.2), the emperor Constantine decided to establish a new imperial city in the east. The center of gravity of the empire now lay increasingly to the east, and Constantine regarded it as essential to locate the new administrative and military hub of the empire closer to its eastern frontiers. In the end, Constantine identified a suitable site on the Bosphorus, straddling the Mediterranean and Black Seas. A settlement had already been established there by the Greeks, which they named "Byzantium."

Constantine took over the site of this older settlement, and redeveloped it. The new Greek-speaking city would be known as "Constantinople" (Greek: *Kōnstantinoupolis*, "the city of Constantine"). From the outset, Constantine referred to his city as *Nova Roma* – the "New Rome" – which would be the capital of the empire. It was consecrated on May 11, 330. As Rome declined in power during the later fourth century, Constantinople's reputation and importance rose.

Did Constantine suspect that the days of the western Roman Empire were numbered? Did he foresee the great invasions from the north, which would lead to the sack of Rome in 410? The evidence suggests that Constantine's primary concern was to ensure that the eastern empire could be efficiently administered and securely defended. Yet in the event, the eastern Roman Empire, based at Constantinople, would outlive the western Roman Empire by a thousand years. It would not fall until 1453 (2.4.7).

Christianity had spread rapidly from its original heartland of Palestine to the Greek-speaking world of the eastern Mediterranean. Christian congregations were established in many of the cities of Asia Minor (modern-day Turkey), Macedonia, and Egypt by the end of the first century. The theological foundations of this form of Christianity were given shape especially during the fourth century by writers such as Basil the Great, Gregory of Nyssa, and Gregory of Nazianzus.

With the expansion of Christianity in the region, the bishops of two of its leading cities – Antioch and Alexandria – began to be regarded as having pre-eminence among their peers (1.3.4). Although Jerusalem remained of great symbolic importance to the early church, its political importance was rapidly declining. So how should the four great "sees" (or "bishoprics") of Alexandria, Antioch, Jerusalem, and Rome relate to each other? Which, if any, had precedence over the others?

These questions of protocol were addressed by the Council of Nicaea, which was convened by Constantine in 325. Although the council's primary concern was to formulate the identity of Jesus of Nazareth in terms that all regarded as acceptable, it also tried to resolve other issues which were becoming causes of concern within the church – including the status of the bishops of the great cities. At this stage, Constantinople was not considered as a leading metropolitan center; this, however, would change as the "New Rome" rose in power and influence later in the fourth century.

In the end, the Council of Nicaea recognized the four great sees of Alexandria, Antioch, Jerusalem, and Rome as having special standing within the worldwide church. In effect, the council conceded that Jerusalem had a place of honor, but not of power. The three "Petrine sees" of Alexandria, Antioch, and Rome were recognized as being both historically significant and politically influential. Traditionally, the churches at Rome and Antioch were held to be founded by the apostle Peter, and the church of Alexandria by his disciple, Mark the Evangelist, author of the second gospel in the New Testament.

With the establishment of the imperial city of Constantinople in the fourth century, the balance of ecclesiastical power began to shift. Constantine had declared that his city would be the "new Rome." Did that not imply that it should enjoy the same ecclesiastical privileges in the east as those enjoyed by Rome in the west? The formal transfer of imperial authority from Rome to Constantinople took place in 330. Rome would remain the administrative center of the western Roman Empire until the threat of invasions from the north led to its relocation to Ravenna in the beginning of the fifth century. Constantinople was now the imperial capital.

Figure 1.7 The great eastern city of Constantinople, from *Notitia Dignitatum*, Switzerland, 1436. The Art Archive/Bodleian Library Oxford

The decision to establish Constantinople as a see – that is, as the seat of a metropolitan bishop – changed this dynamic of power and status irreversibly. The Second Council of Constantinople (381) ruled that the Bishop of Constantinople was to have "the prerogative of honor after the Bishop of Rome, because Constantinople is the New Rome." This ruling was fiercely resisted by other eastern bishops. Nevertheless, the imperial prestige of the new city was such that it was difficult to challenge this trend, especially on account of the growing alignment of secular and religious power within the empire. The Council of Chalcedon endorsed this view in 451 (1.5.9). As a result, many of the religious controversies of the age – particularly the Nestorian controversy – had obvious political dimensions, as the bishops of the older leading cities of the empire sought to assert their authority over and against the upstart see of Constantinople.

By the end of the fourth century, the eastern church had come to recognize a "pentarchy" of sees: Rome, Constantinople, Alexandria, Antioch, and Jerusalem. Although the details of what this meant in practice were sometimes sketchy, spiritual authority was understood to be distributed across these five leading cities, with none having exclusive powers or rights. As only one of these five centers was located in the western empire, it was inevitable that Rome would emerge as the focus of Latin-speaking Christianity, even when the western empire began to disintegrate in the late fifth century. Yet there would be no equivalent of a pope in the eastern church. Spiritual authority was – and remained – distributed, not centralized, in this region.

1.5.   Orthodoxy and Heresy: Patterns in Early Christian Thought

One of the challenges confronting the early church was the consolidation of its religious beliefs. The historical evidence suggests that this was not initially seen as a priority. Even by the middle of the second century, most Christians appear to have been content to live with a certain degree of theological fuzziness. Theological imprecision was not seen as endangering the coherence or existence of the Christian church. This judgment reflects the historic context of that age. The struggle for survival in a hostile cultural and political environment often led to other issues being seen as of lesser significance.

In this section, we shall consider some of the debates which developed within the church over its basic beliefs.

1.5.1.   The Boundaries of Faith: A Growing Issue

The rise of controversy within the Christian churches over a series of matters – especially concerning the identity and significance of Jesus of Nazareth – led to a tightening of the boundaries of what was to be considered as "authentic" Christianity. The periphery of the community of faith, once relatively loose and porous, came to be defined and policed with increasing rigor. Views that were regarded as acceptable in an earlier and less reflective age began to fall out of favor as the rigorous process of examination accompanying the controversies of the age began to expose their vulnerabilities and deficiencies. Ways of expressing certain doctrines which earlier generations regarded as robust began to appear inadequate under relentless examination. It was not necessarily that they were wrong; rather, they were discovered not to be good enough.

A good example of this development can be seen in early Christian reflection on the doctrine of creation. From the outset, Christian writers affirmed that God had created the world. However, there were several ways of understanding what the notion of "creation" entailed. Many early Christian writers took over existing Jewish notions of creation, which tended to see the act of divine creation primarily as the imposition of order on pre-existing matter, or the defeat of chaotic forces. Such views remained dominant within Judaism until the sixteenth century.

Other Christian theologians, however, argued that the New Testament clearly set out the idea of creation as the calling into being of all things from nothing – an idea that later came to be known as "creation *ex nihilo*" (Latin: "out of nothing"). As this idea gained the ascendancy, the older view of creation as "ordering of existing matter" came to be seen initially as deficient, and subsequently as wrong. An idea that was once regarded as mainstream thus gradually came to be sidelined, and eventually rejected altogether. Similar processes can be seen taking place in other areas of Christian thought, especially in relation to the church's understanding of the identity and significance of Jesus of Nazareth.

Early Christian doctrinal development can be compared to an intellectual journey of exploration, in which a range of possible ways of formulating core ideas were examined, some to be affirmed and others to be rejected. This process should not really be thought of in terms of winners and losers; it is better understood as a quest for authenticity during which all options were examined and assessed.

Yet this process of exploration was both natural and necessary. Christianity could not remain frozen in its first-century forms as it entered the second century and beyond. It faced new intellectual challenges which demanded that it proved itself to be capable of engaging with religious and intellectual alternatives to Christianity, especially Platonism and Gnosticism. This process of the conceptual expansion of the contents of the Christian faith proceeded slowly and cautiously. The final crystallization of this process of exploration can be seen in the formation of creeds – public, communally authorized statements of faith, which represented the *consensus fidelium* (Latin: the "consensus of the faithful"), rather than the private beliefs of individuals.

This voyage of intellectual exploration involved investigating paths which ultimately turned out to be barren or dangerous. Sometimes wrong turnings were taken at an early stage, and corrected later. It is easy to understand why many might believe that early patterns of faith are the most authentic. Yet recognizable forms of views that the church later declared to be heretical – such as Ebionitism and Docetism – can be identified within Christian communities as early as the late first century. Although many early Christian writers, such as Tertullian, held that the antiquity of a theological view was a reliable guide to its orthodoxy, this is simply not correct. Mistakes were made, right from the beginning, which later generations had to correct.

The issue of the boundaries of faith became increasingly pressing when Constantine adopted Christianity as the "unifying religion" of the Roman Empire (1.4.4). If Christianity was to be a unifying imperial force, it was clearly important that it should not itself be divided, or the cause for division. Constantine pressed for unity within the church, most obviously by convening the Council of Nicaea (325) to settle Christological disputes. The historical evidence suggests that Constantine did not favor any particular outcome of the council; he simply wanted the matter settled, leading to ecclesiastical unity.

Yet Christianity was not like classical Roman religions, which primarily focused on matters of practice – such as ceremonies, rituals, and binding oaths, all of which were seen as means of creating unity and cohesion within families, cities, and states (1.4.1). Christianity was also about ideas – ways of thinking about the world. At an early stage, it was appreciated that defective ways of conceiving the Christian faith led to inadequate ways of implementing it. Faithfulness and integrity could not be maintained simply by the regulation of practice. Ideas mattered. And the only way of working out which were the best ideas was through debates.

Constantine and his successors thus found themselves in the somewhat uncomfortable position of watching Christian theologians debating ideas about the identity of Jesus Christ and the nature of God – and in doing so, creating division and dissent within the church.

In what follows, we shall consider some of those debates, and their wider importance. The first debate concerned the texts on which subsequent debates would be based – the canon of the New Testament.

1.5.2.   The Canon of the New Testament

The first Christians used the term "scripture" or "writing" (Greek: *graphē*) to refer to a book of the Old Testament, in that these were coming to be regarded as of foundational importance to the Christian church. Debate would continue over the nature of that influence, with a growing consensus that Christianity should appropriate the ideas, but not the practices, of the people of Israel. For example, Christians would not observe Jewish food laws or sacrificial regulations.

But what of the writings of Christians themselves? What was their status? And who was to decide which writings would be normative for the church? While Christianity remained an illegal religion, it was impossible to convene councils to settle such matters. Only in the fourth century could any kind of formal consultations take place between Christian leaders across the empire.

The evidence suggests that this issue was not seen as pressing during the apostolic period, partly because historical continuity with the apostolic tradition was sufficiently strong to ensure continuity of teaching and practice with the first Christians. Irenaeus of Lyons, for example, noted how the churches of the mid-second century were able to trace direct links between their own leaders and those of the apostolic community. Irenaeus wanted to maintain continuity with the ideas and values of the apostolic era, ensuring that the teachings of that formative period were accepted by his own age. For this reason, he placed an emphasis on the importance of institutional continuity between the present church leadership and the apostles. Yet as the historical distance between the churches and the apostles increased, it became increasingly necessary for churches to base their teaching on certain texts. This made it all the more important to reach agreement on which texts they would use to inform their life and thought. The term "canon" (Greek *kanōn*: "rule" or "norm") came to be used to refer to the collections of writings accepted by churches.

A clear distinction emerged early in the second century between an inner core of texts which were widely regarded as authoritative by most Christians, and a more diffuse outer core, which some – but not all – churches regarded as useful. The four gospels and the letters of Paul rapidly acquired normative status throughout the Christian world. Other writings, such as the *Didache* (c. 70), 1 Clement (c. 96), the Epistle of Barnabas (c. 100), the letters of Ignatius of Antioch (c. 110), and the apocalypse of Peter (c. 150) did not secure such universal acceptance, being valued locally rather than universally. The Muratorian Canon – a document which reflects the practices of the Roman churches in the late second century – clearly identifies the gospels, Acts, the Pauline epistles, and three other epistles (1 John; 2 John; Jude) as being valued and accepted across the churches. Other works – such as the Revelation of John and the Apocalypse of Peter – are "received," although with a cautionary comment: "Some do not wish these to be read in churches."

It is not clear what criteria were used in making such selections. What is clear, however, is that by the beginning of the third century, without any form of international consultation, something very similar to today's New Testament canon came to be accepted by most churches. Disagreement centered on the periphery, not the core. The term *antilegomena* (Greek: "writings that are disputed" or "writings that are debated") came to be used for a small group of texts that were not universally accepted by Christians. Some of these – specifically, 2 Peter, 2 John, 3 John, 2 Peter, Jude, and Revelation – eventually achieved general acceptance. Others – such as the *Didache* and the apocalypse of Peter – did not.

By the middle of the fourth century, agreement seemed to be reached on the New Testament canon, without the need for any international council to settle the issue. Athanasius of Alexandria circulated an Easter festal letter of 367, which set out the New Testament canon in the form accepted today. Athanasius does not appear to see himself as determining what books were to be included in the biblical canons. His intention appears to have been to recognize or acknowledge those writings that had already obtained prominence from usage among the various early Christian churches. The formation of the New Testament canon was shaped by the habits of Christian communities, not the decisions of Christian bishops.

Once more, we can see the importance of the legalization of Christianity as an imperial religion on its self-definition. Once Christian leaders were free to meet and discuss their ideas, unresolved questions could be debated and adjudicated. The fixing of the canon of the New Testament and agreement on ideas of the Trinity and the person of Christ all date from this formative period.

It is sometimes suggested that the church tried to exclude or repress certain works which ought to have been recognized as authentic – such as the gospel of Thomas, or the gospel of Judas, which were found in collections of documents at Nag Hammadi in Egypt and elsewhere. The reason for their exclusion is sometimes suggested to be their unorthodox views on the identity of Jesus of Nazareth, which the church found embarrassing. There is little historical evidence for these suggestions. The "Gospel of Judas," for example, is a relatively late document, almost certainly originating within a marginalized Egyptian sect within Christianity which believed it was in possession of secret knowledge denied to outsiders. These documents were not known to Christian congregations in Rome or Antioch in the second century. They appear to have had a local influence among some Christians in Egypt in the third or fourth centuries, but were never taken seriously elsewhere. No serious case can be made for their inclusion in the New Testament canon.

1.5.3. Arianism: The Debate over the Identity of Jesus of Nazareth

One of the greatest challenges faced by the early church was the weaving together of the threads of the New Testament witness to the identity of Jesus of Nazareth into a coherent theological tapestry. Christians gradually came to realize that no existing analogy or model was good enough to meet their needs in expressing the significance of Jesus of Nazareth. The concept of the incarnation began to emerge as of central importance to the church's understanding of Jesus Christ.

While the idea was developed in slightly different ways by different writers, their core theme was that of God entering into history, and taking on human nature in Jesus of Nazareth. This idea caused considerable philosophical difficulties for many of the prevailing schools of Hellenistic philosophy. How, many asked, could an immutable God enter into history? Surely this implied that God underwent change? Contemporary Hellenistic philosophers drew a sharp distinction between the unchanging heavenly realm and the changeable created order. The notion of God entering into and dwelling within this transitory and changing order seemed inconceivable, and proved a significant barrier to some cultured pagans embracing Christianity.

This process of exploration of religious and philosophical categories suitable for expressing the significance of Jesus of Nazareth reached a watershed in the fourth century. The controversy which forced rigorous discussion of the issue was precipitated by Arius (c. 270–336), a priest in one of the larger churches in the great Egyptian city of Alexandria.

Arius's most fundamental belief was that Jesus Christ was not divine in any meaningful sense of the term. He was "first among the creatures" – that is, pre-eminent in rank within the created order, yet someone who was created, rather than being divine. The Father is thus to be regarded as existing before the Son. This is the point made by one of Arius's best-known theological slogans: "There was a time when he was not." Only the Father can be said to be "unbegotten"; the Son, like all other creatures, originates from this one source of being.

Arius's way of locating Jesus of Nazareth on a theological map can be seen, at least in part, as a continuation of the tendency in the second and third centuries towards "subordinationism." This approach recognized a trinity or triad within the Godhead, but regarded their relationship as essentially hierarchical. God the Father was the ultimate source of authority, who chose to act through Jesus of Nazareth and the Holy Spirit. Arius upheld this belief in one God who is superior to Jesus of Nazareth and the Holy Spirit, but defended it by denying the divinity of Jesus. The superiority of the Father was maintained by asserting that the Son was a creature – and hence, by definition, inferior to the Father.

Arius thus drew an absolute distinction between God and the created order. There was no intermediate or hybrid species. For Arius, God was totally transcendent and immutable. So how could such a God enter into history, and become incarnate? As a creature, the Son was changeable, and subject to pain, fear, grief, and weariness. This is simply inconsistent with the notion of an immutable God. Since the notion of a changeable God seemed heretical to Arius, he drew the obvious conclusion: Jesus of Nazareth could not be considered to be divine.

Arius's most indefatigable critic was Athanasius of Alexandria (c. 293–373). For Athanasius, Arius had destroyed the internal coherence of the Christian faith, rupturing the close connection between Christian belief and worship. There are two points of particular importance that underlie Athanasius's critique of Arius.

First, Athanasius argues that it is only God who can save. God, and God alone, can break the power of sin, and bring humanity to eternal life. The fundamental characteristic of human nature is that it requires to be redeemed. No creature can save another creature. Only the creator can redeem the creation. If Christ is not God, he is part of the problem, not its solution.

Having emphasized that it is God alone who can save, Athanasius then made a logical move which the Arians found difficult to counter. The New Testament and the Christian liturgical tradition alike regard Jesus Christ as Savior. Yet, as Athanasius emphasized, only God can save. So how are we to make sense of this? The only possible solution, Athanasius argued, is to accept that Christ is none other than God incarnate. His logic runs as follows.

1. No creature can redeem another creature.
2. According to Arius, Jesus Christ is a creature.
3. Therefore, according to Arius, Jesus Christ cannot redeem humanity.

Now Arius had no problem with the idea that Christ was the savior of humanity. Athanasius's point was not that Arius denied this, but that he rendered the claim incoherent. Salvation, for Athanasius, involves divine intervention – which Athanasius saw affirmed in a critically important biblical text: the "Word became flesh" (John 1:14). God entered into the human situation, in order to change it.

The second point that Athanasius made is that Christians worship and pray to Jesus Christ. This pattern can be traced back to the New Testament itself, and is of considerable importance in clarifying early Christian understandings of the significance of Jesus of Nazareth. By the fourth century, prayer to and adoration of Christ were standard features of Christian public worship. Athanasius argues that if Jesus Christ were a creature, then Christians were guilty of worshipping a creature instead of God – in other words, they had lapsed into idolatry. Did not the Old Testament law explicitly prohibit the worship of anyone or anything other than God? Arius was not in disagreement with the practice of worshipping Jesus; he refused, however, to draw the same conclusions as Athanasius.

An important debate emerged around this time over the best theological term to be used to define the relation of the Father to the Son. The Greek term *homoiousios,* "of like substance" or "of similar being," was seen by many as allowing the proximity between Father and Son to be affirmed without needing further speculation on the precise nature of their relation. However, the rival Greek term *homoousios,* "of the same substance" or "of the same being" eventually gained the upper hand. This was seen as defending a stronger understanding of the relation of Father and Son. When the Nicene Creed – or, more accurately, the Niceno-Constantinopolitan creed – of 381 declared that Christ was "of the same substance" with the Father, it was insisting that the Son was not simply a representative or relative of God; rather, the Son was to be seen as God incarnate. This affirmation has since come to be widely regarded as a benchmark of Christological orthodoxy within all the mainstream Christian churches, whether Protestant, Catholic, or Orthodox.

The politicization of the Arian controversy made its resolution more difficult than many would like. However, in the end, the church rejected Arius's position, holding that this compromised some core Christian affirmations about the identity of Jesus of Nazareth. Constantine did not require the church to adopt one position or the other; he simply wanted the matter resolved, to ensure religious harmony within his empire. Yet many scholars suspect that if Constantine had had a choice in the matter, he would have supported Arius. Why? Because of his emphasis on the sole location of authority in God the Father – a notion of "divine monarchy" which paralleled Constantine's own thinking about the authority and power of the emperor.

1.5.4.   Trinitarianism: A Debate about the Nature of God

The Christian doctrine of God underwent slow development in the first three centuries. Early Christian creeds set out a threefold structure to Christian belief: most of these creeds consisted of three sections, dealing with God the Father, Jesus Christ, and the Holy Spirit (1.5.8). Initially, Christian beliefs about God were framed in terms of God as creator and judge, the almighty ruler of the world to which all earthly rulers were subject, and who was the object of proper worship.

Yet the growing realization that Jesus of Nazareth had to be regarded as divine (1.5.3), in some sense of that word, demanded an expansion of this vision of God. The Council of Nicaea's firm declaration that Jesus Christ was to be regarded as fully divine – without in any way compromising his humanity – raised some fundamental theological questions. If Christ was God, how did this shape Christian thinking about God? Some scholars have suggested that second-century Christianity was really binitarian, committed to belief in God the Father, and God the Son. However, a more reliable reading of the historical evidence is that the early church was implicitly Trinitarian, while being reluctant to formalize this until clarification had been achieved on some important points.

The resolution of the Arian controversy (1.5.3) was one such moment of clarification. Yet this emphatic assertion of the divinity of Christ could be understood merely to confirm a binitarian vision of God – in other words, God as Father and Son. As the fourth-century writer Amphilochius of Iconium pointed out, the Arian controversy had first to be resolved before any serious discussion over the status of the Holy Spirit could get under way. The development of a rigorously Trinitarian theology demanded that the Holy Spirit also be recognized as divine.

Debate initially centered upon a group of writers known as the *pneumatomachoi* (Greek: "opponents of the spirit"), led by Eustathius of Sebaste. These writers argued that neither the person nor the works of the Spirit were to be regarded as having the status or nature of a divine person. In response to this, writers such as Athanasius and Basil of Caesarea made an appeal to the formula which had by then become universally accepted for baptism. Since the time of the New Testament (following the practice of Matthew 28:18–20), Christians were baptized in the name of "the Father, Son and Holy Spirit."

Athanasius argued that this had momentous implications for an understanding of the status of the person of the Holy Spirit. In his *Letter to Serapion,* Athanasius declared that the baptismal formula clearly pointed to the Spirit sharing the same divinity as the Father and the Son. This argument eventually prevailed.

However, early Christian writers were hesitant to speak openly of the Spirit as "God," in that this practice was not sanctioned by Scripture – a point discussed at some length by Basil of Caesarea in his treatise on the Holy Spirit (374–5). Even as late as 380, Gregory of Nazianzus conceded that many Orthodox Christian theologians were uncertain as to whether to treat the Holy Spirit "as an activity, as a creator, or as God."

This caution can be seen in the final statement of the doctrine of the Holy Spirit formulated by a Council meeting at Constantinople in 381. The Spirit was here described, not as "God," but as "the Lord and giver of life, who proceeds from the Father, and is worshipped and glorified with the Father and Son." The language is unequivocal; the Spirit is to be treated as having the same dignity and rank as the Father and Son, even if the term "God" is not to be used explicitly. The precise relation of the Spirit to Father and Son would subsequently become an item of debate in its own right, as the later *filioque* controversy indicates (2.1.10).

The following considerations seem to have been of decisive importance in establishing the divinity of the Holy Spirit during the later fourth century. First, as Gregory of Nazianzus stressed, Scripture applied all the titles of God to the Spirit, with the exception of "unbegotten." Gregory drew particular attention to the use of the word "holy" to refer to the Spirit, arguing that this holiness did not result from any external source, but was the direct consequence of the nature of the Spirit. The Spirit was to be considered as the one who sanctifies, rather than the one who requires to be sanctified.

Second, the functions which are specific to the Holy Spirit establish the divinity of the Spirit. Didymus the Blind (d. 398) was one of many writers to point out that the Spirit was responsible for the creating, renewing, and sanctification of God's creatures. Yet how could one creature renew or sanctify another creature? Only if the Spirit was divine could sense be made of these functions. If the Holy Spirit performed functions which were specific to God, it must follow that the Holy Spirit shares in the divine nature.

The way was now clear to the explicit formulation of a doctrine of the Trinity, consolidating the insights of earlier writers, such as Irenaeus and Tertullian. Yet a number of questions still remained unclear. For example, was the Trinitarian formula an assertion about the actual being of God, or the manner in which God acted in history?

To make sense of the discussion that took place around the time of the Council of Nicaea (325), we need to go back to the early third century concerning the Trinity. The view known as "modalism" held that the divinity of Christ and the Holy Spirit is to be explained in terms of three different "ways" or "modes" of divine self-revelation (hence the term "modalism").

One of the most influential forms of modalism, known as Sabellianism, argued for the following way of understanding the Trinity.

1. The one God is revealed in the manner of creator and lawgiver. This aspect of God is referred to as "the Father."
2. The same God is then revealed in the manner of savior, in the person of Jesus Christ. This aspect of God is referred to as "the Son."
3. The same God is then revealed in the manner of the one who sanctifies and gives eternal life. This aspect of God is referred to as "the Spirit."

There is thus no difference between the three persons of the Trinity, except for their appearance and chronological location. For modalism, the one God is revealed in three different ways at different points in salvation history.

The doctrines of the Trinity which emerged in the early fourth century reasserted the "triunity" of God, moving away from modalism. The work of the Cappadocian Fathers in the eastern church and Augustine of Hippo in the western church did much to consolidate the doctrine of the Trinity. The traditional Trinitarian vocabulary – with its core notions of as "person," "nature," "essence," and "substance" – allowed the theologians of the early church to affirm the fundamental unity of God, while celebrating the richness of God's relationship with the creation. Differences emerged between eastern and western approaches to the Trinity, particularly over the question of the Holy Spirit. Did the Spirit proceed from the Father alone (Basil the Great), or from the Father and the Son (Augustine)? This simmering disagreement would eventually lead to a debate between the eastern and western churches, which would create still further tensions between them, and make no small contribution to the "Great Schism" of 1054 (2.1.10).

1.5.5.   Donatism: A Debate over the Nature of the Church

As we noted earlier, under the Roman emperor Diocletian (284–313), the Christian church was subject to various degrees of harassment and persecution (1.4.1). Under an edict of February 303, Christian leaders were ordered to hand over their books to be burned. Those Christian leaders who handed over their books to be destroyed in this way came to be known as *traditores* (Latin: "those who handed over [their books]").

With the accession of Constantine (1.4.2), the persecution came to an end. But a sensitive issue arose in its aftermath: how were those who had lapsed or otherwise compromised themselves during the persecution to be treated? The matter became especially divisive in Roman North Africa, when Caecilianus was consecrated as bishop by three fellow-bishops, including Felix, Bishop of Aptunga – a *traditor*. Many local Christians were outraged that such a person should have been allowed to be involved in this consecration. They declared that they could not accept the authority of Caecilianus as a result, arguing that the new bishop's authority was compromised on account of the fact that the bishop who had consecrated him had lapsed under the pressure of persecution.

The Donatists were a group who believed that the entire sacramental system of the Catholic church had become corrupted on account of the lapse of its leaders. How could the sacraments be validly administered by people who were tainted in this way? It was therefore necessary to replace these people with more acceptable leaders, who had remained firm in their faith under persecution. It was also necessary to rebaptize and reordain all those who had been baptized and ordained by those who had lapsed.

The issues were still live in Roman North Africa nearly a century later, when Augustine was consecrated bishop of the coastal city of Hippo Regius in 396. Augustine responded to the Donatist challenge by putting forward a theory of the church (or "ecclesiology") which he believed was more firmly grounded than the Donatist viewpoint in the New Testament. In particular, Augustine emphasized the sinfulness of Christians. The church is not meant to be a "pure body," a society of saints, but a "mixed body" (Latin: *corpus permixtum*) of saints and sinners. Augustine finds this image in two biblical parables: the parable of the net which catches many fishes, and the parable of the wheat and the weeds. It is this latter parable (Matthew 13:24–31) which is of especial importance, and requires further discussion.

The parable tells of a farmer who sowed seed, and discovered that the resulting crop included both wheat and weeds. What could be done about it? To attempt to separate the wheat and the weeds while both were still growing would be to court disaster, probably involving damaging the wheat while trying to get rid of the weeds. But at the harvest, all the plants – whether wheat or weeds – are cut down and sorted out, thus avoiding damaging the wheat. The separation of the good and the evil thus takes place at the end of time, not in history.

For Augustine, this parable refers to the church in the world. It must expect to find itself including both saints and sinners. To attempt a separation in this world is premature and improper. That separation would take place in God's own time, at the end of history. No human can make that judgment or separation in God's place.

So in what sense can the church meaningfully be designated as "holy"? For Augustine, the holiness in question is not that of its members, but of Christ. The church cannot be a congregation of saints in this world, in that its members are contaminated with original sin. However, the church is sanctified and made holy by Christ – a holiness which will be perfected and finally realized at the last judgment.

For the Donatists, the sacraments – such as baptism and the eucharist or Lord's Supper – were only effective if they were administered by someone of unquestionable moral and doctrinal purity. Augustine responded by arguing that Donatism laid excessive emphasis upon the qualities of the human agent, and gave insufficient weight to the grace of Jesus Christ. It is, he argued, impossible for fallen human beings to make distinctions concerning who is pure and impure, worthy or unworthy: This view, which is totally consistent with his understanding of the church as a "mixed body" of saints and sinners, holds that the efficacy of a sacrament rests, not upon the merits of the individual administering it, but upon the merits of the one who instituted them in the first place – namely, Jesus Christ. The validity of sacraments is thus not ultimately dependent on the merits of those who administer them.

We see here a major theme of Augustine of Hippo's understanding of the Christian faith: that human nature is fallen, wounded, and frail, standing in need of the healing and restoring grace of God. The church, according to Augustine, is more to be compared to a hospital than to a club of healthy people. It is a place of healing for people who know that they stand in need of forgiveness and renewal. The Christian life is a process of being healed from sin, rather than a life of sinlessness, as if the cure were completed and the patient restored to full health. The church is an infirmary for the sick and for convalescents. It is only in heaven that we will finally be righteous and healthy.

The Donatist approach represents a principled yet ultimately dogmatic refusal to appreciate that all of humanity – including priests and bishops – are in need of the same healing that the gospel provides. The ministers of the Christian church proclaim the same healing which they themselves require. While the Donatist heresy appears to concern our understanding of the church and sacraments, it is more deeply rooted in an understanding of human nature, which ultimately makes the ministration of grace dependent on human merit rather than divine grace. A similar issue arose during the Pelagian controversy, to which we now turn.

1.5.6.　Pelagianism: A Debate over Grace and Human Achievement

The Pelagian controversy, which erupted in the early fifth century, brought a cluster of questions concerning human nature, sin, and grace into sharp focus. Up to this point, there had been relatively little controversy within the church on these matters. The Pelagian controversy changed that, and ensured that these issues were placed firmly on the agenda of the western church.

To understand the background to this debate, we need to consider some of the outcomes of the declaration that Christianity was the state religion of the Roman Empire (1.4.4). Inevitably, this meant that many saw the profession of Christianity as a career opportunity, and adopted it as their religion as a matter of convenience. To flourish within the Roman establishment, some realized, it was necessary to conform to its social and religious norms.

Pelagius, a British monk who arrived in Rome in the closing years of the fourth century, was distressed by the religious and moral nominalism of some Christians. He advocated personal moral reform: Christians ought to be morally upright. Such suggestions were relatively uncontroversial. Yet Pelagius set his demand for moral renewal and perfection within a theological framework that seemed to his opponents – above all, Augustine of Hippo – to convert Christianity into a religion of moral achievement. Several issues emerged as particularly controversial.

First, Pelagius declared that humanity was free to choose to act morally, and was therefore under an absolute moral obligation to do so. It was a matter of self-discipline, and the exercise of will over the lower human nature. Pelagius thus insisted that "since perfection is possible for humanity, it is obligatory."

Augustine disagreed, arguing that human nature was damaged and corrupted by sin. As a result, human freedom was limited. Knowing what we should do did not imply that we were capable of achieving it. Human free will has been weakened and incapacitated – but not eliminated or destroyed – through sin. In order for the human free will to be restored and healed, it requires divine grace. Free will really does exist; it is, however, distorted, compromised, and weakened by sin.

For Pelagius and his followers (such as Julian of Eclanum), however, humanity possessed total freedom of the will, and was totally responsible for its own sins. Human nature was essentially free and well created, and was not compromised or incapacitated by some mysterious weakness. According to Pelagius, any imperfection in humanity would reflect negatively upon the goodness of God.

Second, Augustine developed the idea of the sinfulness of human nature in medical terms. For Augustine, humanity has no control over its sinfulness. It is something which contaminates life from birth, and dominates life thereafter. It is a state over which humans have no decisive control. Augustine understands humanity to be born with an innately sinful disposition, with an inherent bias toward acts of sinning. Sin thus causes sins: the underlying state of sinfulness causes individual acts of sin. Augustine explored this point by using three analogies to illuminate the nature of original sin: disease, power, and guilt. It is ill, and needs to be healed. Until human nature has been renewed and transformed, it is simply incapable of doing good.

In contrast, Pelagius argued that sin was basically a refusal on the part of human beings to do good. We have been commanded to act righteously, and that command implies an ability. For Pelagius, the human power of self-improvement was not compromised. It was always possible for humans to discharge their obligations towards God and their neighbors.

Failure to do so could not be excused on any grounds. Sin was to be understood as an act committed willfully against God.

Augustine replied that it was through realizing its inability to carry out God's will unaided that humanity discovered grace, which Augustine interpreted as the healing and renewing action of God. Pelagius agreed that human beings needed grace, but argued that "grace" was to be understood as God's generous provision of specific moral guidance. Instead of demanding that humanity was to be "perfect," in a very general and unspecific manner, God had made it clear precisely what was intended. The Ten Commandments and the moral example of Jesus of Nazareth were gracious demonstrations of the standards of righteousness that God expected Christians to display.

Although Pelagius's views were well-received at Rome initially, the passing of time led to growing skepticism about his approach. Many began to draw the conclusion that Pelagius basically advocated a rather stern moral authoritarianism, which made no allowance for human weakness or failings on the one hand, or the transforming work of grace of God on the other. The Synod of Arles (470(?)), for example, is generally agreed to have endorsed a slightly modified version of Augustine's theology, and criticized some Pelagian ideas.

Yet Augustine's own ideas on these questions changed further during his lifetime, and led to some tensions with others on issues of grace and free will. In particular, his later doctrine of "double predestination" was seen by many as a theological innovation, which was outside the mainstream of church opinion (1.5.7). Most theologians of the period believed that human free will was damaged or compromised by the Fall; nevertheless, it was not extinguished, but continued to function, even if in a weaker form. Indeed, Augustine's theological innovation proved so controversial to some that a new debate emerged. How could the church protect itself against this kind of theological novelty? We shall consider this in what follows.

1.5.7.   Innovation: A Debate over the Role of Tradition

A series of controversies in the early church brought home the theological importance of the concept of "tradition." The word "tradition" comes from the Latin term *traditio* which means "handing over," "handing down," or "handing on." Both the notion and practice of "handing down" can be found in the New Testament. For example, Paul reminded his readers that he was handing on to them core teachings of the Christian faith which he had himself received from other people of significance (1 Corinthians 15:1–4).

The term "tradition" can refer to both the action of passing teachings on to others – something which Paul insists must be done within the church – and to the body of apostolic teachings which are passed on in this manner (1.1.5). Tradition can thus be understood as a *process* as well as a *body of teaching*. The Pastoral Epistles (three later New Testament letters that are particularly concerned with questions of church structure, and the passing on of Christian teaching: 1 Timothy, 2 Timothy, and Titus) in particular stress the importance of "guarding the good deposit which was entrusted to you" (2 Timothy 1:14). The New Testament also uses the notion of "tradition" in a negative sense, meaning something like "human ideas and practices which are not divinely authorized." Thus Jesus of Nazareth was openly critical of certain traditions within Judaism which he regarded as human constructions (e.g., see Matthew 15:1–6; Mark 7:13).

The importance of the idea of tradition first became obvious in a controversy which broke out during the second century. The Gnostic controversy centered on a number of questions, including how salvation was to be achieved. Christian writers found themselves having to deal with some highly unusual and creative interpretations of the Bible. How were they to deal with these? If the Bible was to be regarded as authoritative, was every interpretation of the Bible to be regarded as of equal value?

Irenaeus of Lyons, one of the early church's greatest theologians, did not think so. As we noted earlier (1.3.2), Irenaeus recognized that the question of how the New Testament was to be interpreted was of the greatest importance. Heretics, he argued, interpreted the Bible in any way that suited them. Orthodox believers, in contrast, interpreted the Bible in line with the apostolic tradition – in other words, in ways that apostolic authors would have recognized and approved. What had been handed down from the apostles through the church was not merely the biblical texts themselves, but a certain way of reading and understanding those texts. This apostolic tradition enables the churches to remain faithful to the original apostolic teaching, and acts as a safeguard against innovations and misrepresentations on the part of heretics. As we shall see in the next section (1.1.8), the emergence of "creeds" reflects this need for public, authoritative statements of the basic points of the Christian faith, expressing the fundamental themes of this apostolic tradition.

This point was further developed in the early fifth century by Vincent of Lérins (died before 450), who was concerned that certain doctrinal innovations were being introduced without good reason. There was a need to have public standards by which such doctrines could be judged.

So what standard was available, by which the church could be safeguarded from such errors? For Vincent, the answer was clear – tradition. Christians ought only to believe ideas that had secured universal consent. "We hold that which has been believed everywhere, always, and by all people." For Vincent, tradition was "a rule for the interpretation of the prophets and the apostles in such a way that is directed by the rule of the universal church." Creeds played an important role in Vincent's understanding of the transmission of tradition, and we shall consider their nature and role further in the next section.

1.5.8.   The Origins and Development of Creeds

The theological debates of the early church emphasized the importance of creeds – authorized, consensual, public statements of the essentials of Christian belief. Short creedal statements can be found, both in the New Testament and the literature of the apostolic age, such as the following:

> I handed on to you as of first importance what I in turn had received: that Christ died for our sins in accordance with the scriptures, and that he was buried, and that he was raised on the third day in accordance with the scriptures. (1 Corinthians 15:3–4)

Yet it became clear that these terse statements needed amplification. As Christian pedagogy became of increasing importance, more structured statements began to emerge. These were often associated with the baptism of new Christians, which was preceded by an extended period of instruction in the basics of faith. By the fourth century the season of Lent was widely seen as a period in which converts who wished to be baptized would attend catechetical lectures in leading Christian basilicas, followed by baptism itself on Easter Day.

At their baptism, candidates would be asked to state their faith. The following account of this practice at Rome, clearly modeled on the baptismal formula of Matthew 28:19, dates from around the year 215:

> When each of them to be baptized has gone down into the water, the one baptizing shall lay hands on each of them, asking, "Do you believe in God the Father Almighty?" And the one being baptized shall reply, "I believe." He shall then baptize each of them once, laying his hand upon each of their heads. Then he shall ask, "Do you believe in Jesus Christ, the Son of God, who was born of the Holy Spirit and the Virgin Mary, who was crucified under Pontius Pilate, and died, and rose on the third day living from the dead, and ascended into heaven, and sat down at the right hand of the Father, the one coming to judge the living and the dead?" When each has replied, "I believe," he shall baptize them a second time. Then he shall ask, "Do you believe in the Holy Spirit and the Holy Church and the resurrection of the flesh?" Then each being baptized shall answer, "I believe." And thus let him baptize for the third time.

This is an example of an interrogative creed – that is to say, a way of publicly affirming the Christian faith, in which the candidates for baptism are required to assent to each of the creedal statements that are put to them. Candidates are baptized in the name of the Father, Son, and Holy Spirit; each clause is then summarized for them, and their consent required. Yet these brief statements of faith are not really "articles of faith"; they are really snapshots of the highlights of the Christian story. The dominant theme is "belief in," not "belief that."

In the end, two creeds emerged as commanding widespread support within Christianity. Their origins and context are quite different. The first to be considered is the Nicene Creed, first formulated by the bishops assembled at the Council of Nicaea in 325. This gathering was convened by Constantine, who wanted to ensure that the unity of the empire was not disrupted by divisions within the church. This creed is clearly shaped by the Arian controversy, and is concerned to emphasize the orthodox understanding of the identity of Jesus Christ over and against Arius and his supporters. As a result, the creed seems slightly skewed, the emphasis on a correct Christology leading to this section of the creed being somewhat longer than necessary. In addition, the creed concludes with a final set of condemnations of unsatisfactory theological positions.

> We believe in one God, the Father, the almighty [Greek: *pantokratōr*], the maker of all things seen and unseen.
>   And in one Lord Jesus Christ, the Son of God; begotten from the Father; only-begotten – that is, from the substance of the Father; God from God; light from light; true God from true God; begotten not made; being of one substance with the Father, through whom all things in heaven and on earth came into being; who on account of us human beings and our

salvation came down and took flesh, becoming a human being; he suffered and rose again on the third day, ascended into the heavens; and will come again to judge the living and the dead. And in the Holy Spirit.

As for those who say that "there was when he was not," and "before being born he was not," and "he came into existence out of nothing," or who declare that the Son of God is of a different substance or nature, or is subject to alteration or change – the catholic and apostolic church condemns these.

This creed was subsequently developed in succeeding decades, generally in response to controversy, before assuming the form in which it is better known today.

The Apostles' Creed, in marked contrast, did not rest on imperial authority, nor did it originate with any council, but appears to have emerged by consensus over an extended period of time, in much the same way as the canon of the New Testament. The most striking difference between the Apostles' and Nicene creeds is that the former shows no signs of any polemical agenda. It does not define Christianity over and against any other position, in the way that the Nicene Creed so clearly defines orthodoxy in the face of an Arian threat. The Apostles' Creed derives its name from a fifth-century belief that each of the Twelve Apostles contributed a statement to the text.

The creeds can thus be seen as serving two central functions: affirming the fundamental themes of faith, and offering a framework by which heretical or deficient versions of Christianity may be identified. The dual object of creeds is thus about defining the center of faith, and policing its periphery. Both these means of defining orthodoxy became increasingly important during the later fourth century, as Christianity's imperial privileges made it necessary to enforce consensus within the church.

Yet there were a number of cases where intellectual persuasion was not enough to enforce orthodoxy within the church. At several points, orthodoxy had to be imposed by force. The most significant example of this development is to be found during the Donatist controversy, when Constantine and his son used coercive measures against the Donatists over a period of decades from 317, having failed to achieve church unity in the region by negotiation.

1.5.9. The Council of Chalcedon, 451

The emperor Constantine convened the Council of Nicaea in 325 to settle debates within the Christian church over the identity of Jesus of Nazareth. Although this Council publicly declared its support for a theological formula which recognized the full divinity and humanity of Christ – while allowing a certain degree of freedom in determining how this was to be expressed – this eventually proved inadequate to settle the matter. Fresh controversy broke out after the council, as Arius and Athanasius debated the theological significance of the divinity of Christ (1.5.3). The bishops of Constantinople, now emerging as the most important metropolitan center in the empire, made it clear that they were committed supporters of Arius.

Once more, it became clear that theological argument was not going to settle the debate. Some kind of official ruling was going to be required. The emperor Theodosius I, who ruled from 379 to 395, made it clear that he expected Nicene orthodoxy to be enforced throughout his empire, and deposed the Arian bishops of Constantinople when they resisted. Like Constantine, Theodosius wished the imperial church to be united on the fundamentals of faith, and was prepared to use his authority to achieve consensus within the church.

Matters were complicated, however, by the simmering tensions between the bishops of Constantinople and Alexandria, both of whom regarded themselves as taking precedence within the Christian world. A major dispute – often referred to as the "Nestorian controversy" – broke out between Cyril, patriarch of Alexandria, and Nestorius, patriarch of Constantinople, in the early fifth century. The issue was whether Nestorius's understanding of the relationship between the humanity and divinity of Christ was adequate. Nestorius had expressed reservations about a traditional term used to refer to Mary, the mother of Jesus of Nazareth. The term *Theotokos* (Greek: "bearer of God") had come to be widely used as a title for Mary, both expressing her own special place in the purposes of God and reaffirming the identity of Jesus as God. In fact, Nestorius's concerns were reasonable. Why not also refer to Mary as *Christotokos*, he asked, to indicate that she was the bearer of the Messiah?

Cyril of Alexandria smelled heresy, and argued that Nestorius did not really believe that Jesus Christ was both divine and human. Nestorius protested both his innocence and his orthodoxy. In the end, Theodosius II, emperor from 408 to 450, convened a council at Ephesus in the summer of 431 to debate the matter. Nestorius presented his case poorly, and lost both the debate, and his bishopric. The 250 bishops present reaffirmed the decisions made at Nicaea in 325, and insisted that the use of the term *Theotokos* was justified.

Once more, the debate was not really resolved. The Council of Ephesus was a holding measure, not a solution. Further controversy developed, especially when a council convened at Ephesus in August 449 with a small number of bishops present was seen by many in the western church to have failed to defend orthodoxy adequately. Shortly after the death of Theodosius, his successor announced that a new council would meet in October 451 in the town of Chalcedon, in the province of Bithynia in Asia Minor. This Council was well attended, and formulated a consensual doctrine which has since become widely accepted within most – though not all – Christian churches.

The "Chalcedonian definition" sets out an agreed formula for making sense of the identity of Jesus of Nazareth, which set out to safeguard his humanity, while affirming his divinity.

> Following the holy Fathers, we all with one voice confess our Lord Jesus Christ to be one and the same Son, perfect in divinity and humanity, truly God and truly human, consisting of a rational soul and a body, being of one substance with the Father in relation to his divinity, and being of one substance with us in relation to his humanity, and is like us in all things apart from sin.

The formulation was widely accepted by both the eastern and western churches, and has come to play a normative role in Christian discussions of the identity and significance of Jesus Christ.

But not all were satisfied. The position generally (though slightly misleadingly) known as "monophysitism" held that Chalcedon had developed a position which failed to do justice to the divinity of Christ (2.1.6). Many in Alexandria felt that Chalcedon had not adequately safeguarded Christ's divinity. The resulting monophysite controversies are somewhat technical theologically, making them difficult to explain simply. Yet perhaps the most important outcome was political: many of the churches of Egypt now considered themselves to be at odds with the churches of Europe and Asia.

This survey of early Christianity has given an overview of some of the main developments to have taken place during this fascinating and formative period. During this era, the Christian faith moved from the margins to the center of imperial culture. Yet with the decline of Roman power, influence, and unity in the west, the church in that region faced new problems. How could it cope without imperial protection? Would it fade away, lacking an imperial protector?

In fact, the western church went on to develop a new sense of identity and purpose. In the following chapter, we shall consider the new social role and theological self-understanding of the western church, which emerged during the Middle Ages.

Sources of Quotations

p. 1: Tacitus, *Annals*, XV.44.
p. 12: Chrysostom, *Homily on the Epistle of St. Paul the Apostle to the Romans*, 31.
p. 24: Justin Martyr, *First Apology*, 66–7.
p. 35: Laura K. McClure, ed. *Sexuality and Gender in the Classical World: Readings and Sources*. Oxford: Wiley-Blackwell, 2008, 158.
p. 39: Pliny, *Epistles*, X.96–7.
p. 67: Hippolytus, *The Apostolic Tradition*, XXI.12–18.

For Further Reading

Ayres, Lewis. *Nicaea and its Legacy: An Approach to Fourth-Century Trinitarian Theology*. Oxford: Oxford University Press, 2004.

Barnes, Timothy D. *Constantine and Eusebius*. Cambridge, MA: Harvard University Press, 2006.

Blasi, Anthony J., Paul-André Turcotte, and Jean Duhaime. *Handbook of Early Christianity: Social Science Approaches*. Walnut Creek, CA: AltaMira Press, 2002.

Botha, Pieter J. J. "Greco-Roman Literacy as Setting for New Testament Writings." *Neotestamentica* 26 (1992): 192–215.

Bradshaw, Paul F. *The Search for the Origins of Christian Worship: Sources and Methods for the Study of Early Liturgy*. New York: Oxford University Press, 2002.

Brent, Allen. *A Political History of Early Christianity*. London: T&T Clark, 2009.

Brent, Allen. *Cyprian and Roman Carthage*. Cambridge: Cambridge University Press, 2010.

Brown, Peter. *The Rise of Western Christendom: Triumph and Diversity, AD 200–1000*. Oxford: Blackwell, 2003.

Burridge, Richard A. *What Are the Gospels? A Comparison with Graeco-Roman Biography*. Grand Rapids, MI: Eerdmans, 2004.

Burtchaell, James Tunstead. *From Synagogue to Church: Public Services and Offices in the*

Earliest Christian Communities. Cambridge: Cambridge University Press, 1992.

Butler, Rex. *The New Prophecy and "New Visions": Evidence of Montanism in the Passion of Saints Perpetua and Felicitas.* Washington, DC: Catholic University of America Press, 2006.

Chadwick, Henry. *The Church in Ancient Society from Galilee to Gregory the Great.* Oxford: Oxford University Press, 2001.

Clark, Elizabeth A. *Reading Renunciation: Asceticism and Scripture in Early Christianity.* Princeton, NJ: Princeton University Press, 1999.

Clark, Gillian. *Women in Late Antiquity: Pagan and Christian Lifestyles.* New York: Oxford University Press, 1994.

Cohick, Lynn H. *Women in the World of the Earliest Christians.* Grand Rapids, MI: Baker Academic, 2009.

Curran, John R. *Pagan City and Christian Capital: Rome in the Fourth Century.* Oxford: Clarendon Press, 2000.

Davis, Stephen J. *Cult of St. Thecla.* New York: Oxford University Press, 2001.

de Ste. Croix, G. E. M., Michael Whitby, and Joseph Streeter. *Christian Persecution, Martyrdom, and Orthodoxy.* Oxford: Oxford University Press, 2006.

Elm, Susanna. *Virgins of God: The Making of Asceticism in Late Antiquity.* New York: Oxford University Press, 1994.

Esler, Philip F., ed. *The Early Christian World.* 2 vols. London: Routledge, 2000.

Evans, G. R. *The First Christian Theologians: An Introduction to Theology in the Early Church.* Oxford: Blackwell, 2004.

Freeman, Charles. *A New History of Early Christianity.* New Haven, CT: Yale University Press, 2009.

Frend, W. H. C. *The Donatist Church: A Movement of Protest in Roman North Africa.* Oxford: Clarendon Press, 2000.

Green, Bernard. *Christianity in Ancient Rome: The First Three Centuries.* New York: T&T Clark, 2010.

Harland, Philip A. *Dynamics of Identity in the World of the Early Christians: Associations,* *Judeans, and Cultural Minorities.* New York: T&T Clark, 2009.

Harmless, William. *Desert Christians: An Introduction to the Literature of Early Monasticism.* New York: Oxford University Press, 2004.

Harris, William V., ed. *The Spread of Christianity in the First Four Centuries: Essays in Explanation.* Leiden: Brill, 2005.

Hultgren, Arland J. *The Rise of Normative Christianity.* Minneapolis: Fortress Press, 1994.

Humphries, Mark. *Early Christianity.* London: Routledge, 2006.

Hunter, David G. *Marriage, Celibacy, and Heresy in Ancient Christianity: The Jovianist Controversy.* New York: Oxford University Press, 2007.

Kelly, J. N. D. *Early Christian Doctrines.* London: Continuum, 2000.

Lampe, Peter. *From Paul to Valentinus: Christians at Rome in the First Two Centuries.* Minneapolis: Fortress Press, 2003.

Levine, Amy-Jill, and Maria Mayo Robbins, eds. *Feminist Companion to Patristic Literature.* New York: T&T Clark, 2008.

Lieu, Judith. *Christian Identity in the Jewish and Graeco-Roman World.* Oxford: Oxford University Press, 2006.

Lössl, Josef. *Early Church: Christianity in Late Antiquity.* London: T&T Clark, 2010.

McGrath, Alister E. *Heresy.* San Francisco: HarperOne, 2008.

Metzger, Bruce M. *The Canon of the New Testament: Its Origin, Development, and Significance.* Oxford: Clarendon Press, 1997.

Nathan, Geoffrey. *The Family in Late Antiquity: The Rise of Christianity and the Endurance of Tradition.* New York: Routledge, 2000.

Odahl, Charles M. *Constantine and the Christian Empire.* London: Routledge, 2004.

Stark, Rodney. *The Rise of Christianity: A Sociologist Reconsiders History.* Princeton, NJ: Princeton University Press, 1996.

Still, Todd D., and David G. Horrell. *After the First Urban Christians: The Social-Scientific*

Study of Pauline Christianity Twenty-Five Years Later. New York: Continuum, 2009.

Vessey, Mark. "The Forging of Orthodoxy in Latin Christian Literature: A Case Study." *Journal of Early Christian Studies* 4 (1996): 495–513.

Wilken, Robert L. *The Spirit of Early Christian Thought: Seeking the Face of God.* New Haven, CT: Yale University Press, 2003.

Williams, Rowan. *Arius: Heresy and Tradition.* Grand Rapids, MI: Eerdmans, 2002.

Young, Frances M. *Biblical Exegesis and the Formation of Christian Culture.* Cambridge: Cambridge University Press, 1997.

Young, Frances, Lewis Ayres, and Andrew Louth, eds. *The Cambridge History of Early Christian Literature.* Cambridge: Cambridge University Press, 2004.

2

The Middle Ages and Renaissance, c. 500–c. 1500

With the collapse and gradual disintegration of the western Roman Empire in the fifth century (1.4.6), the face of Europe began to change. A patchwork of regions and city-states began to emerge, each competing for territory and influence. Yet during this period of fragmentation, the Christian church gradually began to develop a political and temporal role that placed it at the heart of western culture. As some degree of political and economic stability emerged around the year 1100, the church was poised to exercise a major role in shaping the culture of the Middle Ages. In this chapter, we shall explore some aspects of the development of the church in western Europe in this fascinating period, taking our story to the eve of the European Reformation.

By the year 600, Christianity had established itself throughout much of the region of what we now know as the Middle East, including the coastal regions of western North Africa. To the north, Christianity had established its presence up to the Danube and the Rhine. Christian expansion had also taken place to the east of the Roman Empire in Persia, where a form of Christianity that came to be known as "Nestorianism" had gained influence. Christianity is also thought to have become established in India by the end of the third century.

The situation of Christianity in the Mediterranean region changed significantly through the rise of Islam (2.1.3) – the religious belief system based on the teachings of Muhammad (570–632). After Muhammad's death, Islam was spread by military conquest throughout much of the Middle East, including the Roman colonies of North Africa. Islam established itself in Spain, and began to expand into France in the eighth century, until military defeat checked this development.

Christians were regarded by Islam as "People of the Book," and allowed a degree of religious freedom. Yet while they were not forced to convert, they were obliged to pay special taxes, and to wear clothing that distinguished them from Muslims. While Muslims

Christian History: An Introduction, First Edition. Alister E. McGrath.
© 2013 John Wiley & Sons, Ltd. Published 2013 by John Wiley & Sons, Ltd.

were permitted to marry Christian women, Christian men were not permitted to marry Muslim women.

Fear of further Islamic expansion in Europe, whether from Spain in the southwest to Turkey in the southeast was a constant concern throughout the period of the Middle Ages, and extended well into the early modern period. The fall of the great Byzantine city of Constantinople to Islamic armies in 1453 caused concern throughout Europe (2.4.7), as some believed it represented a tipping point, marking the possible end of a Christian Europe.

The emergence of the Middle Ages is a complex and fascinating story, involving the political and social renewal of western Europe, the slow decline and fall of the great Byzantine empire in the east, the rediscovery of the philosophical and scientific writings of the ancient world preserved by Arabic scholars, and the great renewal of letters that we know as the "Renaissance." All of these shaped the narrative of Christian history, as we shall see in what follows.

2.1.   Setting the Context: The Background to the High Middle Ages

The terms "Middle Ages" and "medieval" were invented in the sixteenth century. The European Renaissance (2.5.2) was then at its height. It had captured the hearts and minds of many in western Europe with its program of a return to the cultural glories of ancient Rome and Athens. The term "Middle Ages" was created by humanists to refer disparagingly to what they considered to be the rather uninteresting and dull period in western European history between antiquity and its rediscovery in the Renaissance. Partly because it was a term of abuse, the term is not historically precise. Yet the phrase "the Middle Ages" is so widely used that it cannot be avoided.

So how are the Middle Ages to be defined? When did this period begin? And when did it end? History is continuous; historical periods are the invention of historians. There is no "right" definition of the Middle Ages. In its broadest sense, the period can be said to have begun in 476, with the forced resignation of the emperor Romulus Augustus, and the end of the western Roman Empire. Various markers might be proposed for signaling its end – such as the conquest of Constantinople by the Turks in 1453 (2.4.7), the invention of moveable type by the printer Johann Gutenberg in the 1450s (2.5.1), or the opening up of the great era of maritime exploration, especially Christopher Columbus's voyage to the Americas in 1492 (2.5.7).

If this generous definition of the "Middle Ages" is accepted, it is a period which is over a thousand years long. Although some courses in church history tend to focus on the period 1000–1500, there are many developments of importance in the history of Christianity in western Europe during the period 500–1000, which set the context for the "High Middle Ages." The first section in this discussion (2.1) deals with these important developments, especially during the reign of Charlemagne, which help us understand the later development of Christian history in Europe. We therefore begin by reflecting on how western Christianity adapted to meet the situation which resulted from the decline and fall of the western Roman Empire.

2.1.1. Western Christianity after the Fall of Rome

The forced abdication of the western Roman emperor Romulus Augustus in 476 led to the fragmentation of the Roman administrative system (1.4.6). What had hitherto been a regulated and centralized system of government began to break down, with power passing to local rulers. The church, however, retained its episcopal system, which had been significantly influenced by Roman imperial practices.

Whereas a bishop appears originally to have been the leader of a local congregation, the church increasingly adopted a "monoepiscopal" model, by which a single bishop had authority over Christian priests and congregations in a specified area. Bishops now exercised spiritual authority over specific geographical areas ("dioceses," derived from the Greek word *dioikēsis*, referring to an "area of administration" or "province"), in much the way as a Roman governor ruled provinces. The recognition of Christianity as the state religion of the empire inevitably led to bishops possessing both political (often referred to as "temporal") and spiritual authority, leading to the church developing organizational structures which paralleled those of the state. But the collapse of western imperial structures in the late fifth century was not paralleled by a failure on the part of their ecclesiastical counterparts.

By the middle of the fourth century, the metropolitan bishops of Rome, Constantinople, Alexandria, and Antioch had come to be recognized as possessing a dignity and authority which allowed them to take primacy over other bishops. This authority was formalized by a number of councils, most notably the Council of Chalcedon. The metropolitan bishop of Rome was the only western Christian leader to be given precedence in this way.

In the western church, the bishop of Rome began to be treated as an arbitrator in disputes between bishops and churches, reinforcing the perception that he stood above other bishops – not necessarily by rank, but by convention. A number of factors led to this development during the third century. Some were pragmatic. Rome was, after all, the "eternal city," the capital of the Roman Empire. Others were spiritual. The apostles Peter and Paul were both held to have been martyred and buried in Rome. The term "pope" (Latin: *papa*) was originally used to refer to any revered Christian bishop. Gradually, however, the title came to be seen as especially appropriate for the bishop of Rome. Siricius, who was bishop of Rome from 384–99, formalized this practice, and ruled that the title "pope" should now be used only to refer to him and his successors. The first known papal "decretal" – that is, a letter giving binding rulings on disputes within the church – dates from his reign. While the emperors abandoned Rome in the face of the Visigoth threat in the first decade of the fifth century, the popes remained in Rome, coming to play an important role in negotiations with the invaders.

This centralization of religious authority in Rome continued under Innocent I, pope from 402–17. In January 417, Innocent wrote to the African bishops about religious controversies that had arisen in their region, insisting that:

> Nothing that has been determined even in the most remote and distant provinces should be taken as finally settled unless it has come to the notice of this See, that any correct pronouncement might be confirmed by all the authority of this See, and that other churches might learn from this what they should teach.

This increasing concentration of spiritual and political power in Rome was made possible by the absence of any alternative power structures, following the collapse of the central imperial administration in the late fifth century. Strong popes imposed their authority. Leo the Great, pope from 440–61, played a particularly important role in solidifying the authority of the papacy at both the theoretical and practical levels.

Leo introduced the use of the term *pontifex maximus* (the Roman term for the chief priest of the city in pagan times, and later transferred to the emperor) to refer to the pope. He also framed some of the traditional arguments that subsequently became normative for papal claims to authority. For example, Leo argued that Jesus of Nazareth had made Peter and his successors the rock on which his church would be built. Since the bishop of Rome was the successor of Peter, who had been martyred in the city, it followed that the pope was the ultimate foundation of the church.

Although the Roman Empire had collapsed in the west, the eastern empire was unaffected by the invasions in the west (1.4.7). During the sixth century, emperors based in Constantinople began a military campaign to recapture Italy, and incorporate it into the eastern empire. These campaigns were not totally successful. Nevertheless, by the seventh century, Byzantium had established authority over a large area of territory, which took the form of a diagonal band running roughly from Ravenna in the northeast of Italy to Rome and Naples in the southwest. Yet the emperor found it difficult to assert authority in the western area of Italy, allowing the pope to exercise considerable political and social influence in these regions.

By the end of the sixth century, the church was the only international organization in western Europe to have survived the collapse of the Roman Empire. Increased missionary activity under the reign of Gregory the Great, pope from 590 to 604, and other popes both increased Christianity's reach and influence, and added further to the importance of the church as an agent of social cohesion. Gregory the Great laid the foundations for establishing papal control of the church outside of Italy by sending a mission of Benedictine monks to convert the pagan Anglo-Saxons.

Gregory established a system of church government in England which gradually became standard within the western church. The country was divided into dioceses (analogous to classic Roman provinces), each of which was ruled by a bishop. These bishops were accountable to an archbishop, who was in turn accountable to the pope. Gregory's intention was originally to locate his archbishop in the city of London; in the end, political wrangling with local rulers led him to choose the Kentish town of Canterbury instead.

Christianity had remained a presence in England since Roman days, and had undergone a minor renaissance in the north as a result of Irish missionaries. However, the form of Christianity that Gregory introduced would not be subject to local control, but would be under the authority of the pope in Rome. Despite its evangelistic intentions, the mission of Augustine of Canterbury to England ended up by establishing a new centralized model of ecclesiastical government that could be adapted for use elsewhere in Europe in succeeding centuries.

The task of establishing papal control of the church and extending the Pope's temporal authority was continued by Gregory's successors. In the eighth century, English missionaries brought with them the new English pattern of church government to

Germany and France, consolidating the authority of the pope over the western European church. A further development of importance was the "Donation of Pepin" (754–6), which created the "Papal States" – lands owned and controlled by the papacy. The Frankish ruler Pepin the Short had conquered some territories in northern Italy, which he gave to the Pope, thus establishing a region over which the pope had both temporal and spiritual power.

2.1.2.   The Rise of Celtic Christianity

The rise of Christianity in the Celtic regions of Europe – more specifically, Ireland, Scotland, Cornwall, Brittany, and Wales – is of considerable interest, not least in that this form of Christianity found itself in opposition to the more Romanized forms which rapidly gained the ascendancy in England. Although the origins of Celtic Christianity seem to lie in Wales, it is Ireland which established itself as a major missionary center during the fifth and sixth centuries. Other centers of missionary activity in the Celtic sphere of influence are known from this period, most notably *Candida Casa* (modern-day Whithorn, in the Galloway region of Scotland), which was established by bishop Ninian in the fifth century. The significance of this missionary station was that it lay outside the borders of Roman Britain, and was thus able to operate without having to conform to the norms of Roman forms of Christianity.

The person who is traditionally held to be responsible for the evangelization of Ireland was a Romanized Briton by the name of Magonus Sucatus Patricius, more usually known as "Patrick" (c. 390–c. 460). There are some difficulties in clarifying Patrick's career. Some scholars argue that this confusion arises through some accounts of the works of Palladius, sent by Pope Celestine I as the first bishop to Irish Christians in 431, being mistakenly understood to refer to Patrick. According to the traditional account of his life, Patrick was taken captive in Wales by a raiding party at the age of sixteen, and sold into slavery in Ireland, probably in the region of Connaught. Here, he appears to have discovered the basics of the Christian faith. After six years in captivity, he was able to escape and make his way back to his family.

It is not clear precisely what happened between Patrick's escape from captivity and his subsequent return to Ireland as a missionary. A tradition, dating back to the seventh or eighth century, refers to Patrick spending time in Gaul before his return to Ireland. It is possible that some of Patrick's views on church organization and structures may reflect first-hand acquaintance with the monasticism of certain regions of southern France. There is excellent historical evidence for trading links between Ireland and the Loire Valley around this time.

Patrick returned to Ireland, and – according to the traditional account – established Christianity in the region. Yet it is clear that some form of Christianity was already present in the region. Not only does Patrick's conversion account presuppose that others there knew about the gospel; contemporary records dating from as early as 429 speak of the "Palladius" noted earlier as a bishop of Ireland, indicating that at least some form of rudimentary ecclesiastical structures existed in the region. Irish representatives are also known to have been present at the Synod of Arles (314). Patrick's achievement is perhaps best understood in terms of the consolidation and advancement of Christianity, rather than its establishment in the first place.

The monastic idea took hold very quickly in Ireland. Historical sources indicate that Ireland was largely a nomadic and tribal society at this time, without any permanent settlements of any importance. The monastic quest for solitude and isolation was ideally suited to the Irish way of life, and allowed local noble families to be integrated into monastic structures. Whereas in western Europe as a whole, monasticism tended to lie on the margins of the authority structures of the church, in Ireland it rapidly became its dominant form. The Irish church was monastic in its outlook, with the abbot rather than the bishop being seen as the figure of spiritual authority.

The authority structures which emerged within Celtic Christianity thus differed significantly from those which came to dominate the Roman-British church around this time. The Irish monastic model came to be seen as a threat to the Roman model of the episcopate, in which the government of the church resided firmly in the hands of the bishops. None of the abbots of Iona ever allowed bishops to formally ordain them, rejecting the need for any such official recognition. In Ireland, some of the older bishoprics (including Armagh) were reorganized on a monastic basis, with others being absorbed by monasteries. Abbeys were responsible for the pastoral care of the churches which grew up in their vicinity. The Roman episcopal system was thus marginalized. The Celtic church leaders were openly critical of worldly wealth and status, including the use of horses as a mode of transport, and any form of luxury.

Theologically, Celtic Christianity also stressed the importance of the world of nature as a means of knowing God. This is especially clear from the ancient Irish hymn traditionally ascribed to Patrick, and known as "St. Patrick's Breastplate." The theme of a "breastplate" was common in Celtic Christian spirituality. It is based upon Paul's references to the "armor of God" (Ephesians 6:10–18), and develops the theme of the believer being protected by the presence of God and a whole range of associated powers. Although strongly Trinitarian in its structure, it shows a fascination with the natural world as a means of knowing God. The God who made the world is the same God who will protect Christians from all dangers.

The Irish monasteries acted as centers for missionary activity, often using sea lanes as channels for the transmission of Christianity. Brendan (died c. 580) and Columba (died c. 597) are excellent examples of this type of missionary. In a poem entitled "The Navigation of St. Brendan" (c. 1050), Brendan is praised for his journeys to the "northern and western isles" (usually assumed to be the Orkneys and Hebrides, off the coast of Scotland).

Columba brought Christianity from the north of Ireland to the Western Isles of Scotland, and established the abbey of Iona as a missionary outpost. From there, Christianity spread southwards and eastwards. Aidan (died 651) is an excellent example of a monk from Iona who acted as a missionary in this way. At the invitation of the king of the region of Northumbria, he established a missionary monastery on the island of Lindisfarne, off the east coast of northern England. Celtic Christianity began to penetrate into France, and become increasingly influential in the region.

The tensions between Celtic Christianity and its Roman rivals could not be ignored. Celtic Christianity threatened to undermine the episcopate, reduce the power of Rome, make it more difficult for Christianity to become culturally acceptable, and to make monasticism the norm for Christian living. By 597, the year of Columba's death, the ascendancy of the Celtic vision seemed inevitable. However, the following century saw a series of developments which led to its gradual eclipse outside its heartlands of Ireland. By a coincidence of history, the event which led to its eclipse took place in the same year as Columba's death. In 597, Augustine of Canterbury was sent to England by Pope Gregory to evangelize the English (2.1.1). As Roman forms of Christianity became established in England, tensions arose between northern and southern English Christians, the former remaining faithful to Celtic traditions, and the latter to Roman.

The northeastern English town Streanaeshalch – later renamed "Whitby" – had risen to fame on account of the work of the Anglo-Saxon noblewoman Hild (614–80), who established an abbey and convent there in 657. The Synod of Whitby (664) is widely seen as establishing the institutional dominance of Roman Christianity in England. Although the Synod focused on the question of when Easter should be celebrated (Celtic and Roman traditions differed on the issue), the real issue concerned the growing influence of the archbishopric of Canterbury, which was accountable to Rome. The Saxon invasions of England in the previous century resulted in further major cultural changes in the region. It was probably inevitable that Celtic culture, including its distinctive approach to Christianity, would be relegated to the geographical margins of Britain, as Saxon expansion continued.

2.1.3. The Seventh Century: Islam and Arab Expansion

By the year 600, Christianity had established itself throughout much of the region of what we now know as the Middle East, including the coastal regions of western North Africa. To the north, Christianity was a presence up to the Danube and the Rhine. Christian expansion had also taken place to the east of the Roman Empire in Persia, where a form of Christianity that came to be known as "Nestorianism" had gained influence.

The situation changed significantly through the rise of Islam – the religious belief system based on the teachings of Muhammad (570–632), which provided a new religious identity for the Arab people. Initially, Islamic expansion was confined to the Arabian peninsula. During the Rashidun Caliphate (c. 632–61), immediately following the death of Muhammad, Islam expanded rapidly by military conquest. The ease with which this was achieved was partly a reflection of the weakness of surrounding regions, which were often exhausted by internecine struggles or tensions with their neighbors. By 640, the Caliphate had extended to Mesopotamia, Syria, and Palestine; by 642, to Egypt; and by 643, to the Persian Empire. Three of the five metropolitan sees of the "Pentarchy" – Jerusalem, Alexandria, and Antioch – were now in Islamic hands, and ceased to function as centers of Christian theology and political administration.

The second major period in Islamic expansion took place under the Umayyad Caliphate (c. 661–750), based at Damascus. Islamic armies moved westwards along the North African coast, and crossed the Straits of Gibraltar, establishing a presence in Spain (referred to in Arabic as "Al-Andalus"). This expansion into Europe was brought to an end by the defeat of the Arab army by the Franks at the Battle of Tours in 732. Eventually, the Umayyad

Caliphate was ended by its defeat at the hands of the Abbasids, who relocated the center of the Caliphate from Damascus to Baghdad. Only Al-Andalus remained in the hands of the Umayyads.

The Abbasid Caliphate is widely regarded as a "Golden Age" in the history of Islam, during which scientific research and other forms of scholarship flourished. Texts of classical philosophy and science – such as Aristotle – were preserved and translated. Spain became an important meeting point for Islam and Christianity, and would play an important role in the medieval Christian rediscovery of classical philosophy and science. The Abbasid Caliphate eventually came to an end in 1519, when Turkish armies overwhelmed much of its territory, which was incorporated into the Ottoman Empire, based at Constantinople.

The rise of Islam was of decisive importance for the history of Christianity in the Middle Ages. Perhaps most obviously, Christian regions of Europe began to fear for their safety, in the light of what seemed like inexorable Islamic expansion in Spain and Turkey. The origins of the Crusades lie partly in this growing concern about the stability of Christendom.

Yet Islam also offered intellectual stimulus to Christian theologians, both in the east and west. The rediscovery of Aristotle is widely regarded as resting on Arab scholarship, and we shall consider this development later in this chapter. Islam also provided an intellectual motivation for Christian theologians to develop their ideas, especially concerning the nature of God. Medieval theology often engaged the issues raised by Islamic theologians of the period, particularly al-Ghazali (1058–1111) and Avicenna (the Latinized name of Ibn Sina, c. 980–1058). Medieval debates about the freedom of God often reflect an awareness of the issues raised by these writers, and were often guided by classical resources, which had been preserved in Arabic translations. We shall consider this further at a later point in our discussion (2.2.2).

2.1.4.   The Age of Charlemagne

In the sixth century, the term "Franks" (Latin: *Franci*) came to be used to refer to a group of Germanic tribes who established a stable and significant kingdom between the Rhine and Loire rivers. The increasing importance of the Franks in shaping Christian Europe is best seen from the rise of Charlemagne and the establishment of what would later be known as the "Holy Roman Empire." The emperor Charlemagne (c. 742–814) played a critically important role in shaping the cultural identity of western Europe, and establishing Christianity as the dominant religious faith in the region. The name "Charlemagne" is really a title – "Charles the Great" (French: "Charles le Magne") – and refers to Charles, the son of the Frankish king Pepin the Short, who continued his father's attempt to consolidate groups of small nations into a much larger kingdom.

Charlemagne's reversal of the decentralization of power following the collapse of the western Roman Empire led to the establishment of a new political entity straddling the regions of Italy, France, and Germany, which became known as the "Holy Roman Empire." This consolidation of power was closely linked with the church. Papal support for both Pepin the Short and Charlemagne was important in securing wider acceptance of their authority. On December 25, 799, in Saint Peter's Basilica in Rome, Pope Leo III crowned Charlemagne as *Imperator Romanorum* ("Emperor of the Romans"). It was a

Figure 2.1   Coronation of the emperor Charlemagne (742–814) by Pope Leo III (c. 750–816) at St. Peters, Rome in 800, *Grandes Chroniques de France*, 1375–9, f.106r vellum, French School, fourteenth century. Bibliotheque Municipale, Castres, France/Giraudon/The Bridgeman Art Library

symbolic move of enormous importance. A Christianized Roman Empire was being restored in western Europe. This development consolidated the importance of the pope as a European spiritual leader and power broker, and ensured that the church was firmly embedded in the new social order.

One of Charlemagne's most significant achievements was to reverse the Islamic advance into southwestern Europe. Islamic invaders had occupied most of Spain in the eighth century, and had crossed the Pyrenees into southern France (2.1.3). By the end of Charlemagne's reign, this threat had been neutralized.

The age of Charlemagne witnessed a resurgence in culture in the eighth and ninth centuries – often referred to as the "Carolingian Renaissance" – primarily among the clergy. In part, this development was due to the rising importance of monasteries as centers of learning and culture. Charlemagne invited the leading English scholar Alcuin of York (died 804) to help develop the educational programs of his palace school at Aachen from 782. This reflected a wider realization at the time of the importance of scholarship and learning, reflected in the production of manuscripts at monastic centers throughout western Europe. One of the more interesting developments of this period was the invention of the "Caroline miniscule script" – a form of handwriting particularly suitable for copying manuscripts – at the monastery of Corbie. In view of the importance of the church in bringing about this intellectual renaissance, we shall consider the development of these cathedral schools in more detail.

2.1.5.   The Rise of the Monastic and Cathedral Schools

For modern readers, the universities stand at the center of the world's intellectual reflection and scholarly research. Yet the idea of the university had yet to develop in the ninth century; as we shall see, this new institution would not emerge until the late eleventh century. During the period 800–1100, it was schools attached to monasteries and cathedrals that began to achieve distinction as centers of scholarship.

The development of cathedral schools was often due to the educational vision of the bishop of the diocese. As the traditional educational structures of the Roman Empire began to collapse in the late fifth century, bishops made arrangements to ensure that their clergy would continue to be well educated. In part, this was a pragmatic decision, reflecting the need to have a literate clergy, capable of writing and possessing basic administrative skills. Yet it was often a decision that was also based on a love of learning, and a desire to keep scholarship alive in a time when there were limited opportunities for study and research.

Although the earliest such cathedral schools developed in Spain during the sixth and early seventh centuries, some of the most important schools of this kind developed in England. The conversion of England to Christianity as a result of Gregory the Great's decision to send missionaries to the region created an urgent need for theological education (2.1.1). Provision had to be made for the education of clergy in a region with little recent history of Christian scholarship. Cathedral schools initially developed at Canterbury (597) and Rochester (604) in Kent, in the south of England, soon to be followed by a major school at York Minster in the north of England (627).

The next wave of cathedral schools were established in France, especially at the cathedrals of Chartres, Laon, Liège, Orléans, Paris, Rheims, and Rouen. The cathedral school of Paris would eventually become the University of Paris in the twelfth century. These schools were under the control of the local bishop, and generally focused on educating local clergy.

Yet such cathedral schools were not the only centers of learning. Some of Europe's great monasteries, most of which followed the Order of St. Benedict, emerged as centers of excellence in scholarship, building up large libraries. Indeed, many monasteries considered scholarship to be essential to their calling. Three elements were of particular importance in Benedictine spirituality: liturgical prayer, manual labor, and *lectio divina* (Latin: "divine reading") – a quiet, meditative reading of the Bible. Although many monks were able to commit biblical texts to memory, the important place given to *lectio divina* inevitably created a demand for texts of the Bible, which had to be copied out by hand.

Many monasteries established a *scriptorium* – a special room or section of the library dedicated to the copying of manuscripts – and built up libraries, often including classical works of history and literature alongside biblical texts and works of Christian theology. Monastic libraries of the Carolingian era were filled with Christian and pagan works, which were copied carefully for purposes of transmission. Many of the classical works widely consulted today have survived because of this copying process in the Carolingian period.

For example, two of the earliest manuscripts of Julius Caesar's *Gallic Wars* were both created in France in the ninth century.

2.1.6. Byzantine Christianity: Monophysitism and Iconoclasm

Although the Council of Chalcedon (451) was intended to put an end to divisive Christo-logical debates throughout the Christian world (1.5.9), its formal definition of the identity of Jesus of Nazareth never achieved universal acceptance throughout the eastern empire. Chalcedon affirmed the "two natures" of Christ, in that he was declared to be truly human and truly divine (1.5.9). The "Monophysites," who were especially influential in Egypt and Syria, insisted that Christ had to be understood to possess a single nature. The term "Mono-physite" (Greek: "single nature") was not generally used by those who had misgivings about the Council of Chalcedon's formula for understanding the identity of Jesus of Nazareth; they generally preferred the related term "Miaphysite" (Greek: "one nature").

Although this provoked several attempts at theological diplomacy during the sixth century, aiming to minimize the divergence between the two parties, in the end the divi-sions proved impossible to heal. It led to a schism between Orthodox Christian churches in Europe, and a group of churches in Egypt, Ethiopia, Syria, and Armenia (now often known as "Oriental Orthodox" churches). These divisions remain to this day. The Oriental Orthodox churches recognize the authority of only the first three ecumenical councils: the Council of Nicaea (325), the Council of Constantinople (381), and the Council of Ephesus (431), arguing that things went wrong at the Council of Chalcedon (451).

Yet the most divisive debate of this age concerned the place of icons in Christian worship and devotion. (The Greek word *eikon* means "an image.") One of the most characteristic features of eastern Orthodoxy is its use of icons as "windows of perception," both in public worship and personal devotion. Yet this practice came under intense criticism during the "iconoclastic" (from the Greek terms for "image-breaking") controversies of the eighth and ninth centuries. Although other issues were involved, one of the central questions was whether it was legitimate to create images of Christ for the purposes of devotion. This custom had long been in existence in the eastern church, and was regarded as unproblem-atic by most Christians in the region. Yet in the early eighth century, this practice began to be questioned.

The event that triggered the first iconoclastic controversy took place at some point around the year 730, when the Emperor Leo III ordered the removal of an image of Christ that was prominently positioned over the ceremonial entrance to the Great Palace of Con-stantinople. Leo did not consult with church leaders in removing this image, and probably did not have their support in doing so. One possible motivation for this change was the growing influence of Islam in the region (2.1.3). Given Islam's hostility towards any images of the divine, Leo may have concluded that it might be politic to remove any possible cause for offense to his Islamic neighbors, and hence reduce the likelihood of political tensions and possibly invasions.

Yet Leo faced considerable opposition to his iconoclastic campaign. Icons had come to play an important role in popular devotion, and especially in monastic spirituality. John of Damascus became a leading critic of iconoclasm, pointing out that the doctrine of the incarnation gave a powerful theological rationale for the use of icons in worship and devotion. John was based in Damascus, which by then had become a major Islamic administrative and political center. His *Exposition of the Orthodox Faith* gained widespread recognition as a theological classic, and did much to shape the distinct theological and spiritual outlook of Orthodoxy. Leo's hostility towards icons was maintained by his successors as emperors, until it was finally ended by the empress Irene in 787.

Although the origins of the iconoclastic controversy do not appear to have been primarily theological, it is clear that the debate raised theological issues. One such issue was whether the worship of icons represented some kind of idolatry. The matter was clarified at the Second Council of Nicaea (787), which made a distinction between two kinds of worship. In the first place, worship in the strict sense of the word (Greek: *latria*) was to be given only to God, and was therefore totally inappropriate in the case of icons. Yet there was a weaker sense of the term (Greek: *doulia*) – perhaps best rendered by the English words "veneration" or "reverence" – which was appropriate for icons. The Council appears to have recognized that these two notions were often confused in popular devotion, and needed to be distinguished.

Yet this did not end the controversy. After a period of relative tranquility, a later emperor revived iconoclasm in 815. Once more, it seems that the politically desirable goal of easing relationships with neighboring Islamic territories appears to have been a consideration, although it remains unclear what prompted this development, which had little popular support. Once more, iconoclasm was brought to an end by an empress, when Theodora declared the restoration of icons in 843. After this, the use of idols ceased to be controversial. This controversy had a profound effect on the production of Byzantine icons after their reintroduction in 843. New styles of iconography developed, including the evolution of distinct portrait types for individual saints.

Debates also developed in the western church around this time. In what follows, we shall consider some theological disputes that emerged in a leading school of theology in northern France during the ninth century.

2.1.7.   Ninth-Century Debates: The Real Presence and Predestination

One of the most important French monastic schools of theology was founded in the seventh century at Corbie, in the northern region of Picardy. By the ninth century, the monastery of Corbie had become one of the most important centers of learning in the region, with a large library including many works of classical Latin literature. Several of the leading scholars and thinkers of the age were attracted to the monastery, including Paschasius Radbertus (died 865) and Ratramnus (died 868).

These two scholars found themselves at the center of a divisive debate over the nature of the real presence. Both wrote works with the same title, *Concerning the Body and Blood of Christ*, while developing diametrically opposed understandings of the real presence. Radbertus, whose work was completed around 844, developed the idea that the bread and the wine become the body and blood of Christ in reality; Ratramnus, whose work was written shortly afterwards, defended the view that they were merely symbols of Christ's body and blood. Although Radbertus found it somewhat difficult to provide a convincing explanation of precisely how ordinary bread was transformed into the body of Christ, he had no doubts about the physical reality and spiritual importance of the change.

Ratramnus was not convinced, and took a very different position. The difference between ordinary and consecrated bread lay in the way in which the believer perceived them. The consecrated bread remained bread; however, the believer was enabled to perceive a deeper spiritual meaning as a result of its consecration. The difference between ordinary and consecrated bread was thus subjective, rather than objective, lying within the believer, rather than within the bread itself.

The school of Corbie was also linked to another debate of the ninth century, this time focusing on the question of predestination. The issue under debate arose from what many regarded as an unresolved issue in the theology of grace developed by Augustine of Hippo during the Pelagian controversy (1.5.6). Did God actively predestine some people to damnation? Or were they merely passed over, in the sense that God failed to predestine them to salvation? Augustine tends (although he is not entirely consistent in this respect) to treat predestination as something which is *active* and *positive* – a deliberate decision to redeem on God's part. However, as his critics pointed out, this decision to redeem some was equally a decision *not* to redeem others.

This question surfaced with new force during the great predestinarian controversy of the ninth century, in which the Benedictine monk Godescalc of Orbais (c. 804–c. 869, also known as "Gottschalk") developed a doctrine of double predestination similar to that later to be associated with Calvin and his followers. Although Godescalc was chiefly associated with the monastic school at Orbais in the diocese of Soissons, he also spent some time studying at the monastery at Corbie, and may well have used its library to help him develop his position.

Pursuing with relentless logic the implications of his assertion that God has predestined some to eternal damnation, Godescalc pointed out that it was thus quite improper to speak of Christ dying for such individuals. If he had, and their fate was unaffected, it would follow that he had died in vain – which was unthinkable. Godescalc therefore proposed that Christ died *only for the elect*. The scope of his redeeming work was restricted, limited only to those who were predestined to benefit from his death. Most ninth-century writers reacted critically to this assertion.

2.1.8.   Orthodox Missions to Eastern Europe: Bulgaria and Russia

As we noted earlier, Charlemagne's vision of a new Frankish empire changed the face of western Europe (2.1.4). Many saw Charlemagne as reestablishing the political and cultural authority of the now-vanished Roman Empire, bring new stability to the region. But what of eastern Europe?

The eastern Roman Empire persisted long after the fragmentation of the western empire into territories and regional powers, even reasserting its authority for a while over regions of Italy (1.4.7). But what of the territories to the north of Constantinople? Although Christianity had established a foothold in this region in earlier centuries, the collapse of the Roman Empire had led to the reversion of most peoples to various forms of paganism.

By the ninth century, the peoples of southeastern Europe – such as the Bulgars and Magyars – increasingly found themselves in a difficult political situation. To their west was an increasingly powerful Frankish Empire with obvious territorial ambitions; to their east was the equally powerful Byzantine Empire. The political realities were obvious: some kind of alliance would have to be established with one of these power blocs at some point, if these peoples were to preserve their independence. Yet although both these imperial powers were Christian, they nevertheless represented very different kinds of Christianity. The Franks were Catholic; Constantinople was Orthodox. The peoples of southeastern Europe would have to make a choice.

In 863, a chain of events began which would lead to the gradual Christianization of this region. Ludwig the German (806–76), grandson of the emperor Charlemagne, entered into an alliance with the Bulgars. This caused a significant shift in the power balance in the region. Fearing that the Franks would achieve dominance in the region, Rastislav, prince of the neighboring Slavic region of Great Moravia, decided to ally his nation with the eastern empire. He sent ambassadors to Constantinople asking the emperor Michael III to send missionaries to his nation.

The emperor dispatched Cyril and Methodius, two brothers who were familiar with Slavic dialects. They arrived in Velehrad, the capital of Moravia, in 864, and began translating Christian writings into Slavic. The brothers developed what is now known as the Glagolitic alphabet, based on Greek, in order to write down these translations. The Cyrillic alphabet, used in Russian, is also linked to this development, although it is now considered to have been developed by a disciple of Cyril, rather than by Cyril himself.

Yet the politics of the region began to shift, with the result that Moravia now came under Catholic influence from Rome, rather than Orthodox influence from Constantinople. The Bulgars, having initially decided to adopt Catholicism, now began to show a preference for Orthodoxy. The question which decided the issue was whether the Bulgarians would be allowed to have their own archbishop, or would have an outsider imposed on them by an imperial power.

Basil I, emperor from 867 to 886, found a formula that would satisfy both sides. He declared that any alliance with Constantinople would involve an "autocephalous" (Greek: "self-governing") Bulgarian church, which would be notionally under the control of Constantinople, but would in effect be independent. This model would prove influential in spreading the ideas and practices of Byzantine Christianity in this region, especially in Russia (2.4.3). By adopting Orthodoxy, the Bulgars could retain their autonomy, having their own Orthodox bishops and archbishops.

The conversion of Kievan Rus' – an area that encompassed much of what is now Russia, Ukraine, and Belarus – began to take place in the ninth century, as a result of the work of Greek missionaries from Byzantium. The historical origins of the word "Rus'" are unclear. Some scholars suggest that term "Rus'" derives from a Finnish term for the Swedes, indicating a Viking origin of some of the peoples in the region. Early Byzantine accounts about this region indicate that its inhabitants tended to hold Scandinavian or other non-Slavonic personal names.

The first conversion of Russia is traditionally dated to 988, when Kievan Rus' adopted Orthodox Christianity. The foundations for this development had been laid a generation earlier, through the growth of Christianity among the Kievan nobility. Olga of Kiev was the first ruler of Kievan Rus' to convert to Christianity around 950. Under her grandson, Vladimir the Great, ruler from 980 to 1015, Kievan Rus' first became a Christian state. Kiev was an important trading partner with Constantinople around this time, and this commercial link unquestionably intensified the region's interest in Orthodox Christianity. Kiev became the seat of Russian Christianity, with a metropolitan bishop appointed by the patriarch of Constantinople.

2.1.9. The Tenth Century: Institutional Decline and Decay

The ninth century is now regarded by most historians as a cultural and intellectual high point for Christianity in western Europe. The Carolingian Renaissance saw a rebirth of interest in art, literature, and scholarship (2.1.4). Although this was primarily linked to monastic and cathedral schools (2.1.5), there was a "ripple effect," enabling this new surge of energy to have a wider impact, especially through the imperial court. Although it is easy to place too much importance on the image of Charlemagne as a new Roman emperor, there is no doubt that his military and administrative skills led to the restoration of order throughout much of western Europe. Threats remained, most notably the threat of invasion or attack from Islamic armies in the south, and from the Norsemen in Scandinavia. Yet in the ninth century, these threats were checked.

The church played an important role in the Carolingian renaissance, both as a patron of the arts and scholarship, and as a stabilizing influence on society as a whole. The model of church organization developed by Gregory the Great – based on bishops administering dioceses, under the authority of archbishops who were accountable to the pope – was taking hold in much of western Europe, allowing a greater degree of centralization than had been possible in earlier centuries. A high point in papal influence was reached during the reign of Nicholas I, pope from 858–67. The pope was beginning to emerge as a figure with both temporal and spiritual power. Although this was open to the risk of abuse, it clearly enabled the church to play a significant role in social and political affairs.

Yet the Carolingian renaissance ultimately proved temporary. After Charlemagne's death, his empire began to fragment. Warlords and barons took control of their own regions, and converted them into their personal fiefdoms. Local bishops were often appointed by these lords, with the expectation of receiving spiritual benefits or political influence in return – a practice that is often referred to as "simony." Similarly, the death of Nicholas I led to a series of weak and apparently corrupt popes, elected and controlled by prominent aristocratic families in Rome, who compromised both the integrity and efficiency of the church in western Europe. The requirement that clergy should be celibate was widely flouted, either through marriage or concubines.

This corrupt period in the history of the papacy was put to an end by the emperor Otto I. The springboard for this development was Otto's alarm at the incompetence of John XII, pope from 955 to 964. John XII's father had maneuvered the Roman aristocratic vote to ensure the election of his son as pope, despite the fact that he was a mere eighteen years of age at the time of his election. Contemporary accounts suggest that John became involved in numerous political and sexual intrigues, eventually leading to him being deposed by Otto I, who installed Leo VIII as his successor. This deposition proved controversial, and led to further installations and depositions in the later tenth century. Benedict VI, for example, was installed as pope in 973, and strangled the following year, as the result of political plotting by a prominent Roman family.

Movements for reform sprang up within various sections of the church in response to these developments – including within the papacy itself, particularly during the period 1050–80. Yet others outside the papacy were attempting to reform the church, recovering its spirituality and limiting its secular involvement. One of the most important of these movements was based at the Benedictine monastery of Cluny. This was founded in Burgundy in 909 by William I, Duke of Aquitaine. Most patrons of monastic foundations expected to maintain a long-term connection with the monastery, particularly in ensuring that members of their families were appointed to prominent positions. William, however, explicitly released Cluny from any future obligations to him or his family.

Cluny would be a self-governing community, directly under the authority of the pope – who was unlikely to interfere in its affairs, given the geographical distance of Rome from Burgundy. Its abbots would be elected by the monks themselves, and would not be under any obligation to the secular nobility. The abbot of Cluny would retain authority over any daughter houses founded from Cluny. It is estimated that, by the end of the twelfth century, more than one thousand monasteries were linked to Cluny, which interpreted the Rule of St. Benedict in a more rigorous manner than many other monastic institutions.

Figure 2.2   The Benedictine Abbey of Cluny, founded in 909. View from the southeast: monastery building (eighteenth century) and the towers of Cluny III (built 1088–1130). Photo 2006, from the series Sites Clunisiens (Cluniac Sites). Photo: Yvan Travert/akg-images

We shall consider the Gregorian reforms in more detail presently (2.2.1). But we must now turn to look at a development which brought home the full extent of the growing alienation between the churches of the east and west – the "Great Schism" of 1054.

2.1.10.   The "Great Schism" between East and West (1054)

Relations between western and eastern Christianity were generally problematic throughout the history of early Christianity, often reflecting deep political rivalry between the pope at Rome and the emperor at Constantinople. Although there were clear and genuine theological differences emerging between the two Christian churches from about 700 onwards, these were often not the primary cause of the tensions that culminated in the formal break between the eastern and western churches in 1054.

The first serious rift between the two churches is generally known as the Acacian Schism. This period of ruptured relationships lasted from 484 to 519, and was caused by Pope Felix III's rejection of the emperor Zeno's attempt to resolve the Monophysite controversy (2.1.6). The schism takes its name from Acacius, who was the patriarch of Constantinople from 471 to his death in 489. Irritated as much by their political independence as by their Christological views, Felix III excommunicated both emperor and patriarch. Eventually, the issues were more or less resolved, and a shaky reunion was agreed in 519.

Tensions later rose between east and west over the aftermath of the iconoclastic controversy of the eighth century (2.1.6). Reports which reached the west concerning this controversy suggested that the eastern church was forcing believers to worship images, instead of worshipping God. In part, this western perception arose because of a translation difficulty. It was not easy to express the difference between "worship" and "veneration" in Latin. As a result, many western theologians believed that the Second Council of Nicaea (787) was commending idolatry.

The emperor Charlemagne was alarmed at this interpretation of the iconoclastic controversy. Unaware of the translation difficulty, he considered the decisions of the Second Council of Nicaea as representing a lapse into precisely the form of paganism which he was attempting to overcome in Germany. He convened a council at Frankfurt in 794, which rejected any kind of reverence or veneration of icons. While allowing images to remain in churches for the purposes of ornamentation, or to commemorate saints, believers were forbidden to kneel before them, to kiss them, or to burn lights in front of them. Inevitably, this came to be seen by the eastern church as a criticism of one of its most treasured practices.

Tensions flared again in the ninth century during the Photian Schism (863–7), partly as a result of the western church's introduction of the word *filioque* (Latin: "and from the Son") into its versions of the Creed, without securing approval from the eastern church. The western churches now spoke of the Holy Spirit as "proceeding from the Father and the Son"; the eastern churches retained the older form of words, which spoke of the Holy Spirit as simply "proceeding from the Father." (Ironically, recent research suggests that the introduction of this new and problematic phrase may actually have been due to a local council in the eastern church, around 410.) Debate continues today among scholars about whether the introduction of the phrase *filioque* is of purely semantic significance, or represents a deep theological divergence from traditional Christian belief. Yet there was no doubt of its importance at the time.

The schism of 1054 was, however, a more serious matter than these earlier disputes. While there is little doubt that these debates helped create an atmosphere of suspicion and distrust, they were usually resolved diplomatically without undue difficulty. There was still only one Christian church, even though it was obvious that the east and west were developing in different manners culturally, theologically, and linguistically. These grievances may have created tensions, but they did not lead to schism.

We have already noted the friction over the western church's use of the phrase *filioque* in its creeds (1.5.4). Yet other differences caused further tension. Should unleavened or leavened bread be used at the eucharist? Eastern Christians retained the traditional practice of using leavened bread (that is, bread made from flour to which yeast has been added, causing it to rise); the west increasingly used bread made without any yeast. The east resented the increasingly strident claims to universal authority on the part of popes (sometimes referred to as "Caesaropapalism"), and felt Constantinople's claims to spiritual and political authority were not being given due weight in the west.

Yet many scholars argue that the final breaking point was the intransigence of two leading Christians of the eleventh century: Leo IX, pope from 1049 to 1054, and Michael Cerularius, patriarch of Constantinople from 1043 to 1059. Leo's enforcement of western norms in southern Italian churches (which up to then had generally followed Byzantine liturgical and devotional practices) was seen as tantamount to a claim to papal sovereignty over the entire church. Cerularius seems to have come to the conclusion that the only way of safeguarding the identity of the Byzantine church was to break any remaining relations with Rome, and eliminate any papal influence at Constantinople.

Although various attempts were made during the Middle Ages to mitigate this breach of communion, none of them really achieved very much. In part, this reflected the bitter aftermath of the Fourth Crusade (1202–4). Although intended to neutralize Islamic military expansion in the eastern Mediterranean, the western armies ended up besieging and finally occupying Constantinople (2.2.5). Whether this was an intended goal of the crusades remains disputed among historians. Whether accidental or deliberate, the western sacking of Constantinople solidified the alienation between east and west. Reconciliation between the eastern and western churches now became virtually impossible. As a result, the western church developed along more or less independent lines during the Middle Ages, without feeling under obligation to take Constantinople's views into account.

2.2.   The Dawn of the High Middle Ages

It is generally agreed that the eleventh century marked a transition of major importance in the history of Christianity in western Europe. A number of developments contributed to this changed situation. The threats of invasion of western Europe from Scandinavia or Moorish Spain receded. The power of the eastern empire, based at Constantinople, went into decline. Until the arrival of the Black Death in the late 1320s, western Europe was relatively free of the lethal pandemics that had wreaked havoc in earlier times – such as the "Plague of Justinian" in the sixth and seventh centuries.

By the end of the eleventh century, sustained population growth in the cities of northern Italy had laid the foundation for early forms of capitalism and a more sophisticated urban culture. The papacy reasserted its independence and authority, and became a major religious and political influence throughout western Europe. The reforms introduced by popes during this period deserve closer attention, and we shall consider them further in what follows.

2.2.1. The Eleventh Century: The Gregorian Reforms

During the tenth and early eleventh centuries, the papacy was widely ridiculed as morally and politically bankrupt (2.1.9). Later medieval church historians termed this a "dark age" (Latin: *saeculum obscurum*) in the history of the church. Yet it proved to be a temporary setback. After a period of instability and weakness, a series of reforming popes regained the initiative, and set in place reforms to eliminate the scandals and problems that had plagued the church in the previous century.

The most important of these measures are generally referred to as the "Gregorian Reforms," set in place by Gregory VII, pope from 1073 to 1085. Yet Gregory must not be seen in isolation. His reforms are to be seen as solidifying and extending the attempts of earlier eleventh-century popes to reform the church.

A turning point was reached with the election of the German bishop Bruno of Eguisheim-Dagsburg as pope, who took the name Leo IX. Leo, who was pope from 1049 to 1054, was known to favor reform. He consulted with his clergy, and reaffirmed the traditional view that simony (the practice of deriving spiritual or financial benefits from making church appointments) and clerical marriage were unacceptable. These reforms, which chimed in with the monastic reforming program introduced by the abbey of Cluny (2.1.9), were widely welcomed within the church. Leo's period as pope was complicated by growing theological and political tensions between east and west, which led to the "Great Schism" of 1054. As we noted earlier, although this formal break dates from 1054, the tensions lying behind it had been building up for years.

Nicholas II, pope from 1058 to 1061, reformed the system by which popes were elected. Popes had typically been members of important Roman families, or else political allies of German emperors with armies in the vicinity of Rome. Inevitably, their survival depended on maintaining the goodwill of their sponsors, which opened the way to political manipulation of church policy and appointments. Nicholas was painfully aware of the damage caused by the influence of powerful families and political patrons on the reputation of the papacy, having had to win the papacy by defeating and deposing Benedict X, who had won an earlier papal election through the support of the "Tusculani," a family which had traditionally provided candidates for the papacy, and encouraged the idea that the pope should be chosen from – and by – the noble families of Rome.

In 1059, Nicholas reformed the system by which popes were elected, aiming to eliminate the influence of political patrons. He convened a meeting of bishops in Rome to bring about a change in the election procedure. From now on, popes would be chosen by the most senior clergy of the city of Rome. In later years, this electoral college would be extended geographically. Yet the principle was clear: the election of the pope was a matter for the church, not political sponsors with vested interests. The emperor was to be consulted in making the decision; the decision, however, was to be made by the electoral college.

The most important reforms were introduced by Gregory VII, pope from 1073 to 1085. Gregory was already committed to the cause of reform before his election as pope, and had played a significant role in securing the election of Nicholas II and deposing Benedict X. Gregory regarded Benedict as a pawn of the "Tusculani," and regarded him as an enemy of reform.

Gregory was elected pope in April 1073 at the Lateran Basilica in Rome, following the procedure laid down by Nicholas II in 1059. Contemporary accounts suggest this was a popular election, even though there were some procedural irregularities. For example, Gregory was archdeacon of Rome before his election as pope; he had never held the office of bishop. Nor was the emperor consulted. Gregory fought off several challenges to the legality of his election, and then concentrated on introducing reforms.

While Gregory's reign as pope was, in some respects, a success, in others it was regarded as a failure. His relationship with the emperor Henry IV was fractious. Riled by what he saw as Gregory's high-handed attitude towards him, Henry sought to have him deposed by mobilizing factions within the church that were hostile to Gregory. Gregory responded by excommunicating Henry. In the end, Gregory was forced to leave Rome, and died in exile in Salerno in 1085.

Gregory's reforms, which he was careful to present as recovering past wisdom rather than as controversial innovations, picked up on issues which earlier reforming popes had also considered to be important. Following Leo IX's reforms, Gregory reaffirmed the church's condemnation of simony, and reasserted that priests should be celibate. All significant matters of dispute were to be referred to Rome. This increasing centralization of ecclesiastical administration and government in Rome inevitably led to a weakening of the power of individual bishops. Yet the most important – and controversial – reform concerned the papal rejection of the established practice by which secular lords were able to make church appointments. This issue was central to the "Investiture Controversy," which needs further discussion.

The "Investiture Controversy" centered primarily on the question of who had the right to appoint a bishop. The term "investiture" refers to "putting on the robes of office," raising the question of who is entitled to make such appointments. Especially during the tenth century, this had been seen as the prerogative of a local ruler or patron. By appointing a local bishop or abbot, a patron could expect to exercise influence over their decisions, and possibly benefit financially from them. Gregory confirmed what other eleventh-century popes had already declared – namely, that the right to make such appointments lay with the pope, not with the secular authorities. In 1074, Gregory declared: "Those who have been advanced to any grade of holy orders, or to any office, through simony, that is the payment of money, shall hereafter have no right to officiate in the holy church."

The emperor Henry IV reacted strongly against these proposals, rejecting the pope's right to make such appointments. As if to emphasize his disagreement with the pope, he appointed his personal chaplain as bishop of the Italian city of Milan, knowing that Gregory had already determined that another Milanese priest should have the job. Relations between pope and emperor became so poor that Henry declared his own nominee to be pope, and tried to depose Gregory.

In the end, controversy rumbled on for decades. The matter was finally resolved in the following century. In September 1122, the Concordat of Worms reached agreement that investiture would be eliminated, while allowing a mechanism by which secular leaders could have an unofficial but nevertheless significant influence over the appointment process.

By this time, a major renaissance was under way in western Europe – a matter which needs further discussion in its own right.

2.2.2.   The Cultural Renaissance of the Twelfth Century

The term "renaissance" tends to be used too often for comfort. Nevertheless, there are times when its use seems justified and appropriate. The twelfth century in western Europe is now widely seen as marking a major cultural transition. Although the term "Dark Ages" is no longer regarded as appropriate to describe the period in western European history from the fall of Rome to the dawn of the High Middle Ages, it nevertheless identifies a cultural mood. With rare exceptions – such as the reign of Charlemagne – this period was more concerned with biological, social, economic, and political survival, than with cultural enrichment. Where there was cultural revitalization, it was short-lived. After a short period of renewal, decline set in. The long-term stability that was so important to any kind of renaissance seemed impossible to achieve.

Yet by the twelfth century, a number of transitions had taken place which set in place the foundations for intellectual and cultural renewal. Renewal was now a long-term possibility, and could be expected to be sustained over generations. New cultural possibilities emerged, including a renewal of the ideas and practices of Christianity in western Europe. The main factors of importance were the following.

1. The end of foreign invasions. During earlier centuries, western Europe was constantly under threat from Islamic armies in Spain, or from the Vikings to the north. Yet these threats receded from about 1000. The seriousness of such threats must not be underestimated. On June 8, 793, Vikings destroyed the abbey on the Northumbrian island of Lindisfarne, a famous center of religious learning. Monasteries and churches were attacked by the Vikings, not necessarily because of their religious associations, but because they were seen as economic targets on account of their alleged wealth. By 1100, however, such threats lay largely in the past.
2. Economic renewal. Any cultural renewal depends on an economic foundation, enabling patronage of the arts. Without private or institutional patrons, artists found it difficult to focus on their crafts. International trading became increasingly important during this period, especially with the foundation of the "Hanseatic League" in the late

twelfth century. This trading alliance, based largely in the Baltic city of Lübeck, encouraged trade and economic development throughout the Baltic region, and extended as far west as England.

3. The establishment of universities. One of the most important academic developments of this age was the foundation of universities, primarily in England, Italy, and France (2.2.4). The Universities of Bologna, Oxford, and Paris were among the first to be established, and rapidly developed reputations as centers of academic and theological excellence. These universities would catalyze the theological renaissance of the age, and were an important stimulus to the emergence of scholastic theology.

4. Cultural enrichment. Around this time, western European culture began to discover resources of the classical age, often mediated through Arab channels. Gerard of Cremona (c. 1114–87) traveled to the Spanish city of Toledo to consult an Arabic edition of Ptolomy's *Amalgest* and prepare a Latin translation of the work. Gerard's translation of this work was hugely influential in the Middle Ages, only falling into disuse with the acceptance of Copernicanism in the later sixteenth century. Other scholars produced Latin translations of other major works, especially the writings of Aristotle. These significantly enriched the Middle Ages, opening up new possibilities for philosophical and theological development.

Other developments of this age may also be noted – such as the development of forms of technology (such as the windmill and paper) that enabled more efficient use of resources and labor.

The key point is that a period opened up in western European culture that proved to be relatively stable – politically and economically – which was both open to new stimuli (e.g., Aristotle) and the consolidation and exploration of existing ideas (such as those of Augustine of Hippo, now widely regarded as the father of western theology). This process of consolidation is especially evident in the development of collections of theological and legal material, designed to act as resources for the development of Christian theology and canon law in the new age now opening up.

2.2.3.   The Codification of Theology and Canon Law

It is sometimes suggested that medieval western theology is a set of footnotes to Augustine of Hippo. While this is an exaggeration, there is no doubt that early medieval theologians saw themselves as consolidating and developing the theological heritage of the western church, especially the writings of Augustine. One important resource which began to develop in the tenth and eleventh centuries were collections of "sentences" – that is, sayings of the great teachers of the church, arranged thematically. These became the foundation of theological reflection on these themes.

The most famous of these works is the *Four Books of the Sentences*, assembled by the Parisian theologian Peter Lombard (c. 1100–60). This extended an approach developed earlier in the twelfth century by Anselm of Laon (died 1117), which wove together biblical texts on the one hand, and theological commentary on the other. Peter arranged a series of biblical and patristic texts thematically, dividing his work into four "books." The first of these four books dealt with the Trinity, the second with creation and sin, the third with the doctrine of the incarnation and the Christian life, and the fourth and final book with the sacraments and the last things. Commenting on these sentences became a standard practice for medieval theologians, such as Thomas Aquinas, Bonaventure, and Duns Scotus.

Yet Peter Lombard did more than simply present his readers with a collection of texts. He added a theological commentary, aimed at reconciling or resolving apparent differences between the texts under consideration, and developing their ideas still further. The work is rightly considered to be one of the earliest works of systematic theology, in that it set out the fundamental themes of faith for systematic study, using a framework that was clearly modeled on the Apostles' Creed.

The ethos of the work became characteristic of the early Middle Ages – namely, respecting the theological heritage of the past, and seeing this as the basis for theological consolidation and development in a new intellectual age. The new "scholastic theology" (2.3.1) of the Middle Ages – hailed as a "cathedral of the mind," and seen as one of its most distinctive intellectual achievements – used these "sentences" as its building blocks, and theological commentary as its mortar.

Yet Christian theology was only one area of Christian life and thought where this process of collection and synthesis was taking place. One of the most important achievements of the age was the codification of Canon Law – that is, the law of the church. In the later fourth century, following the legalization of Christianity within the Roman Empire, the church tended to adopt Roman law in resolving disputes and arranging contracts. At points, however, the church established its own norms and conventions – for example, in the canons of Councils, which often established general principles which were binding within the church.

One of the earliest councils to make rulings of this kind took place in 314, a few years after Galerius's edict of toleration was proclaimed (1.4.1). This was a local gathering of bishops from the region of Antioch in the Galatian city of Ancyra. The council issued twenty-five canons that dealt with a variety of recent problems in the church – such as the discipline of the clergy, the alienation of ecclesiastical property, chastity, and adultery. Although these were sometimes regarded as local decisions, binding only on a specific region, ecclesiastical centralization inevitably led to the establishment of norms that were binding for the whole church, with bishops being seen as the administrators responsible for enforcing them.

As the church became increasingly influential following the waning of Roman imperial influence, the church found itself having to go beyond Roman law in a number of respects. Papal decretals – that is, *epistolae decretalis*, letters setting out binding decisions – came to be regarded as establishing some of the basic principles of church legislation. The term "canon law" came to be used to refer to the legal code by which the church governed itself, and conducted its relationship with external bodies. The presumption of canon law was that the church acted according to Roman law, unless it had determined to do otherwise. Even by the sixth century, it became clear that it was necessary to collect these decisions. An important early collection of conciliar canons and papal decretals was made by Cresconius in the eighth century.

As legislative authority within the church came to be increasingly concentrated on the papacy in Rome, it was clear that papal decisions on legal matters needed to be catalogued, codified, and – where necessary – reconciled with each other. Although this task had begun in earlier centuries, it was given a new intellectual rigor through the work of Ivo of Chartres in the late eleventh century, and Gratian of Bologna in the mid-twelfth century. Ivo of Chartre's collection *Panormia* (c. 1091–6) was widely used as a source of ecclesiastical legal decisions in western Europe.

The University of Bologna became a major center for the study of Roman law during the twelfth-century renaissance (2.2.4), and played a significant role in forging the legal norms of the Holy Roman Empire. Bologna championed the "Justinian Code" – a complex body of civil law issued from 529 to 534 by order of the Roman emperor Justinian I. This had fallen out of use in western Europe. Scholars at Bologna developed this code as the basis for a legal system adapted to the times, and it achieved considerable influence, particularly when championed by the emperor Frederick I (Barbarossa) (1122–90). It remains unclear how or why Justinian's code achieved such prominence at Bologna, although it is known that the important northern Italian merchant class regarded it as better adapted to increasingly complex commercial situations than the older German laws of the Holy Roman Empire.

Gratian realized that the renaissance of Roman law made it imperative to establish canon law on the same intellectual basis – that is, the accurate scholarly study of texts. Gratian's *Decretum* was a comprehensive survey of the entire tradition of canon law, which consolidated the material found in four major eleventh- and early twelfth-century canonical collections that were in circulation in Italy. Gratian's definitive collection of material included what are now known to be both genuine and forged papal decretals, as well as the canons of local and ecumenical councils. This process of codification went beyond the mere accumulation of texts. Gratian attempted to sort out apparent inconsistencies in papal decrees, and give a more rigorous foundation to the study of canon law.

In many ways, these two developments are important witnesses to the significance of a new institution to emerge in western Europe at this time – the universities. Given the importance of these institutions for the development of Christianity, we must consider them in more detail.

2.2.4.   The Rise of the University: The Paris and Oxford Schools

In its earlier periods, the main educational centers of Christianity were the cathedral and monastic schools (2.1.5), supplemented by a few royal foundations – such as that of Charlemagne – designed to encourage the emergence of an educated civil service. Although these schools encouraged the study of rhetoric, logic, and grammar, these were seen as subordinate to the study of theology and the practice of the Christian faith. The Middle Ages in western Europe witnessed the emergence of a new kind of educational institution – the university.

It is widely agreed that the modern term "university" has its origins in the Latin term *universitas*, meaning "a totality" or "the whole." This does not, however, refer to the universal scope of a university education, embracing every discipline and subject. Indeed, early universities remained quite specialized, tending to focus on the disciplines of medicine, theology, and law. The term *universitas* is actually an abbreviated form of phrases such as *universitas scholarum* or *universitas magistrorum*, referring to a self-governing community of scholars and teachers whose corporate existence had been recognized and sanctioned by civil or ecclesiastical authority. A "university" was thus an independent community of masters and scholars, who were independent of both church and state. The university was initially an academic guild, similar to the great medieval professional guilds, such as the goldsmiths.

The earliest university is thought to be the University of Bologna. Although this was formally recognized in 1158, it is generally agreed that the origins of the institution date back a further two generations, perhaps to 1080. Bologna initially focused on law and medicine, while providing a general education in the core disciplines of logic, grammar, and rhetoric. These three disciplines were often referred to as the *trivium* ("three ways"), being seen as the basic education needed to proceed to the more advanced studies of arithmetic, astronomy, geometry, and music (the *quadrivium*). The modern English word "trivial" derives from this medieval academic system, meaning "something very elementary." After completing their formal studies in arts, students were able to move on to the more advanced faculties of medicine, theology, and law.

The universities of Paris and Oxford played an especially important role in medieval Christianity. The University of Paris began to emerge in the twelfth century, and was initially based on monastic schools of theology scattered around the cathedral of Notre Dame, such as the famous school of St. Victor. It quickly assumed the status of one of the leading centers of theological education in Europe. Thomas Aquinas, widely regarded as the most eminent medieval theologians, taught at the University of Paris during the years 1245–59, and again from 1269 to 1272.

Paris was a collegiate university, made up of a number of constituent colleges, with the "university" as the corporate glue that held them together. One of its colleges achieved such fame that for many years it became synonymous with the University of Paris. At some point around 1257, Robert of Sorbon founded the Collège de Sorbonne. By the late middle ages, it was common to refer to the university simply as "La Sorbonne." On account of its collegiate structure, the University of Paris was not monolithic in its theology. A number of quite distinct theological schools emerged during the Middle Ages, of which the most important are the Dominican and Franciscan schools. As a result, Paris was seen as the epicenter of medieval theology by most Christian intellectuals in the thirteenth and fourteenth centuries.

The origins of the University of Oxford are not clear, although it is known that academic teaching was taking place there by the end of the twelfth century. Like Paris, Oxford was a collegiate university, which expanded as more colleges were established. Some religious orders founded colleges to ensure their own approaches to theology were represented in the university; other colleges were founded by wealthy patrons without any connection to religious orders. Although Oxford never achieved quite the same international fame as Paris, it was a significant force in the development of medieval theology.

At both Paris and Oxford, theology was taught in "schools" (Latin: *scholae*). The Latin term *schola* was used to designate one of the most distinctive forms of theology to emerge

Figure 2.3   The teaching of philosophy at the medieval University of Paris, from the fourteenth-century French manuscript *Great Chronicles of France*, Northern School. © The Art Archive/Alamy

during the Middle Ages: scholasticism. We shall consider this in section 2.3, which deals with the intellectual achievements of this era. In the meantime, we must consider one of the most significant movements to emerge from the Middle Ages – the Crusades.

2.2.5.   The Crusades: Spain and the Middle East

Although the church in western Europe had established its own identity and concerns by about 1100, it could not ignore developments elsewhere in the region. It was clear that Islamic military expansion posed a major threat to the church throughout the southern flank of Europe, but especially in southern Spain, Sardinia, the Balearic Islands, Sicily, and the Balkans (2.1.3). The origins of the Crusades lie in requests for military assistance during the eleventh century in stemming – or even reversing – Islamic territorial gains.

Although most historians accept that these military campaigns of the Middle Ages were primarily concerned with recapturing territory in various parts of southern Europe invaded by Islamic forces in earlier centuries, the term "Crusade" is often used specifically to designate a series of military campaigns over an extended period of time in the Balkans and the Middle East. Given the symbolic importance of Jerusalem to the Christian church, it was seen as axiomatic that Christians should be allowed access to the Holy Land. The destruction of the church of the Holy Sepulchre in Jerusalem in October 1009 by Caliph Al-Hakim bi-Amr Allah caused considerable resentment (it was later rebuilt). Reports of violence against Christian pilgrims to the region caused concern in western Europe, and created a context sympathetic to military intervention.

The immediate cause of the First Crusade was the defeat of Byzantine armies in 1071 by the Seljuq Turks at the Battle of Manzikert, which led to the loss of the interior of Asia Minor. Constantinople was now vulnerable, no longer having any buffer zone to protect itself against Turkish armies. Alexius I, the Byzantine emperor, appealed to Pope Gregory VII, asking for military assistance in the face of this critical threat. It was not the best time to make such an appeal. Relations between the eastern and western churches had plunged to new depths in 1054 on account of the "Great Schism" (2.1.10). Gregory, preoccupied with the "Investiture controversy" (2.2.1), did not accede to this request.

Nevertheless, his successor – Urban II – responded positively. Alexius I sent ambassadors to the Council of Piacenza in March 1095, once more asking for help in defending what remained of the Byzantine Empire against the Seljuk Turks. On the final day of the Council of Clermont (1095), Urban launched a passionate appeal for Christian princes across Europe to launch a holy war in the Middle East. The First Crusade (1096–9) was fueled by a religious passion which led armies of both knights and peasants to journey to the Middle East. Jerusalem was captured in 1099.

The historical roots of the First Crusade remain contested. Historians have offered various explanations, such as Urban II's desire to extend his religious and political influence eastwards, and rising concern about Islamic encroachment in Europe. Some have suggested that the outcome of the crusade was a further destabilization of the Byzantine rulers, in that it showed them to be militarily and diplomatically incompetent.

Yet most historians agree that the crusade achieved a relatively small and short-lived victory. It would only be a matter of time before the four "Crusader states" which resulted from this incursion – the principality of Antioch, the county of Edessa, the kingdom of Jerusalem, and the county of Tripoli (secured during a later campaign in 1101) – would fall back into Islamic hands. There is also widespread agreement that the religious fervor that led so many civilians to volunteer for military service in the First Crusade diminished significantly in subsequent campaigns, which were generally conducted by military professionals and mercenaries.

The fall of Edessa in 1144 triggered the Second Crusade (1145–9). This was followed by a series of campaigns. Some historians hold that there were nine crusades; we here follow those who suggest that there were eight:

The Third Crusade (1188–92)
The Fourth Crusade (1202–4)
The Fifth Crusade (1217)
The Sixth Crusade (1228–9)
The Seventh Crusade (1249–52)
The Eighth Crusade (1270)

Although the Crusades were presented primarily as an attempt to secure the holy sites of Christianity, and prevent further Islamic expansion in Europe, it is clear that other agendas were being pursued. One of the most significant of these secondary agendas concerns tensions between Rome and Constantinople. Simmering tensions exploded during the Fourth Crusade, when an army that had been raised to capture Jerusalem ended up laying siege to Constantinople in July 1203. (Historians continue to debate whether this was an intended goal of the crusade, or an accidental outcome.) The city fell in April 1204, and was sacked by the Crusaders, with great loss of life – an action that was condemned by Pope Innocent III. The Crusader armies, diverted by their attack on Constantinople, never continued their intended journey to Jerusalem.

The Crusades can be seen as corresponding to a period in history when the power and influence of the papacy was at its height. By the fourteenth century, a degree of decentralization was taking place across Europe, with power increasingly being concentrated in nation-states, anxious to preserve their own identity and interests.

2.2.6.   Secular and Religious Power: Innocent III

The church was a major influence in international politics, in the internal affairs of regions, in fostering a sense of identity at the level of local communities, and in giving individuals a sense of location and purpose within a greater scheme of things. The church had always played an important international role in European society. Medieval Europe bore little relation to its modern counterpart, composed of individual well-defined nation-states. In the Middle Ages, Europe consisted of an aggregate of generally small principalities, city-states, and regions, often defined and given a shared sense of identity more by language and historical factors than by any sense of common political identity.

At the start of the fourteenth century, for example, Italy was little more than a patchwork of independent city-states and petty principalities. These were consolidated into six major political units during the fifteenth century: the kingdoms of Naples and Sicily, the Papal States and the three major city-states of Florence, Venice, and Milan. The modern nation-state of Italy was the result of the *Risorgimento* of the nineteenth century (4.2.6). In much the same way Germany, destined to play a particularly significant role in the events of the age, consisted of a myriad of tiny territories. Even as late as the opening of the nineteenth century, there were still thirty-two German states and territories, which were only finally united into the German empire in the later nineteenth century (4.2.8).

The church was the only international agency to possess any significant trans-national credibility or influence throughout the Middle Ages. It played a decisive role in the settling of international disputes. Under Innocent III (pope from 1198 to 1216), the medieval papacy reached a hitherto unprecedented level of political authority in western Europe. Although the church had vigorously asserted its independence from kings and emperors in previous decades, particularly as a result of the Gregorian reforms noted earlier (2.2.1), secular rulers regularly attempted to encroach on its claims to political influence. Innocent regarded the defense of the *libertas ecclesiae* (Latin: "freedom of the church") as central to his program for the revitalization of the church.

This was given theological justification in the decree *Sicut universitatis conditor*, issued in October 1198, in which Innocent III set out the principle of the subordination of the state to the church. Just as God established "greater" and "lesser" lights in the heavens to rule the day and night – a reference to the sun and moon – so God ordained that the power of the pope exceeded that of any monarch. "Just as the moon derives her light from the sun, and is inferior to the sun in terms of its size and its quality, so the power of the king derives from the authority of the pope." The authority of the church was often recognized with great reluctance by secular rulers; there was, however, no other institution in western Europe with anything remotely approaching its influence.

Innocent's assertion of papal political authority was put to the test in 1201, following the death of the emperor Henry VI in 1197. Henry, who had been king of Germany since 1190, had been crowned emperor by Pope Celestine III in 1191. It was Henry's intention that he would be succeeded as king of Germany by his son, Frederick. Yet Henry's son was an infant at the time of his death. Chaos ensued, as three rival candidates bid for the German crown: Frederick, son of Henry VI; Philip of Hohenstaufen, brother of Henry VI; and Otto of Brunswick, who had no connection with Henry VI.

Innocent intervened. He declared that Frederick was too young for the responsibilities of the position; Philip was corrupt; Otto, however, was noble and pious, and ought to succeed Henry VI. "We therefore decree that he ought to be accepted and supported as king, and ought to be given the crown of empire, after the rights of the Roman church have been secured." The intervention proved decisive. By 1206, however, Innocent realized that he had backed the wrong person, and transferred his support to Philip. In return for his support, Innocent received promises that the king would not interfere with the election of bishops in Germany.

Innocent's reforming agendas were given additional substance at the Fourth Lateran Council of 1215. Aware of the difficulties in securing the attendance of bishops from across Europe, Innocent III issued a summons in April 1213 to bishops and other senior church figures to the council, which would be held in Rome in November 1215. As a result, the council was unusually well attended, and its decisions were seen as a landmark in the consolidation of the internal organization and external influence of the church.

Among the decrees of the Fourth Lateran Council, the following are especially important:

Canon 1: An exposition of the fundamentals of the Catholic faith, including a brief defense of the idea of "transubstantiation" – the doctrine that the substance of the bread and wine of the eucharist are transformed into the body and blood of Christ.

Canon 5: A reaffirmation of papal primacy within Christendom, as recognized by the early church. After the pope, primacy was to be given to the patriarchs in the following order: Constantinople, Alexandria, Antioch, and Jerusalem.

Canon 18: Clergy may not pronounce nor execute a sentence of death; act as judges in extreme criminal cases; or take part in matters connected with judicial tests.

Further reforms of papal elections were introduced in the thirteenth century, especially concerning the rules for papal election. Alarmed by how long it took cardinals to choose a new pope, Gregory X, pope from 1271 to 1276, introduced rules designed to discourage delays. Cardinals were to remain in a closed area (the "conclave") until they had made a decision. Food was to be supplied through a window to avoid contact with the outside world. After three days of the conclave, the cardinals were to receive only one meal a day; after another five days, they were to receive just bread and water.

Yet there were many within the church at the time who were troubled by the soaring power and influence of the papacy, and sought to prevent it getting out of control. The Conciliarist movement argued that ecclesiastical power should be decentralized. Instead of being concentrated in the hands of a single individual, it should be dispersed within the body of the church as a whole, and entrusted to a more representative and accountable group – namely, "general Councils." This movement reached the height of its influence in the fourteenth and fifteenth centuries. Its moment seemed to have arrived when a crisis emerged in the papacy during the fourteenth century. We shall return to this point later in our narrative (2.4.2).

2.2.7.   Franciscans and Dominicans: The Rise of the Mendicant Orders

The religious orders played a major role in maintaining a Christian presence on the eve of the Middle Ages, and continued to be centers of Christian theological and spiritual excellence throughout this period. The Order of St. Benedict – widely known simply as "Benedictines" – were especially important in establishing monasteries throughout western Europe. As we noted earlier, the Benedictine monastery of Cluny played a particularly important role in promoting reform and renewal during the twelfth century (2.1.9). Benedictine spirituality emphasized the importance of corporate worship, spiritual reading, and work in the context of community.

The term "monk" derives from the Greek word *monachos*, meaning "solitary" or "alone." Although some monks led solitary lives, the normative pattern established by the early Middle Ages was that of monks living within a specific self-sufficient community. The ideal of isolation or solitariness was maintained by the monastic cell – a single room to which a monk would withdraw, when not engaged in the worship of the community or communal work. Monasteries offered hospitality to travelers, and often developed hospitals to offer care within and beyond the monastic community.

Yet monasticism was only one form of the religious life. Not all forms of religious life during the Middle Ages followed the monastic model. During the Middle Ages, a second model began to become influential – the mendicant orders. The term "mendicant" derives from the Latin term for "begging." Where monasteries derived their income from their lands, a new group of religious orders emerged during the thirteenth century which depended on the support of wealthy patrons and townspeople. A man who chose to adopt this way of life would be known as a "friar" (from the French word *frère*: "brother").

Whereas a monk would be committed to a particular community in a particular place (such as the Benedictine monastery of Cluny), a friar would be committed to a community dispersed over a wide geographical area known as a "province." Friars undertook an itinerant ministry, typically ministering and preaching in different religious houses owned by the community within his province.

The two most important mendicant orders – the Dominicans and Franciscans – were both established during the thirteenth century. Both were responses to a recognition of changing social norms and the need to extend the pastoral and preaching ministry of the church beyond the enclosed communities of monasteries.

The Franciscans – more correctly known as the "Order of Friars Minor" (Latin: *Ordo Fratrum Minorum*) – arose out of the ministry of Francis of Assisi (1181/2–1226). Francis was the son of a wealthy merchant in the Umbrian town of Assisi, who was captivated by the vision of personal poverty that he found in the teaching of Jesus of Nazareth. He gathered a following as he preached the need for repentance and renewal in the countryside around Umbria, and was given permission to found his own religious order by Innocent III in 1209. Initially, the Franciscans focused their activity on Italy, but the order soon expanded into other parts of Europe. The order was based on a Rule of 1223, drawn up by Francis, which identified its core values and beliefs – but in a manner that proved open to competing interpretations.

As a result, the movement soon found itself mired in internal controversy over one of its core values – poverty. From the outset, the Franciscan order possessed no individual or communal property, holding that the renunciation of property rights was integral to evangelical perfection. If the order was not permitted to own property, how could it build churches? Or establish houses in towns and cities, to allow it to continue its work? Tensions developed within the order between those committed to the ideal of absolute poverty, and more pragmatic voices who recognized the need for property in order to carry out the order's ministry.

Figure 2.4   *St. Francis of Assisi Preaching to the Birds*, predella painting from *The Stigmatization of St. Francis*, by Giotto di Bondone, c. 1295–1300. Paris, Musée du Louvre. © The Gallery Collection/ Corbis

Eventually, a way was found to get round this problem. In 1279 Pope Nicholas III ruled that all property given to the Franciscans was to be regarded as belonging to the Holy See, which in turn allowed the Order to use it as it pleased. Further controversy broke out a generation later, again focusing on the idea of poverty. In 1323, Pope John XXII condemned as heretical the assertion that Christ and the apostles had not owned anything, either individually or in common.

Yet perhaps the most important debate within the order concerned its focus of operations. Should it concern itself primarily with ministry in the rural regions of Italy, following the model of Francis himself? Or should it be concerned with ministry in the cities, especially among the urban poor? The "Conventual Franciscans" – as they came to be known – chose to establish houses in the cities, seeing these as its communal base for preaching and pastoral work. (This name derives from the Latin *convenire*, "to come together," which is also reflected in the word "convent" – namely, a place of gathering or assembly.) Others tended to prefer a solitary ministry in the countryside, without any necessary attachment to a building or community.

The "Order of Preachers" (Latin: *Ordo Praedicatorum*) was founded by Dominic de Guzmán (1170–1221). Dominic was concerned at the spread of the Cathar heresy in southern France. This religious sect appeared in the Languedoc region of France in the eleventh century, and flourished in southern France during the following two centuries. The Cathars adopted views which are recognizably Gnostic, perhaps originating from eastern Europe, such as the notion that matter was intrinsically evil, and the belief in two Gods – an inferior creating divinity and a superior redeeming divinity. The church had attempted to suppress this heresy by force, with little success. Dominic took the view that what would convert the Cathars was neither force nor power, but personal holiness, humility, and good preaching. In 1215, he gathered a small group around him who shared his vision, and eventually received papal permission from Innocent III to found a new religious order in the winter of 1216–17.

One of the social changes that lay behind Dominic's vision was the growing importance of towns as population centers. The influx of rural workers into the towns that was characteristic of this age of increasing prosperity was creating new pastoral problems. Town churches were unable to cope with the population surge. The Dominicans established houses in such towns, using these as a base for their pastoral and preaching ministries. These houses often became centers of theological and spiritual excellence. Leading Dominican theologians and spiritual writers of the Middle Ages included Albert the Great, Thomas Aquinas, Meister Eckhart, Catherine of Siena, and Mechthild of Magdeburg.

2.2.8. Women Mystics and Female Religious Orders

The status of women in medieval western Europe has long been recognized as complex. The single issue of gender is clearly inadequate to categorize what is now known about the historical realities of life in the Middle Ages. In a seminal paper of 1926, the British medieval historian Eileen Power developed views concerning the medieval status of women which has had a major impact on subsequent discussion of the question. Her three main points remain landmarks in contemporary discussion, even if historical research has modified them at points.

1.   A distinction had to be made between medieval ideas about women and the everyday experiences of women. Furthermore, these ideas were often so confused and self-contradictory that they had relatively little direct impact on everyday life.
2.   While medieval women faced some serious challenges – such as a legal system which assumed female inferiority, and a social structure that invested men with considerable power over women's lives – Power noted that most medieval women found themselves in a position "neither of inferiority nor of superiority, but of a certain rough-and-ready equality."
3.   The real issue was not gender, but social class. Power focused her attention on feudal ladies, townswomen, and peasants, ignoring others of potential importance – such as women in religious orders.

Later studies have modified this framework, noting the importance of other factors in shaping the fortunes of women at this time, including ethnicity and regional identity. Yet there is another class of women who played an especially significant role in Christianity during the Middle Ages – women mystics, and members of female religious orders.

Religious orders provided an important context within which women could provide communal leadership and spiritual guidance during the Middle Ages. Some individual female spiritual writers of this period achieved eminence, and were widely regarded as authorities by those looking for religious guidance. Among these, we may note Hildegard of Bingen (1098–1179), Hadewijch of Brabant (early thirteenth century), Mechthild of Magdeburg (c. 1207–c. 1282/1294), Angela of Foligno (c. 1248–1309), and Julian of Norwich (c. 1343–1416). Each of these writers developed an approach to spirituality which attracted a following across Europe.

The term "mystic" is often used to refer to such writers, and it is important to understand what this word really means. In everyday use, the term means something like "someone who is seen to possess spiritual wisdom." However, "mysticism" has a more technical sense in the history of Christian spirituality, meaning a spiritual approach which aims to deepen the direct human experience of God. The term derives from the Greek word *mystikos*, which has overtones of discovering something that is concealed or inaccessible, or being initiated into certain practices. A "mystic" thus means someone who is recognized as developing methods or ideas that help the believer deepen this direct relationship with God.

The twelfth-century mystic Hildegard of Bingen may be singled out for special comment, given the surge of interest in her writings in recent times. Hildegard wrote extensively in almost every genre, including letters, works of natural philosophy, theological treatises, accounts of mystical revelations, and works of drama. Her achievements as an artist, dramatist, mystic, theologian, musician, and correspondent illustrate well how much women could achieve through a monastic vocation. Religious orders provided places of security and stability which had the potential to encourage and enable talented women writers and artists, when society as a whole discouraged any such development.

While Hildegard of Bingen worked within a religious community, other women mystics chose to adopt a more solitary form of existence. Julian of Norwich was an "anchoress" – a woman who chose to withdraw from secular society, and adopt a solitary religious life. Little is known about her circumstances. Some suggest that she chose to do this after the death of her husband, although there is no supporting evidence for this. Julian's celebrated *Revelations of Divine Love*, thought to have been written around 1413, is widely regarded as a spiritual classic, often remembered for its best-known statement: "All shall be well, and all shall be well, and all manner of thing shall be well."

Although the medieval church excluded women from the papacy, the episcopacy, and priesthood, there was no such limitation on the role of women in religious communities. Many women entering religious orders were wealthy and of noble family, and saw the monastic life as an attractive alternative to marriage. (At this time, the social status of marriage and the conventions surrounding it were such that it was much more a commercial and social exchange between the bride's father and husband than an act of romantic love.)

The religious life offered a degree of independence and the possibility of institutional and spiritual leadership which was not available in the secular world of that time. Convents were able to elect their own abbess or prioress, depending on the status of the religious community. Some leaders of religious communities exercised considerable political influence. For example, the noblewoman Sophia I, Abbess of Gandersheim (975–1039), played a major role in the election of Henry II as King of the Romans, and subsequently in the election of Conrad II as Holy Roman Emperor.

A good example of the way in which medieval women exercised spiritual influence can be seen in the founding of the Abbey of Fontevraud in 1100. Philippa of Toulouse persuaded her husband William IX, Duke of Aquitaine, to grant Robert of Abrissel some land to establish a religious community. The abbey was founded as a "double monastery" – that is, with both monks and nuns living on the same site. Robert of Arbrissel declared that the leader of the new abbey should always be a woman and appointed Petronilla de Chemillé (died 1149) as the first abbess. She was succeeded by Matilda of Anjou, the aunt of Henry II, king of England. The abbey became a magnet for rich and powerful women over the years, and played an important social role in western France. It served as a refuge for battered women and prostitutes, as well as a leper hospital.

Other spiritual options were open to women at this time, including the possibility of forming loose supportive communities without taking formal vows of obedience to a spiritual superior, or renouncing their property. The best example of this dates from the early twelfth century, when women who had been widowed on account of the crusades formed communities on the outskirts of towns in the Lowlands. For reasons that are not understood, these women came to be known as "Beguines," and their shared buildings as "Beguinages."

2.3.   Medieval Religious Thought: The Scholastic Achievement

The more settled social and economic conditions of the Middle Ages, coupled with the further development of monastic schools of theology and the emergence of universities

(2.2.4), led to a theological renaissance, which remains a landmark in Christian thought. One of the most distinctive features of the period is the emergence of the genre of "scholastic theology," which merits close attention in its own right.

2.3.1.   Cathedrals of the Mind: The Rise of Scholasticism

Scholastic theology is widely regarded as a medieval landmark. Early generations of theologians had tended to write theological treatises in response to certain specific questions – such as the nature of the church (a question that dominated the Donatist controversy, 1.5.5), or the nature and operation of divine grace (a major theme in the Pelagian controversy, 1.5.6). Some early Christian writers produced more wide-ranging works, introducing the basic themes of Christian theology, often in the form of commentaries on the creeds.

Scholastic theology represented a major departure from these earlier approaches to theology. Most patristic works of theology were occasional (responding to specific debates) or pedagogical (aimed at explaining the core ideas and practices of the Christian faith). Scholastic theology offered a systematic approach to theology, based on a rigorous rational foundation, making full use of the disciplines of rhetoric, dialectic, and logic now taught in most academic contexts. The intricacy and comprehensiveness of leading works of scholastic theology led the great medieval scholar Etienne Gilson (1884–1978) to describe them as "cathedrals of the mind."

There was little reason to expect that this kind of development would take place during the Middle Ages. Dialectical approaches to theology were regarded with suspicion at the opening of the twelfth century. Berengar of Tours (c. 999–1088), for example, was viewed with suspicion, being seen as having reduced the eucharistic mystery to some kind of dialectical puzzle. Similar concerns were expressed about Roscelin of Compiègne's views on the Trinity in the early twelfth century, which critics suggested reduced this theological mystery to little more than a rationalist tritheism.

Yet others were able to develop rational approaches to theology, maintaining both academic rigor and theological orthodoxy. In the late eleventh century, Anselm of Canterbury produced a rational defense of the incarnation, demonstrating that this distinctively Christian doctrine was a proper and necessary consequence of basic beliefs concerning the nature of God and the human predicament. Anselm's positive and orthodox approach to the relation of faith and reason – summarized in the Latin slogan *fides quarens intellectum* ("faith seeking understanding") – created a new awareness of the possibility of a rational approach to theology.

This was taken a stage further through the use of dialectical reasoning to resolve theological contradictions – for example, in the interpretation of biblical passages. Anselm of Laon (died 1117) explored some disputed questions in biblical interpretation, noting how early Christian commentators often offered quite different understandings of biblical passages. Having noted these divergences, Anselm then offered means of resolving them – in effect, producing a synthesis out of a dialectic.

This approach was taken a stage further by Peter Abelard (1079–1142) in his *Sic et Non* (Latin: "Yes and No"), in which he considered 150 debated theological points, and set out the contested points for resolution by his readers. A similar approach lay behind Peter Lombard's twelfth-century textbook *The Four Books of the Sentences*, which set out a variety of patristic statements on various issues, and left it to readers to resolve these (2.2.3). As a result, commentaries on the *Sentences* became one of the most widely used genres of academic theological literature in the Middle Ages.

By the beginning of the thirteenth century, there was a new theological appetite for the systematic articulation of theological positions, justified in terms of their rational and biblical basis, and the views of early Christian writers. Thomas Aquinas's *Summa contra Gentiles* set out a reasoned case for the Christian faith in the face of suggestions that it was irrational.

Yet the most famous work of scholastic theology is Thomas Aquinas's *Summa Theologiae* (Latin: "The Totality of Theology," 1265–74). Aquinas here wove together the reconciliation of competing biblical and patristic statements, within a rational framework which was intended to ensure that the Christian faith could be defended against its rational critics – such as Jews and Muslims, both of whom were present at Paris in the thirteenth century (2.3.3).

Figure 2.5   Thomas Aquinas (c. 1225–74), Italian philosopher and theologian, panel painting by Andrea di Bartolo (c. 1368–1428). Private Collection. © INTERFOTO/Alamy

One of the most influential misrepresentations of scholastic theology is the assertion that it debated how many angels might dance on the head of a pin. This suggestion dates from the seventeenth century, and is not found in any medieval writings. This is not to deny that medieval writers did discuss a number of questions relating to angels. For example, Aquinas sets out a detailed theology of angels, distinguishing nine quite distinct types of angels, and arranging them hierarchically.

Yet one of the most distinctive features of scholastic theologies of the thirteenth century is its growing awareness of additional cultural and intellectual resources made available for Christian theology by increased contact with the Islamic world. One of these was the rediscovery of Aristotle, now rightly recognized as one of the most significant intellectual developments of the Middle Ages. This merits closer discussion in its own right.

2.3.2.   The Handmaid of Theology: The Rediscovery of Aristotle

In 529, the Byzantine emperor Justinian ordered the closing of the philosophical school in Constantinople, forcing many scholars to find intellectual refuge in eastern cities such as the Syrian city of Edessa. There, they were able to continue their work on Plato and Aristotle. Eastern Christianity had tended to regard Aristotle as inferior to Plato. Leading Christian theologians of the eastern church – such as Gregory of Nyssa, or the later Pseudo-Dionysius – were able to use Plato constructively in their theology. Aristotle, however, seemed of little interest. In the west, Aristotle had simply been forgotten, apart from his works on logic.

The Islamic conquest of the Middle East led to a new interest in the works of Aristotle. These were translated, initially into Syrian, and then into Arabic. Many of the works of Aristotle that were preserved in Arabic translation were unknown to the west. In the eleventh century, Islamic writers such as Ibn Sina – better known by his Latinized name "Avicenna" – developed a philosophically rigorous approach to Islamic theology, which was further developed by Ibn Rushd – known to the Middle Ages as Averroes – a Spanish philosopher of the late twelfth century.

The key development in the western rediscovery of Aristotle was the major school of translation established by the bishops of Toledo in Spain in the mid-twelfth century. Increasing contact with Islamic scholarship in Spain led to the translation of many works from Arabic into Latin, with scholars such as Gerard of Cremona (c. 1114–87) playing a leading role in making Aristotle's texts more widely available. Works such as the *Prior Analytics*, *Posterior Analytics*, *Metaphysics*, and *Physics* became accessible to theologians, who quickly realized their potential as "handmaids of theology."

This curious phrase needs further explanation. Christian theology had already discovered that it was possible to use secular philosophy as a dialogue partner in apologetics and theological reflection. Alexandrian theologians in particular had used Platonism as the intellectual scaffolding on which they could build a distinctively Christian theology. In the Middle Ages, this was often expressed using the image of philosophy as the "handmaid of theology" (Latin: *ancilla theologiae*). This image immediately conveyed the idea that philosophy was subordinate to theology, while emphasizing its usefulness.

Aristotle now became appropriated by leading theologians, initially within the Dominican Order. Albert the Great and Thomas Aquinas quickly recognized the importance of Aristotle's approach. Indeed, Aquinas's famous argument for the existence of God based on motion is ultimately grounded in Aristotle's *Physics*. As Aristotle observed, everything that moved is moved by something else. Aquinas saw how this line of thought could easily be adapted for apologetic ends. Just as importantly, Aristotle's notion of a "habit" gave medieval theology an important and useful framework for discussing such questions as the nature of grace, and the place of virtue in the Christian life.

Yet the theological use of Aristotle proved to be controversial. His treatises expressed ideas that did not always fit easily with Christian orthodoxy, and at times completely contradicted it – such as his views about the eternity of the world. Since the world had no beginning, it could not have been created. This led some to wonder if Aristotle had been translated accurately. William of Moerbeke (c. 1215–86) translated some works of Aristotle directly from Greek into Latin at Constantinople in the thirteenth century, partly as a result of concerns that translations based on Arabic texts might be corrupted or distorted. Furthermore, it is now known that a number of works attributed to Aristotle – such as *The Book of Causes* and *On the Universe* – were spurious.

As the thirteenth century proceeded, it became increasingly clear that there were concerns in senior church circles about Aristotle. His logical works were seen as admirable, and came to be the basic texts for many medieval universities, including Paris. Yet many regarded his scientific works as misleading and erroneous. In 1210, a local church council laid down that "neither the books of Aristotle on natural philosophy, nor commentaries on them, are to be read at Paris in public or private, under penalty of excommunication."

A more comprehensive condemnation, drawn up by the bishop of Paris, followed in 1277, listing more than two hundred errors in Aristotle's writings. This condemnation of Aristotle does not appear to have had a long-term impact, and was later abandoned, partly on account of the use made of Aristotelian ideas by Thomas Aquinas. Yet in one respect, the condemnation served a useful purpose: it encouraged theologians to be more critical about Aristotle, subjecting his ideas to careful scrutiny before accepting them. Many scholars argue that the leading Franciscan scholastic theologians Duns Scotus and William of Ockham adopted more rigorous and critical approaches towards Aristotle, anticipating later concerns about the scientific reliability of some of his ideas.

2.3.3.   A Reasonable Faith: Thomas Aquinas

Although the great medieval scholastic theologian Thomas Aquinas is best known for his *Summa Theologiae*, some scholars consider that one of his most significant works is the smaller *Summa contra Gentiles*. Although earlier scholars suggested that this book was written around the year 1264, more recent research has pointed to a later date, perhaps between 1270 and 1273.

Where many theological works of this period are organized around the structure of the Apostles' Creed, the *Summa contra Gentiles* adopts a structure that strongly suggests it is really an *apologetic* work, aimed at defending the Christian faith, rather than a *theological* work, aimed at exploring its contents. This fits in with the traditional account of the circumstances of its composition. Raymond of Peñafort (c. 1175–1275), a senior Dominican with a particular concern to reach out to Jews and Muslims, encouraged both Arabic and Hebrew to be studied and taught at some Dominican colleges. According to tradition, Raymond requested Aquinas to compose a work which would use reason as a means of presenting and defending Christian ideas to these two audiences. Although this cannot be confirmed, it might help explain the unusual structure of the work. Yet there are other aspects of the work that do not fit in easily with this traditional account of its origins – such as its failure to engage with any specifically Islamic ideas.

The work falls into two main parts. The first deals with those truths about God which Aquinas believes to lie within the reach of human reason – such as the existence of God, and the way in which God can be seen in the natural world. The second part deals with core Christian truths that lie beyond the reach of reason, such as the concepts of incarnation and the Trinity. "Some things that are true about God lies beyond the competence of human reason, such as that God is Three and One. Yet there are other things to which human reason can attain, such as the existence and unity of God, which philosophers have demonstrated to be true under the guidance of the light of natural reason." Aquinas's agenda appears to be to lead his readers into the more complex world of Christian truths that lie beyond reason by beginning with the less challenging truths that are accessible to reason.

Yet in the end, perhaps the most important feature of this work is its basic conviction, rather than the specific way in which this is explored – namely, that the Christian faith is eminently reasonable. Where it goes beyond reason, Aquinas argues, this is to be seen as transcending the limits of reason, not contradicting reason. Revelation brings reason to completion. Since both reason and revelation seek the same basic truth, Aquinas argues, they are to be seen as complementary rather than contradictory in their relationship. Although this view can be found throughout Aquinas's writings, it is seen at its clearest in the *Summa contra Gentiles.*

Perhaps the best-known aspect of Aquinas's program of demonstrating the rationality of the Christian faith is his group of five "arguments" for the existence of God, traditionally known as the "Five Ways." In view of their importance and interest, we shall consider them in more detail.

2.3.4. Medieval Proofs for the Existence of God

In the opening pages of his *Summa Theologiae,* Thomas Aquinas sets out five lines of argument in support of the existence of God, each of which draws on some aspect of the world which "points" to the existence of its creator. It is clear that Aquinas does not believe that these are "proofs" of God's existence. Rather, Aquinas believed that it was entirely proper to identify pointers towards the existence of God, drawn from general human experience of the world. His Five Ways represent five lines of thought that demonstrate the consistency of the Christian view of God with what can be observed and known about the world.

So what kind of pointers does Aquinas identify? The basic line of thought guiding Aquinas here is that the world mirrors God, in that it is God's creation. Just as an artist might sign a painting to identify it as his or her handiwork, so God has stamped a divine "signature" upon the creation. What we observe in the world – for example, its signs of ordering – can be explained on the basis that God is its creator. God both brought the world into existence, and impressed the divine image and likeness upon it.

So where might we look in creation to find evidence for the existence of God? Aquinas argues that the ordering of the world is the most convincing evidence of God's existence and wisdom. This basic assumption underlies each of the Five Ways, although it is of particular importance in the case of the argument often referred to as the "argument from design" or the "teleological argument." We shall consider each of these "ways" individually.

The first way begins from the observation that things in the world are in motion or changing. This is normally referred to as the "argument from motion." So how did nature come to be in motion? Why is it not static? Aquinas argues that everything which moves is moved by something else. For every motion, there is a cause. Things don't just change; they are changed by something else. Now each cause of motion must itself have a cause. And that cause must have a cause as well. Aquinas therefore argues that there is a whole series of causes of motion lying behind the world as we know it.

Since there cannot be an infinite number of these causes, Aquinas argues, there must be a single cause right at the origin of the series. From this original cause of motion, all other motion is ultimately derived. This is the origin of the great chain of causality which we see reflected in the way the world behaves. From the fact that things are in motion, Aquinas thus argues for the existence of a single original cause of all this motion – and this, he concludes, is none other than God.

The second of the five ways begins from the idea of causation. One event (the effect) is explained by the influence of another (the cause). The idea of motion, which we looked at briefly above, is a good example of this cause-and-effect sequence. Using a line of reasoning similar to that used above, Aquinas thus argues that all effects may be traced back to a single original cause – which is God.

The third way concerns the existence of contingent beings. The world contains beings (such as animals and humans) which are not there as a matter of necessity. Aquinas contrasts this type of being with a necessary being (one who is there as a matter of necessity). While God is a necessary being, Aquinas argues that humans are contingent beings. The fact that we are here needs explanation. Why are we here? What happened to bring us into existence?

Aquinas argues that a being comes into existence because something which already exists brought it into being. In other words, our existence is caused by another being. We are the effects of a series of causation. Tracing this series back to its origin, Aquinas declares that this original cause of being can only be someone whose existence is necessary – in other words, God.

The fourth way begins from human values, such as truth, goodness, and nobility. Where do these values come from? What causes them? Aquinas argues that there must be something which is in itself true, good, and noble, and that this brings into being our ideas of truth, goodness, and nobility. The origin of these ideas, Aquinas suggests, is God, who is their original cause.

The fifth and final way is often referred to as "the teleological argument" or the "argument from design." Aquinas notes that the world shows obvious traces of intelligent design. Natural processes and objects seem to be adapted with certain definite objectives in mind. They seem to have a purpose. They seem to have been designed. But things don't design themselves: they are caused and designed by someone or something else. Arguing from this observation, Aquinas concludes that the source of this natural ordering must be conceded to be God.

Most of Aquinas's arguments are rather similar in terms of their structure. Each depends on tracing a causal sequence back to its single origin, and identifying this with God. A number of criticisms of the Five Ways were made by Aquinas's critics during the Middle Ages, such as Duns Scotus and William of Ockham. The following are especially important.

1. Why is the idea of an infinite regression of causes impossible? For example, the argument from motion only really works if it can be shown that the sequence of cause and effect stops somewhere. There has to be, according to Aquinas, a prime unmoved mover. But he fails to demonstrate this point.

2. Why do these arguments lead to belief in only *one* God? The argument from motion, for example, could lead to belief in a number of prime unmoved movers. Things could be moved by multiple causes. There seems to be no especially pressing reason for insisting that there can only be one such cause, except for the fundamental Christian insistence that, as a matter of fact, there is only one such God.

3. These arguments do not demonstrate that God *continues to exist*. Having caused things to happen, God might now have ceased to exist. The continuing existence of events does not necessarily imply the continuing existence of their originator. Aquinas's arguments, Ockham suggests, might lead to a belief that God existed once upon a time – but not necessarily now. Ockham developed a somewhat complex argument, based on the idea of God continuing to sustain the universe, which attempts to get round this difficulty.

Other medieval "arguments" for the existence of God could easily be added to this list – such as Anselm of Canterbury's "ontological" argument, which holds that since the reality of God is greater than the mere idea of God, the *idea* of God as "that than which nothing greater can be conceived" necessarily implies the *existence* of God. Yet the main point to note is that these arguments fit within an overall medieval approach to the Christian faith which is based on the assumption that it makes sense in itself, and is able to make sense of what we know about the world as well.

2.3.5. The Consolidation of the Church's Sacramental System

One of the most significant theological achievements of the medieval period was the consolidation of a theology of the church and its practices. In earlier periods, these ideas had tended to be treated in a somewhat disconnected way – for example, during the Donatist controversy (1.5.5). The great scholastic theological systems, in contrast, set out to provide an ordered and coherent account of God, the church, and the world – and saw the theological consolidation of the life of the church as integral to this vision.

One outcome of this was clarification of the nature of Christian ministry. Medieval theologians developed Eusebius of Caesarea's fourth-century views on the orders of ministry, recognizing seven distinct orders, in ascending order: sextons; readers; exorcists; acolytes; subdeacons; deacons; priests. Yet perhaps the most important systematic development was the construction of a sacramental theology which recognized seven sacraments: baptism; confirmation; eucharist; marriage; penance; ordination; and extreme unction.

These developments are to be regarded as the consolidation and extension of earlier approaches to the sacraments. Augustine of Hippo is generally regarded as having laid down the general principles relating to the definition of sacraments in the fifth century. Firstly, Augustine declared, sacraments are signs. "Signs, when applied to divine things, are called sacraments." Secondly, he insisted that these signs must bear some relation to the thing which they are meant to signify. "If sacraments did not bear some resemblance to the things of which they are the sacraments, they would not be sacraments at all."

Yet Augustine's definitions were imprecise and inadequate. For example, does it follow that every "sign of a sacred thing" is to be regarded as a sacrament? In practice, Augustine understood by "sacraments" a number of things that are no longer regarded as sacramental in character; for example, the creeds and the Lord's prayer. As time passed, it became increasingly clear that the definition of a sacrament simply as "a sign of a sacred thing" was inadequate. It was during the earlier Middle Ages that further clarification took place.

In the first half of the twelfth century, the Paris theologian Hugh of St. Victor (1096–1141) revised Augustine's somewhat imprecise definition. He began by noting that "not every sign of a sacred thing can properly be called a sacrament (for the letters in sacred writings, or statues and pictures, are all 'signs of sacred things,' but cannot be called sacraments for that reason)." In the place of this vague definition, Hugh proposed something rather more precise: a sacrament is "a physical or material element set before the external senses, representing by likeness, signifying by its institution, and containing by sanctification, some invisible and spiritual grace."

There are four essential components to Hugh's definition of a sacrament:

1. A "physical or material" element, such as the water of baptism, the bread and wine of the Eucharist, or the oil of extreme unction.
2. A "likeness" to the thing which is signified, so that it can represent the thing signified. Thus the eucharistic wine can be argued to have a "likeness" to the blood of Christ, allowing it to represent that blood in a sacramental context.
3. Authorization to signify the thing in question. In other words, there must be a good reason for believing that the sign in question is authorized by Jesus Christ to represent the spiritual reality to which it points.
4. An efficacy, by which the sacrament is capable of conferring the benefits which it signifies to those who partake in it.

This new systematic statement of the nature and function of sacraments, though welcome, was nevertheless still imperfect. On Hugh's definition, penance could not be a sacrament, as it included no material element. Theory and practice were thus seriously out of line. Peter Lombard (c. 1100–60) resolved the matter by omitting one vital aspect of Hugh's definition – namely, the reference to a "physical or material element."

Peter Lombard's classic definition of a sacrament, which was widely accepted during the Middle Ages, began by affirming that "a sacrament bears a likeness to the thing of which it is a sign." So what is a sacrament? "Something can properly be called a sacrament if it is a sign of the grace of God and a form of invisible grace, so that it bears its image and exists as its cause." This modified definition fits in each of the seven sacraments noted above, and remained virtually unchallenged until the time of the Protestant Reformation of the early sixteenth century.

The important point here is not the theological detail, but the general principle. A coherent theological system was in the process of emerging, which embraced every aspect of Christian thought and practice. Scholasticism had developed a theoretical framework which wove together every aspect of life and thought into a harmonious, ordered whole. The rational scholastic vision set out in Aquinas's *Summa Theologiae* found its imaginative counterpart in Dante's *Divine Comedy* – a work to which we shall return later in this chapter (2.3.8).

2.3.6.   Medieval Biblical Interpretation

The Bible played a major role in personal devotion and theological reflection in the Middle Ages. Most religious orders – especially the Benedictines – laid down that their members must read the Bible, and reflect on its themes. The Benedictine night Office included between three and twelve long readings from the Bible, depending on the day or season. The Bible was read aloud during meals, and monks were encouraged to memorize passages that could subsequently be recalled during periods of work, and used for devotional purposes. In addition, much time was devoted to *lectio divina*, a meditative and devotional form of Bible reading which often mingled the reading of biblical passages with commentaries by leading early Christian writers.

This emphasis on the importance of the Bible during the Middle Ages led to the production of numerous manuscripts of biblical texts, often beautifully illustrated – a good early example being the eighth-century Lindisfarne Gospels. Yet this deep interest in reading biblical texts and exploring their relevance to Christian life and thought raised a question of major importance: how are these texts to be *interpreted*?

This question had been discussed at some length in early Christianity. Once more, the medieval period witnessed the consolidation of these discussions, and the emergence of a codified system of biblical interpretation which gave the institution of the church a particularly significant role in settling theological debates. The standard method of biblical interpretation used during the Middle Ages is usually known as the *Quadriga*, or the "four-fold sense of Scripture." The Latin term *Quadriga* originally mean a chariot drawn by four horses; in Christian usage, it came to mean the reader of Scripture being guided by four quite distinct meanings that lay within the text.

A distinction had long been drawn between the literal and spiritual meanings of biblical passages. The *Quadriga* allowed readers of the Bible to explore four basic meanings of a

Figure 2.6 An illuminated medieval biblical manuscript, showing the construction of the temple of Jerusalem. Miniature from the Bible of St. John XXII, Latin manuscript from the Palace of the Popes of Avignon, France, fifteenth century. The Art Archive/DeA Picture Library/M. Seemuller

given text – its surface meaning, along with three deeper meanings: the *allegorical*, defining what Christians are to believe; the *tropological* or *moral*, defining what Christians are to do; and the *anagogical*, defining what Christians were to hope for. The four senses of Scripture were thus the following:

1. The literal sense of Scripture, in which the text was taken at face value.
2. The allegorical sense, which interpreted certain otherwise obscure passages of Scripture to produce statements of doctrine.
3. The tropological or moral sense, which interpreted such passages to produce ethical guidance for Christian conduct.
4. The anagogical sense, which interpreted passages to indicate the grounds of Christian hope, pointing towards the future fulfillment of the divine promises in the New Jerusalem. This approach to reading the Bible can be seen as expressing one of the deepest beliefs of the medieval Christian outlook – that there is an ordered way of looking at the Bible and the world, which brings stability to both life and thought.

An excellent example of allegorical interpretation can be found in Bernard of Clairvaux's twelfth-century exposition of the biblical book known as the "Song of Songs" or "Song of Solomon." Bernard offered an allegorical interpretation of the sentence "the beams of our houses are of cedar, and our panels are of cypress" (Song of Solomon 1:17). His approach illustrates the way in which doctrinal or spiritual meanings were "read into" otherwise unpromising passages. For Bernard, "houses" were an allegory of "Christian people," and "beams" were an allegory for the "rulers of the church and the state." This might seem to open the way to an arbitrary interpretation of biblical passages, in which readers imposed their own views upon the text. Yet this potential difficulty was avoided by insisting that nothing should be believed on the basis of a non-literal reading of the Bible, unless it could first be established on the basis of its literal sense.

Thus far, our discussion of scholasticism has focused on western Europe. Yet it is not often realized that scholastic ideas were debated at Constantinople, even as late as the fourteenth century. In the section that follows, we shall look at a Byzantine debate which can be seen as a critique of the scholastic approach to theology. We will begin, however, by exploring some aspects of the development of Byzantine theology, leading up to this debate.

2.3.7. A Byzantine Critique of Scholasticism: Hesychasm

Constantinople had become the intellectual and spiritual center of Orthodoxy by the end of the eleventh century (2.1.6). While making extensive use of theologians and spiritual writers who had no connection with the city – such as Gregory of Nazianzus and John of Damascus – Constantinople had begun to develop its own distinct approach to theology and spirituality. Especially under the leadership of its abbot in the early ninth century, Theodore of Stoudios (759–826), the monastery of Stoudios became a significant center for spiritual reflection. It was a focus for the forces opposed to iconoclasm during the bitter controversies of the late eighth and early ninth centuries.

The most significant theologian to emerge within Constantinople itself was Symeon the New Theologian (949–1022), a Byzantine nobleman who came under the influence of the monastery of Stoudios. After a brief period spent at Stoudios, Symeon moved to take charge of the renovation of the run-down monastery of St. Mammas, eventually becoming its abbot. The style of theology that he developed was mystical, placing an emphasis on the direct experience of God in the life of an individual. This was seen as a challenge to the rather more scholastic approach developed by official Byzantine theologians, such as Archbishop Stephen of Nicomedia. Yet though Symeon was a theologian on the margins of both church and society, his long-term influence on the development of Orthodox theology and spirituality was to prove enormous.

Where Stephen, the "official" theologian of the court of Constantinople, saw theology as an essentially abstract, philosophical exploration of ideas, Symeon regarded theology as wisdom infused by the Holy Spirit into a Christian as a result of repentance. His opponents dismissed this as a dangerous novelty, and managed to bring about his exile to the village of Paloukiton in 1009.

Yet Symeon's ideas proved to have a deep appeal. Where many Byzantine theologians developed approaches to theology which paralleled those of western scholasticism, Symeon emphasized the practice of prayer as a means of achieving union with God at a level that was beyond images, concepts, and language. This "apophatic" approach to theology – which highlighted the inability of human language to do justice to God – generated controversy during the Hesychastic Controversy of the fourteenth century. This debate derives its name from the Greek term *hesychia*, which can be translated as "silence," "stillness," "rest," or "quietness."

Hesychasts promoted the idea that the highest goal of the Christian believer is the experiential knowledge of God, which is attained by detaching the mind from the world, and isolating it from distracting thoughts. There are important elements of this idea in the teachings of Symeon, although other writers made a significant contribution to its development.

Negatively, hesychasm emphasized the importance of not being distracted by worldly thoughts; positively, it emphasized the importance of the "Jesus Prayer" – "Lord Jesus Christ, Son of God, have mercy on me, a sinner" – as a means of concentrating the mind and unlocking the heart. The object of this exercise is not to gain a deeper conceptual knowledge of God, but to experience God directly – often in the form of light.

The Hesychast controversy is usually regarded as having begun when Barlaam of Calabria (1290–1348) took exception to the teachings of some hesychastic writers. Barlaam was familiar with western scholastic approaches to theology, and tended to see theology as a science which established correct propositional statements concerning God. The hesychastic approach seemed to him to reduce theology to the subjectivities of experience.

Gregory of Palamas (1296–1359), a monk of Mount Athos, provided a vigorous defense of the central themes of the hesychastic approach against Barlaam's criticisms. (The monasteries of Mount Athos had by this time displaced the monastery of Studious as Orthodoxy's leading center of spirituality.) The differences between Palamas and Barlaam could not be resolved, and were eventually considered by a synod held at Constantinople in May 1341, presided over by the emperor Andronicus III. The synod ruled against Barlaam, who returned to Calabria. He converted to Catholicism, and was subsequently appointed bishop of Gerace.

Although the Hesychastic debate took place in the eastern church, it reflected concerns about the intellectual focus of western scholasticism. By the end of the fourteenth century, many Byzantine theologians were reasserting the close links between theology and spirituality, concerned that dominant western approaches to theology were too concerned with issues of its internal logic and structure, and paid insufficient attention to the affective aspects of faith. These concerns were also expressed within the western church, even if perhaps the most famous critique of the approach originated from the east.

2.3.8.   The Medieval Worldview: Dante's *Divine Comedy*

Many historical writers, if asked to identify one single work as somehow embodying the "medieval worldview," would point to Dante's *Divine Comedy*, composed during the period 1308–21. This massive poem, more than 14 000 lines long, is widely seen as an imaginative poetic vision of a medieval way of thinking about the world, life and death, and especially hell and heaven. The title often puzzles English readers, who assume that the term "Comedy" implies something amusing or funny. However, Dante originally entitled his work with the single Italian word *Commedia*, which is better translated as "Drama." The additional term "divine" appears to have been added by a Venetian publisher at a later stage.

Its author, Dante Aligheri (1265–1321) was born into a well-established family in the city of Florence, which was at that time an independent Italian city-state. Dante became involved in political intrigues in Florence, and incurred the anger of influential Florentine families, who forced him into exile. It was during this enforced absence from Florence that he began to write the major work which we now know as the *Divine Comedy*.

Dante's *Divine Comedy* tells of the poet's journey through Hell, Purgatory, and Paradise. Written in a complex pentameter form known as *terza rima*, the poem is a magnificent synthesis of the medieval outlook, picturing a changeless universe ordered by God. It consists of three interconnected poems, entitled *Inferno* ("Hell"), *Purgatorio* ("Purgatory"), and *Paradiso* ("Paradise"). The poem describes an imaginary spiritual journey which takes place in Holy Week 1300. Clues in the text allow its readers to work out that the journey begins at nightfall on Good Friday – the day on which the Christian church marks the death of Jesus of Nazareth on the cross. After entering Hell, Dante journeys downwards for an entire day, before beginning his ascent towards Purgatory. After climbing Mount Purgatory, Dante rises further until he eventually enters into the presence of God, concluding his journey on the Wednesday following Easter Day.

Throughout the journey, Dante is accompanied by guides. The first guide is Virgil, the great Roman poet who wrote the *Aeneid*. It is widely thought that Dante uses Virgil as a symbol of classic learning and human reason. As they draw close to the peak of Mount Purgatory, Virgil falls behind and Dante finds himself in the company of Beatrice (thought to be based on the young Florentine noblewoman Beatrice Portinari, the idealized object of Dante's affections, who had died in 1290), who leads him through the outer circles of heaven. Finally, he is joined by the great medieval writer and sage Bernard of Clairvaux (1090–1153), who finally leads Dante into the presence of God.

The structure of the poem is intricate and complex, and it can be read at a number of levels. It can, for example, be read as a commentary on medieval Italian politics, particularly the intricacies of Florentine politics over the period 1300–4; or it can be seen as a poetic guide to Christian beliefs concerning the afterlife. More fundamentally, it can be read as a journey of self-discovery and spiritual enlightenment, in which the poet finally discovers and encounters his heart's desire. For our purposes, it is a magnificent representation of medieval beliefs about the afterlife.

Dante's portrayal of the geography of hell is especially interesting, as he conceives of hell as consisting of a group of concentric circles – the perfect shape, according to ancient geometry. Dante portrays himself as descending through successive levels of hell, encountering various individuals who are condemned to its various regions. One of the most interesting aspects of Dante scholarship is to work out why Dante consigns various people to different fates – often reflecting aspects of papal and Florentine politics of the period. For example, "limbo" is seen as a kind of "ante-hell," in which no pain is experienced and which is illuminated by a "hemisphere of light" corresponding to the light of human reason.

Dante populates this region with virtuous non-Christians, particularly pagan philosophers such as Aristotle, Seneca, Euclid, and Virgil. Beyond this lies the second circle of hell, to which Dante consigns all those who have "made reason slave to appetite." Dante includes Achilles, Cleopatra, Helen of Troy, and Tristan (a hero of many medieval romances) among the inhabitants of this region.

One of the historical myths about the Middle Ages, still encountered in some outdated textbooks, is that it was believed that the earth was flat. No serious Christian thinker of the age held that opinion. *Purgatory*, the second book of Dante's *Divine Comedy*, is of particular interest as a witness to the medieval knowledge of a spherical Earth. During this poem, Dante discusses the different stars visible in the southern hemisphere, the altered position of the sun, and the various time zones of the Earth. Dante points out that, when the sun sets at Jerusalem, it is midnight on the River Ganges, and the sun is rising in Purgatory.

In the third book, *Paradise*, Dante sets out the medieval understanding of the structure of the universe. The cosmos is depicted as a series of concentric spheres, arranged in hierarchical order. The innermost sphere consists of formless matter. As Dante travels through these spheres, he moves initially from matter to plants to animals to human beings. The spheres above humanity contain heavenly beings, such as the angels and finally, God. Dante's final vision of God is framed in terms of Aristotle's idea of the "unmoved mover," with a distinctively Christian gloss – "the love that moves the sun and the other stars."

Dante's *Divine Comedy* merits close reading. For our purposes, it is best seen as a magnificent poetic depiction of the medieval understanding of the physical and spiritual worlds. Its astronomy is Ptolemaic, not Copernican. The earth stands at the center of everything. Yet this physical universe is supplemented by a complex spiritual understanding of the deeper structure of reality, in which everything derives its existence from God. Dante's journey of 1300 is an exploration of the medieval vision of reality, both physical and spiritual.

2.4.   The Later Middle Ages

Many accounts of the history of the Middle Ages make a distinction between the "High Middle Ages" (from about 1100 to 1300, often portrayed as a period of cultural and social achievement) and the "Later Middle Ages" (from about 1300 to 1500, often portrayed as a period of decay or stagnation). There is some truth in these traditional representations of the medieval period, even if there is at least some degree of arbitrariness about the exact date of this transition. Western Europe experienced a series of disasters shortly after 1300, such as the Great Famine of 1315–17 and the Black Death, which arrived in Europe from China in the late 1320s, and was at its height in 1348–50. Some estimates suggest that the population of western Europe may have been reduced by some two hundred million people – roughly 30 percent of the population – by these catastrophes. The situation was made worse by widespread social unrest, and the outbreak of the destructive Hundred Years' War – actually a series of wars – over the period 1337 to 1453.

Christianity in western Europe was deeply affected by these developments. In the case of the Catholic church, an additional complication arose through what is known as the

"Great Schism." As we shall see, political infighting led to conflict over the identity of the pope, and the influence of the church over international politics. In this section, we shall consider the fortunes of the western church, and how it coped with what many still regard as a period of ecclesiastical decline and decay.

2.4.1. The Avignon Papacy and the Great Schism

As we saw earlier, the election of popes was a contentious matter in the Middle Ages, and potentially open to manipulation by political or familial power groups (2.1.9). While the Gregorian reforms had sought to minimize this danger (2.2.1), it never really disappeared. The opening of the fourteenth century witnessed developments which seemed to many to illustrate the power that secular rulers wielded over supposedly spiritual elections.

Some scholars believe that the high water mark of papal political influence was reached in November 1302, when Boniface VIII (c. 1234–1303) issued the bull *Unam Sanctam*, in which he proclaimed that "every human creature is subject to the Roman pontiff." This viewpoint, and the manner in which it was asserted, provoked open dispute with many influential political leaders of the age, including the Emperor Albert I of Habsburg, the powerful Colonna family of Rome, and Philip IV of France. The Florentine poet Dante Alighieri (2.3.8) – author of the *Divine Comedy* – penned his essay *De Monarchia* ("On Monarchy") in response, challenging Boniface's claims of papal supremacy.

Philip IV launched a campaign designed to discredit Boniface, and minimize his influence. Guillaume de Nogaret, Philip's chief minister, declared that Boniface was a heretic; Boniface responded by excommunicating both Philip and de Nogaret. Philip teamed up with the Colonna family to arrange for two thousand mercenaries to ambush Boniface while he was staying in the town of Anagni, southeast of Rome. It worked. Boniface was taken captive. Although he was eventually released, he died shortly afterwards.

His successor, Benedict XI, was widely regarded as the puppet of Philip IV of France. He promptly revoked the order of excommunication that Boniface had imposed on Philip, and did nothing to implement Boniface's declaration of papal supremacy over secular rulers. However, in 1304, Benedict excommunicated de Nogaret and the prominent Italians who had played a part in the seizure of Boniface VIII at Anagni. He died shortly afterwards. Rumors rapidly spread that he had been poisoned.

A power struggle now developed between French and Italian cardinals over who should succeed Benedict. After nearly a year of wrangling within the deadlocked papal conclave, the French archbishop of Bordeaux was elected pope, and took the papal name Clement V. One of his first acts was to remove the papal establishment from Rome to France. Initially, the papacy was based at Poitiers. In 1309, it moved to the southern French city of Avignon. The "Avignon Papacy" would continue until 1377, by which time it had become widely discredited as a tool of the French monarchy. The seven Avignon popes, all French, were: Clement V (1305–14); John XXII (1316–34); Benedict XII (1334–42); Clement VI (1342–52); Innocent VI (1352–62); Urban V (1362–70); and Gregory XI (1370–8).

In the end, Gregory XI finally brought the curtain down on the Avignon papacy, returning to Rome in January 1377. The long period of the Avignon papacy had severely eroded the notion of the pope as a unifying Christian leader in western Europe, partly because

Figure 2.7   The medieval papal palace of Avignon, overlooking the city of Avignon and the Rhone River. © Gail Mooney/Corbis

of its obvious collusion with French political interests. Many hoped that the return of the papacy to Rome would end this damaging episode in the history of the western church.

Following Gregory's death in early 1378, a papal conclave met in Rome to choose his successor. The building in which the conclave was taking place was surrounded by a mob, who demanded that the new pope should be Italian, not French. The cardinals gave in to this popular pressure, and elected Bartolomeo Prignano, who took the name Urban VI. Although initially liked, Urban rapidly gained a reputation for arrogance, which alienated him from many of the cardinals. In August 1378, they issued a declaration that Urban's election was invalid, as it had taken place under pressure from a mob.

The French cardinals proceeded to elect a Frenchman, and reestablished the Avignon papacy with Clement VII as pope, whilst Urban remained in Rome, maintaining the legitimacy of his election. Western Christendom proved incapable of deciding which of the two popes was legitimate, leading to growing disquiet over the role of the papacy in spiritual and temporal affairs.

The ensuing period of the "Great Schism" led to the western church being split between two rival popes (often referred to as "pope" and "anti-pope"), each presenting himself as the only legitimate successor to St. Peter, and rejecting the authority of his rival. England, Germany, Hungary, most of Italy, Poland, and the Scandinavian countries supported Urban VI at Rome; France, Scotland, Spain, and southern Italy supported the "anti-pope" Clement

VII at Avignon. This situation continued for nearly forty years, and led to a dwindling in respect for the institution of the papacy. How could absolute power be entrusted to such an institution, which had clearly become open to corruption and the exercise of improper influence?

But what was the alternative? As we shall see, the "Great Schism" prompted many to explore other models of church government, the most important of which was "conciliarism."

2.4.2.   The Rise of Conciliarism

The Avignon papacy and the "Great Schism" (2.4.1) caused many in the western church to reflect on the potential for abuse and corruption which resulted from concentrating such spiritual and temporal power in the hands of a single individual. If there were two claimants to the papacy, and no human authority was to be recognized as superior to the papacy, how could things be sorted out? There seemed to be no existing mechanism by which the conflict could be resolved.

Yet many wondered if there might be a way in which power could be exercised more accountably on behalf of the church. Was the traditional system of focusing power on the pope really the best model of ecclesiastical governance? During the fourteenth century, one option began to emerge as a serious alternative to the existing papal model. What if authority within the church was not invested in a single individual, but in a group of accountable individuals – in other words, in a *council*? The movement widely known as "conciliarism" held that the ultimate focus on authority within the church was a General Council.

The origins of conciliarism can be traced back to the early church. The Council of Nicaea (325) was convened by the emperor Constantine (1.4.2). It consisted of bishops drawn from throughout the Christian world, who were charged with reaching consensus on a number of issues, especially doctrinal formulations concerning the identity of Jesus of Nazareth. Faced with the papal authoritarianism of the fourteenth century, many senior church figures came to the conclusion that the notion of absolute papal authority needed checks and balances if abuse was to be avoided. General Councils, convened on behalf of the church, would ensure that authority was exercised more responsibly. Although some suggested that such General Councils might eventually replace the papacy in the western church, most writers of the fourteenth century simply preferred to redefine the pope's privileges and responsibilities within a conciliar context. Their concern was to increase papal accountability to the church, not to replace the papacy with an alternative institution.

In the end, the momentum to resolve the Great Schism arose primarily within France. A number of French churchmen, inclined to think that France was partly responsible for the chaotic situation by encouraging the Avignon papacy, took the initiative in rectifying things. During the reign of the French anti-pope Clement V, the French academics Jean Gerson (1363–1429) and Pierre d'Ailly (1351–1420) invited the University of Paris – then widely regarded as the leading academic authority in western Europe – to discuss how the situation might be remedied.

The University of Paris declared that the schism could be ended in three ways. Firstly, the two rival popes could renounce the office unconditionally (an option referred to as "cession"), clearing the way to a new election by accountable and acceptable means. Secondly, the matter could be resolved by each pope agreeing to an impartial arbitrator, who would resolve the issue. Thirdly, a general council might meet to discuss the issue, and issue a binding recommendation.

Clement's death in September 1394 gave the conciliarists the opportunity for which they had been waiting. However, in the end, nothing came of it. Two weeks after Clement's death, Pedro de Luna was unanimously elected as pope by twenty-four cardinals at Avignon, taking the name Benedict XIII. A letter from the king of France, requesting the cardinals not to proceed to an election, was deliberately not opened until after the decision had been reached. In 1395, however, the national assembly of France and the French clergy endorsed the University of Paris's strategy for ending the Great Schism, either through cession of office, or through convening a general council. Yet neither Benedict XIII nor Gregory XIII was willing to give up his claim to the papacy. Nor would either agree to call a General Council to resolve the issue.

In the end, a group of disaffected cardinals decided to take the initiative. They convened a Council to meet at Pisa in 1409, with the explicit objective of seeking a resolution of the contested papacy. Benedict XIII and Gregory XIII called rival councils, hoping to discredit Pisa. Yet international support grew for Pisa, with the universities of Paris and Oxford throwing in their weight, backed up by many secular rulers. In the end, a large and representative body of bishops gathered in Pisa to hear the case for each of the rival claimants. After due consideration, the council declared that both had shown themselves unfit for this high office. Both were deposed. In their place, the council elected Cardinal Peter Philarghi (1339–1410) as pope, who took the name of Alexander V.

It seemed that the matter had been resolved, and that a new principle had been established – that a general council had authority over popes. Yet Alexander V had rather different ideas on this question, and promptly began to exercise the same authoritarian rule that had given birth to conciliarism in the first place. Alexander's death a year later in 1410 led to the election of a new pope, John XXIII – but not to the resolution of the issue. For, following the death of Alexander, there were now three claimants to the papacy: Benedict XIII and Gregory XIII (neither of whom recognized the validity of the Council of Pisa), and John XXIII.

By now, impatience with the situation was widespread. Another reforming council was convened by John XXIII at Constance from November 1414 to April 1418. Once more, the legitimacy of the council was called into question. Sigismund of Luxemburg, king of Germany (and later Holy Roman Emperor) attended the council, and made clear his support for its final decision – that all three popes should resign, opening the way for a fresh election. In the end, a new pope was elected, thus bringing the western schism to an end.

Yet the new pope – Martin V – had little enthusiasm for conciliarism, and found it relatively easy to revert to traditional ideas of absolute papal authority. Support for conciliarism had been largely the result of concerns about the destabilizing impact of the Great Schism on western Europe. With the ending of the schism, enthusiasm for conciliarism waned. The traditional model of the papacy reestablished itself.

2.4.3. Eastern Europe: The Rise of Russia as a Christian Nation

As we noted earlier, Orthodox Christianity became established as the dominant religion of the area known as Kievan Rus' during the tenth century (2.1.8). The Russian church was headed by the metropolitans of Kiev, the traditional metropolitan center of Christianity in this region. Yet the stability of this entire region was undermined during the early thirteenth century as Mongol armies under Genghis Khan (1162?–1227) and his successors moved westwards.

The Mongol invasions of the 1220s hastened the political and economic decline of Kiev, and the break-up of Kievan Rus' into three separate regions. The Mongols inflicted a decisive defeat on the army of Rus' at the Battle of the Kalka River (1223); however, they did not press home their advantage. A fresh incursion took place in 1238, with the forces of Rus' being defeated once more at the Battle of the Sit River. This time, the region was subjected to Mongol rule. Kievan Rus' ceased to exist; its constituent territories began to develop in different directions, eventually leading to the formation of the three regions now known as Russia, Ukraine, and Belarus.

The period of the "Tatar yoke" witnessed significant changes in the organization of Christianity in the region. The most important of these is generally agreed to be the relocation of the metropolitan center of Russian Orthodoxy to Moscow. Although Moscow was seen as subordinate to Constantinople, it became increasingly clear to Russian observers that Constantinople's future was threatened by Turkish expansion. In 1448, a council of Russian bishops declared the independence of the Russian church from Constantinople, and appointed its own metropolitan bishop with the title of "Metropolitan of Moscow and All Russia."

Throughout this period, the spiritual identity of the Russian Orthodox church was sustained by a network of monasteries. The Mongolian Empire was religiously tolerant, and showed little interest in interfering with Russian affairs. Although the Mongolian people were primarily Shamanistic in their religion, Christianity was a significant influence within the higher social classes of the empire, as a result of Nestorian missions to the region. This tolerance left the monasteries free to develop as centers of mission, scholarship, and spirituality. Monastic visionaries and reformers, such as Sergei Radonezhsky (also known as "Sergius of Radonezh," died 1392), established monasteries throughout central and northern Russia.

With the fall of Constantinople in 1453 (2.4.7), the Russian Orthodox church began to see itself as the "Third Rome." Although some suggest that the city of Moscow itself was the successor to the cities of Rome and Constantinople, it is more accurate to suggest that it was the nation of Russia – rather than its leading city – which was seen in this way. Mindful of Constantine's designation of his city as the "Second Rome" more than a millennium earlier, Russian Christians came to see themselves as his true successors.

Figure 2.8   The icon of the Trinity by Andrei Rublev (1360–c. 1430), one of the most famous expressions of medieval Russian monastic spirituality. Tretyakov State Gallery, Moscow. © 2012. Photo: Scala, Florence

This trend was given added significance during the reign of Ivan III of Russia (1440–1505). With the final defeat of the Mongols at the Battle of the Ukra River in 1480, Russia emerged as the dominant power in the region. Ivan had married Sophia Paleologue, niece of Constantine XI, the last Byzantine emperor. This family link allowed Ivan to present himself as the successor to the emperor, and the see of Moscow as the successor to Constantinople. It was only a matter of time before the rulers of Russia began to refer to themselves as "emperors." (The Russian term "czar," like the German term "Kaiser," is derived from the Latin word *Caesar*.) Grand Duke Ivan IV (called "the Terrible") was proclaimed the first Russian czar in January 1547.

As Russian power expanded still further in the sixteenth century, few in the region were prepared to argue with its claims to religious supremacy. With the consent of other Orthodox patriarchs, the Russian Orthodox church was recognized as an autocephalous Orthodox church in 1589.

2.4.4.   Heresy: Waldensians, Hussites, and Wycliffites

Although the Council of Constance had been preoccupied with issues concerning the papal succession, other matters had emerged as important – above all, the threat of heresy. The Bohemian reformer Jan Hus (c. 1369–1415) was gaining a significant following for his program of reform within the church. Significantly, Hus's demands were given added importance by a growing tide of nationalism in this region.

Heresy began to emerge as a significant problem for the church in western Europe in the eleventh century, having had a remarkably low profile in the previous three centuries. Some have suggested that the year 1000 was seen as possessing mystical significance, triggering a wave of heretical speculation during the "millennial generation" (1000–33). The study of heresy in western Europe during the Middle Ages raises some important questions of definition. Some of the movements that were declared to be heretical seem to represent renewal or modification of older heresies.

An excellent example of this is provided by the Cathars, a religious sect which appeared in the Languedoc region of France in the eleventh century, and flourished in southern France during the following two centuries. This sect adopted views which are recognizably Gnostic, perhaps originating from eastern Europe – such as the notion that matter was intrinsically evil, and a dialectic between an inferior creating divinity and a superior redeeming divinity.

Others, however, seem to fall into a more political category – movements which posed a threat to the temporal authority of the church. This challenge might take the form of an alternative vision of society, or of the privileged place of the church in the interpretation of Scripture. An example of such a movement is the Waldensians, a reform movement which emerged in southern France about the year 1170 as a result of the activity of a wealthy Lyonnais merchant by the name of Valdes.

Valdes embarked on a reforming ministry which was based upon a literal reading of the Bible (particularly its injunctions to poverty) and biblically based preaching in the vernacular. This ethos contrasted sharply with the somewhat loose morality of the clergy at that time, and attracted considerable support in southern France and Lombardy. Although this was little more than a grass-roots movement seeking reform, it was regarded as a significant threat to the power and status of the church.

The politicization of the notion of heresy is perhaps best seen in the church's reaction to John Wycliffe (c. 1320–81), an English theologian who is often credited with inspiring the first English translation of the Bible. Wycliffe argued extensively – in both English and Latin – for the translation of the Bible into his native English. (Wycliffe used the Latin Vulgate text of the Bible, not having access to the original Hebrew and Greek texts.)

For Wycliffe, the English people had a right to read the Bible in their own language, rather than be forced to listen to what their clergy wished them to hear. As Wycliffe pointed out, the ecclesiastical establishment had considerable vested interests in not allowing the laity access to the Bible. They might discover that there was a massive discrepancy between the lifestyles of bishops and clergy and those commended – and practiced – by Christ and the apostles.

Wycliffe thus threatened to call into question the clerical domination of theology and church life in England. Although Wycliffe's motivations for translating the Bible were mainly theological, there was a strong political and social dimension to his program. The translation of the Bible into English would be a social leveler on a hitherto unknown scale. All would be able to read Christendom's sacred text, and judge both the lifestyle and teachings of the medieval church on its basis.

The defining issue for Wycliffe was who has the right to read and interpret the text of the Bible – all believers, or merely a spiritual elite? There was a fundamental issue of power here. By insisting that the Bible should be translated into English, Wycliffe was expanding the circle of those who had access to this text, and those who believed they had the right to interpret it. Those who resisted Wycliffe's demands for the democratization of biblical interpretation offered a traditionalist theological defense of their elitist conception of the right to interpret the Bible. Nevertheless, the motivation of issues of power and the consolidation of the *status quo* can hardly be overlooked. The effect of the Wycliffite "heresy" was to weaken the church's grip on the control of how the Bible was to be interpreted. Wycliffe's supporters – who came to be known as "Lollards" – played a significant role in creating demand for reform in the later medieval English church, and may well have prepared the ground for the English reception of Martin Luther's reforming ideas in the 1520s.

Although the Middle Ages did indeed see the revival, often with local transmutations, of older heresies, many movements were branded as heretical for political reasons. The establishment of the Inquisition can be seen as marking a confirmation of the increasing political and institutional significance of heresies deemed to pose a threat to papal authority. This represents a significant move away from early Christian attempts to encapsulate the essence of heresy, which focused on the threat it posed to the Christian faith as a whole – not to Christian individuals or institutions. The use of the term "heresy" to denote a threat to the church was to be seen as an inquisitorial, rather than a theological, definition of heresy. As Herbert Grundmann pointed out in 1935, many of the religious movements of the Middle Ages that were branded "heretical" were really nothing of the sort. There was a serious case to be made for abandoning the use of the word "heresy" to designate many of them.

2.4.5.   The Modern Devotion: The Brethren of the Common Life

As we noted earlier, monasteries and convents played a critical role in maintaining and propagating Christian ideas during the Middle Ages (2.1.5). Yet this concentration of theological and spiritual excellence within the monastic tradition had some unintended consequences. For example, the everyday life of the laity was often left virtually totally untouched by the spiritual riches being developed behind monastic walls. Monastic spirituality often presupposed a lifestyle and outlook quite alien to lay people.

Yet many reforming movements in the later Middle Ages sought to bridge the gap between the religious orders and lay people. Both the Dominicans and Franciscans represented serious attempts to reconnect the Christian faith with wider culture, partly by encouraging a religious presence within society. One of the most important of these developments took place during the fourteenth century in the Low Countries – the movement often known by the Latin phrase *Devotio Moderna* ("Modern Devotion"), and the Brethren of the Common Life.

The Modern Devotion had its origins in the flourishing commercial towns of the Low Countries. Gerard Groote (1340–84) was the son of a prominent merchant of Deventer, a trading center on the River Ussel which was a member of the Hanseatic League. Groote's family had risen to become one of the leading cloth merchants of Deventer, and were wealthy as a result. In 1374, while seriously ill, Groote had a conversion experience, which caused him to abandon his comfortable lifestyle and adopt an ascetic way of living.

Groote chose to enter the Carthusian monastery at Monnikhuizen shortly after his conversion. He went there as a guest, apparently without any real intention of becoming a member of the Carthusian order. Yet the monastic disciplines of prayer, fasting, and manual labor helped shape his religious ideals, which became central to the spirituality of the Modern Devotion. He was strongly pragmatic in his outlook, and regarded theology and philosophy as being somewhat peripheral to more important matters. Groote saw Christianity as primarily practical in its outlook, and developed an emphasis upon the service of God in society.

Groote's legacy was two quite distinct types of communities. The first was the movement known as the "Brethren of the Common Life." The Brethren – who were mainly lay – devoted themselves to religious exercises, the quest for personal renewal by reflecting on the person of Christ, manual work, and service to others. Many scholars have described the Brethren of the Common Life as "practical mystics," in that their concern for personal union with God was linked with their efforts to reform the church through educating young people and instructing the laity in the basics of the Christian faith. This led to the Brethren developing an emphasis on education – either through founding schools and colleges of their own in the Lowlands, Germany, and France, or through members becoming teachers at existing institutions run by other religious communities.

The second type of community that resulted from Groote's ministry followed a more traditional monastic model. The monasteries established by his followers were grouped in the congregation of Windesheim, which became a major center for monastic reform. By 1500, just under one hundred monasteries had links with the movement, sharing its emphasis on a deep and personal religious experience and faith, combined with biblical and theological learning.

The impact of this religious order affected even the University of Paris, widely regarded as the greatest academic center of the Middle Ages (2.2.4). Jan Standonck (1453–1504), a native of Brabant, was deeply influenced by the ideals of the "Modern Devotion." In 1483, Standonck became Master of the Collège de Montaigu, one of the colleges of the University of Paris, where he set about refurbishing its buildings, and encouraging the academic vocations of poor students. By 1485, Standonck had been elected Rector of the University of Paris.

One of the most influential spiritual works of the late Middle Ages had its origins within the *Devotio Moderna*. Thomas à Kempis (c. 1380–1471), who came into contact with the movement while studying at Deventer, is thought to have written the spiritual classic *The Imitation of Christ* at some point during the period 1418–27. While some uncertainties about the work's true authorship remain, the work is widely attributed to à Kempis. The work was enormously influential, and was copied extensively in the fifteenth century. The invention of printing increased its influence still further, and it is now widely cited as one of the most influential works of Christian spirituality of all time.

Thomas à Kempis's *Imitation of Christ* is characterized by its emphasis on the interior life and withdrawal from the world, which marks it off from other works of monastic spirituality which encouraged an active imitation of the example of Christ. The influence of Groote can be seen at a number of points, particularly its criticism of theological speculation and affirmation of the importance of love for God. This is best seen in his famous comment on the doctrine of the Trinity.

> What good does it do you if you dispute loftily about the Trinity, but lack humility and therefore displease the Trinity? It is not lofty words that make you righteous or holy or dear to God, but a virtuous life. I would much rather experience contrition than be able to give a definition of it.

2.4.6.   Popular Religion: The Cult of the Saints

To make sense of how Christianity developed during the Middle Ages, it is important to appreciate how it impacted on different groups of people. We have already reflected on its impact on the life of the mind and the politics of Europe. But what of its popular appeal? How did Christianity relate to the everyday world outside the universities, monasteries, and royal courts? In recent years, scholarship has given increased attention to the phenomenon of "popular religion" or "folk religion," in which Christian ideas and practices were adapted and implemented in rural life.

Although the late fourteenth and fifteenth centuries tended to be regarded as a period of religious degeneration by an earlier generation of historians, more recent research has decisively overturned this verdict. Towards the end of this period, on the eve of the Protestant Reformation, religion was perhaps more firmly rooted in the experience and lives of ordinary people than at any time in the past. Earlier medieval Christianity had been primarily monastic, focused on the life, worship, and writings of Europe's monasteries and convents. Church building programs flourished in the later fifteenth century, as did pilgrimages and the vogue for collecting relics. The fifteenth century has been referred to as "the inflation-period of mystic literature," reflecting the growing popular interest in religion. There was a widespread popular appropriation of religious beliefs and practices, not always in orthodox forms.

The phenomenon of "folk religion" often bore a tangential relationship to the more precise yet abstract statements of Christian doctrine that the church preferred – but that many lay people found unintelligible or unattractive. In parts of Europe, something close to "fertility cults" emerged, connected and enmeshed with the patterns and concerns of everyday life. The agrarian needs of rural communities – such as haymaking and harvesting – were firmly associated with popular religion.

For example, in the French diocese of Meaux in the early sixteenth century, the saints were regularly invoked in order to ward off animal and infant diseases, the plague and eye trouble, or to ensure that young women find appropriate husbands. The direct connection of religion and everyday life was taken for granted. The spiritual and the material were interconnected at every level.

The medieval Catholic church was encountered by ordinary people through its practices and images, rather than its abstract theological ideas. The liturgy of the church, especially the Mass, enacted dramatically a visual "grand narrative" of human history and experience. Its ritual observance and symbolic gestures shaped the congregation's perception of the world, and their own location within it. It offered spectacle and instruction, theater and dogma, in a form which reaffirmed the medieval worldview, and the necessary place of the institutional church as an instrument and vehicle of salvation. Outside that church, there was no salvation.

The drama of the liturgy was supplemented by images – often images of gospel scenes, painted on church walls, illustrating gospel scenes for the benefit of those who could not read; or images of saints, especially Mary, whose intercessory powers were affirmed and proclaimed by the church. Saints were mediators of divine grace, who would hear and mediate the prayers of ordinary people. In churches throughout western Europe, the cult of the saints was represented iconically – through paintings, altarpieces, and statues.

So what was this "cult of the saints," which had such a huge impact at the time? The recognition of the importance of the saints (Latin: *sancti*, "holy ones") dated back to early Christianity, where vigils were often held at the tombs of prominent Christian leaders, especially those who had been martyred for their faith (1.4.4). Gradually, a cult of veneration of the saints developed, with three distinct elements.

1. Commemoration. Here, a specific day would be set aside in the church's calendar to recall the life and teachings of a saint. Some saints were recognized as having universal significance; others were seen as being of local importance.
2. The cult of relics. Relics (Latin: *reliquae*, "things that are left behind") were material objects associated with the saints which were seen as "pledges" or "tokens" of the saint's intercessory power. Such relics included body parts, as well as objects which had belonged to or been used by the saint, such as clothes or books.
3. Pilgrimages to shrines associated with saints. In the Middle Ages, there were many such sacred sites – such as the Santiago de Compostela in northern Spain, linked with the apostle James, or the tomb of the martyred archbishop Thomas à Becket at Canterbury.

The cult of the saints played a major role in medieval Christianity, especially at the popular level. One way of understanding this phenomenon is to consider the idea of a heavenly court. For many in the Middle Ages, God was to be compared to a monarch, surrounded by a glittering company of courtiers – namely, the saints. One of the key themes of the "cult of the saints" is the notion of a saint's intercessory power – in other words, his or her ability to gain a hearing at the court of heaven. The idea of saints as advocates gained a huge following in the Middle Ages.

This idea is perhaps best seen in the notion of a "patron saint" – that is, a heavenly intercessor or advocate in heaven on behalf of a nation, place, or profession. Some examples of this development may be noted.

1. A place. During the Middle Ages, it was common for a city which grew to prominence to acquire the remains of a famous saint who had lived and was buried elsewhere, and transfer them to its cathedral. This was seen as conferring considerable prestige on the city. The best-known example of this is the city of Venice, which is traditionally held to have secured the remains of Saint Mark from Egypt in the ninth century. The iconic St. Mark's Basilica was built to house these relics. The patron saint of Venice had originally been the martyr Theodore of Amasea; once the relics of Mark arrived, however, the city decided to upgrade its patron saint.
2. A profession. Luke – the author of both the gospel bearing his name and the Acts of the Apostles – was a physician, often leading to his being spoken of as a "physician of the soul" in Christian spiritual and devotional writings. It was natural that he would be adopted as the patron saint of the medical profession. Hospital chapels were often dedicated to Luke for this reason.

The notion of an "indulgence" also came to be linked with the cult of the saints. Strictly speaking, an "indulgence" was understood as the relaxation or remission of any penance required of sinners. They were not understood as the cause of the forgiveness of sins, which was seen as God's prerogative. The medieval church, building on established customs of the early church, imposed penances on those who confessed their sins, partly as a sign of genuine contrition or repentance. In the early thirteenth century, this notion was developed further. The Dominican theologian Hugh of St. Cher (c. 1200–63) argued that there was a "treasury" of grace at the church's disposal, as a result of the merits of Christ and the saints.

The idea of an "indulgence" was easily misunderstood as the purchase of forgiveness of sins – something that was never intended or sanctioned by the church. This misunderstanding probably arose through the sale of indulgences as a way of raising funds for ecclesiastical projects – such as the construction of St. Peter's Basilica in Rome in the early sixteenth century. At the popular level, this came to be seen as a way of securing remission of any penalties linked with sin. The indulgence traffic became hugely popular in France and Germany – and controversial. Martin Luther's protest against the sale of indulgences in Germany in 1517 fits into a broader pattern of concern about this trade (3.3.1).

In France, an indulgence campaign was arranged by Leo X and Francis I in 1515, with a view to financing a crusade. In 1518, however, the Parisian faculty of theology protested against some of the superstitious ideas to which this campaign gave rise. It condemned as "false and scandalous" the teaching that "whoever puts into the collection for the crusade one teston or the value of one soul in purgatory sets that soul free immediately, and it goes unfailingly to paradise." Yet although regarded as questionable by academic theologians, such beliefs held a deep fascination for ordinary people. An "unofficial" theology thus came to develop, largely unrelated to the approved theology textbooks, but deeply rooted in the hopes and fears of society in general.

2.4.7. The Rise of the Ottoman Empire: The Fall of Constantinople (1453)

By the beginning of the fifteenth century, many had concluded that Constantinople was unable to survive as an independent city. The city had already fallen to Crusaders in 1204, and was no longer regarded as invincible – despite its formidable system of defenses. By the late fifteenth century, Islamic leadership was in the process of passing from the Abbasid Caliphate to the Ottomans, who regarded the conquest of Christendom's greatest city as a jihad – a holy war. The expansionist policies of the Ottoman Turks led to the city being surrounded, and deprived of any economic or political hinterland. The "Second Rome" was isolated. It had earlier been fatally weakened through a natural disaster. Between 1348–50, the "Black Death" spread within the city, killing as much as half the population. It was just a matter of time before the city fell.

The Ottoman sultan Mehmed II (1432–81) constructed a fortress in Ottoman territory just north of Constantinople in 1452, which served the dual purpose of cutting off the city's links with Black Sea ports on the one hand, and acting as the launching point for the siege of Constantinople a year later on the other. Mehmed II laid siege to Constantinople in April and May 1453. After fifty-seven days, the city fell. Strained relations between the Christian west and east led to a marked absence of support, political or military, for the besieged city. Having secured the city, Mehmed continued to expand Ottoman influence in the region now known as the Balkans. Bosnia was conquered in 1463; Albania in 1478; Herzegovina in 1482; and Montenegro in 1498.

Although western rulers had relatively little sympathy for the ailing Byzantine Empire, which many regarded as religiously heterodox and politically degenerate, the advance of Ottoman forces into the western sphere of influence caused alarm. In 1521, Belgrade was captured. In 1529, Vienna was under siege. A surprise Ottoman naval victory at the Battle of Preveza in 1538 gave them control of much of the Mediterranean Sea. It seemed to some that the further advance of the Ottoman Empire was unstoppable. An Islamic Europe seemed a real possibility.

Yet all was not well for the Ottoman Empire. The siege of Vienna fizzled out inconclusively. An attempt to capture the island of Malta in 1565 pitted a large Ottoman force of around 50 000 with a much smaller Maltese army of around 6000, including the crusader order of the Knights of St. John. The siege failed. The turning point was the Battle of Lepanto (1571), when a naval force put together by southern European nations inflicted a decisive defeat on the Ottoman navy off the coast of southern Greece. This defeat is widely regarded as checking Ottoman expansion in the region.

Yet land-based expansion continued. Ottoman armies invaded the southern Ukraine, and mounted a second siege of Vienna in the late summer of 1683. After two months, the large besieging army was attacked by a substantial army mustered by the emperor Leopold I (1640–1705). In 1699, following the Ottoman defeat at the Battle of Senta (1697), a peace treaty was signed between the Ottomans and Habsburgs ending the Ottoman control of large parts of central Europe.

The Ottoman Empire left a complex legacy in eastern Europe. Many small nations in the Balkans developed complex religious demographies, with Islamic, Orthodox Christian, and occasionally Jewish populations existing alongside one another. The Ottoman Empire was generally tolerant towards religious minorities through its "millet" system, which allowed religious communities a significant degree of religious freedom and political autonomy. However, the Ottoman occupation generated unrest, leading to growing demands for national sovereignty in parts of southeastern Europe, especially Serbia and Greece. In both cases, as we shall see later, the Orthodox church would be a leading force in nourishing and sustaining nationalist sentiments (4.2.2).

2.5.   The Renaissance: Cultural Renewal and Christian Expansion

As we saw in the previous section, western Europe was plagued with problems in the later Middle Ages. Economic downturns, wars, and plagues caused instability in many regions. Yet many began to feel that a turning point was reached in the later fifteenth century. Signs of economic renewal began to appear, accompanied by the emergence of movements working for cultural regeneration and renewal. Scholars often use the phrase "the Renaissance" to refer to this new injection of energy and creativity into the life of the church and culture around this time.

The term "Renaissance" is now universally used to designate the literary and artistic revival that initially developed in fourteenth- and fifteenth-century Italy, and then spread to most of Europe in the late fifteenth and early sixteenth centuries. The Renaissance was a remarkable period of cultural regeneration, which reached the peak of its influence in the 1500s. Its central theme was that today's culture could be renewed by a creative engagement with the cultural legacy of the past, above all the heritage of ancient Greece and Rome.

The related term "humanism" is widely used to refer to the philosophy of the Renaissance. This term is easily misunderstood by modern readers. In the twenty-first century, this word is often used to mean something like "atheism" or "secularism," identifying a worldview that excludes belief in – or at least reference to – the divine. At the time of the Renaissance, the word "humanism" had a very different connotation. It referred to the underlying ideas of the Renaissance, by which western European culture might be renewed by an appeal to its origins in classical Rome and Athens. Humanism was a quest for eloquence and excellence, grounded in the application of the wisdom of the classics to the present.

This renewal of confidence in many parts of western Europe was evident in another development: the great "voyages of discovery" of Portuguese and Spanish mariners during the 1490s (2.5.7), which opened up new trade routes to southern Africa and Asia, as well as discovering the Americas and West Indies. Portugal and Spain were both strongly Catholic nations, and encouraged the evangelization of these regions by religious orders. By the end of the Middle Ages, Christianity was no longer geographically restricted to Europe; it was in the process of becoming a global faith.

Yet we begin our analysis of this age of expansion by considering a new invention which transformed the way in which information was shared and spread – moveable metal type. Although some popular historical accounts refer to the "invention of printing" at this time, the real innovation was not printing itself, but one component of the new type of printing presses: reusable metal type, which could be used again and again. In what follows, we shall consider the religious importance of this new technology.

2.5.1.   A New Technology: The Religious Importance of Printing

Recent technological developments in the field of data processing and transfer – such as the Internet – have revolutionized many aspects of modern life. A similar situation emerged in the late fifteenth century in western Europe, through the invention of printing using moveable type. This would have a very substantial impact on the development and propagation of religious ideas during the great debates of the sixteenth century, when Protestantism emerged as a serious challenge to Catholicism. The printing press played a significant role in making the ideas of both sides more widely available.

The late Middle Ages saw a soaring demand for books, reflecting a significant rise in literacy throughout much of western Europe. Yet this new market for reading material simply could not be met. Existing book production techniques were painfully slow, and the price of books correspondingly high. Text and illustrations had to be painstakingly copied out by hand by specially trained scribes. Demand far outstripped the supply.

The surge of interest in books caused many to wonder whether it was possible to develop a new way of producing them, which would cut out the hugely expensive copying process. A short-term answer was found in the early part of the fifteenth century. Text and illustrations were engraved on wooden blocks, using a knife and gouge. A water-based brown ink, made from the bark of trees, was then applied to the block using an inking cushion. The block was then used to print copies of the image on single sheets of paper, which were bound together to produce a book. But it was only an interim solution. The blocks were costly to produce, and once cut to order, could not be used for any other purpose. It was ideal for short books – but for long works, such as the Bible, it was unrealistically cumbersome. A better solution had to be found.

Johann Gutenberg (c. 1398–1468) developed a printing system which brought together a number of existing technologies, as well as one major innovation – moveable metal type. After printing a page, the type-frame could be broken down into its constituent elements, and used all over again to print a different page. The invention of moveable metal type on its own would not have been enough to enable this breakthrough. Gutenberg's genius lay in creating a system which incorporated both new and old ideas, enabling a task to be performed with unprecedented efficiency.

The first printed book using moveable type was produced by Gutenberg in the city of Mainz around 1454. In 1456, the same press produced a printed Latin Bible. This was followed in 1457 by the so-called Mainz Psalter, which established the custom of identifying the printer, the location of the press, and the date of publication on the title page of the work. No longer would copies of sacred texts be dependent on copyists; a more reliable, economical, and efficient means of production was now available.

From Germany, the technology spread quickly. William Caxton set up his printing shop at Westminster, London, in 1476. The famous Aldine Press was established at Venice in 1495 by Aldo Manuzio (1449–1515). This press was responsible for two important developments: the "lower case" letters (so-called because they were kept in the lower of two cases containing type), and the sloping "italic" type (so-called in English-language works, on account of Venice being located in Italy; Manuzio himself called the type "Chancery").

Why would printing have such a major impact upon western Christianity? Two major points should be noted. First, it now became possible to produce more accurate editions of religious works – such as the text of the New Testament, or of important religious writers from the past, such as Augustine of Hippo – through the elimination of copying errors. By comparing the printed text of a work with manuscript sources, the best possible text could be established and used as the basis of theological reflection. In the late fifteenth and early sixteenth centuries, humanist scholars rummaged through the libraries of Europe in search of early Christian manuscripts which they could edit and publish. The tedious process of copying manuscripts by hand was no longer necessary. Further, the errors introduced by the copying process were eliminated; once a work was set up in type, any number of error-free copies could be run off.

As a result, these sources were made much more widely available than had ever been possible before. By the 1520s, just about anyone could gain access to a reliable edition of the Greek text of the New Testament or the writings of Augustine of Hippo. The eleven volumes of the collected works of Augustine were published at Basel by the Amerbach brothers between 1490 and 1506. Although only two hundred copies of each volume seem to have been published, they were widely used to gain access to the most reliable text of this important writer.

Second, the printing press had the potential to transmit ideas across national boundaries. Many scholars argue that the great religious controversies of the sixteenth century were internationalized through the smuggling of books. For example, the Protestant writer John Calvin (1509–64) never left the city of Geneva after his return from exile in Strasbourg in 1541 (3.3.5). Yet his ideas were debated across Europe, as his books found their way into private libraries.

There is no doubt that the invention of printing was of major importance to the development of western Christianity. Yet another development, taking place around the same time, also proved a significant catalyst for change. The rise of the movement we now call the "Renaissance" led to a new injection of intellectual energy into western Christianity, and led to renewed calls for reform of the life and thought of the church.

2.5.2. The Origins of the Italian Renaissance

By the end of the fourteenth century, it was clear that a major new cultural movement was in the process of emerging in Italy. Historians now refer to this as the "Italian Renaissance." A major theme of this cultural movement was the need for the renewal of secular and religious culture using the resources of the classical "Golden Age." The Italian Renaissance developed a program of renewal and regeneration of both society and the church, whose influence came to be felt throughout much of western Europe. The term "Renaissance" is widely used to refer to movements throughout Europe influenced by these ideas originating in Italy. Its ideas percolated through culture through printed books, and especially the appointment of leading Renaissance thinkers to university and other posts of social influence.

The literary and cultural program of the Italian Renaissance can be summarized in the Latin slogan *ad fontes* – "back to the fountainhead." This slogan sums up the retrospective admiration for antiquity that is so characteristic of this age. Renaissance writers invented the term "Middle Ages" as a way of dismissing the cultural and intellectual merits of the period between the glories of antiquity and the present day. Applied to the Christian church, the slogan *ad fontes* meant a direct return to the title-deeds of Christianity – the writers of the early church and, supremely, the New Testament.

It seemed to many that the sterile form of Christianity associated with the Middle Ages could be replaced with a new, vital, and dynamic form, through the study of Scripture. *Ad fontes* was more than a slogan: it was a lifeline to those who despaired of the state of the late medieval church. The apostolic era, by then widely seen as the "Golden Age of the church," could once more become a present reality.

Although it had limited popular impact, the Renaissance brought about a dramatic transformation of high western European culture. The effects of this broad program of cultural renewal could be seen at an astonishing variety of levels. Classical architectural styles came to be preferred over the prevailing Gothic. Cicero's elegant Latin style displaced the rather mechanical, barbarous form of Latin used by scholastic writers. Roman law and Greek philosophy were eagerly studied at universities. In every case, the same basic principle can be seen at work: the assumption that the fountainhead of western culture in the classical period has the capacity to refresh and redirect it, when it has become tired, spent, and directionless.

Certain historians, most notably Jacob Burckhardt (1818–97), have argued that the Renaissance gave birth to the modern era. It was in this era, Burckhardt argued, that human beings first began to think of themselves as *individuals*. The communal consciousness of the medieval period gave way to the individual consciousness of the Renaissance. In many ways, Burckhardt's definition of the Renaissance in purely individualist terms is highly questionable, in view of powerful evidence for the strongly collective values of aspects of Italian Renaissance humanism. But in one sense, Burckhardt is unquestionably correct: *something* novel and exciting developed in Renaissance Italy, which proved capable of exercising a fascination over generations of thinkers.

It is not entirely clear why Italy in general, or Florence in particular, became the cradle of this brilliant new movement in the history of ideas. A number of factors have been identified as having some bearing on the question:

1. Italy was saturated with visible and tangible reminders of the greatness of antiquity. The ruins of ancient Roman buildings and monuments were scattered throughout the land. As historians have noted, these ruins represented vital links with a great past. They appear to have kindled interest in the civilization of ancient Rome at the time of the Renaissance, and acted as a vital stimulus to its thinkers to recover the vitality of classical Roman culture at a time which they regarded as being culturally arid and barren.
2. Scholastic theology – the major intellectual force of the medieval period – was never particularly influential in Italy. Although many Italians achieved fame as theologians (such as Thomas Aquinas and Gregory of Rimini), they were generally active in the

universities of northern Europe. There was thus an intellectual vacuum in Italy during the fourteenth century. Vacuums tend to be filled – and it was Renaissance humanism which filled this particular gap.

3. The political stability of Florence depended upon the maintenance of her republican government. It was thus natural to turn to the study of the Roman Republic, including its literature and culture, as a model for Florence.

4. The economic prosperity of Florence created a demand for literature and the arts. Patronage of culture and the arts was seen as an appropriate use for surplus wealth.

5. Following the Turkish invasion of Asia Minor, and especially after the fall of Constantinople in 1453, there was an exodus of Greek-speaking intellectuals westward. Many such émigrés settled in Italian cities. A revival of the study of the Greek language thus became possible, and with it renewed interest in the Greek classics.

This broad cultural program of renewal and regeneration through returning to the "fountainhead" could also be applied to Christianity. As we shall see, this led to a significant movement for renewal developing within the church, including a revitalized interest in the New Testament, and growing criticism of scholasticism. But before we consider the significance of the Renaissance for western Christianity, we need to reflect a little further on the nature of humanism.

2.5.3.   The Nature of Humanism

The Italian term *umanista* – meaning "a university teacher of the humanities," such as rhetoric and poetry – began to be used extensively in the fourteenth century. The use of the word "humanism" to refer to the worldview underlying the Renaissance is a later development. Yet this worldview is not so much a set of ideas as a general method. Humanism at this time is best understood as a quest for cultural eloquence and excellence, rooted in the belief that the best models lay in the classic civilizations of Rome and Athens. Its basic method can be summed up in the Latin slogan *ad fontes* ("back to the sources"). A stream is at its purest at its source. Humanists argued for the by-passing of the "Middle Ages" – that telling phrase, by the way, is a humanist creation, designed to belittle this irritating historical interlude between the glories of the ancient world and their renewal in the Renaissance – in order to allow the present to be renewed and reinvigorated by drinking deeply at the wellspring of antiquity.

It is beyond doubt that the Renaissance witnessed the rise of classical scholarship. The Greek and Latin classics were widely studied in their original languages. Although some early studies suggested that humanism originated outside a university context, the evidence now available points unquestionably to a close link between humanism and the universities of northern Italy. It might therefore seem that humanism was essentially a scholarly movement devoted to the study of the classical period. This, however, would be to overlook the question of *why* the humanists wished to study the classics in the first place.

The evidence available makes it clear that such study was regarded as *a means to an end*, rather than *an end in itself*. That end was the promotion of contemporary written and spoken eloquence. In other words, the humanists studied the classics as models of written eloquence, in order to gain inspiration and instruction. Classical learning and philological competence were simply the tools used to exploit the resources of antiquity. As has often been pointed out, the writings of the humanists devoted to the promotion of eloquence, written or spoken, far exceed those devoted to classical scholarship or philology.

The view of humanism developed by Paul Oskar Kristeller (1905–99) has gained wide acceptance within North American and European scholarship, and has yet to be discredited. Kristeller envisages humanism as a cultural and educational movement, primarily concerned with the promotion of eloquence in its various forms. Its interest in morals, philosophy, and politics is of secondary importance. To be a humanist is to be concerned with eloquence first and foremost, and with other matters incidentally. Humanism was essentially a cultural program, which appealed to classical antiquity as a model of eloquence.

In art and architecture, as in the written and spoken word, antiquity was seen as a cultural resource, which could be appropriated by the Renaissance. Petrarch referred to Cicero as his father and Virgil as his brother. The architects of the *Quattrocènto* studiously ignored the Gothic style of northern Europe, in order to return to the classical styles of antiquity. Cicero was studied as an orator, rather than a political or moral writer.

Humanism was thus concerned with *how ideas were obtained and expressed*, rather than with *the actual substance of those ideas*. A humanist might be a Platonist or an Aristotelian – but in either case, the ideas involved derived from antiquity. A humanist might be a skeptic or a religious believer – but both attitudes could be defended from antiquity. The enormous attractiveness of Kristeller's view of humanism derives from the fact that it accounts brilliantly for the remarkable diversity of the Renaissance. The diversity of *ideas* which is so characteristic of Renaissance humanism is based upon a general consensus concerning *how to derive and express those ideas*.

As we have seen, the Renaissance encouraged a new level of engagement with the foundational resources of culture, urging social and intellectual renewal on the basis of classical models – including the New Testament. Yet the Renaissance also witnessed the rise of a new conception of humanity, with a radically altered understanding of its place within the cosmos. To explore this, we shall consider the famous "Manifesto of the Renaissance" (1486), which resonated throughout much of Europe.

Giovanni Pico della Mirandola (1463–94), one of the leading voices of the Italian Renaissance, delivered his precocious "oration on the dignity of humanity" in 1486 at the age of twenty-four. This "Manifesto," written in highly polished and elegant Latin, depicted humanity as a creature with the capacity to determine its own identity, rather than to receive this in any given fixed form. The human creature possesses no determinate image, and is urged by its creator to pursue its own perfection. God, the creator of humanity, is portrayed as mandating it to shape its own destiny: "You are constrained by no limits, and shall determine the limits of your nature for yourself, in accordance with your own free will, in whose hand we have placed you."

The ideas of this oration proved to be enormously influential in the late Renaissance, and, in the longer term, can be seen as setting the scene for the Enlightenment assertion of human autonomy in the eighteenth century. In the short term, however, it galvanized a new understanding of human nature and capacities. There was no "fixed" order of things;

everything could be changed. Humanity was mandated by God to change the social and physical world. This new vision of humanity as God's agent for changing the world empowered many who felt called to transform society.

Yet the medieval church was seen to be strongly conservative, lending theological support to the existing social order. The physical and social orders were held to be fixed and permanent, sanctioned by divine command. The traditional authority of influential families, monarchs, and principalities was not to be challenged. It was a source of frustration for the entrepreneurial middle classes, who were held back by the stifling force of tradition. A religious ideology that legitimated, or perhaps even *encouraged*, change would undermine such a static worldview, and open the way to a dynamic alternative.

2.5.4. Erasmus of Rotterdam

If any figure stands head and shoulders above other northern European humanists, it was Erasmus of Rotterdam. Although Erasmus is often presented as reflecting northern European humanism at its best, the situation is perhaps more complex than is generally realized. There were significant tensions within northern European humanism. Two are of particular interest: one concerning the question of national languages, the other concerning the question of national boundaries. On both counts, Erasmus pitted himself against other humanists with different ideas.

Erasmus regarded himself as a citizen of the world, and Ciceronian Latin as the language of that world. He saw national languages as presenting an obstacle to his vision of a cosmopolitan Europe united by the Latin language. Yet this was not something that all humanists agreed on. Other humanists, especially in Germany and Switzerland, saw national languages as promoting a sense of national identity. Erasmus's cosmopolitan vision of humanism contrasted sharply with more nationalist approaches.

For Erasmus, the vision of a cosmopolitan Europe was threatened by political and cultural nationalism, which only served to reinforce outdated concepts such as a sense of national identity and associated ideas such as national boundaries. Other northern humanists, by contrast, saw themselves as engaged in a struggle to *promote* national identity. Where Erasmus would have preferred to concentrate upon *eliminating* nationalist ideas and values, Swiss humanists saw themselves as having a sacred duty to defend Swiss national identity and culture by literary means.

This tension between the "cosmopolitan" and "nationalist" visions of humanism, between those wishing to *abolish* and those wishing to *consolidate* national identities, reflects the conflicting views current within northern European humanism of this period. It also demonstrates that Erasmus cannot be regarded as a totally representative spokesman for humanism, as some scholars suggest.

The most influential humanist work to circulate in Europe during the first decades of the sixteenth century was Erasmus's *Enchiridion militis Christiani* (Latin: "Handbook of the Christian Soldier"). Although the work was first published in 1503, and was then reprinted in 1509, the real impact of the work dates from its third printing in 1515. From that moment onwards, it became a cult work, apparently going through twenty-three editions in the next six years.

Figure 2.9   Erasmus of Rotterdam, humanist, philologist, and church critic. Copperplate engraving, 1526, by Albrecht Dürer (1471–1528). 24.9 × 19.3 cm. Photo: akg-images

Its appeal was primarily to educated lay men and women, whom Erasmus regarded as the most important resource that the church possessed. Its amazing popularity in the years after 1515 suggests that a radical alteration in lay self-perception may have taken place as a result. Erasmus's success also highlighted the growing importance of printing as a means of disseminating radical new ideas.

The *Enchiridion* developed the attractive thesis that the church of the day could be reformed by a collective return to the writings of the Fathers and Scripture. The regular reading of Scripture is put forward as the key to a new lay piety, on the basis of which the church may be renewed and reformed. Erasmus conceived of his work as a lay person's guide to Scripture; it provided a simple yet learned exposition of the "philosophy of Christ." This "philosophy" was really a form of practical morality, rather than an academic philosophy; the New Testament concerns the knowledge of good and evil, in order that its readers may eschew the latter and love the former.

The New Testament, according to Erasmus, is the *lex Christi*, "the law of Christ," which Christians are called to obey. Christ is the example whom Christians are called to imitate.

Yet Erasmus does not understand Christian faith to be mere external observance of some kind of morality. His characteristically humanist emphasis upon inner religion leads him to suggest that reading of Scripture *transforms* its readers, giving them a new motivation to love God and their neighbors.

A number of features of this book are of particular importance. First, Erasmus understands the future vitality of Christianity to lie with the laity, not the clergy. The clergy are seen as educators, whose function is to allow the laity to achieve the same level of understanding as themselves. There is no room for any superstitions which give the clergy a permanent status superior to that of their lay charges. Second, Erasmus's strong emphasis on inner religion results in an understanding of Christianity which makes no reference to the church – its rites, its priests, or its institutions. Why confess sins to another human being, asks Erasmus, when you can confess them directly to God? Religion is a matter of the individual's heart and mind; it is an inward state. Erasmus pointedly avoids any significant reference to the sacraments in his exposition of Christian living. Similarly, he discounts the view that the "religious life" (in other words, the calling to be a monk or a nun) is the highest form of the Christian life. For Erasmus, the lay person who reads Scripture is just as faithful to his or her calling as any monk.

The revolutionary character of Erasmus's *Enchiridion* lies in its daring new suggestion that the recognition of the Christian vocation of the lay person holds the key to the revival of the church. Clerical and ecclesiastical authority is discounted. Scripture should and must be made available to all, in order that all may return *ad fontes*, to drink of the fresh and living waters of the Christian faith, rather than the stagnant ponds of late medieval religion.

Erasmus came to recognize, however, that there were serious obstacles in the path of the course he proposed, and he was responsible for a number of major developments to remove them. First, there was a need to be able to study the New Testament in its original language, rather than in the inaccurate Vulgate translation. This required two tools, neither of which was then available: the necessary philological competence to handle the Greek text of the New Testament and direct access to that text itself.

2.5.5.   The Renaissance and Religious Renewal

Most humanists of the era – such as the great Erasmus of Rotterdam – were Christians, concerned for the renewal and reform of the church. So why not apply the same method of regeneration to Christianity? Why not return *ad fontes*, to the original sources of faith, and allow them to reinvigorate a burned-out and run-down church? Could the vitality and simplicity of the apostolic age be recaptured? It was a powerful, inspirational vision, and it captivated the imagination of many lay people in the fifteenth and early sixteenth centuries.

But how was this to be done? What was the religious analogue of the culture of the classical world? What was the fountainhead of Christianity? Christian humanists had little doubt: the Bible, especially the New Testament. This was the ultimate source of faith. The writings of medieval theologians could be set to one side with the greatest of ease, to allow a direct engagement with the ideas of the New Testament. The ecclesiastically safe and familiar interpretations of the Bible found in scholastic theology would be marginalized in favor of reading the text directly.

For conservative churchmen, this was a dangerous, threatening move, which had the potential to destabilize the delicately balanced theological equilibrium, achieved over many centuries. The humanist demand to return to the Bible turned out to be far more radical than many senior churchmen could stomach.

Two themes of the Renaissance proved especially important in the new developments which began to reshape Christianity, especially in the late fifteenth and early sixteenth centuries.

1. Growing criticism of scholasticism. Humanist authors had little time for this theological movement. One of the criticisms that they leveled against scholasticism is of particular importance. Humanists regarded scholasticism as impeding access to early Christian writers – such as Augustine of Hippo – by presenting later interpretations as a definitive interpretation of his writings. The Renaissance urged a direct engagement with Augustine and other writers, and produced editions of his texts to make this possible.
2. A return to the New Testament. Renaissance Christian writers regarded the New Testament as the title-deeds of Christianity, and insisted that theology and spirituality should be based on a direct engagement with this text, preferably in its original Greek. This second point is of particular importance, and we shall consider it further below.

The humanists were primarily scholars, men of letters, who insisted that this systematic return to the Bible should be done on the basis of the best possible scholarship. The actual content of the Bible would have to be established by the most reliable textual methods, and it would have to be read in its original languages. Immediately, the authority of the Latin Vulgate translation came under threat. As humanist scholars began to examine the history of the text in detail, problems began to emerge. Probing questions were pressed with increasing vigor concerning its textual integrity and philological reliability. As the Vulgate text was painstakingly compared with the best Greek manuscripts, errors began to be noticed. Variant readings were identified.

In 1516, Erasmus himself produced an edition of the Greek text of the New Testament, which caused something of a storm. Though it had many faults, it caused a sea-change in attitudes by challenging the Latin Vulgate translation of the Bible at several points. To put the issue as bluntly as possible: if Erasmus was right, certain statements that earlier generations had accepted as "biblical" might not be part of the original text of the New Testament at all. So what, many wondered, did this mean for those church doctrines based on such statements?

One text, often used by medieval theologians to defend the doctrine of the Trinity, was of particular importance: "For there are three that bear record in heaven, the Father, the Word, and the Holy Spirit: and these three are one. And there are three that bear witness in earth, the Spirit, and the water, and the blood: and these three agree as one" (1 John 5:7–8). Erasmus pointed out that the words "the Father, the Word, and the Holy Ghost: and these three are one. And there are three that bear witness in earth" are not found in any Greek manuscript. They were added later to the Latin Vulgate, probably after 800, despite not being known in any ancient Greek version.

The most likely explanation is that these words were initially added as a "gloss" (a brief comment set alongside or above the text), which a later scribe assumed to be part of the text itself, and thus included in later Latin texts, unaware that they were not part of the original Greek text of the New Testament. If this passage were to be declared to be "unbiblical," some feared that this most difficult of Christian doctrines might become dangerously vulnerable. Erasmus came under intense pressure to revise his revision; in the end, he gave in, and restored this section in later editions of his text.

The demand that the Bible be read in its original languages found wide acceptance throughout western Europe. Those wanting to advance the ideals of the Renaissance aimed to be *trium linguarum gnarus* ("knowing three languages") – that is, competent in Greek, Hebrew, and Latin. This led to the founding of trilingual colleges or, in some cases, of a chair in three languages at, for example, the universities of Alcalá in Spain (1499), Wittenberg in Germany (1502), Oxford in England (Corpus Christi College, 1517), Louvain in modern-day Belgium (1517), and the royal Collège de France at Paris (1530).

It was not long before possibly serious translation errors were uncovered in the Vulgate, which might force revision of existing church teachings. Erasmus pointed out some of these in 1516. An excellent example is found in the Vulgate translation of the opening words of Jesus's ministry in Galilee (Matthew 4:17) as: "do penance, for the kingdom of heaven is at hand." This translation creates a direct link between the coming of God's kingdom, and the sacrament of penance. Erasmus pointed out that the original Greek text should be translated as: "repent, for the Kingdom of heaven is at hand." Where the Vulgate seemed to refer to an outward ecclesiastical practice (the sacrament of penance), Erasmus insisted that the reference was to an inward psychological attitude – that of "being repentant."

Another problem concerned the implications of Erasmus's new translation of the Greek text for sacramental theology. Much medieval theology justified the inclusion of marriage in the list of sacraments on the basis of a New Testament text which – in the Vulgate translation – spoke of marriage being a *sacramentum* (Ephesians 5:31–2). Erasmus argued that that the Greek word (*mysterion*) here translated as "sacrament" simply meant "mystery." There was no intended reference to marriage being a "sacrament." One of the classic proof texts used by medieval theologians to justify the inclusion of matrimony in the list of sacraments was thus rendered virtually useless for this purpose.

Yet there proved to be more to the humanist vision of biblical scholarship than the need for better translations. The rise of the "new learning" promoted an alternative vision of interpretative authority in the 1510s – that of the scholarly community, rather than the church. The academy already held the key to the reconstruction of the biblical text and its translation into the vernacular. It would be only a small step to claim the right to interpret that text, using the new hermeneutical techniques of the Renaissance that were then emerging.

The rise of humanism forced a more radical program of reform on the church than any had anticipated. While many believed that there was an urgent need to eliminate abuse, simplify structures, and increase levels of education within the church, others now began to suggest that another layer of review was necessary. At least some teachings of the church might rest upon less than adequate biblical foundations. People were well used to complaints about the many moral and spiritual failings of the church; this was something new, which threatened to spark off deeply disturbing debates and developments that were without precedent in western Christendom. As we shall see, the Protestant Reformation of the sixteenth century would draw on humanist scholarship to propose significant changes in Christian belief and practice.

2.5.6. Christian Arts in the Middle Ages and Renaissance

The present section of this work has surveyed the history of Christianity throughout the Middle Ages. So how did Christian arts develop during this period? How did faith impact on culture? What were its implications for visual culture and for music?

It is now widely recognized that the Middle Ages was a period of immense artistic creativity. This is especially evident in the visual arts. Churches made use of art for both devotional and pedagogical purposes. Many church walls were illustrated with gospel scenes to supplement sermons on their themes. Panel painting was widely used to depict narratives concerning Jesus, or static portraits of Jesus and his mother. In the early Middle Ages, the two dominant religious images were the Madonna and child, and Christ on a cross (Latin: *crucifixus*), which were often placed on church altarpieces as devotional aids.

Renaissance artists regarded many incidents in the life of Jesus as of potential importance. Particular attention was paid to the Annunciation (that is, to the scene in Luke's gospel in which Gabriel informs Mary that she is to bear a son), the baptism of Jesus, and the resurrection. This theme is treated in works such as Sandro Botticelli's *Annunciation* (1493) and Matthias Grünewald's *Crucifixion* (1515–16). The appearance of the risen Jesus to Mary Magdalene (John 20:17) was also the subject of many classic works, including Fra Angelico's fresco *noli me tangere* ("do not touch me"), painted over the period 1440–1 in the convent of San Marco in Florence. In the eastern church, the visual arts found their expression especially in the painting of icons. Russian and Byzantine iconography emerged as a distinct art form over this period.

Church architecture underwent significant changes during this period. One particularly important function of church architecture at this time was to stress the transcendence of God. The great soaring arches and spires of medieval cathedrals were intended to stress the greatness of God, and raise the thoughts of worshippers heavenwards. The symbolism is that of the eternal impinging upon the temporal, with the church building symbolizing the mediation between heaven and earth offered through the gospel. This emphasis on representing the transcendent here on earth is especially associated with the Gothic style of church architecture, characterized by pointed arches, extended door and window space, structural complexity, immense size, and (especially in northern Europe) by large stained-glass windows and sculptured doorways.

Within a period of a century (1130–1230) some twenty-five Gothic cathedrals were built in France. One of the most distinctive features of this architectural style is its deliberate and programmatic use of height and light to generate and sustain a sense of the presence of God and heaven on earth. The extensive use of buttresses allowed the weight of the building to be borne by outside supports, thus allowing the external walls to have large glass windows, which ensured that the building was saturated with the radiance of the sun. The use of stained glass helped generate an other-worldly brilliance within the cathedral, while simultaneously allowing gospel scenes to be depicted to worshippers. The use of tall, thin internal columns created an immense sense of spaciousness, again intended to evoke the hope of heaven. The cathedral thus became a sacred space, bringing the vast spaciousness and brilliance of heaven within the reach of believers.

The flourishing of the Gothic architectural style encouraged the development of stained-glass technology. As churches became taller and lighter, walls became thinner, and windows larger. The technology of creating stained-glass windows was well established by the year 1100. Glass was colored during its manufacture, by adding metallic salts or oxides. The addition of gold produced a cranberry color, silver produced yellows and golds, while cobalt produced a deep blue, ideal for representing the heavens. The increased use of glass led to the exploration of how this might be used to depict devotional scenes. One hundred and fifty-two of the original windows of the great French cathedral of Chartres are still intact, including the three great rose windows, which date from around 1200.

The "Mystery Play" was a well-established feature of late medieval English life. One of the most ambitious was that performed at the great cathedral city of York. The origins of the York Mystery Plays are to be found in the increasingly prosperous economic situation enjoyed by York in the later Middle Ages. By the fifteenth century, the city was second only to London. The text of the mystery plays is thought to have reached its final form by 1415, and was performed annually until it declined in the later sixteenth century, and was eventually abandoned.

This play was divided into sections, with one of the city's professional guilds being given the responsibility for each. The crucifixion of Christ, generally regarded as one of the finest sections of the entire cycle, was assigned to the Guild of Pinners – that is, to those who made nails. The dry humor of this would have been obvious to the crowd watching, as the dominant theme of this section is the nailing of Christ to the cross. The scenes depicting the death of Christ were allocated to the Butchers, and would probably have been enacted in the section of the city of York now known as "The Shambles," which was the site of a number of slaughter-houses in the Middle Ages.

Music developed significantly during the Middle Ages, both in secular society and within the church. The importance of music in worship had long been recognized. In the late classical period, the musical form now known as "plainsong" emerged. Religious texts – especially the Psalms – would be sung "monophonically." In other words, the music consisted of a single, unaccompanied melodic line. There was no harmony; each singer would pitch the same note, and follow the same rhythm. The most famous of these monophonic forms of church music is usually referred to as "Gregorian Chant."

Yet new developments began to emerge during this period. The single chant line was supplemented or varied in a number of ways, to make the outcome more interesting. In some cases, this involved retaining the same single unaccompanied melodic line, but using different groups of singers. Two approaches became particularly significant.

1. Responsorial. Here, the melody alternated between a single singer, and a group of singers. The first part of a verse would be sung by a soloist, and the chorus would respond with the second part.
2. Antiphonal. This also involved alternation of the melody, in this case between two groups of singers. In a monastic context, the singers on one side of the chapel would chant the first part of the verse, followed by the singers on the other side of the chapel chanting the second.

The development of polyphony, which is thought to date from the ninth century, brought new complexity and richness to worship. Here, the chant consisted of two or more independent melodic voices. This opened the way to the increased use of variations in harmony and rhythm.

2.5.7.   Christian Expansion: Portuguese and Spanish Voyages of Discovery

As we have seen, the Renaissance of the later Middle Ages led to significant demands for renewal and reform, as well as the reinvigoration of Christian arts. Yet other developments which took place around this time opened up new possibilities for western European Christianity – above all, the possibility of physical expansion, as new trade routes were established with Asia, and as new lands were discovered.

The European powers that spearheaded the "Age of Discovery" were Spain and Portugal, two staunchly Catholic nations, who regarded the spread of the Catholic faith as a natural expansion of national influence. They were later joined by another Catholic maritime power, France.

The great Portuguese navigator Vasco da Gama (c. 1460–1524) opened up trade routes with the east coast of Africa, and subsequently across the Indian ocean to India itself. In addition to establishing the highly profitable spice trade route, da Gama's exploration led to Portugal establishing the east African colony of Mozambique as a staging post on the route to India.

Christopher Columbus (1451–1506, often referred to by his Spanish name, Cristobal Colón) initially intended to establish a western trade route to India. Based on a mistaken figure for the size of the earth, Columbus reckoned it would be just as quick to sail westwards to India than eastward. Although some popular accounts of Columbus's voyages suggest that people believed the world was flat, this is clearly incorrect. The spherical shape of the world was widely accepted in the Middle Ages. Columbus intended to sail around the world to India, using a route that he believed would be faster. In the end, he discovered the Americas, and laid the foundation for the Spanish colonization and economic exploitation of this vast new territory, which soon became known as the "New World." Portuguese navigators such as Pedro Álvares Cabral (c. 1467–c. 1524) made landfall further south, and established the colony of Brazil.

Catholicism developed an early concern for the spread of the Christian faith outside Europe. Spanish and Portuguese rivalry became so great that, during the early 1490s, two popes made rulings concerning the extent of their political and economic influence over

Figure 2.10   Monument to the Discoveries, Lisbon, Portugal, commemorating the achievements of the Portuguese navigators of the late fifteenth and early sixteenth centuries. © age fotostock/ SuperStock

newly discovered territories. The Treaty of Tordesillas (1494) finally resolved the issue, dividing the world beyond Europe between the Portuguese and the Spanish along a north–south meridian 370 leagues (1560 km) west of the Cape Verde Islands. This was a treaty between Spain and Portugal, and did not involve the pope.

Yet these voyages of discovery were not merely of political and economic importance. They were partly motivated by religious concerns, given additional impetus by a growing awareness within the Catholic church of its missionary responsibilities. Individual popes were firmly committed to the importance of global evangelization. As we shall see in the next chapter, the Council of Trent laid the groundwork for Catholic missionary work through religious orders, especially the Society of Jesus (3.4.4). As a result, Catholicism underwent considerable expansion during the sixteenth century, establishing bases in the Americas, Africa, and Asia.

The Jesuits spearheaded Catholic expansion in Asia. In 1542, Francis Xavier (1506–52) arrived at Goa on the west coast of India, by then established as a Portuguese trading center in Asia. Over the next ten years, Xavier initiated a series of missionary projects in the region, including many missions in India and other parts of Asia. During the years 1546–7, Xavier established a mission in Ambon, a large island that is now part of Indonesia. In 1549, he began missionary work in Japan. He died in 1552, as he was preparing to undertake missionary work in China. Another Jesuit, Matteo Ricci (1552–1610) continued Xavier's work.

After arriving at Macao, Ricci began a program of immersion in the Chinese language and culture, aiming to work out how best to express Christian ideas in Chinese culture. Ricci established missions in several major Chinese cities.

In 1521, the great Spanish explorer Ferdinand Magellan discovered a group of some 3141 islands in southeast Asia. The islands, now known as "the Philippines," became a Spanish colony. Under Spanish rule, a program of evangelization was undertaken by various religious orders, especially the Franciscans and Dominicans.

The most significant expansion of Christianity during the early modern period took place in the Americas. Spain, Portugal, and France claimed sovereignty over vast areas of territory, within which Catholicism began to take root. Bishoprics were established by 1511 in the islands of Dominica, San Juan, and Haiti. Spain's empire in the Americas included a vast region known as "New Spain," which included Central America, Mexico, Florida, and much of what is now the southwestern part of the United States. Catholic priests built missions in all these areas to convert Native Americans. One of the best known of these is the Alamo in Texas, which was originally constructed as a Franciscan mission in 1722. Spanish influence also extended to the West Indies. Portugal colonized most of the southeast coast of South America, with Spain taking over the northern regions and the western coast.

The implications of these new discoveries could not be overlooked. Who did they belong to? Which European powers had rights over these new territories? In 1481, Pope Sixtus IV confirmed Spanish rights over the Canary Islands, and granted Portugal rights over all further territorial acquisitions made in Africa and eastward to the Indies. Yet the voyages of Christopher Columbus raised new questions about rights over hitherto unknown lands to the west. Pope Alexander VI, whose sympathies lay with Spain, ruled that any lands discovered after 1492 should belong to Spain. Portugal refused to accept this ruling. Bilateral discussions between Spain and Portugal eventually led to the Treaty of Tordesillas (1494), which allocated each nation certain areas of these new territories (which had yet to be mapped and explored).

Although there was uncertainty about precisely how this treaty was to be interpreted, in practice this led to Portugal taking possession of the vast tract of land along the Amazon River now known as Brazil, and Spain taking possession of territories to the north and west of this region, including what is now known as "Latin America." The Treaty of Saragossa, signed on April 22, 1529, divided up territories to the east. Although the pope was not party to these discussions, this division of territory is sometimes inaccurately referred to as the "Papal Line of Demarcation."

This massive expansion of a Christian presence beyond Europe would have a transformative impact. Christianity had ceased to be a European phenomenon, and was in the process of becoming a global faith.

Sources of Quotations

p. 73: Innocent I, *Epistle* 29.
p. 128: Thomas à Kempis, *The Imitation of Christ*, I, 1–2.

For Further Reading

Barron, Caroline M., and Jenny Stratford, eds. *The Church and Learning in Later Medieval Society*. Donington: Shaun Tyas, 2002.

Bartlett, Robert. *The Making of Europe: Conquest, Colonization, and Cultural Change, 950–1350*. Princeton, NJ: Princeton University Press, 1993.

Bitel, Lisa. *Women in Early Medieval Europe, 400–1000*. Cambridge: Cambridge University Press, 2002.

Cant, Geneviève de. *A World of Independent Women from the 12th Century to the Present Day: The Flemish Beguinages*. Riverside, CT: Herve van Caloen Foundation, 2003.

Colish, Marcia L. *Medieval Foundations of the Western Intellectual Tradition, 400–1400*. New Haven, CT: Yale University Press, 1997.

Cook, William R., and Ronald B. Herzman. *The Medieval World View: An Introduction*. New York: Oxford University Press, 2012.

Cowdrey, H. E. J. *Pope Gregory VII, 1073–1085*. Oxford: Clarendon Press, 1998.

Duffy, Eamon. *The Stripping of the Altars: Traditional Religion in England c.1400–c.1580*. New Haven, CT: Yale University Press, 1992.

Eastwood, B. S. *Ordering the Heavens: Roman Astronomy and Cosmology in the Carolingian Renaissance*. Leiden: Brill, 2007.

Evans, G. R. *The Medieval Theologians*. Oxford: Blackwell, 2001.

Foltz, Richard. *Religions of the Silk Road: Overland Trade and Cultural Exchange from Antiquity to the Fifteenth Century*. New York: St. Martin's Press, 1999.

Gill, Meredith J. *Augustine in the Italian Renaissance: Art and Philosophy from Petrarch to Michelangelo*. Cambridge: Cambridge University Press, 2005.

Grant, Edward. *Planets, Stars and Orbs: The Medieval Cosmos, 1200–1687*. Cambridge: Cambridge University Press, 1996.

Gregory, Timothy E. *A History of Byzantium*. Oxford: Wiley-Blackwell, 2010.

Hankins, James, ed. *The Cambridge Companion to Renaissance Philosophy*. Cambridge: Cambridge University Press, 2007.

Herrin, Judith. *Byzantium: The Surprising Life of a Medieval Empire*. Princeton, NJ: Princeton University Press, 2008.

Inglis, John, ed. *Medieval Philosophy and the Classical Tradition in Islam, Judaism, and Christianity*. London: Routledge, 2002.

Kamerick, Kathleen. *Popular Piety and Art in the Late Middle Ages: Image Worship and Idolatry in England, 1350–1500*. New York: Palgrave Macmillan, 2002.

Kraye, Jill, ed. *The Cambridge Companion to Renaissance Humanism*. Cambridge: Cambridge University Press, 1996.

Lambert, Malcolm. *Medieval Heresy: Popular Movements from the Gregorian Reform to the Reformation*. Oxford: Blackwell, 2002.

Lewis, C. S. *The Discarded Image: An Introduction to Medieval and Renaissance Literature*. Cambridge: Cambridge University Press, 1997.

Leyser, Henrietta. *Medieval Women: A Social History of Women in England 450–1500*. New York: St. Martin's Press, 1995.

Logan, F. Donald. *A History of the Church in the Middle Ages*. London: Routledge, 2012.

Lubbock, Jules. *Storytelling in Christian Art from Giotto to Donatello*. New Haven, CT: Yale University Press, 2006.

Mayr-Harting, Henry. *Church and Cosmos in Early Ottonian Germany: The View from Cologne*. Oxford: Oxford University Press, 2007.

Nauert, Charles G. *Humanism and the Culture of Renaissance Europe*. Cambridge: Cambridge University Press, 2006.

O'Callaghan, Joseph F. *Reconquest and Crusade in Medieval Spain*. Philadelphia: University of Pennsylvania Press, 2003.

Pieper, Josef. *Scholasticism: Personalities and Problems of Medieval Philosophy*. South Bend, IN: St. Augustine's Press, 2001.

Power, Eileen. "The Position of Women." In *The Legacy of the Middle Ages*, edited by C. G. Crump and E. F. Jacob, 401–33. Oxford: Clarendon Press, 1926.

Ranft, Patricia. *Women and the Religious Life in Premodern Europe*. New York: St. Martin's Press, 1996.

Riddle, John M. *A History of the Middle Ages, 300–1500*. Lanham, MD: Rowman & Littlefield, 2008.

Riley-Smith, Jonathan. *The First Crusaders, 1095–1131*. Cambridge: Cambridge University Press, 1998.

Riley-Smith, Jonathan. *The Oxford History of the Crusades*. Oxford: Oxford University Press, 1999.

Rolker, Christof. *Canon Law and the Letters of Ivo of Chartres*. Cambridge: Cambridge University Press, 2010.

Rosemann, Philipp W. *The Story of a Great Medieval Book: Peter Lombard's "Sentences."* Toronto: University of Toronto Press, 2007.

Rosenthal, Joel T., ed. *Medieval Women and the Sources of Medieval History*. Athens, GA: University of Georgia Press, 1990.

Shubin, Daniel H. *A History of Russian Christianity*. 4 vols. New York: Algora Publishing, 2004.

Tanner, Norman P. *The Church in the Later Middle Ages*. London: I. B. Tauris, 2008.

van Nieuwenhove, Rik. *An Introduction to Medieval Theology*. Cambridge: Cambridge University Press, 2012.

Venarde, Bruce L. *Women's Monasticism and Medieval Society: Nunneries in France and England, 890–1215*. Ithaca, NY: Cornell University Press, 1997.

Volz, Carl A. *The Medieval Church: From the Dawn of the Middle Ages to the Eve of the Reformation*. Nashville: Abingdon Press, 1997.

Weiss, Roberto. *The Renaissance Discovery of Classical Antiquity*. Oxford: Blackwell, 1988.

Welsh, Evelyn. *Art in Renaissance Italy 1350–1500*. Oxford: Oxford University Press, 2001.

3

Competing Visions of Reform, c. 1500–c. 1650

The sixteenth century and its immediate aftermath represent one of the most fascinating periods in the history of western Christianity. The Renaissance emphasis on returning to classic sources for inspiration and renewal began to take on a more specifically religious focus (2.4.2). As pressure grew for reform of the church "in head and members," the humanist program of returning to the simpler form of Christianity represented in the New Testament seemed increasingly attractive to many.

Yet there were other factors emerging as significant for church life at this time. Nationalism was on the rise in many parts of northern Europe, including Germany, France, and England. An emerging middle class was resentful at the power and privilege of the traditional aristocracy, and wanted to flex its muscles. Lay literacy was increasing, and there was a growing mood for change within both church and society. Forms of Christianity began to develop which offered new ways of thinking about the place of individuals in society, and especially their ability to change things.

It is against this background that the movement we now refer to as the "Reformation" emerged. Demands for reform, fueled partly by political and social agendas, were given additional energy through theological concerns – such as a desire to return to the simplicity of apostolic Christianity. Although most saw this process of reform as taking place within the mainstream of church life, the political and ecclesiastical situation of the time led to some embarking on such reforming programs outside the mainstream. This "Age of Reformation" thus led to the emergence of the complex movement generally known as "Protestantism" on the one hand, and a renewed and reinvigorated Catholicism on the other. In this chapter, we will explore these developments, which are of major importance for the shaping of global Christianity.

Although a variety of terms were used to refer to the movements for reform within the church in the sixteenth century, historians now tend to refer to them using the phrases

Christian History: An Introduction, First Edition. Alister E. McGrath.
© 2013 John Wiley & Sons, Ltd. Published 2013 by John Wiley & Sons, Ltd.

"Reformation" or "European Reformation." From an historical point of view, the movements in question are often designated in terms of their geographical region – for example, "the German Reformation," "the Reformation in England," or "the French Reformation."

The broad movement known as the "Reformation" is generally agreed to include four distinct elements: Lutheranism, the Reformed church (often referred to as "Calvinism"), the "radical Reformation" (often – though not entirely accurately – referred to as "Anabaptism"), and the "Counter-Reformation" or "Catholic Reformation." In its broadest sense, the term "Reformation" is used to refer to all four movements, all of which will be considered in this chapter. The term "Protestant Reformation" is generally used to refer to the first three movements, taken together.

Some recent studies of this age have used the plural form "Reformations" to suggest that the Reformation was a multi-faceted movement – perhaps even that it was a loosely connected set of distinct reforming movements, rather than a single coherent movement with local adaptations. The Reformation in England illustrates this point neatly, as this developed in its own characteristic manner. The interaction of religion and politics in England was such that a local variant of the Reformation arose, quite distinct from its counterparts in Switzerland or Germany.

The present volume follows the general practice of using the term "Reformation" to refer to the major upheavals which changed the shape of western Christianity in the sixteenth century, spilling over into the seventeenth. We begin our reflections on this phase in the history of western Christianity by reflecting on its background in the later Middle Ages.

3.1.   Setting the Context: The Background to the Reformation

In recent scholarship, there has been a growing emphasis upon the need to place the Reformation movements of the sixteenth century in their late medieval context. Although many popular accounts of the origins of Protestantism often identify Martin Luther's posting of the Ninety-Five Theses against indulgences (October 31, 1517) as marking the origins of the European Reformation, the truth is somewhat more complex. The origins of the Reformation lie largely in the intellectual and social upheavals of that era, which both created a crisis for existing forms of Christianity, and offered means by which it might be resolved.

3.1.1.   The Pressure for Reform of the Church

The fifteenth century witnessed many calls for reform of the late medieval church. A substantial "grievance literature" began to develop, expressing concerns about many aspects of church life, from the pope down to the most menial of the clergy. The Renaissance papacy was widely criticized for its financial excesses, and preoccupation with social status and political power. Pope Alexander VI, a member of the Borgia family, perhaps chiefly remembered for its lethal dinner parties, managed to bribe his way to victory in the election to the papacy in 1492 despite the awkwardness of having several mistresses and at least seven

Figure 3.1   Portrait of Leo X, one of the later Renaissance popes. Oil on canvas, Italian School, sixteenth century. Private Collection/The Bridgeman Art Library

known illegitimate children. Niccolò Machiavelli, the age's greatest theorist of naked power, put the immorality of his age down to the appalling example set them by the papacy.

It is easy to find much to criticize among the senior clergy of the age, whose appointments often rested on the influence of family, fortune, and power, rather than any merit on the part of the individuals appointed. In 1451, Duke Amadeus VIII of Savoy secured the appointment of his son to the senior position of bishop of the city of Geneva, later to be noted for its association with John Calvin. The appointment was particularly successful – which is perhaps unsurprising, given that the new bishop was only eight years old.

In many parts of France, the senior clergy were generally outsiders, often nobility imposed upon the dioceses by royal patronage. Rarely resident within their dioceses, these clergy regarded their spiritual and temporal charges as little more than sources of unearned income, useful for furthering political ambitions elsewhere. In France, Antoine du Prat (1463–1535), archbishop of Sens, was so preoccupied with state duties that he found time to attend only one service at his cathedral. Appropriately enough, it was his funeral.

Lower clergy were often the butt of crude criticism. Monasteries were regularly depicted as lice-infested dens of homosexual activity. The poor quality of the parish clergy generally arose from their low social status: in early sixteenth-century Milan, chaplains had incomes lower than those of unskilled laborers. Many resorted to horse and cattle trading to make ends meet. Illiteracy was rife among the clergy. Many had learned the Latin words of the

Mass off by heart from older colleagues, and were known to make mistakes as time passed, and memories failed.

As the laity became increasingly literate in the late fifteenth century, so they became increasingly critical of their clergy. These criticisms were generally directed particularly at their perceived incompetence and the privileges they enjoyed. The tax breaks enjoyed by clergy were the source of particular irritation, especially in times of economic difficulty. In the French diocese of Meaux, which would become a center for reforming activists in the period 1521–46, the clergy were exempted from all forms of taxation, provoking considerable local resentment. In the diocese of Rouen in Normandy, there was popular outcry over the windfall profits made by the church by selling grain at a period of severe shortage.

Yet it is important not to exaggerate the extent of such anti-clericalism. While there were undoubtedly areas in which such hostility was particularly pronounced – particularly in cities – the clergy were often valued and respected. In rural areas, where levels of lay literacy were low, the clergy remained the most highly educated members of the local community. More importantly, many of the great monasteries of Europe were respected on account of their social outreach, and their significant contributions to the local economy. Yet when all this is taken into account, a rumbling discontent remained, often expressed in the "grievance literature."

A growing popular interest in religion led to lay criticism of the institutional church where it was felt to be falling short of its obligations. Yet this reflects a new interest in religion which was reflective, where in the past it might have been somewhat uncritical. Christians became dissatisfied with approaches to their faith which stressed its purely external aspects – such as just attending church. They demanded a form of Christianity which was relevant to their personal experience and private worlds, and capable of being adapted or mastered to meet their personal needs. If anything, it was adaptation, rather than reformation, which seemed to be the primary concern of the articulate laity. Not only were people more interested in their faith; levels of lay literacy had risen significantly, enabling the laity to be more critical and informed about what they believed, and what they expected of their clergy.

Studies of inventories of personal libraries of the age show a growing appetite for spiritual reading on the part of the laity. With the invention and increasing use of printing (2.5.1), books became more widely available, now lying well within the reach of an economically empowered middle class. Devotional books, collections of sermons, traditional "books of hours," and New Testaments feature prominently in these inventories. Lay people were beginning to think for themselves, and no longer regarded themselves as subservient to the clergy in matters of Christian education. Erasmus's *Enchiridion* found a wide and enthusiastic readership in the 1510s, particularly among those who saw themselves as the equals of the clergy in terms of their learning.

Important though these developments were, in themselves and of themselves they do not adequately explain, still less necessarily entail, the rise of Protestantism. The root and branch "reformation" demanded by so many at that time could easily have taken the form of an internal review of the church's teachings and practices, not unlike the Gregorian reforms of the eleventh century. The key question is why and how this group of movements working for renewal and reform within the church came to develop *outside* the church structures of its day, and manage to survive.

The points of difficulty noted above could have been addressed, and possibly resolved, by a gradual process of reappraisal and reform within the church, similar to those introduced in Castille, Spain, in the 1480s by Francisco Ximénez de Cisneros (1436–1517), which radically transformed the Spanish church during this era of transition. Cisneros is widely regarded as having laid the foundations for the church's predominant role in the Spanish Golden Age of the sixteenth and early seventeenth centuries.

Most of Cisneros's major reforming measures were put in place after he became archbishop of Toledo in 1495. Although nearly sixty years of age at that time, he spent the remainder of his life reforming the church, encouraging learning and a revival of religious vocations, and maintaining Spanish political unity at a time of rapid change and potential instability. Cisneros's educational reforms led to both the foundation of the University of Alcalà and the Complutensian Polyglot (a multi-lingual version of the Bible). While these reforms were not entirely successful, and took a long time to take root, they point to the capacity of the church to transform itself in response to the great challenges facing Spain at that time – most notably, after the re-Christianization of Spain following the military defeat of Islamic invaders from North Africa.

In part, the radical developments of the sixteenth century are to be explained on account of the changing social context of western Europe, which was creating new pressures and possibilities for cultural and religious change. We shall consider some of these in what follows.

3.1.2.   The Changing Social Order of the Early Sixteenth Century

The religious debates of the sixteenth century often reveal a deep-seated tension between a medieval notion of a fixed social and intellectual order, and the new understanding of a social order based on change as a means of pursuing the good. The medieval worldview was static. Someone was allocated a position within society on the basis of their birth and social tradition. These were not matters that could be changed. By the end of the fifteenth century, however, an ideology of transition was in the process of developing, which held that individuals could determine their social position and status by their own efforts. They were not trapped by their social origins or circumstances, but could better themselves.

Demands for social change began to build up apace around 1500, especially in the cities. The rise of a mercantile class in cities such as Zurich posed a challenge to the power and influence of traditional aristocratic families. In the closing decade of the fifteenth century, the Swiss city of Zurich replaced the old patrician government by a Great Council of some two hundred city fathers, chosen for life by the merchant guilds, and by a Small Council of Fifty, selected by the Great Council and the guilds. A similar pattern emerged in other cities around this time, creating an expectation of change and improvement.

Luther's cardinal doctrine of the "priesthood of all believers" marked a decisive break with the medieval idea of vocation as a calling to a monastic life; for Luther, Christians were called to serve God actively in the world and its affairs. The Protestant work ethic (3.2.6), which emerged definitively in the 1530s, gave a new religious motivation to active lay engagement in politics, business, finance, and other professional and artistic spheres. This theology of lay empowerment resonated strongly with the aspirations of a newly emerged and increasingly confident middle class. The new religious ideas associated with Luther, Zwingli, and their circles connected with this longing for social progress and reform, particularly in the cities of western Europe.

3.1.3. The Reformation and the Cities of Europe

The northern European Reformation was based largely in the cities. French Protestantism began as a predominantly urban movement, with its roots in major cities such as Lyons, Orléans, Paris, Poitiers, and Rouen. In Germany, more than fifty of the sixty-five "Imperial Cities" responded positively to the Reformation, with only five choosing to ignore it altogether. In Switzerland, the Reformation originated in an urban context (Zurich), and spread through a process of public debate within other Swiss cities such as Bern and Basel, and other cities or regions – such as Geneva and St. Gallen – linked to these cities by treaty obligations.

It is becoming increasingly clear that the success or failure of the Reformation in these cities was dependent in part upon political and social factors. By the late fifteenth and early sixteenth centuries, the city councils of the imperial cities had managed to gain a substantial degree of independence. In effect, each city seems to have regarded itself as a miniature city-state, with the city council functioning as a government and the remainder of the inhabitants as subjects.

The growth in the size and importance of the cities of Germany is one of the more significant elements in late fourteenth- and fifteenth-century history. An extended food crisis, linked with the ravages of the Black Death, led to an agrarian crisis. Wheat prices dropped alarmingly in the period 1450–1520, leading to rural depopulation as agricultural workers migrated to the cities in the hope of finding food and employment. Denied access both to the trade guilds and to the city councils, discontent grew within this new urban proletariat.

The early sixteenth century thus witnessed growing social unrest in many cities, as demands for broader-based and more representative government gained momentum. In many cases, the Reformation came to be linked with these demands for social change, so that religious and social change went together, hand in hand. We must not think that religious concerns swamped all other mental activities – they simply provided a focal point for them. Economic, social, and political factors help explain why the Reformation succeeded, for example, in Nuremberg and Strasbourg, yet failed in Erfurt.

Despite important local variations, some significant common features emerge from a study of the origins and development of the Reformation in major northern European cities such as Augsburg, Basel, Bern, Erfurt, Frankfurt, Geneva, Hamburg, and Zurich. It is helpful to explore them.

First, the Reformation in the cities appears to have been a response to some form of popular pressure for change. Dissatisfaction among urban populations of the early sixteenth century was not necessarily purely religious in character. Social, economic, and political grievances were unquestionably elements within the unrest of the time. City councils generally reacted in response to this popular pressure, often channeling it in directions appropriate to their own needs and purposes. This subtle manipulation of such pressure was an obvious way of co-opting and controlling a potentially dangerous popular protest movement. Existing urban regimes were often relatively unchanged by the introduction of new religious ideas and practices, which suggests that city councils were able to respond to such popular pressure without radical changes in the existing social orders.

Second, the success of the Reformation within a city was dependent upon a number of historical contingencies. To adopt the Reformation was to risk a disastrous change in political alignment, in that existing treaties or relationships – military, political, and commercial – with territories or cities which chose to remain Catholic were usually deemed to be broken as a result. A city's trading relationships – upon which her economic existence might depend – might thus be compromised fatally.

Third, it is important to appreciate that the city council played a decisive role in the religious debates of the sixteenth century, from the initial decision to implement a process of reform to subsequent decisions concerning the nature and the pace of reforming proposals. Zwingli's Reformation in Zurich (3.3.4) proceeded considerably more slowly than he would have liked on account of the cautious approach adopted by the council at crucial moments. Martin Bucer's freedom of action in Strasbourg was similarly limited. As Calvin would discover, city councils were perfectly willing to expel reformers from their precincts if they stepped out of line with publicly stated council policy or decisions.

In practice, the relationship between city council and reformer was generally symbiotic. The reformer, by presenting a coherent vision of the Christian gospel and its implications for the religious, social, and political structures and practices of a city, was able to prevent a potentially revolutionary situation from degenerating into chaos. The constant threat of reversion to Catholicism, or subversion by radical Anabaptist movements rendered the need for a reformer inevitable. Someone had to give religious direction to a movement which, unchecked and lacking direction, might otherwise degenerate into chaos, with momentous and unacceptable consequences for the existing power structures of the city and the individuals who controlled them. The relation between reformer and city council was thus delicate, easily prone to disruption, with real power permanently in the hands of the latter.

3.1.4.   A Crisis of Authority within the Church

We noted earlier how a crisis of authority began to develop in the late medieval church, partly as a result of the Avignon papacy, and the "Great Schism" (2.4.1). The authority of the pope was called into question through the division of western Christendom resulting from the Great Schism (1378–1417) and its aftermath. An Italian faction was led by Urban VI, a French faction by Clement VII. This situation continued until 1417, when the Council of Constance elected Martin V as pope. For a brief period around 1409, there were three claimants to the papacy. The Council of Constance (1414–17) was convened to choose between the rival candidates for the papacy, and conveniently resolved the matter by passing over all three, and choosing its own candidate (Martin V).

The scene was thus set for the development of two rival theories of authority within the church (2.4.2): those who held that supreme doctrinal authority resided in a General Council (the "conciliarist" position) and those who argued that it resided in the person of the pope (the "curialist" position). As the recognition of the need for reform of the church grew in the fifteenth century, the conciliarist party argued that the only hope for such reform lay in calling a reforming general council. Martin Luther adopted a conciliarist position in his 1520 *Appeal to the German Nobility,* in which he argued that the German princes had the right to convoke such a council. The emperor Constantine had convened the Council of Nicaea in 325 (1.4.2). Why should not the emperor or the German nobility convene a council today?

The ultimate failure of the conciliarist movement during the late fifteenth century is generally regarded as a central cause of the Reformation. Conciliarism would never work without the support of Europe's monarchs; they became distracted by other concerns within their borders. The early promise of conciliarism led to hopes being raised that the church might be reformed from within – and when such hopes were dashed, many began to look for ways of *imposing* reform upon the church, perhaps through an appeal to the secular authorities as agents of change. It also posed a challenge to the doctrinal authority of the pope, thereby contributing to the theological confusion of the later medieval period. It became increasingly unclear what views circulating in the late medieval church were merely the private opinions of theologians, and which were the official teaching of the church.

A further factor of importance here is the rise in the power of the secular rulers of Europe, who increasingly came to regard the pope's problems as of somewhat limited relevance. The ability of the popes to call on secular rulers to enforce their religious will was ebbing away. Nationalism became an increasingly important factor in reducing papal authority north of the Alps in the early sixteenth century, as the situation in France demonstrates. The dramatic victory of the French monarch Francis I over the combined papal and Swiss forces at the battle of Marignano in September 1515 established him as a force to be reckoned with in Italian affairs, and enhanced his authority over the French church. The ensuing Concordat of Bologna (1516) gave Francis I the right to appoint all the senior clergy of the French church, effectively weakening the direct papal control over church affairs in France.

Francis, aware of the need to enforce religious orthodoxy within his realm, delegated responsibility for this matter to the Faculty of Theology of the University of Paris. As a result, reforming movements within France were treated as a matter concerning Francis I, rather than the pope. Had the pope wished to intervene in the affairs of the French church, a formidable series of diplomatic and legal obstacles awaited him. Having just defeated the pope in battle, Francis showed relatively little interest in defending papal interests in France, save when they happened to coincide with those of the French monarchy.

A further illustration of the severe restrictions placed upon papal authority by secular rulers can be seen in the case of Henry VIII's attempts to divorce Catherine of Aragon (3.4.2), which took place from 1527 to 1530. At the time when Henry petitioned the pope for a divorce (which would normally have been forthcoming without undue difficulty), the pope found himself under enormous pressure from the emperor Charles V – who happened to be related to Catherine of Aragon. As Charles had recently sacked Rome and retained a large military presence in the region, the pope was faced with the choice of offending either the English king (who had not, and was never likely to have, armies anywhere near Rome) or the emperor (who had such armies, and was perfectly prepared to use them). The outcome was a foregone conclusion. Henry VIII did not get his divorce. As we shall see later (3.4.2), this failure was instrumental in persuading Henry to make some fundamental changes to the religious fabric of England.

There was thus a two-fold crisis of authority in the later medieval church. There was obvious confusion concerning the nature, location, and manner of exercise of *theological* authority, just as there was either a reluctance or an inability to exercise the *political* authority required to suppress the new ideas of the Reformation. In the midst of this ecclesiastical confusion and powerlessness, the Reformation proceeded with increasing pace, until its local suppression was no longer a realistic possibility.

3.1.5.   The Origins of a Term: Protestantism

The term "Protestant" is widely used to refer to the new forms of Christianity that emerged during the early sixteenth century. The origins of this word date from the second Diet of Speyer, held in 1529. (A "Diet" was a legislative assembly.) The historical context of this term needs to be appreciated. The Diet of Worms (1521) issued an edict declaring Martin Luther to be a dangerous heretic, and a threat to the safety of the Holy Roman Empire. Any who supported him were threatened with severe punishment. It was an unpopular move with many German princes, a growing number of whom were sympathetic to at least some of Luther's demands for reform.

One of them, Frederick the Wise, Elector of Saxony, arranged for Luther to be abducted and given safety in Wartburg Castle, where he began his great German translation of the Bible. This hostility on the part of many German rulers towards its policies led Emperor Charles V to dilute the Edict of Worms. In 1526, the Diet of Speyer decreed that it was up to individual princes whether they should enforce its draconian anti-Lutheran measures. The outcome – though clearly not the intention – of this measure was to allow Luther's reforming vision and program to gain strength in many regions of Germany.

At this time, the emperor Charles V was seriously preoccupied with other matters, and was distracted from dealing with the rise of this unpredictable new form of religious faith within Germany. His empire was under immediate and serious threat. One worrying challenge came from a perhaps unexpected source: Rome itself had challenged his authority. Exasperated, in 1527 Charles V sent a task force of 20 000 mercenaries to sack Rome, and place the pope (Clement VII) under house arrest. The episode undoubtedly dampened any slight enthusiasm Charles might have had for dealing with the pope's enemies in Germany.

Yet a far greater danger lay to the east, where decidedly ominous storm clouds were gathering. Following their capture of the great Byzantine city of Constantinople in 1453 (2.4.7), Islamic armies were pressing westwards, making deep inroads into hitherto Christian areas of eastern Europe as they pursued their *jihad*. Much of the Balkans were occupied, and Islamic spheres of influence established – a development that has resounded throughout the subsequent history of the area, especially the Bosnian civil war (1992–5). Following their defeat of the Hungarians in 1526, Turkish armies headed north. By 1529, they had laid siege to Vienna. The Islamic conquest of western Europe suddenly became a real possibility. Urgent action was required to deal with this clear and present danger to western Christendom.

The second Diet of Speyer was hurriedly convened in March 1529. Its primary objective was to secure, as quickly as possible, a united front against the new threat from the east. Some, however, saw this as a convenient opportunity to deal with another, lesser, threat in their own backyards. It was easy to argue that the reforming movements that were gaining influence throughout the region threatened to bring about destabilization and religious anarchy. They demanded the rigorous enforcement of the Edict of Worms throughout the empire. Suppression of religious dissent would lead to the national unity that was essential in the face of the new threats they faced from the east.

Six German princes and fourteen representatives of imperial cities entered a formal protest against this unexpected radical curtailment of religious liberty. The Latin term *protestantes* ("protesters") was immediately applied to them and the movement they represented. Although the term "Protestant" reflects the specifics of the religious situation in Germany, it rapidly came to be applied to related reforming movements, such as those associated with Huldrych Zwingli in Switzerland, the more radical reforming movements known as "Anabaptism," and the later movement linked with John Calvin in the city of Geneva.

3.2.   Protestantism: An Overview of a Movement

The first major group of "reformations" that we shall consider are often gathered together under the term "Protestantism." This term is widely used, both to refer to the debates of the sixteenth century and certain forms of Christianity which resulted from this. We shall consider each specific form of Protestantism in later sections. At this stage, we shall try to get a sense of the overall concerns, agendas, and ideas of the movement.

It is important to appreciate that early Protestantism was not a homogeneous movement. Reforming movements throughout Europe often had local agendas, and did not necessarily see themselves as part of a bigger movement. An idea that was of fundamental importance to Martin Luther – for example, the doctrine of justification by faith – was not always seen as equally important by others, particularly within the radical wing of the movement. Nevertheless, there are a number of shared features of the Protestant movement that allow us to offer a general overview of its ideas and concerns in this way.

3.2.1.   A Return to the Bible

The Renaissance, as we noted earlier, emphasized the importance of returning to the roots of culture, in order to secure its renewal – a program often summarized in the slogan *ad fontes* (2.5.2–3). Cultural renewal could be achieved by returning to the ideas and values of the classical period. Yet this program of renewal and reconstruction could also be applied to Christianity itself. The renewal of the church, it was argued by many Renaissance writers, lay in a return to its title deeds in the New Testament. A stream was purest at its source. Why not by-pass medieval scholasticism, and return to the simpler ideas and structures of the New Testament itself? In the end, this approach would prove central to the reforming movements on all sides in the sixteenth century.

One of the themes common to most reforming movements in the sixteenth century was a desire to get away from abstract theological speculation and get back to ways of thinking and living that were more deeply rooted in the Bible, particularly the New Testament. Writers such as Martin Luther and John Calvin asserted that the Bible was the "word of God" addressed to humanity, which trumped the "human words" of church tradition or papal decrees. The authority of the Pope could be resisted and undermined by asserting that all Christians were ultimately under the authority of the "word of God," and were to be judged by it.

Two Latin slogans summarized this approach. One, widely used by most Protestants, emphasized that the Bible was to be given priority over all other sources of authority. *Sola scriptura* – "by Scripture alone" – summarized the high value that early Protestantism placed on the Bible as a source of teaching and moral guidance. A second slogan was limited to Lutheranism. The Latin slogan *Verbum Domini manet in aeternum* – "The Word of the Lord abides in eternity" – was widely adopted within Lutheranism in the 1520s. Lutherans wore their hearts on their sleeves, by embroidering the letters VDMA – representing the initial letters of the main words of the Latin slogan just noted – on their coats, and even carving them on household items.

Given the importance of the notion of the "Word of the Lord" for the fledgling movement, it is not surprising that the first phase of Protestantism saw the appearance of a wide variety of resources designed to enable and encourage ordinary believers to become familiar with the Bible. Aware of the difficulties that many experienced in reading and making sense of the Bible, Protestant theologians and preachers produced a rich range of material aiming to make an engagement with the Bible as simple and productive as possible. The role of the printing press in allowing the ready production and dissemination of these resources was of critical importance to the success of the Protestant enterprise at this point. Three main categories of resources emerged as particularly significant.

1.   Biblical translations. Although a number of vernacular translations of the Bible were produced during the Middle Ages, these were often unreliable, and occasionally even illegal. The democratizing agenda of Protestantism demanded that every believer should have access to the text of the Bible; this necessitated its translation into the vernacular.

2.   Biblical commentaries. From the outset, Protestantism produced a wide range of study aids for the interpretation of the Bible, of which the "Bible commentary" remains one of the most enduring. These works explained difficult or unfamiliar ideas encountered in the biblical text, commented on translation issues, addressed theological issues, and made practical applications. Some were primarily academic in tone; others were more devotional.

3.   Works of biblical theology. John Calvin's *Institutes of the Christian Religion*, which appeared in its first edition in 1536 (3.3.6), was intended to be a guide to the ideas of the Bible, allowing its readers to build up a systematic overview of Christian doctrine through

Figure 3.2   An early modern printer's workshop. Engraving from Gottfried's "Historical Chronicle," Frankfurt 1619. © Lebrecht Music and Arts Photo Library/Alamy

an engagement with the biblical text. Many others have followed in its wake, aiming to weave together the themes of the Bible in order to give a systematic and coherent account of the themes of the Christian faith.

The Protestant *sola scriptura* principle is linked with two subsidiary ideas. The "sufficiency of Scripture," already noted, affirms that no doctrines other than those clearly set out in the Bible are necessary for salvation. The Church of England's "Thirty-Nine Articles" (1571) set out this position with classic precision:

> Holy Scripture containeth all things necessary to salvation: so that whatsoever is not read therein, nor may be proved thereby, is not to be required of any man, that it should be believed as an article of the faith, or be thought requisite or necessary to salvation.

The second idea is that of the "clarity of Scripture," sometimes also referred to as the "perspicuity of Scripture." This holds that the basic meaning of the Bible can be ascertained by ordinary Christians without the need for assistance. The core teachings of the Bible are clear, and those parts of it which were difficult to understand could be interpreted in the light of other, more accessible passages.

Both these ideas were vigorously disputed by Catholic writers. The Catholic theologian Melchior Cano (1509–60) argued that the Bible was far from clear, and that ordinary people needed help with its interpretation. Protestantism, he argued, ends up making the individual believer the judge of the meaning of the Bible, and had no real place for the corporate judgment of the church. A similar criticism was made later by the Jesuit writer Cardinal Roberto Bellarmine (1542–1621). It was, he argued, obvious that the Bible was difficult to interpret, a fact that Protestantism tried to conceal by following a herd instinct, and pretending this amounted to divine guidance.

3.2.2.   The Doctrine of Justification by Faith

One of the most distinguishing features of western Christianity is its insistence that the basis of salvation is not any form of human privilege, merit, or achievement, but the graciousness of God. The idea is found throughout the New Testament, particularly in the letters of Paul. "By grace you have been saved through faith, and this is not your own doing; it is the gift of God – not the result of works" (Ephesians 2:8–9).

As we noted earlier, the implications of these ideas were explored and clarified during the Pelagian controversy (1.5.6), in which Augustine of Hippo argued that such actions and behavior were the result, not the cause, of being accepted by God. Divine acceptance was an act of grace, which resulted in the moral and spiritual transformation of the sinner. God's grace was essential at every stage in the Christian life. Humanity was fallen, damaged and wounded by sin, and needed healing and restoration – something they could not achieve themselves.

In many ways, the Reformation can be seen as a replay of some of the leading themes of the Pelagian controversy. Protestantism sided with Augustine in this dispute, regarding him as a generally trustworthy interpreter of the Bible, and defender of divine grace. These issues lay at the heart of the reforming program of Martin Luther at Wittenberg (3.3.2). Throughout the late 1510s, Luther and his colleagues sought to renew Augustine's reforming agenda in the face of what they believed to be a fresh outbreak of Pelagianism within the contemporary church. Although historians have noted that this represents an unacceptable generalization, involving an unjustified extrapolation from a local situation to the entire church, there is little doubt that Luther and his colleagues had some valid grounds for concern.

What gave the Lutheran reformation its distinctive character was its decision to change the terms used in discussing the question of human salvation. Up to this point, the Christian tradition had focused on the Pauline notion of "salvation by grace" (Ephesians 2:8), and used this vocabulary in its discussion of how humanity was reconciled to God. Luther and his colleagues now used a different Pauline category to express substantially the same notion: "justification by faith" (Romans 5:1). The reasons for this shift in vocabulary are not fully understood.

Luther was adamant that the doctrine of justification by faith was integral to the recovery of Christian identity and integrity at the time of the Reformation. If humanity became righteous in the sight of God because of its good actions, the whole gospel of grace was compromised. Salvation was a gift, not something that was earned through achievements or merit. Arguing that contemporary Catholicism taught "justification by works," Luther insisted that Paul's doctrine of "justification by faith" was definitive for Christianity. To avoid any misunderstanding, Luther added the word "alone," to avoid any suggestion that faith was simply one among a number of causes of justification – including works. This teaching was often summed up in the Latin slogan *sola fide*, "by faith alone."

Luther's translation of Romans 3:28 angered his critics. A literal translation of the Greek text reads as follows: "someone is justified by faith without the works of the law." Luther translated this as "someone is justified by faith alone without the works of the law." This addition to the text of Scripture caused outrage on the part of Luther's critics. Catholics pointed out that the New Testament nowhere taught "justification by faith *alone*"; indeed, the letter of James explicitly condemned this idea.

Luther responded by making the point that his slogan encapsulated neatly the substance of the New Testament, even if it did not use precisely its original words. His translation conveyed the sense of Paul's original, even if it departed from what he had actually written. And as for the letter of James, was it not "an epistle of straw," which ought not to be there in the New Testament anyway? This second argument caused considerable unease within Protestant circles, and was not maintained by Luther's successors.

Luther's doctrine of justification won wide – but not universal – acceptance within early Protestantism. Although John Calvin gave the doctrine enthusiastic support, the Swiss reformer Huldrych Zwingli was critical of the idea, believing that it might be misunderstood to suggest that Christians had no obligation to do good works. Some Anabaptist writers also distanced themselves from it, again expressing anxieties about its biblical foundations and moral implications (3.4.1).

Luther responded by calming such fears, particularly in his "Sermon on Good Works," arguing that all he was saying was that good works were the natural result of having been justified, not the cause of that justification. Far from destroying morality, Luther simply saw himself as setting it in its proper context. Believers performed good works as an act of thankfulness to God for having forgiven them, rather than in an attempt to persuade or entice God to forgive them in the first place.

3.2.3. Democratization: The "Priesthood of All Believers" and the Use of the Vernacular

One of the most distinctive features of early Protestantism is its strongly democratizing outlook. The riches of the Christian faith were not to be restricted to those who spoke Latin – the language of the academy and church. As a matter of principle, religious resources were to be presented in a language understood by ordinary people – in other words, the vernacular. Most Protestants attached especial importance to three such resources: the Bible; the liturgy; and the sermon. For Luther and other early Protestant reformers, all believers had a right to have access to the Bible, to worship, and to Christian education – and that meant that these resources had to be made accessible to them, by delivering them in a language they could understand.

This theme of spiritual democratization is also evident in Luther's doctrine of the "priesthood of all believers." There was no basis, Luther argued, for asserting that the clergy were superior to the laity, as if they were some kind of spiritual elite, or that their ordination conferred upon them some special "indelible character." The clergy are merely laity who have been recognized by other laity within the community of the church as having special gifts, and are authorized by their colleagues to exercise a pastoral or teaching ministry among them. The authority to make such decisions thus rests with all Christians, not with an autocratic elite or putative spiritual aristocracy.

Luther develops this point using a civil analogy: the clergy are "office-holders," who are elected by the laity as their representatives, teachers, and leaders. There is no fundamental difference between clergy and laity in terms of their status; the difference lies entirely in the former being elected to the "office" of a priest. All believers already have this status, on account of their baptism. This election to office is reversible; those who are thus chosen can be de-selected if the occasion demands it.

On the basis of this doctrine of the universal priesthood of believers, Luther insists that every Christian has the right to interpret the Bible, and to raise concerns about any aspect of the church's teaching or practice which appears to be inconsistent with the Bible. There is no question of any "spiritual" authority, distinct from or superior to ordinary Christians, who can impose certain readings of the Bible upon the church. The right to read and interpret the Bible is the birthright of all Christians.

At this stage, Luther clearly believed that the Bible is sufficiently clear for ordinary Christians to be able to read and understand it. Following through on his democratizing agenda, Luther insists that all believers have the right to read the Bible in a language they can understand, and to interpret its meaning for themselves. The church is thus held to be accountable to its members for its interpretation of its sacred text, and is open to challenge at every point.

Yet Luther's emphasis on the vernacular also had a polemical dimension. He wanted to be able to take his arguments directly to the people. Luther had learned from Erasmus the importance of the printing press in projecting intellectual influence within society. In 1520, he began to advance the cause of his reformation by appealing directly to the German people, over the heads of clerics and academics, through the medium of print and the German language.

Why was this development so important? The language of the academy, the church, and the state in western Europe throughout the Middle Ages was Latin. There was an obvious need for a common language to allow communication across this vast and diverse region of the world. Latin was the language of the great Roman poets, rhetoricians, politicians, and philosophers, and of highly influential Christian theologians such as Augustine of Hippo, Ambrose of Milan, and Tertullian. Luther knew that anything he wrote in Latin would be understood by the educated elite across Europe.

Yet Luther wanted to reach beyond an academic readership, and touch the hearts and minds of ordinary people. The decision to publish in German was iconic, making a statement about the inclusive and democratic nature of the reformation that Luther proposed to pursue. To publish in Latin was to exclude the ordinary people. To publish in his native German was to democratize the debate about the future of the church, by including those who were traditionally marginalized by the use of the ancient scholarly language. From that moment onwards, one of the hallmarks of Protestantism would be its use of the vernacular at every level. Most importantly of all, the Bible would also be translated into the language of the people.

The importance of this point is too easily overlooked. In England, for example, it was illegal to translate the Bible into English. In 1407, Thomas Arundel, archbishop of Canterbury, ruled that "nobody shall from this day forth translate any text of Holy Scripture on his own authority into the English, or any other, language, whether in the form of a book, pamphlet or tract," and that any such book "shall not be read in part or in whole, in public or in private." English thus became the language of the religious underground in the later Middle Ages. To write in English was tantamount to holding heretical views. Even as late as 1513, John Colet (1467–1519) – then dean of St. Paul's Cathedral, London – was suspended from his position for translating the Lord's Prayer into English.

The real point was that the use of the vernacular was about empowering the laity. The importance of this point can be illustrated from Calvin's decision to produce a French-language edition of his *Institutes of the Christian Religion* in 1541. Up to this point, the work was only available in Latin. When it appeared in French, its ideas were accessible and available to anyone in France who could either afford to buy it, or persuade one of their colleagues to lend it to them. Calvin's use of his native French language opened the floodgates to religious debate within France, with Calvin's vernacular writings being a major resource for those arguing for religious and social change.

One of the major implications of this emphasis on the vernacular was the need for biblical translation. One of the most distinctive features of the Protestant Reformation was its insistence that the Bible should be made available in the everyday languages of Europe. Luther himself pioneered the translation of the Bible into German. Others followed his example. William Tyndale (1492–1536) produced one of the most important early English translations of the New Testament, which was published anonymously in mainland Europe in 1526, and smuggled into England.

It is not difficult to see why more conservative English Catholics were alarmed by this development. Tyndale's English translation of the New Testament challenged traditional ecclesiastical structures. For example, Tyndale insisted that the Greek word *presbuteros*, used in Paul's letters to refer to an office within the Christian church and traditionally translated as "priest," should be rendered instead as "senior." The English word "priest" should, Tyndale argued, be reserved solely for translating the Greek term *hiereus*, which was used in the New Testament exclusively to refer to Jewish or pagan priests. The Greek term *ekklēsia*, traditionally translated as "church," was now rendered as "congregation." As a result, many New Testament references which could have been taken as endorsing the institution of the church were now to be understood as referring to local congregations of believers. The use of the vernacular was thus seen as religiously subversive, undermining some traditional medieval ideas about church structure and authority.

3.2.4.　The Rejection of Papal Authority

One of the most distinctive features of the church in western Europe during the Middle Ages was its high view of the spiritual and temporal authority of the pope. Although some were alarmed at this exclusive concentration of power in the hands of a potentially

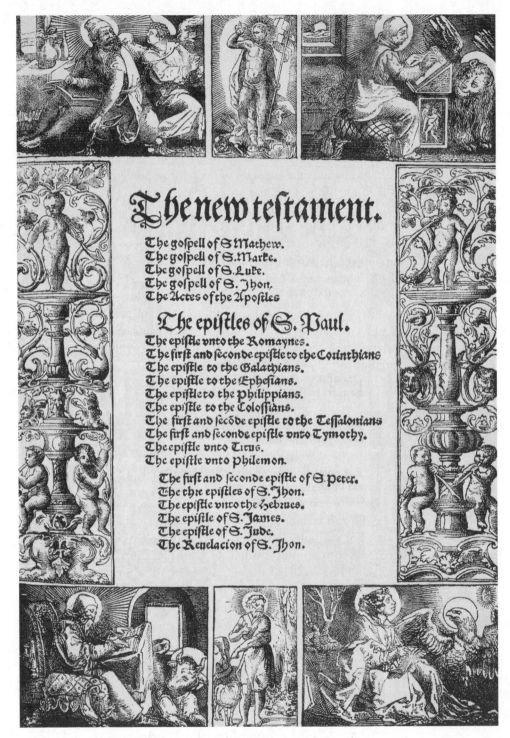

Figure 3.3 Title page of William Tyndale's New Testament, printed in 1530s, from *The National and Domestic History of England* by William Hickman Smith Aubrey (1858–1916), published London, c. 1890 (litho), English School, nineteenth century. Private Collection/Ken Welsh/The Bridgeman Art Library

autocratic ruler, others regarded it as a proper and necessary measure to maintain the identity and discipline of the church. The eastern church never recognized the notion of absolute papal authority, tending to see spiritual authority as distributed and dispersed across essentially autonomous churches.

In line with its emphasis on the democratization of faith, Protestantism rejected any notion of absolute papal authority. This theme plays a particularly significant role in Martin Luther's 1520 work *An Appeal to the Nobility of the German Nation*. The pope, Luther argues, has no more right to interpret the Bible than any other Christian. The fundamentally democratic nature of early Protestantism dictated that theology was an enterprise that may be undertaken by any person, on the basis of a publicly available resource – the Bible.

There is no question of any one interpretation being "privileged," or of any secret additional sources of divine knowledge, accessible only to the initiated, upon which salvation ultimately depends. Nor is there any idea of a spiritual elite, as if there were some group of believers who had the right to impose their views – whether on account of their academic qualifications or their institutional seniority. From the outset, Protestantism was adamant that the office-holders of the church are accountable to their members for the interpretations of the Bible they offer in their preaching and teaching, and may be challenged and corrected on its basis.

The basic idea of the "clarity of Scripture" was held to entail that the meaning of biblical passages could be ascertained without undue difficulty on the part of a wise and learned reader. Luther appears to suggest that ordinary pious Christian believers are perfectly capable of reading Scripture and making perfect sense of what they found within its pages. A similar position is defended by Zwingli in his important treatise of 1522, *On the Clarity and Certainty of the Word of God*. For Zwingli, Scripture is perfectly clear. "The Word of God, as soon as it shines upon an individual's understanding, illuminates it in such a way that he understands it."

Yet this position caused difficulties for many, especially as disputes arose within Protestantism over the interpretation of the Bible. If there was no authority set over and above the Bible, who could decide whether the Bible was being correctly interpreted? Many of the debates within early Protestantism centered on questions of biblical interpretation, and seemed to lie beyond resolution – at least, theoretically.

An example of such a debate concerned the interpretation of the words of Jesus of Nazareth at the Last Supper. What did Jesus mean, in declaring that "this is my body" (Matthew 26:26)? Luther argued that the meaning was perfectly clear. The reference was to the bread which was broken and shared at the Last Supper, and the meaning of Jesus's words was that the bread used in communion services had become the body of Christ. Zwingli disagreed. The meaning, he argued, was equally clear. The bread used at communion services was a symbol or reminder of the death of Christ. Where Luther interpreted the passage in a generally literal sense, Zwingli interpreted it in a generally metaphorical sense. But which was right?

One way of resolving this difficulty was to provide readers of Scripture with a filter or lens, by means of which they might interpret Scripture correctly. One example of such a "filter" is Luther's *Lesser Catechism* (1529), which provided its readers with a framework by which they could make sense of Scripture. Luther's pedagogical work allowed its readers to weave together biblical passages, and see them as part of Luther's theological framework. Of course, there were other frameworks that could be used to make sense of these biblical passages, but these were not set out by Luther himself.

The most famous Protestant theological guide to Scripture, however, was John Calvin's *Institutes of the Christian Religion*, especially the definitive edition of 1559. Calvin is known to have initially modeled this pedagogical work on Luther's catechism. In the preface to the French edition of 1541, he states that the *Institutes* "could be like a key and an entrance to give access to all the children of God, in order that they might really understand Holy Scripture." Yet not everyone was persuaded that Calvin's judgments in this influential book were correct.

In the end, Protestantism took the view that it was better to live with such questions than to have someone impose a decision from above. Most early Protestant writers took the view that the Bible was clear on matters that were of ultimate significance, and that disagreement could be accepted on peripheral matters. The term *adiaphora* (Greek: "matters of indifference") was used by some Protestant writers, such as Philip Melanchthon, to refer to areas of theology in which Protestants ought to agree to disagree.

3.2.5.   Two Sacraments – and Reception in Both Kinds

Earlier, we noted how the theologians of the early Middle Ages reached agreement on a definition of a sacrament which allowed seven such sacraments to be identified: baptism; confirmation; the eucharist; marriage; penance; ordination; and extreme unction (2.3.5). This understanding of the nature of a sacrament was subjected to critical scrutiny by early Protestant writers. The result of this process of review and revision was that only two sacraments were recognized by Protestants: baptism and the eucharist (or Lord's Supper).

Yet there was a second matter relating to the sacraments that emerged as significant in the sixteenth-century debates. In a communion service, were the laity allowed to receive both bread and wine, or only the bread? Early Protestant writers were severely critical of the medieval practice of "communion in one kind" (in other words, giving the laity bread alone, and not bread and wine). Until the twelfth century, it was the general practice to allow all present at Mass to consume both the consecrated bread and the consecrated wine. However, it seems that during the eleventh century, increasing offense arose through some of the laity being careless with the wine when receiving it, and spilling what was now, according to the emerging theology of transubstantiation, the blood of Christ over church floors. By the thirteenth century, only clergy were permitted to receive wine.

According to Luther, this was indefensible, partly in that it lacked any biblical or historical precedent. Yet Luther also declared that the clerical refusal to offer the chalice (the vessel containing the wine) to the laity was unacceptable on theological grounds. If the laity were prevented from having access to the wine, they were also prevented from having access to *what the wine signified*.

Since all of Christ's benefits were intended to be available for all of Christ's people, it was essential that the laity should be allowed to receive both bread and wine. The sacramental symbolism had to correspond to the theological reality. So influential did Luther's attitude become that the practice of offering the laity the chalice became a hallmark of a congregation's allegiance to the Reformation.

3.2.6. A New Work Ethic and the Development of Capitalism

One of the more distinctive features of early Protestantism was its rejection of the medieval distinction between the "sacred" and "secular" realms. While this can easily be interpreted as the desacralization of the sacred, it is important to note that it can equally well be understood as the sacralization of the secular. As early as 1520, Luther had laid the basic conceptual foundations for creating sacred space within the secular. As we noted earlier, his doctrine of the "priesthood of all believers" asserted that there was no genuine difference of status between the "spiritual" and the "temporal" order. All Christians were called to be priests – and could exercise that calling within the everyday world.

This had significant implications for the notion of "calling." During the Middle Ages, the Latin term *vocatio* ("call" or "calling") was understood to mean a call to the monastic life, which involved leaving the world behind. Those who chose to remain in the world tended to be regarded as second-rate Christians, who lacked the commitment to enter the religious life. Luther's abolition of the distinction between the "spiritual" and "temporal" estates forced a revision of the notion of vocation.

The idea of "calling" was thus affirmed, yet fundamentally redefined, by Protestantism. No longer was it about being called to serve God by leaving the world; it was now about serving God within the everyday world. Inevitably, this core principle led to a rejection – or at least marginalization – of any form of monastic life within Protestantism. It served no useful purpose, and distracted believers from their real sphere of responsibilities and activities – in the world.

For Luther, God calls people to express their faith in their lives. Luther stated this point when commenting on Genesis 13:13: "what seem to be secular works are actually the praise of God and represent an obedience which is well pleasing to him." Luther even extolled the religious value of housework, declaring that although "it had no obvious appearance of holiness, yet these very household chores are more to be valued than all the works of monks and nuns." Luther's English follower William Tyndale commented that while the "washing of dishes and preaching the word of God" clearly represented different human activities, he went on to insist that "as touching to please God," there was no essential difference between them.

The idea was developed further by John Calvin, who emphasized the importance of a Christian engagement with and presence within the everyday world. Calvin's theology led directly from a view of work as a socially demeaning, if pragmatically necessary, activity, best left to one's social inferiors, to a dignified and glorious means of praising and affirming God in and through his creation, while adding further to its well-being. It is no accident that those regions of Europe which adopted Protestantism soon found themselves prospering economically – a spin-off, rather than an intended and premeditated consequence, of the new religious importance attached to work.

This led many historians to consider whether there is some intrinsic connection between the spread of Protestantism and the rise of capitalism. The evidence is certainly suggestive. Flanders was torn apart in the second half of the sixteenth century by Protestant revolt and

Catholic reconquest by the Spaniards. For the best part of two hundred years thereafter, the Protestant zone was bustling and prosperous, and the Catholic area depressed and unproductive. Even in robustly Catholic nations, such as France or Austria, economic entrepreneurialism was primarily due to Calvinists. Capitalism and Calvinism were virtually co-extensive by the middle of the seventeenth century.

So is there some deeper connection between Calvinism and capitalism? Or is this simply an accident of history? The German sociologist Max Weber (1864–1920) famously suggested that Calvinism created the psychological preconditions essential to the development of modern capitalism. Catholicism regarded the accumulation of capital as being intrinsically sinful; Calvinism considered it as being praiseworthy.

Weber saw this fundamental change in attitude particularly well illustrated by a number of seventeenth-century Calvinist writers such as the American politician and writer Benjamin Franklin (1706–90), whose writings affirmed the accumulation of capital through engagement with the world, while criticizing its consumption. Capital was to be seen as something that was to be increased, not something that was to be consumed. While Weber's thesis remains contested, there is little doubt that one of the most interesting features of Protestantism is its impact on the world of work and money.

Thus far, we have considered some general features of the thought and practice of Protestantism which were shared across the movement. In what follows, we shall consider each element of Protestantism in more detail, before moving on to consider the Catholic reformation. We begin by reflecting on the development and ideas of the mainline reformation in Germany and Switzerland.

3.3.   The Mainstream Reformation: Luther, Zwingli, and Calvin

History is shaped by a combination of forces – social, economic, political, and religious. All of these factors helped to shape the development of the upheavals of the sixteenth century. However, it is widely agreed that three individual thinkers played a significant role in shaping and directing this movement: Martin Luther (1483–1546), Huldrych Zwingli (1484–1531), and John Calvin (1509–64). In what follows, we shall consider these three figures, and their impact on Christian history during the sixteenth century.

All three of these thinkers belong to the mainstream reforming movement that is often referred to as the "magisterial Reformation," in which a close relationship was envisaged between the church and state, with the "magistracy" – in other words, the civil authorities, whether this takes the form of a monarchy or a city council – having a significant influence over the church, and the implementation of the Christian faith in their local region. As we shall see in a later section, more radical wings of the Reformation often rejected any such relationship.

3.3.1.   Martin Luther: A Brief History

Martin Luther was born on November 10, 1483, in the German town of Eisleben. Luther began his university education at Erfurt in 1501. He was ordained as a priest in 1507, and was awarded the degree of Doctor of Divinity in 1512. This allowed him to take up an academic teaching position at the newly founded University of Wittenberg.

Luther was initially propelled to fame through a controversy concerning the sale of indulgences in 1517. Archbishop Albert of Mainz had given permission for the sales of indulgences in his territories, partly as a means of funding the rebuilding of St. Peter's basilica in Rome (2.4.6). Johann Tetzel, who had been given responsibility for selling these indulgences, crafted a catchy slogan, making the merits of his product clear even to the simplest of people:

> As soon as the coin in the coffer rings,
> The soul from purgatory springs!

Luther regarded the sale of indulgences as theologically questionable, running the risk of the commodification of forgiveness – in effect, treating God's forgiveness of sins as something that could be purchased. In 1517, Luther wrote to Archbishop Albert, protesting against the practice and giving notice of a set of "theses against indulgences" which he proposed to dispute at the University of Wittenberg. These constitute the famous "Ninety-Five Theses," regarded by some historians as marking the origins of the Reformation in 1517.

Although popular accounts of the significance of the "Ninety-Five Theses," as these have come to be known, suggest that they were very radical, their criticisms of the indulgence trade were echoed elsewhere at the time. Luther had two fundamental objections against the selling of indulgences. First, they were financially exploitative of the German nation. If the pope realized the severe poverty of the German people, he would prefer that St. Peter's remained in ruins than that it should be rebuilt out of the "skin, flesh, and bones of his sheep." Second, Luther argued that the pope had no authority over purgatory, so was in no position to influence how long anyone spent there.

Luther's profile was raised considerably in 1519 at the Leipzig Disputation. This disputation – which focused on issues relation to the reform of the church – pitted Luther and his Wittenberg colleague Andreas Bodenstein von Karlstadt against Johann Eck, a highly regarded Catholic theologian from Ingolstadt. During the course of a complicated debate over the nature of authority, Eck managed to get Luther to admit that, in his view, both popes and general councils could err. Even more, Luther indicated a degree of support for Jan Hus, the Bohemian reformer who had been condemned as a heretic some time previously (2.4.4). Eck clearly regarded himself to have won the debate, in that he had forced Luther to state views on papal authority which were unorthodox by the standards of the day.

Others, however, were delighted by Luther's criticisms. Of particular importance was the reaction of many German humanists, who saw Luther's criticisms as indicating that he was one of their number. In fact, this was not the case. Nevertheless, this "constructive misunderstanding" led Luther to be lionized by humanists around this time.

In 1520, Luther published three major works which established his reputation as a major popular reformer. Shrewdly, Luther wrote these in German, making his ideas accessible to a wide public (3.2.3). Where Latin was the language of the intellectual and ecclesiastical

Figure 3.4   Martin Luther, reformer (1483–1546). Painting of Luther with biretta, 1528, studio of Lucas Cranach the Elder (1472–1553). Oil on wood, 34.3 × 24.4 cm. Photo: akg-images

elite of Europe, German was the language of the common people. In his *Appeal to the German Nobility*, Luther argued passionately for the need for reform of the church. In both its doctrine and its practices, the church of the early sixteenth century had cast itself adrift from the New Testament. His pithy and witty German gave added popular appeal to some intensely serious theological ideas.

Encouraged by the remarkable success of this work, Luther followed it up with *The Babylonian Captivity of the Christian Church*. In this powerful piece of writing, Luther argued that the gospel had become captive to the institutional church. The medieval church, he argued, had imprisoned the gospel in a complex system of priests and sacraments. The church had become the master of the gospel, where it should be its servant. This point was further developed in *The Liberty of a Christian*, in which Luther stressed both the freedom and obligations of the believer.

By now, Luther was at the center of both controversy and condemnation. On June 15, 1520, Luther was censured by a papal bull (Latin: *bulla*, "seal," referring to the seal which authenticated the letter to which it was attached), and ordered to retract his views. Luther refused, and publicly burned the bull as an act of defiance. As a result, he was excommunicated in January of the following year, and summoned to appear before the Diet of

Worms. Once more, he refused to withdraw his views. Luther's position became increasingly serious. Realizing this, Frederick the Wise, the elector of Saxony, arranged for him to be "kidnapped," and removed him to the safety of the Wartburg, a castle near Eisenach, for eight months. By the time Luther returned to Wittenberg in 1522 to take charge of the Reformation in that town, his ideas were gaining considerable support throughout Europe.

Luther's influence on the Reformation at this early stage was fundamental. His period of isolation at the Wartburg allowed him to work on a number of major reforming projects, including liturgical revision, biblical translation, and other reforming treatises. The New Testament appeared in German in 1522, although it was not until 1534 that the entire Bible was translated and published. In 1524, Luther argued for the need to establish schools in German towns, and to extend education to women. His two Catechisms of 1529 developed new approaches to religious instruction, which would have a major impact on western Christian educational practice.

Yet not all was well. The Peasants' War of 1525 caused Luther's reputation to suffer severely. Luther argued that the feudal lords had every right to end the peasants' revolt, by force where necessary. Luther's writings on this matter – such as his tract *Against the Thieving and Murderous Hordes of Peasants* – had virtually no impact on the revolt itself, but tarnished his image severely.

Perhaps the most significant controversy erupted over the very different views on the nature of the real presence held by Luther and Huldrych Zwingli. Luther's strong commitment to the real presence of Christ in the eucharist contrasted sharply with Zwingli's metaphorical or symbolic approach. Although many sought to reconcile the two views, or at least to limit the damage caused by the differences – these eventually came to nothing. The Colloquy of Marburg (1529), arranged by Philip of Hesse as a means of getting Luther and Zwingli to settle their differences, was of particular importance. Its failure can be argued to have led to the permanent alienation of the German and Swiss reforming factions at a time when increasingly adverse political and military considerations made collaboration imperative.

By 1527, Luther married a former nun, Katharina von Bora (1499–1552). Although Luther went on to produce a number of major theological works in his later period (most notably, his commentary on Galatians), his attention was increasingly taken up with his personal health, and the politics of the Reformation struggles. He died of natural causes in 1546 while attempting to mediate in a somewhat minor quarrel which had broken out between some members of the German nobility in the city of Mansfeld.

3.3.2. Luther's Reformation at Wittenberg

Luther's reforms, set out in three reforming treatises of 1520 and enacted at Wittenberg during the period 1522–4, rapidly became a template for reforming individuals and congregations throughout Europe. Luther demonstrated that his fundamental theological principles could be actualized in changes to the church and society.

Luther's vision for renewal of the church's life and thought was about reforming an existing Christian church, which had lost its bearings and moorings during the Middle Ages. His fundamental conviction was that the church of his day had lost sight of some –

but not all – of the fundamental themes of the Christian gospel. Not every aspect of the church's life and thought required reform. Renewal, not innovation, was Luther's watchword. Luther's program for reform was not simply about restructuring institutions and calling for moral reform. It was, at heart, about a rediscovery of the central theological themes of the Christian faith, through a return to the Bible.

Perhaps the most obvious theme of Luther's reforms is the central place he allocated to the Bible (3.2.1). For Luther, the Bible was central to the life and thought of the church, as it was to the personal devotion of the individual Christian. Much of Luther's early work concerned making the Bible accessible to German Christians – above all, by translating it into the German language. Luther's emphasis on making theological and spiritual resources available to German Christians in their own language was a fundamental motivation for his translation of the Bible into German in the 1520s.

When it became clear that ordinary Christians experienced difficulty in interpreting the Bible, Luther produced catechisms, devotional tracts, and biblical commentaries, aimed at aiding the faithful to get the most from this treasure that had now been placed in their hands.

The educational aspects of Luther's reforms proved highly influential, and were widely adopted and adapted throughout western Europe. A visitation of Lutheran churches in Saxony over the period 1528–9 showed that most pastors and just about every layperson were ignorant of basic Christian teachings. Luther was shocked by his findings, and decided to put in place measures to increase public knowledge of basic Christian teachings.

In May 1529, Luther published what has come to be known as the *Lesser Catechism*. This work, written in German, showed a lightness of touch, an ease of communication, and a general simplicity of expression which ensured that it was widely used and appreciated. Its question-and-answer format was ideally suited to learning by rote, and the work was widely used in churches and schools.

Yet Luther's emphasis on the Bible was primarily about the means by which God's promises were mediated to people. What of the substance of those promises? Here, we come to a core feature of Luther's reforming program – his emphasis on the doctrine of justification by faith alone.

Intense study of Luther's theological development over the period 1513–18 makes it clear that Luther experienced some kind of theological breakthrough around this time (though the precise date is contested). The essence of this change concerns his understanding of Paul's declaration that the "righteousness of God" is revealed in the gospel (Romans 1:17). Luther initially believed that this referred to the standards of righteousness that was required of people if they were to be accepted by God. However, his engagement with the New Testament over this period led him to conclude that "justifying righteousness" should be understood as a divine *gift to humanity*, not a divine *requirement of humanity*.

Luther's theology now came to be dominated by his realization that salvation was a free, unmerited gift of God, received by faith. This is the central theme of his doctrine of "justification by faith alone," which was central to Luther's own reforming agenda (3.2.2). If this idea was misunderstood or denied, the church would lose its identity, and the gospel would be compromised – which was precisely what Luther believed to have taken place during the later Middle Ages. The controversy about indulgences of 1517 arose because Luther believed that the church was implying that forgiveness of sins could be *purchased*, when it was in fact a free gift.

Yet Luther's reforming program also extended to the life of the church. Perhaps the most obvious development was Luther's rejection of the idea that continuity with the apostolic church was safeguarded by institutional means. To break away from this church was to lose any right to be called a "Christian" church. But for Luther, the medieval church had lost its way, ethically and theologically. Luther justified the existence of his breakaway church by insisting that it maintained continuity with the apostles by remaining faithful to their teaching – something he believed the church of his day had conspicuously failed to do.

As we noted earlier, Luther went on to insist that there is no fundamental spiritual distinction between clergy and laity (3.2.3). All believers are priests, on account of their baptism; that some function as priests is simply a matter of church order, not theological or spiritual superiority. This idea, articulated in Luther's doctrine of the "priesthood of all believers," had momentous implications. Clergy and laity alike should receive communion in both kinds (3.2.5).

Luther also insisted that clergy should be able to marry, like anyone else. Luther himself married Katharina von Bora (1499–1552), a former nun, who came to be regarded as a role model for women in the new Protestant order then emerging. Each congregation should be able to elect its own preachers and pastors, and deselect them if circumstances required. Once more, the fundamental theme is that of democratization – the subversion of any notion of a "spiritual elite."

Luther also gave thought to the political aspects of his vision for the church. What was the relation of the Christian community to the state? To the German princes of the time? In answering this question, Luther developed his doctrine of the "two kingdoms." Having rejected the medieval distinction between the "temporal" and "spiritual" estates, Luther developed an alternative theory of spheres of authority, based upon a distinction between the "spiritual" and the "worldly" government of society. God's spiritual government is effected through the Word of God and the guidance of the Holy Spirit. God's worldly government is effected through kings, princes, and magistrates, through the use of the sword and the civil law.

This proved to be perhaps one of the least satisfactory aspects of Luther's reforming program, in that it seemed to give German princes the upper hand in their relationship with the church, and prevented the church from criticizing the state when it used repression against its people – as many believed it had done in the suppression of the Peasants' Revolt of 1525.

3.3.3.   Huldrych Zwingli: A Brief History

The Swiss reformer Huldrych (or "Ulrich") Zwingli played a major role in developing a reforming movement within the Swiss Confederation, especially in the city and canton of Zurich. Zwingli was born on New Year's Day, 1484, in the Toggenburg Valley in the canton of St. Gallen, in the eastern part of modern-day Switzerland. Strictly speaking, St. Gallen was not part of the Swiss Confederation at this time. However, in the treaty of 1451, St. Gallen had allied itself to some of the Swiss cantons, and Zwingli always appears to have regarded himself as Swiss.

After an initial period of education at Bern, Zwingli attended the University of Vienna (1498–1502). Vienna was widely regarded as one of the most exciting universities close to Switzerland, on account of the university reforms then taking place.

Under the guidance of leading humanists, such as Conrad Celtis, the university was adopting humanist reforms (2.5.3). Zwingli then moved to the University of Basel (1502–6), where he strengthened his humanist position. In 1506, he was ordained priest, and served in this capacity at Glarus for the next ten years, before moving to serve as "people's priest" at the Benedictine monastery at Einsiedeln in 1516.

During his time as parish priest of Glarus, Zwingli served as a chaplain to Swiss soldiers serving as mercenaries in the Franco-Italian war. He was present at the disaster of Marignano (1515), in which large numbers of Swiss mercenary soldiers died. This event, which confirmed Zwingli's opposition to the mercenary trade, was of fundamental importance in the development of Swiss isolationism in the sixteenth century. In the light of what happened at Marignano, it was decided that the Swiss would take no part in other nations' wars again.

By 1516, Zwingli had become convinced of the need for reform of the church, along the lines suggested by biblical humanists such as Erasmus (2.5.4). He purchased Erasmus's edition of the Greek New Testament, and studied the writings of both Greek and Latin early Christian authors. By the time he left Einsiedeln for Zurich, Zwingli had become convinced of the need to base Christian belief and practice on Scripture, not human traditions.

On January 1, 1519, Zwingli took up his new position as "people's priest" at the Great Minster in Zurich. From the outset, his commitment to a program of reform was obvious. He began to preach a course of sermons on Matthew's gospel, ignoring the conventional lectionary altogether. Zwingli's career at Zurich came close to being ended abruptly; he nearly died during an outbreak of the plague at Zurich in the summer of 1519. This narrow escape from death is known to have had a significant impact on his thinking on the nature of divine providence.

It was not long before Zwingli's reforms became more radical. In 1522, he was actively preaching against virtually every aspect of traditional Catholic religion, including the cult of the saints, the practice of fasting, and the worship of Mary. His preaching caused controversy within the city, and alarmed the city council. Anxious at the unrest which was growing within the city, the city council determined to settle the matter. In January 1523, a great public disputation was arranged between Zwingli and his Catholic opponents. The City Council sat in judgment, as Zwingli debated his program of reform with some local Catholic clergy.

It soon became clear that Zwingli had gained the upper hand. Able to translate into the local Zurich dialect without difficulty from Hebrew, Greek, or Latin, Zwingli displayed a mastery of the Bible which his opponents simply could not match. There could only be one outcome. The City Council decided that a program of reform based on Scripture, such as that outlined by Zwingli, would become official city policy.

In 1525, Zurich city council finally abolished the Mass, and substituted Zwingli's version of the Lord's Supper. Zwingli's views on the religious significance of the eucharist would prove to be immensely controversial; indeed, Zwingli is perhaps best remembered for his radical "memorialist" view of the Lord's Supper, which he regarded as a remembrance of Christ's death in his absence.

Encouraged by his reforming successes, Zwingli persuaded other city councils to have public debates along the same lines. A major breakthrough took place in 1528, when the city of Bern decided to adopt the Reformation after a similar public disputation. Bern was a major center of political and military power in the region. Its political and military support for beleaguered Geneva in 1536 would subsequently prove to be decisive in establishing Calvin's influence over the second phase of the Reformation. Zwingli was killed in battle on October 11, 1531, defending his reformation.

3.3.4.   Zwingli's Reformation at Zurich

Zwingli initiated a program of reform at Zurich which represents a distinctive approach to the reformation of the church, reflecting currents of thought characteristic of eastern Switzerland at that time. There is no evidence that Zwingli had heard of Luther's ideas and methods as he began to agitate for change to both the ecclesiastical and civic life of Zurich.

In common with Luther and Erasmus, Zwingli held that the church needed to realign itself with the teachings and practices of the New Testament. Yet Zwingli's understanding of how that process should happen, and what form it would take, bore little relation to Luther's approach. It was much closer to Erasmus's vision for institutional and moral reform, based on an educational program grounded in the classics and the New Testament (2.5.4–5).

Zwingli, like many reformers in eastern Switzerland, had a vision of reform that was primarily institutional and moral. The church needed to return to the simple ways of the New Testament, and behave according to the moral teachings of Christ. The New Testament was to be valued because of its clear teaching about Christian discipleship and ethics. Reformation was about the church and its members reshaping their lives in the light of that ethical teaching. Unlike Luther, Zwingli did not see doctrinal reformation as being of central importance. Zwingli did not share Luther's sense that theological inadequacy compromised the essence of Christian identity.

On the day after his arrival at Zurich in 1519, Zwingli announced his intention to deliver a continuous course of sermons on the gospel according to Matthew. Instead of relying on commentaries, he would base his sermons directly on the scriptural text. For Zwingli, scripture was a living and liberating text, by means of which God would speak to his people, and enable them to break free from bondage to false ideas and practices. In particular, he held that Christ's "sermon on the mount" set out a vision for the moral life that was binding on all Christians.

In his 1522 treatise *The Clarity and Certainty of the Word of God*, Zwingli argued for the capacity of the Bible to interpret itself lucidly and unambivalently in all matters of importance. Like Erasmus, he insisted that the best possible aids to the interpretation of the Bible – such as a knowledge of the Hebrew and Greek languages, and an understanding of the various figures of speech employed in Scripture – needed to be brought to the task of establishing the natural sense of Scripture. Like Luther, he held that the church had no authority other than (or above) the Bible.

Luther and Zwingli, however, despite their shared emphasis upon the centrality of the Bible (3.2.1), used quite different techniques of biblical interpretation. Though both appealed to the same source as authoritative, the outcomes of their engagement with the biblical text were very different – and led to very different visions of reform. For Luther, the Bible primarily contained the *promises* of God, leading to salvation; for Zwingli, the Bible primarily contained the *commands* of God, leading to ethical living.

One particularly important divergence between Luther and Zwingli concerns their attitudes to the use of images in worship. Where Luther was prepared to tolerate religious images in churches, seeing these as having a valuable educational role, Zwingli held that the Old Testament ban on images was binding on all Christians. In June 1524, the city of Zurich ruled that all religious imagery was to be removed from churches. Iconoclastic riots spread throughout the region – including the cities of Bern (1528), Basel (1529), and Geneva (1535) – marking the spreading of the Reformation by popular acts of violence and desecration.

Yet perhaps the most striking difference between Luther and Zwingli concerned the nature of the "real presence." In what sense, if any, is Christ really present in the bread and wine of the Mass? As we noted earlier (3.2.3), Luther was strongly critical of the medieval doctrine of "transubstantiation," believing that it was excessively dependent on the Aristotelian philosophical notions of "substance" and "accidents." Yet his own view was the body and blood of Christ were conveyed in, through, or under the bread and the wine. When Christ offered bread to his disciples, he declared that "this is my body" (Matthew 26:26). Was not the obvious, correct way of making sense of this core text that the bread in question was Christ's body?

Zwingli responded by pointing out that this was by no means the only way of interpreting this text. The Bible was full of statements which might seem to suggest one thing but, on closer inspection, meant another. For Zwingli, the phrase "this is my body" did not mean that the bread was identical with the body of Christ; rather, it pointed to, or signified, that body. Christ's words were to be understood as meaning that the bread of the "Supper" or "Remembrance" – Zwingli did not wish to retain the traditional term "Mass" – was a symbol of Christ's body, just as the wine symbolized his blood. Christ was being remembered in his absence, and his future return anticipated.

It will be obvious that these represent very different understandings of this same text. Luther's interpretation was traditional, Zwingli's more radical. But which was right? Which was Protestant? We see here the fundamental difficulty that the Reformation faced: the absence of any authoritative interpreter of Scripture, which could give rulings on contested matters of biblical interpretation. If this question was to be answered, an authoritative rule or principle had to be proposed which stood *above* Scripture – the very idea of which was ultimately anathema to Protestantism.

The solution offered by Zwingli was elegant and simple: the community of faith would decide the matter by a vote. In January 1523, the great debate usually known as the "First Zurich Disputation" got under way. Its outcome was of great importance for the development of the Reformation. It was decided that the church in Zurich would be bound by the "word of God," and would be obedient to Scripture. But who was to interpret the Bible? The city council, seeing itself as a duly elected representative body of the Christians of Zurich, declared that it possessed the corporate right to settle the question of the interpretation of the Bible. The interpretation of the Bible would thus be a local matter, to be settled democratically.

This was an approach that endeared itself to city councils throughout the region, as the Reformation began to spread. Religious authority was transferred from the pope or local bishop to elected representatives of the people. It was yet another example of the "democratization of faith" which was so characteristic of the reforms then taking place, and gave a place of no small significance to the city council within the urban "sacral community."

3.3.5.   John Calvin: A Brief History

John Calvin was born on July 10, 1509, in the French cathedral city of Noyon, about seventy miles (112 kilometers) northeast of Paris. At some point in the early 1520s (probably 1523), the young Calvin was sent up to the University of Paris. After a thorough grounding in Latin grammar at the hands of Mathurin Cordier, Calvin entered the Collège de Montaigu. After completing his rigorous education in the arts, Calvin moved to the University of Orléans to study civil law, probably at some point in 1528.

Calvin returned to Paris in 1531 to continue his studies, and became increasingly sympathetic to the reforming ideas then gaining a hearing in the city. The university and city authorities, however, were intensely hostile to Luther's ideas. On November 2, 1533, Calvin was obliged to leave Paris suddenly. The rector of the University of Paris, Nicolas Cop (1501–40), had delivered a university address in which he openly supported Luther's doctrine of justification by faith. The Parliament at Paris immediately took action against Cop. A copy of Cop's address exists in Calvin's handwriting, suggesting that he may have composed the address. Calvin fled Paris, fearful for his safety.

By 1534 Calvin had become an enthusiastic supporter of the principles of the Reformation. During the following year, he settled down in the Swiss city of Basel, safe from any French threat. Making the best use of his enforced leisure, he published a book destined to exercise a decisive effect upon the Reformation: the *Institutes of the Christian Religion*. First published in May 1536, this work was a systematic and lucid exposition of the main points of the Christian faith. It attracted considerable attention to its author, who revised and expanded the work considerably during the remainder of his life. The first edition of the book had six chapters; the final edition, published in 1559 (and translated by Calvin into his native French in 1560), had eighty. It is generally regarded as one of the most influential works to emerge from the Reformation.

After winding up his affairs in Noyon early in 1536, Calvin decided to settle down to a life of private study in the city of Strasbourg. Unfortunately, the direct route from Noyon to Strasbourg was impassable, due to the outbreak of war between Francis I of France and the emperor Charles V. Calvin had to make an extended detour, passing through the city of Geneva which had recently gained its independence from the neighboring territory of Savoy. Geneva was then in a state of confusion, having just evicted its local bishop and begun a controversial program of reform under the Frenchmen Guillaume Farel and Pierre Viret. On hearing that Calvin was in the city, they demanded that he stay, and help the cause of the Reformation. Calvin reluctantly agreed.

His attempts to provide the Genevan church with a solid basis of doctrine and discipline met intense resistance. Having just thrown out their local bishop, the last thing that many Genevans wanted was the imposition of new religious obligations. Calvin's attempts to reform the doctrine and discipline of the Genevan church were fiercely resisted by a well-organized opposition. After a series of quarrels, matters reached a head on Easter Day 1538: Calvin was expelled from the city, and sought refuge in Strasbourg.

Having arrived in Strasbourg two years later than he had anticipated, Calvin began to make up for lost time. In quick succession he produced a series of major theological works. He revised and expanded his *Institutes* (1539), and produced the first French translation of this work (1541); he produced a major defense of reformation principles in his famous *Reply to Sadoleto* (Cardinal Sadoleto had written to the Genevans, inviting them to return to the Catholic church); and his skills as a biblical exegete were demonstrated in his *Commentary on the Epistle to the Romans*. As pastor to the French-speaking congregation in the city, Calvin was able to gain experience of the practical problems facing reformed pastors. Through his friendship with Martin Bucer (1491–1551), the Strasbourg reformer, Calvin was able to develop his thinking on the relation between the city and church.

In September 1541, Calvin was invited to return to Geneva. In his absence, the religious and political situation had deteriorated. The city appealed to him to return, and restore order and confidence within the city. The Calvin who returned to Geneva was a wiser and more experienced young man, far better equipped for the massive tasks awaiting him than he had been three years earlier. Although Calvin would still find himself quarreling with the city authorities for more than a decade, it was from a position of strength. Finally, opposition to his program of reform died out. For the last decade of his life, he had virtually a free hand in the religious affairs of the city.

During this second period in Geneva, Calvin was able to develop both his own theology and the organization of the Genevan reformed church. He established the Consistory as a means of enforcing church discipline, and founded the Genevan Academy to educate pastors in reformed churches. Calvin also produced expanded and revised editions of the *Institutes of the Christian Religion*, which became one of the most significant religious works of the sixteenth century.

This final period in Geneva was not without its controversies. Calvin found himself embroiled in serious theological debate over the correct interpretation of Christ's descent into hell, and whether the Song of Songs was canonical. A furious and very public debate broke out with Jérôme-Hermès Bolsec (died 1584) over the doctrine of predestination, of such ferocity that Bolsec ended up having to leave Geneva. A more serious controversy concerned Michael Servetus (1511–53), accused by Calvin of heresy, who was finally burned at the stake in 1553. Although Calvin's role in this matter was less significant than some of his critics have implied, the Servetus affair continues to stain Calvin's reputation.

By the early spring of 1564, it was obvious that Calvin was seriously ill. He preached for the last time from the pulpit of Saint-Pierre on the morning of Sunday February 6. By April, it was clear that Calvin had not much longer to live. He found breathing difficult,

Figure 3.5   Portrait of John Calvin (Noyon, 1509–Geneva, 1564), French theologian and religious reformer, by Henriette Rath (1773–1856). Miniature. Photo: akg-images/De Agostini Picture Library

and became chronically short of breath. Calvin died at eight o'clock on the evening of May 27, 1564. At his own request, he was buried in a common grave, with no stone to mark its location.

3.3.6.   Calvin's Reformation at Geneva

Calvin was a second-generation reformer, and his achievements are best considered as a consolidation of the insights of earlier reformers, such as Luther and Zwingli. Calvin is a system-builder, not an original thinker. Perhaps his most significant achievement was providing a systematic defense of the new understanding of the Christian church, partially developed by Luther, which allowed the new reformed communities throughout Europe to assert their Christian identity, without the need to have institutional continuity with the medieval church.

For Calvin, there were two – and only two – essential elements of a Christian church: the preaching of the word of God, and the proper administration of the sacraments.

> Wherever we see the Word of God purely preached and listened to, and the sacraments administered according to Christ's institution, it is in no way to be doubted that a church of God exists. For his promise cannot fail: "Wherever two or three are gathered in my name, there I am in the midst of them" (Matthew 18:20).

Calvin's definition is significant as much for what it does *not* say as for what it does explicitly affirm. There is no reference to the necessity of any historical or institutional continuity with the apostles. For Calvin, it was more important to teach what the apostles taught than to be able to show an unbroken line of institutional continuity with them. Institutional continuity, Calvin insisted, did not guarantee theological fidelity. For Calvin, the Catholic church had suffered from institutional drift, losing its grounding in the fundamental ideas of the apostles, which were, of course, expressed in the Bible.

This radical new understanding of the church in effect envisaged it as a community which gathered around the preaching of the word of God, and celebrated and proclaimed the gospel through the sacraments. Where the gospel is truly preached, there a church will gather. Protestant theologians, sensitive to the charge that this new approach represented a distortion of a proper theology of the church, pointed to a classic statement of the first-century Christian writer Ignatius of Antioch: "wherever Christ is, there is also the church" (*ubi Christus ibi ecclesia*). Gathering together in the name of Christ ensures his presence – and with that presence, a church comes into being.

Yet perhaps the greatest of Calvin's achievements at Geneva, when viewed in the context of Christian history as a whole, was a book – the *Institutes of the Christian Religion*. As we noted earlier, the printed book of the most significant factors in molding intellectual opinion across sixteenth-century Europe (2.5.1). Books were easily transported, capable of crossing national frontiers undetected, and finding their way to private libraries where they were eagerly, if secretively, devoured. The printed word was integral to the spreading of the ideas of the Reformation across the religious and political boundaries of Europe.

The first edition of the *Institutes* was published at Basel in 1536. Modeled on Luther's influential catechisms of 1529, its six chapters included commentaries on the Ten Commandments, the Apostles' Creed, and some disputed matters of theology. Calvin revised the work substantially during his time in Strasbourg. It is the second edition that established the work as one of the most important Protestant works of the era. Completely restructured, the work's seventeen chapters set out a clear, accessible account of the basics of Christian belief, including the doctrine of God, the Trinity, the relation of the Old and New Testaments, penitence, justification by faith, the nature and relation of providence and predestination, human nature, and the nature of the Christian life. Calvin's distinctive emphases on the sovereignty of God and the authority of the Bible are evident from even a cursory reading of the work, and would remain central as it underwent development in later editions.

This edition of the *Institutes* is not so much a work of *theology*; it is a work of *pedagogy*, based on careful reflection on how to communicate and commend ideas. The work offers a clear and immensely readable account of ideas that might otherwise be inaccessible and unintelligible. This concern for effective communication with a lay audience is especially evident in the French translation of the *Institutes* (1541), which shows Calvin adapting his ideas and language to his intended audience. Greek words and references to Aristotle were left out, and a healthy dose of French proverbs and idioms added. This translation is regularly hailed as a model of pedagogical clarity.

Yet it was not simply the many educational and presentational virtues of the book that propelled it to prominence. It addressed head-on the central weakness of Protestantism up to this point: the problem of the multiplicity of interpretations of the Bible. How can one speak of the Bible as having any authority, when it is so clearly at the mercy of its interpreters? Calvin established the credentials of his interpretations of the Bible not by an assertion of his personal authority or wisdom, but by careful engagement with biblical passages, informed by a good knowledge of how these passages had been interpreted by well-regarded older Christian writers, such as Augustine of Hippo.

Readers of the *Institutes* were presented with reasoned, defended, and superbly presented accounts of central Christian teachings, firmly rooted in the Bible. Alternatives were presented and critiqued, reassuring readers of the plausibility of Calvin's preferred interpretations in the face of their rivals. Calvin did not merely defend his ideas; he showed how he derived them in the first place.

So what are the central ideas that Calvin develops? The most important is the fundamental assertion that a consistent and coherent theological system can be derived and defended on the basis of the Bible. Calvin's greatest legacy to Protestantism is arguably not any specific doctrines, but rather his demonstration of how the Bible can serve as the foundation of a stable understanding of Christian beliefs and structures. In particular, Calvin holds that the New Testament lays down a specific, defensible church order. Calvin's theology is similar to Luther's at many points, while taking a theologically subtle and diplomatic view on the issue that caused such a furious row between Luther and Zwingli – the question of the real presence.

The growing importance of the *Institutes* led Calvin to revise and expand the work, culminating in the definitive edition of 1559, consisting of eighty chapters arranged in four books. The final Latin edition was five times larger than the first. This final edition shows a marked improvement over previous editions as a result of the complete reorganization of the work, allowing the inner coherence of Calvin's approach to be appreciated, while at the same time making it easier to find specific discussions.

The work also included some additions, reflecting later controversies. It must be said that some of these later additions are rather less elegant and more acerbic than earlier parts of the work, and do not reflect Calvin at his best. Calvin is believed to have suffered from irritable bowel syndrome later in life, and this may underlie this unfortunate development.

While Luther, Zwingli, and Calvin played an important role in shaping the new forms of Christianity developing in Europe in the sixteenth century, local factors also affected the shaping of the new religious order. In the next section, we shall explore some further aspects of this complex new religious landscape.

3.4.   Reformations across Europe: The Bigger Picture

As we noted earlier, a number of reforming movements sprang up within western Europe in the early sixteenth century. Although these are sometimes grouped together as "the Reformation," this implies a far greater degree of shared values and collaboration than was actually the case. Often, reforming movements were concerned with purely local affairs. Some aligned themselves with reforming movements elsewhere; others found themselves drawn into broader conflicts and disputes, thus becoming part of a wider movement. In what follows, we shall try to identify some components of the western European reforming movements of this period which lay beyond those initiated and directed by Luther, Zwingli, and Calvin.

3.4.1. The Radical Reformation

The term "Radical Reformation" is now often used to refer to the group of loosely associated reforming movements in Germany and Switzerland which believed that reformers such as Luther and Zwingli had compromised their own basic reforming principles. They had, more radical thinkers argued, implemented only a half-reformation. The "Radical Reformation" is more widely known as "Anabaptism" – a term which owes its origins to Zwingli. This term literally means "re-baptism," and refers to what was perhaps the most distinctive aspect of Anabaptist practice – the insistence that only those who had made a personal public profession of faith should be baptized. Infant baptism was not enough; a second baptism was necessary as the mark of an authentic Christian believer.

Strictly speaking, Anabaptism represents only one manifestation of the Radical Reformation. For example, the movement also included groups that were critical of the doctrine of the Trinity ("anti-Trinitarians"), which they regarded as unbiblical. Nevertheless, Anabaptism is the best known and most significant aspect of the Radical Reformation, and we shall retain the convention of using this term to refer loosely to the broader movement with which it is associated.

Although Anabaptism arose primarily in Germany and Switzerland, it subsequently became influential in other regions, such as the Lowlands. The movement produced relatively few theologians, partly because the movement was forcibly suppressed by civil authorities as being a threat to public order. The three most significant are generally agreed to be Balthasar Hubmaier (c. 1480–1528), Pilgram Marbeck (died 1556), and Menno Simons (1496–1561).

A number of common elements can be discerned within the various strands of the Anabaptist movement: a general distrust of external authority, the rejection of infant baptism in favor of the baptism of adult believers, the common ownership of property, and an emphasis upon pacifism and non-resistance. To take up one of these points: in 1527, the governments of the cities of Zurich, Bern, and St. Gallen accused the Anabaptists of believing "that no true Christian can either give or receive interest or income on a sum of capital; that all temporal goods are free and common, and that all can have full property rights to them."

It is for this reason that "Anabaptism" is often referred to as the "left wing of the Reformation" (Roland H. Bainton) or the "radical Reformation" (George Hunston Williams). For Williams, the "radical Reformation" was to be contrasted with the "magisterial Reformation," which he broadly identified with the Lutheran and Reformed movements.

Anabaptism seems to have first emerged within the city of Zurich, in the aftermath of Zwingli's reforms of the early 1520s (3.3.4). It centered on a group of individuals (especially Conrad Grebel, c. 1498–1526) who argued that Zwingli was not being faithful to his own reforming principles. He preached one thing, and practiced another. Although Zwingli pretended to accept the *sola scriptura* principle, Grebel argued, he retained a number of practices – including infant baptism, the close link between church and magistracy, and the participation of Christians in warfare – which were not sanctioned or ordained by Scripture. Grebel demanded consistency here. Either you limited yourself to what the Bible explicitly taught, or you allowed other ideas and practices which had an *implied* – but not an *actual* – biblical warrant. Grebel had no doubt about which of these was the correct approach.

In the hands of radical thinkers such as Grebel, the *sola scriptura* principle (3.2.1) became radicalized. Christians were to believe and practice only what was explicitly taught in Scripture. There was no place for tradition or continuity with the past in the interpretation of the Bible. Every individual or community was free to interpret the Bible without reference to the Christian past. Old traditions might well be little more than ancient mistakes. This view reflects the distinctive view of the Radical Reformation that the true church ceased to exist shortly after the period of the apostles. Why appeal to the views of past writers, when these either had tarnished credentials, or were not even proper Christians? This point is of considerable importance, and needs further comment.

For the magisterial reformers, such as Luther and Calvin, the task of the Reformation was to reform a church which had become corrupted or disfigured as a result of developments in the Middle Ages. The essential presupposition underlying this program should be noted carefully: *to reform a church is to presuppose that a church already exists.* Luther and Calvin were both clear that the medieval church was indeed a Christian church. It had lost its way and required to be reformed.

The theologians of the radical wing of the Reformation, however, did not share this basic assumption. For them, the church had simply ceased to exist. How could the church be reformed, when there was no longer a church? It needed restoration, not reformation. By "reforming" the medieval church, Luther had merely altered the external appearance of a corrupt institution which had no right to call itself a Christian church. There was, radical writers declared, a need to recreate the church by purging non-biblical practices and beliefs.

Anabaptist writers argued that a proper interpretation of the *sola scriptura* principle demanded that beliefs and practices – such as the baptism of infants – which were not specifically stated or endorsed in the Bible were to be uprooted. As the radical leader Balthasar Hubmaier (1480–1528) put this point in his *Dialogue with Zwingli* (November 1525): "Christ does not say, 'All plants which my heavenly Father has forbidden should be uprooted.' Rather he says, 'All plants which my heavenly Father has not planted should be uprooted.'"

Zwingli was alarmed by this radical approach to the interpretation of the Bible, which he saw as destabilizing. It threatened to cut the Reformed church at Zurich off from its historical roots and its continuity with the Christian tradition. Yet the Anabaptists had good reason to accuse Zwingli of compromise. In 1522, Zwingli wrote a work known as *Apologeticus Archeteles*, in which he recognized the idea of a "community of goods" as an authentic Christian ideal. "No-one calls any possessions his own," he wrote, "all things are held in common." But by 1525, Zwingli had changed his mind, and come round to the idea that private property was not such a bad thing, after all.

Probably the most influential document to emerge from the Radical Reformation is the Schleitheim Confession, drawn up by Michael Sattler (1490–1527) on February 24, 1527. The Confession takes its name from the small town of that name in the canton of Schaffhausen. Its function was to distinguish Anabaptists from those around them – supremely from what the document refers to as "papists and antipapists" (that is, unreformed Catholics and magisterial Protestants). In effect, the Schleitheim Confession amounts to "articles of separation" – that is to say, a set of beliefs and attitudes which distinguish Anabaptists from their opponents inside and outside the Reformation, and function as a core of unity, whatever their other differences might be.

Many princes and city councils regarded Anabaptism with a mixture of open contempt and hidden fear, especially when some within the movement began to proclaim the imminent return of Christ and the destruction of existing power structures. These were particularly serious concerns within the city of Strasbourg, which was home to a large community of Anabaptists. In 1530, a furrier named Melchior Hoffman began to preach that God had chosen Strasbourg as the New Jerusalem, and called for the overthrow of the city authorities. Alarm bells began to ring throughout the city.

The event that really galvanized nervous monarchs and city authorities throughout Europe took place in 1534, when Anabaptists took over the city of Münster. Anabaptist leaders declared that everyone remaining in the city would have to be rebaptized, or face execution. All property was to be distributed equally among the population. The seizure sent shock waves throughout the region. It was not until the spring of 1535 that the Anabaptist seizure of Münster was ended by force. The episode created intense hostility towards Anabaptism, which was now seen as a threat to social and national security and stability.

3.4.2.   The English Reformation: Henry VIII

Recent studies of English church life on the eve of the Reformation have pointed to its vitality and diversity. There is no doubt that there was some degree of internal dissatisfaction with the state of the English church in the late Middle Ages. Visitation records show a degree of concern on the part of English bishops over the low quality of the clergy, and misgivings over various aspects of church life. There were also clear signs of external dissatisfaction. Hostility towards the clergy in many places, most notably in London, was the cause of much concern. Nevertheless, animosity towards the clergy was by no means universal. In parts of England – such as Lancashire and Yorkshire – the clergy were, on the whole, well-liked, and there was no great enthusiasm for any radical change.

Luther's ideas began to be discussed in England in the early 1520s. Perhaps the greatest interest in his writings at this stage was among academics, particularly at Cambridge University. It is possible that this appeal may have been enhanced through the influence of Lollardy (2.4.4), a late medieval religious movement indigenous to England which was severely critical of many aspects of church life. Nevertheless, the evidence strongly points to the personal influence of Henry VIII having been of fundamental importance to the origins and subsequent direction of the English Reformation.

The background lies in Henry's concern to ensure a smooth transition of power after his death through producing a son as heir to the English throne. His marriage to Catherine

Figure 3.6 Henry VIII, king of England (1509–47), portrait 1536, by Hans Holbein the Younger (1497–1543). Resin tempera on wood, 26 × 19 cm. Thyssen-Bornemisza Collection. Photo: akg-images/André Held

of Aragon had produced a daughter, the future queen, Mary Tudor. The marriage had not only failed to produce the requisite son and heir; it also reflected the political realities of an earlier generation, which saw an alliance between England and Spain as essential to a sound foreign policy. The weakness of this assumption had become clear by 1525, when Charles V declined to marry Henry's daughter by Catherine. Henry therefore began the process by which he could divorce Catherine.

Under normal circumstances, this procedure might not have encountered any formidable obstacles. An appeal to the pope to annul the marriage could have been expected to have secured the desired outcome. However, the situation was anything but normal. Rome was under virtual siege by the army of Charles V, and the pope (Clement VII) was feeling somewhat insecure. Catherine of Aragon was the aunt of Charles V, and it was inevitable that the pope would wish to avoid offending the emperor at such a sensitive moment. The request for a divorce failed.

Henry's response was to begin a program of persuasion, designed to assert both the independence of England as a separate province of the church, and the autonomy of the English king. On November 3, 1529, Henry argued that the English clergy, by virtue of their support for Rome, were guilty of *praemunire* (a technical offense which can be thought of as a form of treason, in that it involves allegiance to a foreign power – namely, the pope). With this threat hanging over them, the clergy reluctantly agreed to at least some of Henry's demands for recognition of his ecclesiastical authority.

Henry was presented with an opportunity for the advancement of his aims when the archbishop of Canterbury, William Warham, died in August 1532. Henry replaced Warham with Thomas Cranmer, who had earlier indicated his strong support for Henry's divorce proceedings. Cranmer was finally consecrated as archbishop (possibly against his will) on March 30, 1533. Meanwhile, Henry had begun an affair with Anne Boleyn. Anne became pregnant in December 1532. The pregnancy raised all kinds of legal niceties. Henry's marriage to Catherine of Aragon was annulled by an English court in May 1533, allowing Anne to be crowned queen on June 1. Her daughter, Elizabeth Tudor, was born on September 7.

Henry now determined to follow through the course of action on which he had embarked, by which his supreme political and religious authority within England would be recognized. A series of Acts were imposed in 1534. The Succession Act declared that the crown would pass to Henry's children. The Supremacy Act declared that Henry was to be recognized as the "supreme head" of the English church. The Treasons Act made denial of Henry's supremacy an act of treason, punishable by death. This final act established the legal basis for the execution of two prominent Catholics, the statesman Sir Thomas More (1478–1535) and the bishop John Fisher (1469–1535), both of whom refused to recognize Henry as "supreme head" of the English church – a title which they believed belonged only to the pope.

These actions alienated the pope, and gave other Catholic states a pretext for military action against England. Henry now found himself under threat of invasion from neighboring Catholic nations. The mandate of restoring papal authority would have been a more than adequate pretext for either France or Spain to launch a crusade against England. Henry was thus obliged to undertake a series of defensive measures to ensure the nation's safety. These measures reached their climax in 1536. The dissolution of the monasteries provided Henry with funds for his military preparations. Negotiations with German Lutherans were begun with the object of entering into military alliances.

From this brief account of the origins of the English Reformation under Henry VIII, it will be clear that there are reasons for supposing that Henry's aims were of critical importance for the genesis of that Reformation. Henry's agenda was political, and was dominated by the desire to safeguard the succession. Theological ideas never played a dominant role in religious reform, as they had in Germany. This does not mean that Lutheran ideas were without influence in England. Many significant English churchmen were sympathetic to the new ideas, and made it a matter of principle to secure a favorable hearing for them in both church and society at large.

Yet the *origins* of Henry's reforming policies are not themselves religious in nature. Furthermore, the evidence indicates that Henry VIII remained fundamentally sympathetic to Catholicism throughout his life, despite his separation from Rome. Many of the tenuous reforms during his reign reflect his theological conservatism, and his desire to rein in reforming elements within his realm. Having declared himself, rather than the pope, as head of the English church, Henry had no further ecclesiastical agendas to pursue, apart from the economic exploitation of their resources, evident during the suppression and dissolution of the monasteries (1536–41).

In the end, the English Reformation under Henry VIII was an Act of State. The comparison with the situation in Germany is highly instructive. Luther's reformation was conducted on the basis of a theological foundation and platform. The fundamental impetus was religious (in that it addressed the life of the church directly) and theological (in that the proposals for reform rested on a set of theological presuppositions). In England, the reformation was primarily political and pragmatic. The reformation of the church was, in effect, the price paid by Henry (rather against his instincts) in order to secure and safeguard his personal authority within England.

3.4.3.   The English Reformation: Edward VI to Elizabeth I

With the death of Henry VIII, an important era in the English Reformation came to an end. In many ways, the first phase of the English Reformation was both driven and directed by the personal agendas of Henry, and the various compromises he was forced to make to ensure his succession. At the time of his death in January 1547, Henry had failed to make the fundamental changes which would institutionalize his reforms. The diocesan and parish structures of England had been left virtually as they were, particularly in relation to their forms of worship. Thomas Cranmer might well have had ambitious ideas for the reform of the liturgy and theology of the English church; Henry VIII gave him no opportunity to pursue them.

During the final years of Henry's reign, a subtle power struggle had developed within the court, with a clique based on Edward Seymour (c. 1500–52), brother of Jane Seymour (Henry VIII's third wife) gradually gaining the ascendancy. The Seymour family had strongly Protestant inclinations. As Edward VI was still a child on the death of his father, Henry VIII, his authority was delegated to the Privy Council, which was initially dominated by Seymour (who had by then become Duke of Somerset, and Lord Protector).

The Church of England now began to move in a distinctively Protestant direction. Cranmer, finally able to flex his theological muscles in a manner which had been impossible under Henry VIII, began to introduce a series of reforms moving the Church of England in a theological direction that was closer to the ideas associated with Zwingli and Zurich than with Luther and Wittenberg. Although English Protestants initially aligned themselves with Lutheranism, the Reformed form of Protestantism began to gain traction in the later 1540s.

Cranmer's changes included the revision of the Prayer Books in 1549 and again in 1552. The revisions proved to be of considerable importance, particularly in relation to eucharistic theology. Yet Cranmer was also responsible for a series of further developments, designed to consolidate Protestantism. Recognizing the theological weakness of the reforms introduced to date, Cranmer invited leading Protestant theologians from continental Europe to settle in England, and give a new theological direction and foundation to the English Reformation. Two of these appointments were of particular significance: Peter Martyr was appointed as Regius Professor of Divinity at Oxford University, and Martin Bucer as Regius Professor of Divinity at Cambridge University. Their arrival pointed to a new determination to align the English Reformation with its European counterpart, particularly its Reformed constituency. The Forty-Two Articles (1553) drawn up by Cranmer were strongly Protestant in orientation, as were the Book of Homilies (a set of approved sermons for delivery in parish churches).

Yet Edward's early death in 1553 put an end to this state-sponsored Protestantization of the English national church. Mary Tudor, who succeeded to the throne, appointed Reginald Pole – a loyal Catholic bishop deposed under Henry VIII – as archbishop of Canterbury. She put in place a series of measures designed to bring about a restoration of Catholicism within England. These measures became particularly unpopular when Cranmer was executed by being publicly burned at Oxford.

By then, most rich Protestants had fled England and sought refuge in Europe. Some eight hundred are known to have accepted exile in this way, waiting their chance to return to England and begin the Reformation all over again. While waiting for the death of Mary in exile in cities such as Geneva and Zurich, they came into contact with leading representatives of continental Protestantism, especially in its Reformed versions. This period of exile gave rise to a theologically literate and highly motivated Fifth Column that was merely awaiting an opportunity to put their ideas into practice. The famous Geneva Bible (1560) is an excellent example of the theological works which emerged from within these Protestant émigré communities.

Perhaps to their surprise, that opportunity came sooner rather than later. Mary Tudor and Reginald Pole both died on November 17, 1558. Both monarch and primate had been removed from the scene, which was now set for a radical change in direction. Henry VIII's will made it clear that the heir to the throne was his daughter. Elizabeth, initially cautious in revealing her religious inclinations, soon put in place measures to establish a "Settlement of Religion," which would eventually lead to the creation of a more explicitly Protestant state church.

The basic elements of this Settlement were the Act of Supremacy, which affirmed Elizabeth's sovereignty over the national church, and abolished any papal power; and the Act of Uniformity, which aimed to enforce religious uniformity throughout the nation, making church attendance compulsory on Sundays and saints' days. The effect of such measures was that the queen laid down what the church should believe, how it should be governed, and how its services were to be conducted.

Elizabeth's own religious inclinations were unquestionably Protestant. Nevertheless, she had no interest in causing offense to Catholic Spain, which might pose a significant military threat to England. This concern probably reflects her chosen title as "Supreme Governor" of the church: her refusal to be called "supreme head" avoided offending Protestants (who used this title to refer to Jesus Christ) or Catholics (who used it to refer to the pope). The Church of England would be reformed in its theology, yet catholic in its institutions, especially its episcopacy.

Elizabeth's "Settlement of Religion" was always precarious, relying much on veiled promises and hints of future favors and concessions which somehow never materialized. It was a political, rather than a theological, statement, aimed at generating consensus and stability, assisted to no small extent by theological vagueness or evasion. Elsewhere, Protestantism might be riven and cleft by theological disputes; England would be religiously undivided, at least publicly. The origins of what many now call "Anglicanism" belong to this period in English religious history.

3.4.4.   The Catholic Reformation: The Life of the Church

Reform was under way within Catholicism by the 1520s, partly in response to internal demands for renewal and overhaul, and partly in response to the perception that the new movement that would soon be known as "Protestantism" posed a serious threat to Catholicism, especially in parts of northern Europe. The term "Catholic Reformation" is often used to refer to an extended period of reform, renewal, and reconfiguration, lasting roughly a century, in which the Catholic church reasserted its influence and authority in the face of the Protestant threat. Many historians regard the Catholic Reformation as beginning with the opening of the Council of Trent in 1543, and ending with the close of the Thirty Years War in 1648.

Although some degree of internal reform had been under way within parts of the Catholic world since the 1490s, the rise of Protestantism catalyzed a systemic review of the church's life and thought throughout western Europe. While this renewal was partly driven by an internal recognition of the need for change within the church, the importance of external factors cannot be overlooked. In northern Europe, the Catholic Reformation generally expressed itself as a Counter-Reformation, concerned with neutralizing and reversing the impact of Protestantism in hitherto Catholic territories.

When the Catholic Reformation assumed this polemical nature, Protestantism was "the other." The term "Protestant" came to mean a third, deficient, and deviant form of Christianity, that was neither Catholic nor Orthodox. Catholics regarded the movement as an essentially homogeneous "non-church" that posed a clear and present danger to the *real* church. A group of essentially distinct, even potentially divergent movements were thus bracketed together for essentially polemical reasons, to encourage Catholic unity and vigilance. Their obvious differences were glossed over, in a generally successful attempt to portray Protestantism as a single, well-defined enemy – a serious threat that demanded Catholic unity if it was to be neutralized.

The reforming Council of Trent gave a new sense of theological direction and intellectual security to the church. The Council met during three separate periods: 1545–7, under Paul III; 1551–2, under Julius III; and 1562–3, under Pius IV. All of its decrees were formally confirmed by Pope Pius IV in 1564. Its reforming measures are widely seen as laying the basis for the consolidation of Catholicism in response to the rise of Protestantism.

So why was the Council of Trent not convened before 1543? Why did the Catholic church wait so long before calling a reforming council to engage with the challenges raised by the rise of Protestantism? The answer lies mainly in tensions between leading

Catholic nations resulting from a series of wars in the late fifteenth and early sixteenth centuries. These are often referred to as the "Italian Wars," although they are sometime known as the "Hapsburg–Valois Wars" after the main participants. The wars revolved around tensions between France and Spain, which spilled over into Italy. It would have been impossible to convene a council of leading bishops in Italy during such campaigns.

A further point which may help us understand the delay concerns the memory of the Conciliarist movement of the fifteenth century. At times, councils of bishops ended up challenging or undermining the authority of the pope. Furthermore, Luther's reforming program played into the Conciliarist agenda, in that it emphasized the importance of convening a reforming council to address issues of concern (2.4.2). By the time the Council of Trent began to meet, however, the situation had moved on, and these anxieties seem to have receded into the background.

The Council of Trent proposed a series of reforms in response to the challenge of Protestantism. Most obviously, clerical abuses were checked through a series of measures designed to eliminate the main causes of criticism and complaint. Bishops were now required to live in their dioceses, rather than being allowed to absent themselves in order to reside at court. Limits were placed on the "plurality of benefices" – the practice by which a priest might receive the income from several parishes, without residing in, or having any personal spiritual obligations towards, them all.

The emphasis placed within Protestantism on religious education led to the Catholic church introducing changes to ensure their clergy and congregations were at least as well schooled in the basics of the Catholic faith. Seminaries were established for the proper theological education and spiritual formation of priests. Peter Canisius's *Catechism* (1555) proved an especially effective challenge to its Protestant rivals.

Existing religious orders were reformed, and new ones established. The Carmelite order, founded in the late twelfth or early thirteenth century, is an example of a religious order to undergo reform in the aftermath of the Council of Trent. Teresa of Avilà (1515–82) and John of the Cross (1542–91) were instrumental in introducing greater rigor through the "discalced" movement within the order, which required its members to go barefoot. Both these writers achieved fame as spiritual writers, Teresa for her *Autobiography*, and John for his *Dark Night of the Soul*.

One of the most important new religious orders of the day was the Society of Jesus (4.1.6), founded by the Spanish knight Ignatius Loyola (1491–1556). Following a religious conversion experience while recovering from injuries received at the Battle of Pamplona (1521), Loyola conceived the idea of founding a new religious order "for the defence and propagation of the faith and for the progress of souls in Christian life and doctrine." Members of the Society of Jesus – traditionally known as "Jesuits" – became a leading force in the Counter-Reformation, and played a significant role in missionary work during the exploration of the Americas, India, and Asia in the later sixteenth century.

Yet the achievement of the Council of Trent went beyond reforming the life of the church. It also provided a firm statement of Catholic doctrine in the face of Protestant challenges.

Figure 3.7   Ignatius of Loyola (1491–1556), founder of the Society of Jesus. Copper engraving, 1621, by Lucas Vorstermann (1595–1675) after a contemporary portrait. Photo: akg-images/ullstein bild

3.4.5.   The Catholic Reformation: The Thought of the Church

Protestantism provided a challenge to Catholic teaching in a number of areas, of which the most important are the following:

1.   The critique of the Vulgate Latin version of the Bible, which was argued to be an inaccurate and unreliable translation of the original Hebrew and Greek texts.
2.   The assertion that the Bible could be understood by any pious person, and that neither the church nor the pope had any magisterial role to play in its interpretation.
3.   The rejection of any source of revelation beyond the Bible, which challenged the medieval view that there existed an "unwritten tradition" that was an additional source of knowledge of God.
4.   The Protestant doctrine of justification by faith alone was seen to challenge several core features of traditional Catholic teaching about the nature of justification.
5.   Protestantism recognized only two sacraments, and was severely critical of the doctrine of transubstantiation.

The Council of Trent provided a robust response to all these challenges, setting out the traditional Catholic position with clarity.

1.   The Vulgate translation of Scripture was affirmed to be reliable and authoritative. The council declared that "the old Latin Vulgate edition, which has been used for many centuries, has been approved by the church, and should be defended as authentic in public lectures, disputations, sermons or expositions, and that no one should dare or presume, under any circumstances, to reject it."

2.   The authority of the church to interpret Scripture was vigorously defended, against what the Council of Trent clearly regarded as the rampant individualism of Protestant interpreters (3.2.1). "No one, relying on his or her own judgement, in matters of faith and morals relating to Christian doctrine (distorting the Holy Scriptures in accordance with their own ideas), shall presume to interpret Scripture contrary to that sense which Holy Mother Church, to whom it belongs to judge of their true sense and interpretation, has held and now holds."

3.   The Council of Trent argued that Scripture could not be regarded as the only source of revelation. The role of unwritten traditions, originating from Christ and the apostles, had to be given due weight. "All saving truths and rules of conduct . . . are contained in the written books and in the unwritten traditions, received from the mouth of Christ himself or from the apostles themselves." Protestantism, Trent argued, had cut itself off from this second source of revelation. Furthermore, Protestant confusion over biblical interpretation reinforced the Catholic case for the church as the authorized interpreter of the Bible.

4.   A number of criticisms were directed against Protestant teaching on justification by faith (3.2.2). The most important are the following.

(a)   Protestantism mistakenly limited justification to the remission of sins, and failed to recognize that it embraced the idea of transformation and renewal. Protestantism defined justification as the event of the forgiveness of sins and imputation of righteousness, and sanctification as the process of making the believer righteous. Trent argued that justification included both this event and process. It was about making the believer righteous, both in reality and in the sight of God.

(b)   Justifying righteousness is not external to the believer, but is internal. It is on the basis of an imparted, not an imputed, righteousness that a believer is rendered acceptable to God.

(c)   Trent rejected what it called the "ungodly confidence" of the reformers in believing that they could be certain of their salvation. The Council conceded that no one should doubt God's goodness and generosity, but argued that the reformers erred seriously when they taught that "nobody is absolved from sins and justified unless they believe with certainty that they are absolved and justified, and that absolution and justification are effected by this faith alone." Trent insisted that "nobody can know with a certainty of faith which is not subject to error, whether they have obtained the grace of God."

5.   The Council of Trent reiterated that there were seven genuine sacraments, and vigorously defended both the doctrine and the terminology of transubstantiation against its Protestant critics (3.2.5). "By the consecration of the bread and wine a change is brought

about of the whole substance of the bread into the substance of the body of Christ and of the whole substance of the wine into the blood of Christ. This change the Holy Catholic church properly and appropriately calls transubstantiation."

It was one thing to set out such doctrinal statements; it was quite another to make sure that these were communicated effectively to parish priests and congregations. Recognizing the importance of this point, the council decided in 1546 to produce a catechism which would convey the basics of the Catholic faith, as clarified by Trent, to children and uneducated adults. Twenty years later, work began on this project under the leadership of Charles Borromeo (1538–84), archbishop of Milan. The resulting catechism was widely praised for its accessibility and clarity, and did much to counter the low levels of theological awareness then typical of many clergy and laity.

3.4.6. Women and the Reformation

The competing visions of Reformation jostling for influence across western Europe caused many traditional attitudes and beliefs to be reexamined. So what impact did these upheavals have on the status and roles of women? This question remains controversial, partly because of the difficulty in establishing reliable data on the one hand, and interpreting the material on the other. At present, the general scholarly consensus is that the sixteenth century was neither uniformly beneficial or detrimental to women; in some ways, things were better; in others, worse.

One significant change took place at the level of religious iconography. Devotion to the Virgin Mary – often referred to as "Marian devotion" – had a deep popular appeal in the Middle Ages. Mary was seen as a mediator between God and humanity – one of the greatest saints of the church, to whom churches were dedicated throughout Europe. Popular piety often focused on this female figure. The form of prayer known as the "Rosary" (Latin: *rosarium*, "a rose garden"), which probably dates from the fourteenth century, became a highly popular Christian imaginative prayer, focusing on Mary. Protestantism dismantled this Marian emphasis, thus effectively removing female iconography from the devotional life of churches and individuals.

As we noted earlier, two institutions offered women significant social and religious roles during the Middle Ages: royalty, and religious orders (2.2.8). The social upheavals of the sixteenth century involved many changes to the social fabric of western Europe. For example, the power of city councils increased considerably, and gave a new social prominence to the rising mercantile classes. These economically active middle classes posed a challenge to the traditional authority of the aristocracy.

Yet these upheavals had relatively little impact on royalty. Royal families might change their religious allegiance; this did not, however, bring the institution of royalty into question. Royal women played a significant role within both Catholicism and Protestantism, having considerable impact on the shaping of national religious identity. As we noted earlier (3.4.3), Mary Tudor, queen of England from 1553 to 1558, was instrumental in reasserting Catholicism in England; her half-sister Elizabeth, queen of England from 1558 to 1603, steered England in a firmly Protestant direction. Other royal women played significant roles at this time – such as Catherine de Medici (1519–89) of France, Jeanne d'Albret of Navarre (1528–72), and Mary Queen of Scots (1542–87).

The second institution which gave women a significant voice during the Middle Ages were female religious orders. The reform of the religious orders which resulted from the Council of Trent is generally agreed to have strengthened their positions, and given increased respect to abbesses and prioresses. Women religious authors, such as Teresa of Avilà (1515–82), came to exercise considerable spiritual influence. Teresa's *Interior Castle of the Soul* was widely admired, partly on account of its controlling image. The spiritual life is to be compared to the exploration of a complex castle, in which doors lead into courtyards that bring the explorer closer to its center.

The Protestant Reformation, with its emphasis on living out the Christian life in the everyday world, had little time for religious orders. In 1525, Martin Luther married a former nun, Katharina von Bora (1499–1552). Katharina had been a nun at the Cistercian convent of Marienthron, but had become disillusioned with the religious life, seeing marriage as a better option. Religious orders either dwindled into insignificance or were forcibly suppressed in Protestant territories. As a result, women were denied a significant leadership role within both church and society at large. Protestant churches retained exclusively male leadership models, forcing women into the background.

This was counterbalanced by the Protestant emphasis of the importance of marriage, and especially the role of women in running households. This was often seen as a social and commercial partnership, symbolized by commissioning "diptych portraits" – a single painting depicting both husband and wife, with equal emphasis being given to both. This partnership of husband and wife stood at the heart of the household. The correspondence between a prosperous Nuremberg couple, Magdalena Paumgartner (1555–1642) and her husband Balthasar Paumgartner (1551–1600), illustrates how they shared the rule of their household, the rearing of their children, and the management of their business operations. Many commercial operations would continue to be run by widows after the death of their husbands, partly out of economic necessity, but partly because of their existing experience of managing such enterprises.

The religious empowerment of women as result of Protestantism is suggested by the high profile of female advocates of reform, who often attracted considerable followings. Argula von Grumbach (1492–1554), a Bavarian noblewoman, was incensed when the University of Ingolstadt attempted to repress Protestantism. She wrote a forceful letter to the rector and senate of the university, demanding that they reconsider their views. The letter was published as a pamphlet in 1523, and went through fourteen editions in two months.

One of the more disturbing features of the sixteenth and seventeenth century was its obsession with witches, who were seen as a serious threat to public wellbeing. Yet the origins of this trend are to be traced back to the later Middle Ages, especially the *Malleus Maleficarum* ("Hammer of Witches"), published in 1484. This book, written by Heinrich Kramer (c. 1430–1505), an inquisitor who seems to have had an obsession with the sexual habits of "witches," is generally thought to have contributed to the popular fascination with magic and the occult, which continued in later periods. In practice, those accused of being "witches" often appear to have been older women, usually widows, often living alone.

Although this obsession was particularly prevalent in Germany, the most notorious incident took place in colonial North America. The Salem Witch Trials of 1692, instigated by the clergy of a small village in colonial Massachusetts, resulted in the execution of nineteen people. The British governor, Sir William Phips (1641–95), eventually put an end to the hysteria, which eventually led to clerical apologies and recantations which seriously diminished the standing and reputation of the town's clergy.

As this brief discussion makes clear, the question of the status of women as a result of the Protestant Reformation is complex, and not easily summarized in snappy slogans. In some ways, women prospered as a result of the new religious outlook; in others, their potential for leadership was reduced.

3.5.   The Post-Reformation Era

The Reformation marked a landmark in western European religious, social, and political history. So what was its impact on subsequent developments? How did the currents of thought and practice developed during this period of radical religious change work out in the longer term? In the present section, we shall consider the impact of the Reformation on the shape of Christianity in western Europe and beyond.

3.5.1.   Confessionalism: The Second Reformation

European Protestantism underwent significant development after the death of John Calvin in 1564, partly in response to the changing political context. European monarchs became increasingly aware of the threat of destabilization of their nations and regions through religious controversies. It became increasingly common for European nations to impose religious uniformity as a means of containing these tensions. As we saw earlier, this was the situation that developed in England under Elizabeth I (3.4.3). There would be one "official" or "established" church, with Elizabeth as its "supreme governor." No religious alternatives would be permitted.

A similar process can be seen taking place elsewhere in Europe, especially in Germany during the 1560s and 1570s. The terms "Confessionalization" or "the Second Reformation" are often used to refer to this process of aligning religious beliefs and practices with the objectives of the state. The basic idea was that of a territorial religion based on an authorized declaration of doctrines (usually referred to as a "Confession of Faith"), which would be binding on all subjects and enforced by an established church which was accountable to the prince or the magistrates.

This led to growing demand for a legally defined and enforceable system of beliefs and practices. As a result, "state churches" began to develop, leading to greater social cohesion. In many ways, this can be seen as a redevelopment of the medieval idea of Christendom, but now implemented at the regional, rather than continental, level. Each region was a mini-Christendom, governed by its own particular understanding of what Christianity actually was. Although these regional churches regarded the Bible and creeds as having supreme importance, they also recognized the importance of local "Confessions of Faith," which identified the specific beliefs or practices of these regional churches.

The emergence of these Protestant "state churches" was a response to the situation in Germany in the 1570s. Whatever its benefits, it created a link between the church and political power which would prove problematic in years to come. Protestant churches were now part of the establishment, with vested interests that might easily compromise its integrity. The phenomenon of the "state church" might well have helped achieve political and social stability in the short term; in the longer term, it helped to create the conditions for wars of religion, because of the connections forged between religion and natural identity. A link had been created between theological beliefs and the state.

Many religious beliefs and practices, which earlier had been considered as "matters of indifference" (*adiaphora*; 3.2.4), now became treated as criteria of demarcation between the emerging Protestant confessional churches. The need to distinguish the two major confessional churches of the age – Lutheranism and Calvinism – led to differences being sought. Once these differences had been identified, they were often given an emphasis which reflected a need to draw a line between one church and another. The result was that differences in theology, liturgy, or church government became explicitly politicized as the early modern state sought to impose greater social control within its sphere of influence.

By the 1590s, there seemed little doubt as to which of the two major forms of Protestantism was gaining the ascendancy in western Europe. By 1591, Calvinism seemed to have made irreversible gains throughout Europe. The rise of Calvin's vision of Protestantism forced Lutheranism to define and defend itself against two rivals, instead of its traditional single opponent – Catholicism. Both Lutheran and Reformed communities now defined themselves by doctrinal formulations. The Heidelberg Catechism (1563), widely regarded as one of the finest Protestant pedagogical documents, was a Reformed catechism developed in Germany during this period, aimed at teaching its readers both the truth of Calvin's vision of theology, and the errors of his Lutheran and Catholic opponents.

The rise of Protestant orthodoxy dates from this period, and reflects a growing concern to develop robust theological systems, similar to those of medieval scholasticism. Beliefs were codified, and set out in works of dogmatic theology. Lutherans argued that their vision of theology was superior to those of Catholicism and Calvinism, and demonstrated this through theological polemics which went over the heads of most ordinary religious believers.

These tensions between Lutheran and Reformed churches in Germany can be seen as the inevitable outcome of a quest for self-definition on the part of two ecclesial bodies within the same geographical region, both claiming to be legitimate outcomes of the Reformation. At the social and political level, the communities were difficult to distinguish; doctrine therefore provided the most reliable means by which they might define themselves over and against one another. The notion of a core concept of "Protestantism," with two major branches, became difficult to sustain, given the embittered hostility between the two factions, and their open competition for territory and influence.

Perhaps more importantly, given the central role of the Bible for Protestantism (3.2.1), this new trend meant that the Bible tended to be read through the prism of "confessions" –

statements of faith, which frequently influenced, and sometimes determined, how certain passages of the Bible were to be interpreted. This shift was a contributing factor to the rise of "proof-texting," in which isolated, decontextualized verses of the Bible were cited in support of often controversial confessional positions. Paradoxically, this development actually lessened the influence of the Bible within Protestantism, in that its statements were accommodated to existing doctrinal frameworks, rather than being allowed to determine, and even to challenge them.

As a result, pressure grew to find ways of placing clear blue water between the two forms of Protestantism, to avoid any confusion between them. As the intellectual warfare between Lutheran and Calvinist polemic intensified, two areas of doctrine emerged as potentially reliable demarcators: the doctrine of predestination, and the concept of the "real presence." In each case, there was a clear distinction between the Lutheran and Calvinist position.

3.5.2.   Puritanism in England and North America

As we noted earlier, Elizabeth I created a form of Protestantism that emphasized its continuity with the Christian past, retaining a remarkable amount of organization, custom, and tradition from the pre-Reformation era (3.4.3). Much to the irritation of more radical English Protestants, influenced by developments in Calvin's Geneva (3.3.5), Elizabeth retained bishops and insisted on distinctive clergy dress. The traditional ecclesiastical structuring of dioceses with their bishops, and parishes with their parish priests continued to function. An ordered and uniform liturgy was prescribed by the Book of Common Prayer.

The term "Puritanism" now began to be used to refer to dissident Protestants within the Church of England, who wanted to implement Calvin's vision of Protestantism within England. They objected to many aspects of the "Elizabethan Settlement," and campaigned against what they regarded as unacceptable beliefs and practices. For a start, they wanted to get rid of bishops, who they considered to be a vestige of medieval Catholicism. They also objected to the practice of making the sign of the cross in baptism, the wearing of clerical robes, using a ring in the marriage service, and bowing at the name of Jesus. All these were unbiblical, they argued, and therefore could not be imposed on any minister of the church.

The impact of Puritanism on Elizabethan England was slight. However, Elizabeth's death plunged England into religious uncertainty. When it was announced that Elizabeth would be succeeded by James VI of Scotland, English Puritans believed their moment had come. James had earlier supported the reforms of the Calvinist preacher and reformer John Knox (1514–72) who had created a Scottish reformed church modeled on Calvin's Geneva. Surely he could be relied upon to do the same in England? The Puritans decided to seize the initiative, and steal a march on their Anglican opponents.

On his way from Edinburgh to London in April 1603, James was met by a Puritan delegation, who presented him with the "Millenary Petition," signed by more than one thousand ministers of the Church of England. They had, they declared, served their church faithfully, despite their serious misgivings concerning its practices; the time had now come to change things.

In the end, James I managed to marginalize Puritanism. The Puritans were offered scraps of consolation and promises of future change which either never materialized, or amounted to surprisingly little. As we shall see, James promised a new English translation of the Bible, which some Puritans may unwisely have hoped would strengthen their position. When the famous "King James Version" was published in 1611 (3.5.3), it turned out to use the traditional language favored by Anglicans, rather than the more radical terms preferred by Puritans. We shall consider this famous translation of the Bible in the following section.

Puritanism might have been checked in terms of its influence in England. It was, however, far from being a spent force. It continued to develop during the reigns of James I and Charles I, fueled by growing popular resentment at the autocratic behavior of the monarchy. Both James I and Charles I justified their actions through an appeal to the "divine right of kings." Puritan writers had little difficulty in challenging this notion, pointing out both its lack of biblical warrant and its unacceptable implications of royal absolutism. For Puritan critics, the king's excesses highlighted the virtues of the republicanism of Calvin's Geneva. The idea of republicanism began to gain political traction among England's increasingly alienated gentry. Yet it was not until the 1640s that its moment would come.

Yet Puritanism was no longer limited to England. In the first half of the seventeenth century, during the reigns of James I and Charles I, Puritans began to leave their native England to seek a new life in the American colonies. There, they believed, they would be able to live out their religious vocations without fear of persecution or oppression. They were like the people of Israel, leaving behind the bondage of Egypt and journeying to the promised land.

One such wave of emigration achieved iconic status. In 1607 or 1608, a Puritan congregation from the Nottinghamshire town of Scrooby, weary of the hostile religious policies of James I, migrated to Amsterdam, which had by then displaced Geneva as the center of the Reformed world. In 1609, they moved on to Leiden, where they developed a sense of identity as God's chosen people, aliens in a strange land. Never regarding themselves as Dutch, and unwilling to return to the hostile ecclesiastical environment of England, they conceived a solution, as desperate as it was brilliant. Those of their number who believed that they were called to do so would travel to the American colony of Virginia, and establish a settlement in the Hudson Valley.

After an initial unsuccessful attempt to set sail in a smaller vessel, they left Plymouth in the *Mayflower*. Due to a navigation error, the "Pilgrim Fathers" arrived at Cape Cod, Massachusetts, in November 1620, some considerable distance north of their intended destination. A month later, they finally landed at Plymouth Rock, and established a community there. The Puritan settlement of New England was under way.

Between 1627 and 1640 some four thousand individuals made the hazardous crossing of the Atlantic Ocean, and settled on the coastline of Massachusetts Bay. For these settlers, there was a clear alignment between the narratives of their journey and that of the Bible. England was the land in which they struggled under oppression; America would be the land in which they found freedom. Expelled from their Egypt by a cruel pharaoh (as they saw both James I and Charles I), they had settled in a promised land flowing with milk and honey. They would build a new Jerusalem, a city upon a hill, in this strange land. The Pilgrim Fathers were an inspiration to many who followed them to the new world.

The Pilgrim Fathers were not, it must be appreciated, typical of English Puritanism at this time. They were separatists, with beliefs more characteristic of the Anabaptists than of Calvin, convinced that each congregation had the democratic right to determine its own beliefs and choose its own ministers. Most English Puritans of the age were Presbyterian, committed to the notion of a single mother church with local outposts – a "universal church" with "particular congregations," bound together by shared beliefs and leaders. It was only a matter of time before the defining conflicts of the Old World would find themselves being replayed in the New. But this time, decentralization would win.

One of the most remarkable features of the early history of New England Protestantism in the 1620s and 1630s is that most Puritan communities appear to have abandoned a Presbyterian view of church government within months of their arrival, and adopted a congregational polity instead. The Plymouth Colony Separatists appear to have been significant in bringing about a major shift in how congregations organized themselves and related to other congregations.

Reacting strongly against the rigid hierarchical structures of the European state churches, the American settlers opted instead for a democratic congregationalism. Local congregations made their own decisions. Instead of centralized authority structures – such as presbyteries or dioceses – the Puritans of the Massachusetts Bay area developed a highly decentralized congregational church order. The new situation in America thus allowed the unfettered exploration of religious possibilities that were simply unthinkable in England, leading to diversification of religious beliefs and customs in response to local circumstances.

Roger Williams (1603–84) was one of the leading proponents of a pure separatist church, arguing that the Church of England was apostate, and that any kind of fellowship with it – whether in England or in America – was a serious sin. Christian believers were under an obligation to separate from apostate churches and from a secular state. Church and state should be separate; above all, the state should not be able to enforce the first four of the Ten Commandments. Disenchanted by Massachusetts' unwavering commitment to the mutual interpenetration of church and state, Williams established the colony of Rhode Island in 1636, insisting upon complete religious freedom – extending this far beyond traditional Christian denominations to embrace Jews and other religious minorities.

3.5.3.   The King James Bible (1611)

One of the landmark religious and literary achievements of the English church was the production of a new translation of the Bible, published in 1611. The King James Bible, as it has come to be known, stands in a long line of English translations, beginning with William Tyndale's translation of the New Testament in 1525, and continuing through the Great Bible of 1539, and the Bishops' Bible of 1568. In view of the enormous cultural significance of this translation, we shall consider its origins and style.

The origins of the new translation lay in James I's desire to secure religious peace in England in the opening years of his reign. The Hampton Court Conference of January

1604 was convened by James in an attempt to secure some degree of religious consensus towards the beginning of his reign, and to show willingness on his part to hear the concerns of the Puritan party (3.5.2). On the final day of the conference, in what seems to have been a totally unexpected development, James announced his decision that there would be a new English translation of the Bible. The reasons for this decision remain unclear. There was no pressure for any such translation from either Anglicans or Puritans. James clearly believed, however, that such a new translation of the Bible would help secure religious unity within England.

The decision to translate having been taken, James I entrusted the process to Richard Bancroft (1544–1610), archbishop of Canterbury. Bancroft recruited some fifty translators to undertake this process, including the regius professors of Greek and Hebrew from Oxford and Cambridge. Two were based at Westminster, in London; two at Cambridge; and two at Oxford. Three of these "companies of translators" were assigned to the Old Testament; two to the New Testament; and one to the Apocrypha. In 1610, each company sent representatives to a central meeting at Stationers' Hall in London, at which the translations were presented for comment and improvement.

Bancroft had limited the freedom of his translators by laying down certain "rules" which would govern their translation. He was fully aware that certain English terms – such as "church" or "bishop" – were heavily freighted with significance (3.2.3). Puritans would much prefer that these were replaced with words more adapted to their own agendas – such as "congregation," and "supervisors" or "overseers." In using this modified vocabulary, Puritans hoped that any popular belief that the existing structures of the Church of England rested on firm biblical foundations would be undermined.

Bancroft therefore insisted that the traditional vocabulary would continue to be used: "The old ecclesiastical words to be kept, namely, as the word *church* not to be translated *congregation &c.*" Verbal alterations to the text of Scripture, as Bancroft wisely realized, could become the prelude to structural alterations to the established forms of church life. Retention of traditional ecclesiastical language came to be seen as a bulwark against the agenda of more radical reformers – such as the increasingly influential Puritan wing of the established church.

Bancroft also made sure that the translators would not start their translations from ground zero, with complete freedom to render passages as they saw best. They were required to base themselves on earlier English translations, which they might improve where necessary, but could not disregard. This forestalled any suspicion of radical innovation or whimsical changes on the part of the translators.

The King James translators generally produced a literal translation of the original biblical text, offering an English word for every word of the Greek or Hebrew originals, even when this might have seemed strange to English ears. For example, consider the following familiar text concerning the reaction of the Wise Men to seeing the star of Bethlehem: "they rejoiced with exceeding great joy" (Matthew 2:10). The rhythm of the resulting English prose is slightly curious, and might be judged by some to read less satisfactorily than Tyndale's more natural translation of 1525: "they were marvellously glad." Yet the Second Oxford Company of translators chose to render each element of the original Greek precisely as they found it. For every Greek word in the original, King James's translators offered an English equivalent, even duplicating the root "joy," when this could easily have been avoided.

This literal translation underlies two of the more interesting features of the King James Bible. Perhaps the more obvious is easily noted by anyone who has looked at printed editions of this Bible – namely, that words added by the translators to bring out the meaning of the text, but which are not themselves present in the original, are typeset in such a way that they are visually distinguished from the remainder of the text. The translators felt it right to make an absolute distinction between the biblical text itself, and those slight additions they felt obligated to make to bring out its true meaning, even if the interposed words were generally uncontroversial. The "word of God" would be set in Black Letter type, conveying the solid impression of an official declaration; any supplementary words of the translators would be typeset in a smaller, less prominent typeface, thus both conceding their syntactical necessity while at the same time indicating their lesser *theological* importance.

The King James translators also tended to retain some verbal characteristics of the original texts, even where these were generally better and more accurately expressed in English through minor alterations. For example, a number of phrases were translated directly from the original Hebrew or Greek, without any attempt to adapt them to the normal patterns of spoken English. Most of these were repeated from earlier translations, particularly Tyndale. Familiar examples from the Hebrew include: "to lick the dust" (Psalm 72:9; Isaiah 49:23; Micah 7:17); "to fall flat on his face" (Numbers 22:31); "a man after his own heart" (1 Samuel 13:14); "to pour out one's heart" (Psalm 62:8; Lamentations 2:19); and "the land of the living" (Job 28:13; Psalm 27:13; Psalm 52:5). From the Greek, we might note "the powers that be" (Romans 13:1) and "a thorn in the flesh" (2 Corinthians 12:7).

The impact of such literal translation of Hebrew and Greek phrases was thus to cause English to adapt in order to accommodate them. Despite their initial strangeness, such terms became accepted through increased familiarization and use, becoming naturalized in the English language and enriching its voice. This was clearly an unintended consequence of the translation process, which is known to have raised concerns at the time. Yet the growing familiarity of the King James Bible led to its more memorable phrases being picked up and incorporated, particularly at the literary level. Later generations generally had no idea that standard set English phrases such as "the apple of my eye," a "den of thieves," or "led like a lamb to the slaughter" reflected fundamentally Hebraic modes of speech.

This important English translation is widely regarded as a literary and cultural landmark, and is an important illustration of how religious ideas and texts can have a significant cultural impact. This naturally leads us to consider the broader impact of the theological ideas of this period on the shaping of culture.

3.5.4. Christianity and the Arts

The medieval Catholic church was encountered by ordinary people primarily through its practices and images. While few read works of theology, the liturgy of the church offered them both spectacle and instruction, drama and dogma, in a highly accessible form which reaffirmed the medieval worldview (2.3.8), and the proper place of the institutional church as the only means of salvation. The drama of the liturgy was supplemented by images – often images of gospel scenes, painted on church walls, illustrating these scenes for the benefit of those who could not read.

The importance of the arts in mediating Christian ideas and values to the people was widely recognized in the Middle Ages, and would continue to be affirmed by the Catholic church in the sixteenth and seventeenth centuries. The architecture of churches was seen as an important way of embodying and affirming religious values and ideas. The Council of Trent (3.4.4–5) criticized artists who used elaborate techniques which lessened the religious impact of their works. But there was no doubt of the importance the council attributed to art in encouraging personal devotion and helping theological reflection. The Catholic Reformation witnessed a renaissance of religious art and music.

Protestantism, however, moved in a very different direction, tending to limit art and music to secular contexts. The Protestant critique of Catholic art reflected both hostility towards the theology that it embodied, and the means used for expressing it. While Luther and his circle remained persuaded of the importance of religious art in propagating the ideas and values of the Reformation, both Zwingli and Calvin regarded it as tantamount to idolatry. Images of any kind would be rigorously excluded from Reformed churches, which often had undecorated, whitewashed walls (3.3.4).

However, the Reformed hostility to pictorial representations of God was fundamentally theological in its foundation, and did not extend to other subject matters. No significant restrictions were placed upon the activities of Reformed artists outside the specific sphere of ecclesiastical ornamentation. John Calvin was perfectly clear on this matter: painting and sculpture were perfectly permissible – he even called them "gifts of God" – provided that the objects represented were "visible to our eyes." Calvinist painters might thus well find themselves having serious theological misgivings about representing God in their paintings; they had no such difficulties with the enterprise of painting itself. Other possibilities lay wide open to them, as the emerging interest in landscapes, townscapes, domestic scenes, and portraits characteristic of seventeenth-century Flemish art makes clear.

There were also mixed views within Protestantism over how music was to be used in church. Luther saw no difficulty about using music in worship: "Next to the Word of God, music deserves the highest praise," he wrote. "I do not believe that all the arts should be removed or forbidden on account of the Gospel, as some fanatics suggest. On the contrary, I would gladly see all arts, especially music, in the service of Him who has given and created them."

Luther urged others within the reforming movement to write hymns based upon the Psalms, in order that the whole of Christendom might be enlightened and inspired. Luther's best-known hymn is a paraphrase of Psalm 46, which opens with the words "God is our refuge and strength, a very present help in trouble." Luther's, set to a tune of his own composing, became a landmark in Christian hymnody: "A mighty fortress is our God."

This hymn is important in another respect, in that it represents an example of Luther's most significant liturgical innovation – the "chorale." This was a piece of German-language verse in stanza form, generally set to music similar to that of popular German secular songs of the period, and sung by the whole congregation during church services. The first such collection appeared in 1524 as the *Little Book of Spiritual Songs*, which includes "A mighty fortress." The chorale tradition was raised to new heights in later Lutheranism by Johann Sebastian Bach.

From the reign of Edward VI, English Protestantism tended to follow the Reformed, rather than Lutheran, model. The Psalms were seen as a divinely authorized hymnal, providing resources for the praise of God. Luther's use of hymns was dismissed as implying that God's work was incomplete or inadequate. Worship might therefore include a psalmody, but not a hymnody. Furthermore early English psalmody was almost exclusively vocal. Most Reformed clergy believed that instruments were appropriate only for secular music, and not for public worship. The psalms were therefore sung without accompaniment – not unlike the plainchant of medieval monasteries.

Wherever possible, the Church of England directed that the words of the psalms would be chanted, not paraphrased, despite the metrical difficulties that this created for singing. This non-metrical approach preserved the integrity of the actual words of Scripture, and required no alteration of the biblical text – always a theologically sensitive issue in the Reformed tradition.

Yet the fundamental Protestant desire to involve all believers in the worship of the church soon led to the development of paraphrased psalms that could be sung by congregations to easily learned tunes. The psalm text was now retranslated, not in order to achieve total verbal accuracy, but to render it in a poetic meter so that it could be sung to tunes. The simplicity of these metered tunes made it easier to sing *and remember* the psalms – one of the key goals of Protestants.

In England, John Day produced a *Book of Psalms* (1562), based on psalm texts translated by Thomas Sternhold, John Hopkins, and others, with tunes drawn from the *Genevan Psalter* and from familiar English sources, including popular ballads. Day's *Psalms* remained in general use for more than two hundred and fifty years, and is thought to have gone through more than five hundred editions. Perhaps the most famous paraphrase of all is found in the *Scots Psalter* of 1650, authorized for general use by the Church of Scotland. This collection of paraphrases of all 150 psalms includes the following familiar version of Psalm 23.

> The Lord's my shepherd, I'll not want.
> He makes me down to lie
> In pastures green: he leadeth me
> the quiet waters by.

In Germany, theological divisions within Protestantism over the role of church music caused no small problems for professional musicians, including Johann Sebastian Bach (1685–1750). Although Bach dates from a slightly later period, the issues he encountered were the direct result of the religious developments noted in this chapter. As Bach's career led him throughout Germany, the musical implications of German "Confessionalization" became increasingly clear. Confessional differences between regions of Germany resulted in very different attitudes towards music in Christian worship.

As a devout Lutheran, Bach saw his task as setting the Bible to music in such a way that its meaning and power might be fully appreciated by congregations. By this time, Lutheranism had developed a rich musical tradition, which Bach augmented further, particularly through his Cantatas and Passions. Bach's last and greatest appointment was as organist and choir-master at the Lutheran Thomaskirche in Leipzig. Major works which date from this period include the Magnificat in D, the St. John Passion, the St. Matthew Passion, the B-Minor Mass, and the Christmas Oratorio. Yet not all of Bach's appointments were in Lutheran contexts.

From 1717 to 1723, however, Bach was employed at the Reformed court of Anhalt-Köthen. Though the court was strongly supportive of music, their Reformed views dictated that it should not be used in public worship. Bach thus found himself focusing on secular works during this period, in that he was unable to express his musical talents liturgically. Bach used this period to write the six Brandenburg Concertos, and the first book of the Well Tempered Clavier. It proved to be an enormously productive period of his life, even if he was not able to exercise his art in his own favored context – congregational worship.

3.5.5.   Christianity and the Sciences

It is widely agreed that the "Scientific Revolution" of the late seventeenth century was of major importance in shaping modern culture. There is much to be said for this view, and we shall consider the role of Christianity in catalyzing this development in a later chapter. Yet the Scientific Revolution built upon developments during the later Middle Ages, and especially during the sixteenth century. One theme that is known to have been significant in catalyzing the emergence of the scientific method is the fundamental Christian belief that the universe has been created with an inbuilt ordering which can be grasped and represented by the human mind.

The field of science most affected by Christianity in the sixteenth and early seventeenth centuries was astronomy. The retrieval of ancient scientific works from Arabic or Greek sources in the early Middle Ages (2.3.2) led to considerable interest being taken in the views of the Egyptian astronomy Ptolemy, who held that the earth is at the center of the universe, and that all heavenly bodies rotate in circular paths around the earth. This geocentric view was regarded as scientifically established, and was incorporated into medieval biblical exegesis. The Bible was interpreted on the assumption that the earth stood at the center of the universe.

Yet during the sixteenth century, this view began to be challenged. It became clear that Ptolemy's theory could not account for detailed observational evidence that had built up in the early sixteenth century. Initially, the theory was modified by the introduction of a complicated and rather clumsy series of "circles within circles" (technically known as "epicycles"). But some began to suggest that a better way of thinking about things would have to be found.

Nicholas Copernicus (1473–1543), a Polish scholar, argued that the planets moved in concentric circles around the sun. The earth, in addition to rotating about the sun, also rotated on its own axis. The apparent motion of the stars and planets was thus due to a combination of the rotation of the earth on its own axis, and its rotation around the sun. In the end, it was found that Copernicus's heliocentric theory could not account for the observational evidence. Yet it initiated a theological debate that is relevant to our discussion.

The suggestion that the earth rotated around the sun was seen by some Christian theologians as incompatible with the Bible. Advocates of a geocentric way of looking at things claimed that there were biblical passages which clearly stated that the earth is in a state of rest, and it is the sun that moves. Examples of such texts include Psalm 93:1: "[God] has established the world; it shall never be moved." This was understood in a spatial sense, meaning that the earth does not physically move.

The real problem was that the Christian church had tended to read the Bible from a geocentric perspective, and had assumed that the Bible endorsed this perspective. As a result, biblical passages were interpreted in a way that was consistent with a geocentric way of looking at things, even when this was not actually required by the text itself. For example, the text just noted – "[God] has established the world; it shall never be moved" – was interpreted as implying that the earth was stationary. In fact, the text refers simply to the stability of the earth.

The church's reading of the Bible thus had to be liberated from such geocentric presuppositions. Yet the problem was deeper than this. In the first place, it was necessary to avoid treating the Bible as some sort of scientific textbook; in the second, the church found that it had to counter excessively literal readings of biblical passages which seemed to endorse geocentric outlooks.

These obstacles were overcome through an approach whose origins can be traced back to John Calvin in the 1540s. Calvin encouraged the scientific study of nature by emphasizing the orderliness of creation. Both the physical world and the human body testify to the wisdom and character of God. More importantly, Calvin argued that the Bible is primarily concerned with the knowledge of Jesus Christ. It is not an astronomical, geographical, or biological textbook. And when the Bible is interpreted, it must be borne in mind that God "adjusts" to the capacities of the human mind and heart.

This idea of "accommodation" was not invented by Calvin, but has a long history of use in biblical interpretation, Christian and Jewish. God chose to use words in Scripture which represented an accommodation or adaptation to the non-technical perspectives of the readers. Certain passages in the Bible use language and imagery which were appropriate to the cultural conditions of its original audience. These were not to be taken "literally," Calvin suggested, but were rather to be interpreted by extracting the key ideas which have been expressed in forms and terms which are specifically adapted or "accommodated" to the original audience. The Bible might seem to say that the sun goes round the earth – but that is simply an adaptation of speech.

The impact of Calvin's approach upon scientific theorizing, especially during the seventeenth century, was considerable. For example, the English scientific writer Edward Wright (1558–1615) defended Copernicus's heliocentric theory of the solar system against biblical literalists by arguing, in the first place, that Scripture was not concerned with physics, and in the second, that its manner of speaking was "accommodated to the understanding and way of speech of the common people, like nurses to little children." Both these arguments derive directly from Calvin, who may be argued to have made a fundamental contribution to the emergence of the natural sciences in this respect.

Yet the controversy over a heliocentric view was not limited to Protestantism. Within Catholicism, controversy arose over the views of Galileo Galilei (1564–1642), who mounted a major defense of the Copernican theory of the solar system. Galileo's views were initially received sympathetically within senior church circles, partly on account of the fact that he was held in high regard by a papal favorite, Giovanni Ciampoli (1589–1643). Ciampoli's fall from power led to Galileo losing support within papal circles, and is widely regarded as opening the way to Galileo's condemnation by his enemies.

Although the controversy centering on Galileo is often portrayed as science versus religion, or libertarianism versus authoritarianism, the real issue concerned the correct interpretation of the Bible. Galileo's critics within the Catholic church argued that some biblical passages contradicted him. For example, they argued, Joshua 10:12 spoke of the sun standing still at Joshua's command. Did not that prove beyond reasonable doubt that it was the sun which moved around the earth?

Galileo countered with an argument resembling Calvin's. This, he suggested, was simply a common way of speaking. Joshua could not be expected to know the intricacies of celestial mechanics, and therefore used an "accommodated" way of speaking. His critics responded by suggesting he had fallen into a Protestant error – that of changing the church's interpretation of Scripture. Galileo had become entangled in the religious politics of the age, which made a balanced discussion of these important questions impossible.

Yet it is too easy to focus on religious controversies of this age, and fail to appreciate how Christianity in general offered an intellectual framework that was conducive to scientific development. The theme of "regularity within nature," widely regarded as an essential theme of the natural sciences, is articulated and affirmed by a Christian doctrine of creation. Christian writers of this age affirmed there was something about the world – and the nature of the human mind – which allows people to discern patterns within nature, for which explanations may be advanced and evaluated.

One of the most significant parallels between the natural sciences and Christian thought is a fundamental conviction that the world is characterized by regularity and intelligibility. The great astronomer Johann Kepler (1557–1630) argued that, since geometry had its origins in the mind of God, it was only to be expected that the created order would conform to its patterns:

> In that geometry is part of the divine mind from the origins of time, even from before the origins of time (for what is there in God that is not also from God?) has provided God with the patterns for the creation of the world, and has been transferred to humanity with the image of God.

This perception of ordering and intelligibility is of immense significance, both at the scientific and religious levels. As the physicist Paul Davies pointed out, "in Renaissance Europe, the justification for what we today call the scientific approach to inquiry was the belief in a rational God whose created order could be discerned from a careful study of nature."

Figure 3.8 Johann Kepler (1571–1630). Hand-colored engraving. Photo: akg-images/North Wind Picture Archives

3.5.6. The Wars of Religion

The religious tensions of the sixteenth century regularly threatened to lead to warfare. The French Wars of Religion (1562–98) arose from the rapid growth of Calvinism within France during the 1550s, which was secretly encouraged and resourced from Calvin's Geneva. Geneva covertly supplied reformed pastors and preachers to cities and congregations throughout France. Safe houses, complete with hiding places, were established in the deep valleys of Provence, set a day's journey apart. An underground network, similar to that employed by the French Resistance during the Second World War, allowed pastors from Geneva to slip across the ill-defined frontier into France.

By 1562, the number of fully established reformed congregations in Calvin's native France had risen to 1785. Calvin's ideas proved particularly attractive to the French nobility. By the 1560s, more than half of the nobility were Protestant. (The term "Huguenot" was now widely used to refer to French Protestants.) As Calvinism grew in importance, so did hostility towards its presence in France. The outbreak of hostilities is traditionally dated to March 1562, when the Duke of Guise massacred a Huguenot congregation at Wassy. A later atrocity of August 1572, in which possibly 10 000 French Protestants were killed, came to be known as the "Saint Bartholomew's Day Massacre." The French Wars of Religion demonstrated the severe damage to social cohesion that resulted from religious conflict.

Figure 3.9   Saint Bartholomew's Day Massacre, August 24, 1572, Paris, France. Wars of Religion in France 1562–98, as depicted by François Dubois (1529–84). The Art Archive/Musée des Beaux Arts Lausanne/Gianni Dagli Orti

Yet the most important religious conflicts took place during the first half of the seventeenth century. We shall note two such wars: one involving conflict between different visions of Protestantism, and the other a conflict between Protestantism and Catholicism.

The English Civil War (1642–51) is best seen as a war of religion which pitted two rival visions of Protestant identity against each other. Puritan and Anglican battled for the soul of England (3.5.2). The death of James I in 1625 precipitated a new wave of religious uncertainty in England, in that Charles I (1600–49) was known to be much more pro-Catholic and anti-Puritan than his father. Added to that, he had married a foreign queen, Henrietta Maria of France – a Catholic. Religious criticism of the marriage surged, fueled by anxieties about what it might portend for English religious life and foreign policy.

Yet the real problem was that Charles was seen as an absolute monarch, who saw himself as being above parliament. Charles's hand was forced by war – first in Scotland, and then Ireland. In November 1640, he summoned the "Long Parliament" to finance war. Sensing Charles's weakness, parliament abolished the Star Chamber and other institutions that had been instruments of Charles's absolutism. To demonstrate where ultimate power really lay, parliament tried to impeach some of Charles's favorites. One of these was Thomas Wentworth, Earl of Strafford (1593–1642), who was impeached and eventually executed for treason in 1641.

In 1641, John Pym (1584–1643) led a parliamentary rebellion against Charles's efforts to raise an army to deal with the rebellion in Ireland, convinced that Charles would first use this army to crush his opponents in England, before turning his attention to Ireland. Parliament issued a "Grand Remonstrance" repeating their grievances against Charles, impeaching twelve bishops, and even attempting to impeach the queen. An abortive attempt by Charles to enter the House of Commons and arrest Pym and four parliamentary acolytes polarized matters to a point at which diplomacy was impossible. In August 1642, the English Civil War broke out.

Initially, the war went well for Charles. Realizing the organizational weakness of its army, parliament revoked existing military command structures, and created the "New Model Army" under Oliver Cromwell (1599–1658) in 1645. From now on, a soldier's rank would be based on his ability, not his social status. The king now suffered severe military reversals. Under Sir Thomas Fairfax and Oliver Cromwell, the parliamentarian forces won victories at Marston Moor (1644) and Naseby (1645). The capture of Charles's correspondence at Naseby revealed his attempts to raise foreign support for his cause, thus alienating many of his more moderate supporters. In May 1646, Charles gave himself up to the Scottish army, who eventually handed him over to parliament. He was held captive at Hampton Court. He was eventually executed on January 30, 1649.

In the end, the Puritan military victory could not be sustained politically, and Anglicanism regained the religious ascendancy after a remarkably short and ineffective interregnum. Yet while other intra-Protestant tensions might not have led to violence or warfare on such a dramatic scale, the tensions were real, and seemed incapable of resolution. Protestantism was a house divided against itself – regionally, culturally, and theologically. Protestantism was not merely the victim of a war of religion; it caused one of its own, which pitted one style of Protestantism against another in a battle for the very soul of the movement in England.

The Thirty Years War (1618–48) was both an international religious conflict and a German civil war, involving Lutheran, Reformed, and Catholic regions and nations. The origins of the war were religious, although other factors contributed significantly to the cause of the war, and its severe prolongation. It is widely regarded as one of the most destructive events in modern European history. The populations of many regions were decimated through this war of attrition, and their economies brought to the brink of total collapse. The outcomes of this sterile and inconclusive conflict between Protestants and Catholics were meager for all concerned.

When the war was finally resolved through the Peace of Westphalia (1648), any remaining enthusiasm for religious warfare had evaporated. People had had enough. A yearning for peace led to a new emphasis on toleration, and growing impatience with religious disputes. The scene was set for the Enlightenment insistence that religion was to be a matter of private belief, rather than state policy. In both intellectual and political circles, religion came to be viewed as a source of international and national conflict, a burden rather than a blessing. A dislike of religious fanaticism emerged, which was easily transmuted into a dislike of religion itself.

The necessity for Catholics and Protestants of various traditions to coexist throughout Europe was now so obvious that it required little argument. No-one wanted a repeat of the pointless brutalization and destruction that had just ended. Many came to the conclusion that the best way of resolving disputes in the future was to avoid basing arguments on purely religious authorities. Reason seemed to many to be a neutral resource, accessible to everyone. An appeal to reason could avoid the acrimonious religious disagreements that had caused such damage in the past.

A massive shift in the tectonic plates of western European culture took place, as an age of faith gave way to the age of reason. The shift is evident from the political writings of each age. In 1649, the Puritan writer and activist Gerrard Winstanley had set out a vision for a commonwealth in which religious values were "really and materially to be fulfilled." Yet a mere forty years later, with the failed Puritan social experiment in mind, the English philosopher John Locke (1632–1704) argued that the "great and chief end of men uniting into governments and putting themselves under government is the preservation of their property." The scene was set for the rise of an increasingly secular Europe – the topic of the next chapter of this book.

Sources of Quotations

p. 161: *Thirty-Nine Articles*, article 6.
p. 181: John Calvin, *Institutes of the Christian Religion* (1559 edition), IV.i.9–10.
p. 208: Johann Kepler, *Gesammelte Werke*. Munich: C. H. Beck, 1937–83, vol. 6, 233.

For Further Reading

Alford, Stephen. *Kingship and Politics in the Reign of Edward VI*. Cambridge: Cambridge University Press, 2002.

Bireley, Robert. *The Refashioning of Catholicism, 1450–1700: A Reassessment of the Counter Reformation*. Basingstoke: Macmillan, 1999.

Bouwsma, William J. *The Waning of the Renaissance, 1550–1640*. New Haven, CT: Yale University Press, 2002.

Breen, Louise A. *Transgressing the Bounds: Subversive Enterprises among the Puritan Elite in Massachusetts, 1630–1692*. New York: Oxford University Press, 2001.

Cameron, Euan. *The European Reformation*. Oxford: Clarendon Press, 2012.

Coffey, John, and Paul Chang-Ha Lim, eds. *The Cambridge Companion to Puritanism*. Cambridge: Cambridge University Press, 2008.

Dodds, Gregory D. *Exploiting Erasmus: The Erasmian Legacy and Religious Change in Early Modern England*. Toronto: University of Toronto Press, 2009.

Doran, Susan, and Christopher Durston. *Princes, Pastors, and People: The Church and Religion in England, 1500–1700*. London: Routledge, 2003.

Evans, G. R. *The Roots of the Reformation: Tradition, Emergence and Rupture*. Downers Grove, IL: InterVarsity, 2012.

Furey, Constance M. *Erasmus, Contarini, and the Religious Republic of Letters*. Cambridge: Cambridge University Press, 2005.

Gordon, Bruce, ed. *Protestant History and Identity in Sixteenth-Century Europe*. 2 vols. Aldershot: Ashgate, 1996.

Gordon, Bruce. *The Swiss Reformation*. Manchester: Manchester University Press, 2002.

Heal, Felicity. *Reformation in Britain and Ireland*. Oxford: Clarendon Press, 2003.

Howell, Kenneth J. *God's Two Books: Copernican Cosmology and Biblical Interpretation in Early Modern Science*. Notre Dame, IN: University of Notre Dame Press, 2002.

Hsia, R. Po-chia. *The World of Catholic Renewal, 1540–1770*. Cambridge: Cambridge University Press, 2005.

Jones, Norman L. *The English Reformation: Religion and Cultural Adaptation*. Oxford: Blackwell, 2002.

Kaartinen, Marjo. *Religious Life and English Culture in the Reformation*. Basingstoke: Palgrave, 2002.

Louthan, Howard, and Randall C. Zachman. *Conciliation and Confession: The Struggle for Unity in the Age of Reform, 1415–1648*. Notre Dame, IN: University of Notre Dame Press, 2004.

MacCulloch, Diarmaid. *Reformation: Europe's House Divided, 1490–1700*. London: Allen Lane, 2003.

McGrath, Alister E. *The Intellectual Origins of the European Reformation*. Oxford: Blackwell, 2003.

McGrath, Alister E. *Iustitia Dei: A History of the Christian Doctrine of Justification*. Cambridge: Cambridge University Press, 2008.

Michalski, Sergiusz. *The Reformation and the Visual Arts: The Protestant Image Question in Western and Eastern Europe*. London: Routledge, 1993.

Mullett, Michael A. *The Catholic Reformation*. London: Routledge, 1999.

Naphy, William G. *Calvin and the Consolidation of the Genevan Reformation*. Louisville, KY: Westminster John Knox, 2003.

Newton, Diana. *Papists, Protestants and Puritans, 1559–1714*. Cambridge: Cambridge University Press, 1998.

Pettegree, Andrew. *Reformation and the Culture of Persuasion*. Cambridge: Cambridge University Press, 2005.

Rex, Richard. *Henry VIII and the English Reformation*. New York: Palgrave Macmillan, 2006.

Ryrie, Alec. *The Age of Reformation: The Tudor and Stewart Realms, 1485–1603*. London: Longman, 2009.

Smith, Jeffrey Chipps. *Sensuous Worship: Jesuits and the Art of the Early Catholic Reformation in Germany*. Princeton, NJ: Princeton University Press, 2002.

Stjerna, Kirsi Irmeli. *Women and the Reformation*. Oxford: Blackwell, 2009.

Williams, George H. *The Radical Reformation*. Kirksville, MO: Sixteenth Century Journal Publishers, 2001.

Wright, A. D. *The Counter-Reformation Catholic Europe and the Non-Christian World*. Burlington, VT: Ashgate, 2005.

4

The Modern Age, c. 1650–1914

At the opening of the sixteenth century, Christianity was largely confined to Europe. While Spain was no longer under Moorish control, other parts of Europe were under threat. The Byzantine Empire had crumbled, with Turkish Ottoman armies deeply embedded in the Balkans. With the fall of Constantinople in 1453, there was little resistance to the Ottoman advance into eastern Europe (2.4.7). In the late 1520s, there was genuine concern that the great city of Vienna would soon fall, and become a staging post for further Turkish incursions into central Europe. It was a time of considerable anxiety for many in western Europe, especially in Germany – the next obvious target of Turkish invasion.

The decisive defeat of Ottoman naval forces at the Battle of Lepanto (1571) allowed western European powers to refocus their attention on the expansion of their spheres of influence in America, Africa, and Asia. The Catholic naval powers Spain and Portugal were in the process of launching major maritime explorations, eventually leading to colonization and a massive expansion of their political influence and economic resources. The "Age of Discovery," which reached its climax during the sixteenth and early seventeenth centuries, saw an enlargement of the European presence and influence in the Americas, Africa, and Asia.

In view of the importance of North America to the history of Christianity, we may consider how Christianity came to be planted there in a little more detail. By the end of the sixteenth century, Catholic mission stations had been established in many places colonized by France and Spain. Portugal did not colonize North America, restricting its influence to the south. Much of the southern parts of North America – such as Texas and Florida – were occupied by the Spanish. A French colonial presence was established in Louisiana, and much further north along the Mississippi Valley, the St. Lawrence Valley, and the Great Lakes.

Christian History: An Introduction, First Edition. Alister E. McGrath.
© 2013 John Wiley & Sons, Ltd. Published 2013 by John Wiley & Sons, Ltd.

From the beginning of the seventeenth century, England also began to establish colonies in the "New England" region. Although these were Crown Colonies, their religious identity was complex. The Church of England was regarded as the established colonial church. However, many of the most active religious congregations were émigré communities, primarily consisting of refugees from religious persecution or discrimination in England. Tensions began to develop between Puritans and Anglicans that would contribute to the origins of the American Revolution of 1776. The global expansion of Christian European nations led to a new era opening up in the history of Christianity, raising new questions about the interaction of faith and culture.

Yet in Europe itself, new challenges were emerging. One of the most important of these was a new suspicion of religion as a cause of violence and social fragmentation. Growing sympathy was developing for approaches to beliefs and ethics which made their appeal to what was then regarded as a universal human faculty – reason. If all beliefs and values could be established scientifically by reason, the great religious disputes of the past could be avoided. We therefore open our discussion of this important period in the history of Christianity by considering the "Age of Reason," and the challenges that it raised for Christianity in western Europe and beyond.

4.1. The Age of Reason: The Enlightenment

By the middle of the seventeenth century Christianity, especially Catholicism, was making new inroads globally, expanding its sphere of influence. Yet back in its original heartlands in Europe, tensions were developing that would lead to a sea change in attitudes towards religion in the region. The massive damage caused to European economies by the "Wars of Religion" of the seventeenth century (3.5.6) caused many to wonder how such traumas might be avoided in the future.

One answer began to attract considerable support to a war-weary Europe: limit the power of religion, and find an alternative source of authority that would command universal consent. The "Age of Reason" believed that it had found such a source of authority in human reason. Rationalism would be the key to a new approach to morality and politics.

4.1.1. The Rise of Indifference towards Religion

By 1700, western Europe was exhausted by seemingly endless wars of religion, which caused social disintegration and economic hardship. The Thirty Years War (1618–48) was both an international religious conflict and a German civil war, involving Lutheran, Reformed, and Catholic regions and nations (3.5.6). The populations of many regions were decimated through this war of attrition, and their economies brought to the brink of total collapse. The outcomes of this sterile and inconclusive conflict were decidedly meager for all concerned. When the war was finally resolved through the Peace of Westphalia (1648), any remaining enthusiasm for religious warfare had evaporated. People had had enough. A yearning for peace led to a new emphasis on toleration, and growing impatience with religious disputes.

The scene was set for the Enlightenment insistence that religion was to be a matter of private belief, rather than state policy. In both intellectual and political circles, religion came to be viewed as a source of international and national conflict, a burden rather than a blessing. A dislike of religious fanaticism emerged, which was easily transmuted into a dislike of religion itself – especially when religion was seen or portrayed as the enemy of peace and progress.

In England, the Civil War and its debilitating aftermath had exhausted any enthusiasm for religious partisanship. The conflict between Puritan and Anglican, between Parliamentarians and Royalists, had exhausted the country. The restoration of the monarchy in 1660 was greeted with enthusiasm by Anglican and Puritan alike, largely because it restored political and economic stability to the nation. Yet within decades, a new religious crisis had developed. When Charles II died in 1685, he was succeeded by James II, a Catholic, who appointed coreligionists to prominent positions in the state, army, and universities. This prompted widespread concern, and gave rise to furious rumors of a secret plot to convert England to Roman Catholicism. A new religious civil war seemed inevitable.

A characteristically English solution, however, emerged, which defused the situation. James II's daughter Mary had earlier married William III, prince of Orange, a firmly committed Protestant with a reputation for tolerance and generosity. A secret approach was made by leading political figures to William. If he were to invade England, he could be assured that strategically placed well-wishers would rally the nation around him. Encouraged by such overtures, William landed in the west of England in 1688, to widespread public support. James soon realized that his cause was utterly lost. In January 1689, he fled England for France.

William and Mary were declared king and queen of England in February – but only after agreeing to sign a "Bill of Rights" which guaranteed free elections and freedom of speech. The "Glorious Revolution" had averted another civil war, and limited both the power of religion and the monarchy in English public life.

It was no accident that John Locke's *Letters of Toleration* were published at this precise moment, arguing for the need to tolerate at least some degree of diversity in religion, rather than allowing it to lead to conflict. Locke argued for limited religious toleration on three grounds.

1. It is impossible for the state to adjudicate between competing religious truth-claims. Locke argued that no earthly judge can be brought forward to settle such debates. For this reason, religious diversity is to be tolerated.
2. Even if it could be established that one religion was superior to all others, the legal enforcement of this religion would not lead to the desired objective of that religion.
3. The results of trying to impose religious uniformity are far worse than those which result from the continuing existence of diversity. Religious coercion leads to internal discord, or even civil war.

Yet Locke was clear that toleration was *not* to be extended to Catholics and atheists, both of whom he regarded as threats to the still-unstable social order in England at the time. While Locke is often singled out as a prophetic advocate of toleration, it is important to note that these views are limited by his entrenched views of the past.

Locke's conclusion resonated with the anti-dogmatic mood of an age tired and disgusted with religious controversies. Religious toleration, within limits, was the only way of coping with the religious diversity of early modern Europe. It is important to note that Locke's analysis leads to the view that religion is a private matter of public indifference. What individuals believe should be regarded as private, with no relevance to the public domain. This approach at one and the same time upheld religious toleration, while indicating that religion was a purely private matter.

The necessity for Catholics and Protestants of various traditions to coexist throughout Europe was now so obvious that it required little argument. Locke's arguments did not need to persuade; they chimed in with the spirit of the age. Few wanted a repeat of the pointless brutalization and destruction that had just ended. So what common ground might be found, by which future debates might be resolved?

Wearied with religious controversy, many leading western European thinkers of the eighteenth century came to believe that civil peace and religious toleration would be based on a non-dogmatic faith – such as some form of Deism. One of the most powerful and persuasive statements of this case was due to the Enlightenment writer Gotthold Ephraim Lessing (1729–81). Lessing's play *Nathan the Wise* (1779), set in Jerusalem during the Third Crusade (2.2.5), explores how the wise Jewish merchant Nathan, an Islamic sultan and a Templar knight manage to bridge the gap between their Jewish, Islamic, and Christian faiths.

The centerpiece of the play is the famous "Parable of the Three Rings," related by Nathan when asked which of their three religions is true. A father tells each of his three sons that he is giving them a special ring, never revealing which is the true ring. Each believes he alone is the possessor of the special ring. Yet the narrative of the play gives no clue as to which – if any – of the three rings is genuine. Nathan suggests that the true test of the ring's authenticity is whether its owner lived as the father would have wished.

This new mood was expressed in a growing interest in using human reason – rather than the contested claims of divine revelation or ecclesiastical authority – as the basis of human philosophy and ethics. Not only would this set these important areas of thought apart from the violence and fanaticism of religion; it would place them on a single, universal basis. Reason, it was then believed, transcended the divisions of creed, geography, and culture. Surely everyone – whether Lutheran, Reformed, Anglican, or Catholic – could agree on the power of reason to guide and illuminate? And so the movement now known as the "Enlightenment" was born.

4.1.2.   The Enlightenment and Christianity

The movement that is known in English as "the Enlightenment" is generally understood to refer to the cultural and intellectual movement that emerged in eighteenth-century

Europe and North America, which placed an emphasis on human reason as a means of overcoming the particularism of religious belief. It is widely regarded as having shaped some of the defining features of the modern world, especially through its confidence in the power of human reason, its commitment to individual freedom of expression against ecclesiastical or royal tyranny, and its assumption that these values would improve the human condition everywhere. The movement is often considered to have inspired and justified the fundamental nineteenth- and twentieth-century achievements of industrialization, liberalism, and democracy.

Religious life and thought were both affected by this change in cultural mood. Western Christianity has been deeply shaped by the ideas of the Enlightenment – both its positive emphasis upon the competency of reason and the possibility of objectivity of judgment, and its negative critiques of the concept of supernatural revelation, and the capacity of the Bible or any religious tradition to disclose truths that allegedly lay beyond reason.

The use of the singular term "Enlightenment" needs comment. Recent scholarship has suggested that this movement is better understood as a "family of Enlightenments," sharing a common commitment to a core of ideas and values, yet demonstrating diversity at other points. The English, German, and French Enlightenments took quite distinct forms, and emphasized different ideas. The idea that the Enlightenment was characterized by a definite single set of ideas has proved very difficult to sustain historically. It is perhaps better to think of the movement as "an attitude of mind" rather than as a "coherent set of beliefs."

The origins of the Enlightenment lie partly in English Deism, a movement which developed in the late seventeenth century. Sir Isaac Newton (1643–1727) had argued that the universe was like a vast machine, rationally designed and constructed by an intelligent creator. Deism minimized the supernatural dimensions of faith, and presented Christianity essentially as a rational and moral religion, easily harmonized with human reason. God was the creator of the kind of regular, ordered universe that Newtonian mechanics had uncovered.

Many English writers began to develop approaches to religion which accepted the notion of a creator God, who had implanted reason within the human soul as a basis of judgment. Thereafter, God was of no relevance. God may have created the world, but that was as far as it went. The famous image of God as the divine watchmaker began to emerge in the late seventeenth century. God had created a wonderful mechanical universe which, once created, could regulate itself without further divine attention. Reason was the light of the human soul. It may have originated from God, and continued to serve as a witness to the reality of God. But reason transcended the specifics of culture.

More importantly, the critical use of reason allowed Enlightenment thinkers to dispose of what they regarded as the unnecessary supernatural baggage of the Christian faith. A number of stages in the development of this belief may be discerned.

In the first phase of the Enlightenment, during the late seventeenth century, it was argued that the beliefs of Christianity were rational, and thus capable of standing up to critical examination. This type of approach may be found in John Locke's *Reasonableness of Christianity* (1695), and within some philosophical schools of thought in early eighteenth-century Germany. Christianity was a reasonable supplement to natural religion. The notion of divine revelation was thus affirmed, while any idea that it offered *exclusive* access to the truth was rejected.

In its second phase, it was argued that the basic ideas of Christianity, being rational, could be derived from reason itself. There was no need to invoke the idea of divine revelation. Christianity, according to John Toland in his *Christianity Not Mysterious* (1696) and Matthew Tindal in his *Christianity as Old as Creation* (1730), was essentially the republication of the religion of nature. It did not transcend natural religion, but was merely an example of it. All so-called "revealed religion" was actually nothing other than the reconfirmation of what can be known through rational reflection on nature. "Revelation" was simply a rational reaffirmation of moral truths already available to enlightened reason.

In the final phase of this transition, which was essentially complete by the middle of the eighteenth century, leading representatives of the Enlightenment confidently affirmed the ability of reason to judge revelation. Thomas Paine's *Age of Reason*, published in three parts in 1794–1807, is seen by many as a classical statement of this position. Reason and nature teach us all we need to know; any other claims to revelation are to be dismissed as fraudulent and forgeries.

> Deism, then, teaches us, without the possibility of being deceived, all that is necessary or proper to be known. The creation is the Bible of the deist. He there reads, in the handwriting of the Creator himself, the certainty of his existence and the immutability of his power, and all other Bibles and Testaments are to him forgeries.

Critical reason was seen as a basis on which it was possible to judge Christian beliefs and practices, with a view to eliminating any irrational or superstitious elements. This view, associated with Hermann Samuel Reimarus (1694–1768) in Germany and many eighteenth-century French rationalist writers (often referred to collectively as *les philosophes*), placed reason firmly above revelation. This attitude would later be symbolized in one of the landmark events of the French Revolution (4.1.8) – the enthronement of the Goddess of Reason in the cathedral of Notre Dame de Paris in 1793.

The iconic significance of this emphasis upon reason for the eighteenth century is best seen from the frontispiece to Christian Wolff's *Rational Thoughts on God, the World, and the Soul* (1719). This superb piece of intellectual propaganda shows a beaming, benevolent sun smiling upon the world, removing clouds and shadows. A new age has dawned! The darkness of earlier generations will vanish, as surely as night gives way to day! It was a powerful vision, which resonated with the hopes and fears of a war-weary Europe. Might this be the way to social, religious, and political stability?

It was a vision that proved compelling to many conflict-weary Protestants, deeply disillusioned by the violence and fanaticism of the recent religious past. Some Anglican clergy and bishops found its ideas compelling. Deism – a belief in a generic creator God – seemed much less intellectually demanding and tiresome than the Trinitarian God of the Christian tradition. It resonated well with the new emphasis on the divine ordering of the world, now emerging from the "mechanical philosophy" of Isaac Newton and his school.

God could be thought of as the divine clockmaker, who had constructed a particularly elegant piece of machinery, and made no demands of anyone other than a due appreciation of the beauty of the creation. Religions of all kinds tended to be seen as corruptions of an original "religion of nature," which had no priests or creeds. These latter were later distortions, introduced by self-serving clerics, anxious to secure their social status and exploit the gullible.

Yet the appeal of the Enlightenment proved greatest within Reformed circles. For reasons that remain unclear, rationalism gained wider acceptance at many former strongholds of Calvinism. Geneva and Edinburgh, both international centers of Calvinism in the late sixteenth and early seventeenth centuries, became epicenters of European rationalism in the late eighteenth. The religious worldviews of John Calvin and John Knox gave way to those of rationalists and skeptics, such as Jean-Jacques Rousseau and David Hume. In marked contrast, the Enlightenment had relatively little impact on Catholicism during the eighteenth century, except in France, where Deist writers such as Voltaire argued for the need for reform of the church on the basis of its backward-looking attitude towards progress.

4.1.3.   Christian Beliefs in the "Age of Reason"

The phrase "Age of Reason," often used as a synonym for the Enlightenment, is a little misleading. It implies that reason had been hitherto ignored or marginalized. As we saw in an earlier chapter, the Middle Ages can quite legitimately be thought of as an "Age of Reason" in its own terms. It is important to appreciate that the Enlightenment developed the notion of the autonomy of reason in a way that went far beyond the ideas of rationality found in classical Greek philosophy or the thought of the Middle Ages. A defining characteristic of the Enlightenment is its emphasis on the ability of human reason to penetrate the mysteries of the world (4.1.2). Humanity is able to think for itself, without the need for any assistance from God. Unaided human reason is able to make sense of the world – including those aspects of that world traditionally reserved for theologians.

Although such criticisms would apply to any religious system that accepted the notion of divine revelation – including Judaism and Islam – Christianity was the historically dominant religion in those parts of the world in which the Enlightenment gained hold. Unsurprisingly, most Enlightenment critics of religion in general chose to direct those criticisms against many aspects of traditional Christian belief and practice.

A classic example of such a criticism is found in the rationalist criticism of the traditional Christian doctrine of God as a trinity – Father, Son, and Holy Spirit. This was widely ridiculed by Enlightenment thinkers, who held it to be logically absurd. How could any rational person accept such mathematical nonsense? Thomas Jefferson (1743–1826), third president of the United States, regarded the Trinity as an irrational and outdated obstacle to proper Christian devotion. In a letter to Timothy Pickering, dated February 27, 1821, Jefferson complained of the apparent irrationality of the notion, demanding to get rid of the "incomprehensible jargon of the Trinitarian arithmetic."

Under the pressure of such rationalist criticism, many orthodox Christian thinkers de-emphasized the doctrine of the Trinity, believing that it was impossible to mount an effective defense of this doctrine, given the spirit of the age.

Throughout the period of the Enlightenment, rationalist pressure led to many Christian theologians developing approaches to the doctrine of God which came close to Deism (4.1.2). God was the supreme governor of the universe, the creator of all things. This approach is especially evident in eighteenth-century English theology, which saw God simply as the "divine watchmaker," the constructor of an ordered and regular universe. Trinitarian theology went into hibernation for much of the Enlightenment period, and only reemerged in the early twentieth century, as confidence in the Enlightenment world-view began to collapse after the trauma of the First World War.

A second area of Christian belief to come under critical examination was the identity of Jesus of Nazareth. As we noted earlier, the Council of Nicaea (325) had declared that Christianity was committed to, and based upon, the firm conviction that Jesus was both divine and human (1.5.3; 1.5.9). This idea was regarded as irrational and illogical by writers sympathetic to the Enlightenment. There was, they declared, a serious discrepancy between the real Jesus of history and the New Testament interpretation of his significance. Reimarus and others argued that it was possible to go behind the New Testament accounts of Jesus and uncover a simpler, more human Jesus, who would be acceptable to the new spirit of the age. For Reimarus, the gospel accounts of the resurrection were simply attempts to cover up his shameful death, which had thrown his followers into confusion.

This conviction triggered the "Quest of the Historical Jesus" – an intellectual search for a more rational understanding of the person of Jesus, from which all traditional trappings had been stripped. Jesus of Nazareth was not a divine savior, nor even a divine revealer. He was simply one among many religious teachers, without any supreme authority.

Other areas of Christian thought that were subjected to criticism included the notion of divine revelation, and any idea that the Christian Bible was an "inspired" text. The concept of revelation had long been of central importance to traditional Christian theology. While many Christian theologians (such as Thomas Aquinas and John Calvin) recognized the possibility of a natural knowledge of God, they insisted that this required supplementation by supernatural divine revelation, such as that witnessed to in Scripture.

The Enlightenment was characterized by an increasingly critical attitude to the very idea of supernatural revelation. In the first place, it was unnecessary. In the second, it lacked the universality of human reason. Everyone had access to reason; only a select few had access to revelation. The phrase "the scandal of particularity" was used by Enlightenment writers in expressing their concerns about the traditional notion of revelation at this point.

Yet if there was no need for divine revelation, what was the point of the Christian Bible, traditionally regarded as a revelatory text? Within Orthodox Christianity, whether Protestant or Roman Catholic, the Bible was seen as a divinely inspired source of doctrine and morals, to be differentiated from other types of literature. The Enlightenment saw this assumption called into question, with the rise of the critical approach to Scripture. Developing ideas already current within English Deism, the theologians of the German Enlightenment developed the thesis that the Bible was the work of many hands, at times demonstrating internal contradiction, and that it was open to precisely the same method of textual analysis and interpretation as any other piece of literature.

Yet perhaps the most important aspects of the Enlightenment critique of Christianity were political. The Enlightenment rejected the idea of tradition as having any binding authority. If something was right, it could be proved to be such by reason. There was no reason to allow past ideas, attitudes, or institutions to be seen as possessing some special divine authority. Theologically, this led to the rejection of tradition as a source of doctrine; politically, it led to the criticism of any institutions or authorities whose existence or legitimacy could not be defended by reason.

It was a revolutionary idea. Kings and the political order they embodied might well be deeply rooted in history. Some might argue that kings possessed some form of "divine right" to government. Yet none of these claims would stand up in the court of reason. The foundations for a radical challenge to the traditional political and social structures of Europe had been laid.

We shall consider the American and French revolutions, and their importance for Christianity, later in this chapter (4.1.7; 4.1.8). First, however, we must consider a religious movement that emerged at the time of the Enlightenment, which many regarded as laying the foundations for revival, rather than revolution.

4.1.4.   Pietism and Revival in Germany and England

Many in late seventeenth-century Germany were unhappy with the austerity of Lutheran orthodoxy of this age, feeling it was out of touch with the popular mood. Its cold theological logic failed to connect up with a population which had been traumatized by the destructiveness of the Thirty Years War (1618–48). A number of movements arose, concerned with reconnecting the Christian faith with the laity. The most important of these revivalist movements is known as "Pietism," which emerged in the immediate aftermath of the Thirty Years War in Germany (3.5.6). Faced with widespread disenchantment with the spiritually arid forms of Protestantism in this region, Philip Jakob Spener (1635–1705) published his *Pia Desideria* ("Pious Wishes," 1675). In this work, Spener lamented the state of the German Lutheran Church in the aftermath of the Thirty Years War and set out his proposals for the revitalization of the church of his day.

Spener argued that German Lutheranism's obsession with rigid theological orthodoxy (3.5.1) had to give way to a new concern for the devotional life, deepening a personal relationship with Jesus Christ. Chief among his proposals was a new emphasis upon personal Bible study as a means of deepening a personal, living faith in God. Bible study groups would be *ecclesiolae in ecclesiae* (Latin: "little churches" within the church"), serving as springboards and catalysts for renewal. These proposals were treated with derision by academic theologians; nevertheless, they were to prove influential in German church circles, reflecting a growing disillusionment and impatience with the sterility of Lutheran orthodoxy in the face of the shocking social conditions endured during the war.

Pietism developed in a number of different directions, especially in England and Germany. In Germany, Nikolaus Ludwig Graf von Zinzendorf (1700–60) founded the Pietist community generally known as the "Herrnhuter," named after the village of Herrnhut in Saxony. Alienated from what he regarded as the arid rationalism and barren Protestant religious formalism of his time, Zinzendorf stressed the importance of a "religion of the heart," based on an intimate and personal relationship between Christ and the believer. A new emphasis was placed upon the role of "feeling" (as opposed to reason or doctrinal orthodoxy) within the Christian life. (This is often seen as laying the foundations for Romanticism in later German religious thought.) Zinzendorf expressed his idea of a personally appropriated faith in the slogan "a living faith," an idea which he contrasted unfavorably with the views of Protestant orthodoxy. For orthodoxy, faith was about formal assent to the creeds; for Zinzendorf, it was about a personal, transforming encounter with God, with creedal assent playing a minor role.

Zinzendorf's ideas soon began to find acceptance in England. John Wesley (1703–91) was a founder and early leader of the Methodist movement within the Church of England, which subsequently gave birth to Methodism as a denomination in its own right. Convinced that he "lacked the faith whereby alone we are saved," Wesley paid a visit to Herrnhut in 1738, and was deeply impressed by what he found there. Wesley found the Pietist emphasis upon the need for a "living faith" and the role of experience in the Christian life to be very persuasive. His conversion experience at a meeting in Aldersgate Street, London, in May 1738, in which he felt his heart to be "strangely warmed," led to him traveling throughout England, preaching his new understanding of the Protestant religion.

Wesley's emphasis upon the experiential side of Christian faith, which contrasted sharply with what he saw as the spiritual dullness of contemporary English Deism (4.1.2), led to a minor religious revival in England during the eighteenth century. Wesley was joined in his ministry by his brother Charles; between them, they wrote some of the best-known hymns in the English language, many of which express the transformative nature of faith, and the need for personal conversion. Their structured and disciplined approach to Christian devotion earned them the nickname "Methodists."

One of Methodism's strongest supporters was Lady Selina Hastings, Countess of Huntingdon (1707–91), who had a right as a peeress of the realm to appoint Anglican clergymen as household chaplains and assign their duties. She also had the right to purchase presentation rights to chapels, enabling her to decide who would conduct services and preach. The Countess of Huntington began to appoint Methodists to various preaching positions, seeing this as a means of securing revival within the national church. Among the many chaplains, mostly of a Calvinist theological hue, who she appointed and continued to finance for many decades was John Wesley's associate, George Whitfield.

In 1779, after sixty chapels were already functioning under her patronage, a consistory court of London declared the arrangement to be illegal. This legal barrier was, however, not difficult to evade. Under the Toleration Act, designed to reduce religious tension within England by permitting "non-conformists" to worship freely, these chapels were formally registered as dissenting places of worship, coming to be known as "The Countess of Huntingdon's Connexion."

Methodism's emphasis on the experiential side of religion raised the specter of "enthusiasm" – a dramatic, religiously inspired fervor, often accompanied by agitated body movements, faintings, and swoonings. The phenomenon of "enthusiasm" was widely ridiculed by English religious commentators, and was devastatingly caricatured in William Hogarth's etching "Enthusiasm Delineat'd." Many revivalist preachers – including John Wesley and George Whitfield – found themselves torn between sympathy for the idea that a direct experience of God might induce such dramatic effects, and a concern that its bizarre manifestations would alienate a religiously suspicious public. Somehow, a middle way had to be found, avoiding the religious excesses of "enthusiasm" on the one hand, and the impoverishment of "formalism" on the other.

Despite their differences, the various branches of Pietism succeeded in making Christian faith relevant to the experiential world of ordinary believers – in some ways, anticipating the success of Pentecostalism two centuries later. Pietism succeeded in lodging Protestantism in the everyday realities of life for many people. It is of no small importance to note that the strongly anti-religious tone of the French Revolution (4.1.8) in the late eighteenth century is partly due to the absence of any real equivalent of Pietism in French Catholicism at that time. In England and Germany, faith was being reconnected with everyday life; in France, that link appears to have been fractured – with massive implications for the future of Christianity in that region, as we shall see when we consider the French Revolution of 1789 in more detail (4.1.8).

Yet revival was not breaking out merely in Germany and England in the early eighteenth century. In America, the "Great Awakening" ushered in a new period of religious devotion, which many scholars see as the backdrop to the American Revolution of 1776.

4.1.5. America: The "Great Awakening"

One of the most distinctive features of North American Protestant Christianity is the phenomenon of the "Awakening." To date, three such "Awakenings" have been documented, each leading initially to religious renewal, and subsequently to social change. The first of these religious revivals, traditionally known as the "Great Awakening," took place in New England in the late 1730s and early 1740s. To appreciate its importance, we must consider the background against which it took place.

By 1700, American Protestantism appeared to be stagnant. The first generation of Puritan immigrants possessed a driving religious vision which was not always shared by their children. Church membership began to decline as the spiritual fervor of an earlier generation of Puritan immigrants (3.5.2) was displaced by the pragmatism of their descendents. Increased immigration from Europe led to the middle Atlantic states become religiously diverse to an extent without parallel anywhere else, raising awkward questions about earlier Puritan visions of a "holy commonwealth." More significantly, a series of scandals rocked the credibility of Puritan institutions. The worst of these was the Salem Witch Trials of 1693, instigated by the clergy of that town, which led to the execution of nineteen people (3.4.6).

Tensions began to emerge over church membership. In the early seventeenth century New England congregations generally had a policy of admitting to full membership only those individuals who could provide a narrative of personal conversion. As the century progressed, fewer and fewer individuals could testify to such an experience. Yet most individuals wanted some connection or association with the church, not least on account of the close ties between church membership and citizenship in most communities. As church attendance began to decline, tensions emerged between those who wanted to maintain religious purity at any cost, and those who believed that the churches could only survive by broadening their membership base through adopting less strict criteria.

A compromise was reached. In 1662, a "half-way" membership was accepted by some congregations. This compromise allowed those prepared to accept formally the truth of Christianity and the moral discipline of the church to have their children baptized. The result of this idea of a "half-way covenant" was perhaps inevitable: by the beginning of the eighteenth century a large proportion of church members were "nominal" or "half-way" Protestants. Protestantism was on its way to becoming the civil religion of New England, its primary functions being social and moral.

All this was changed through the "Great Awakening." From about 1735 to 1745, much of New England was engulfed in religious renewal. Contemporary records speak of mass outdoor meetings, occasionally attracting 20 000 people, open-air sermons, deserted taverns, and packed churches. Historians have pointed out that the connections between these events are often difficult to establish, and that using the later term "Great Awakening" retrospectively imposes a single narrative structure upon what may really have been a complex set of happenings. It is, however, clear that some significant events took place, reversing the downward trend in church attendance and the declining public profile of religion in the region.

One of the central figures of this revival was Jonathan Edwards (1703–58), the pastor of the Massachusetts town of Northampton, which experienced a revival during the winter of 1734–5. As the revival spread across New England, it was given a new sense of direction by George Whitfield (1717–70), recently arrived from England, where the "evangelical revival" (4.1.4) was changing the religious landscape.

By 1760, it was clear that the Awakening was bringing about significant changes in American Christianity. It was not simply that people were returning to church, or that religion was playing an increasingly significant role in public life. The revival changed the nature of American Christianity, bringing about a changed understanding of the relation between the individual, congregation, and state.

The new emphasis on individuals having undergone a personal conversion led to the emergence of "conversion narratives" as a means of proving religious commitment and affirming personal identity. Whereas in the 1630s, a congregation would test a person's beliefs to determine whether they were indeed a truly converted, orthodox believer prior to admitting them to full membership, the emphasis now fell upon the individual's personal experience. For this reason, some scholars argue that the Awakening led to the weakening of the intellectual side of faith, and to an emphasis being placed instead upon its emotional and relational aspects.

Whereas the French Revolution (4.1.8) took place against a background of growing popular disenchantment with, and alienation from, the Christian church, the American Revolution would take place against the backdrop of growing religious enthusiasm and commitment. Where some would argue that the French Revolution saw Christianity as its enemy, the American Revolution was not in any way anti-religious. Indeed, religious fervor fueled resentment against the privileges accorded to one established church, and denied to

Figure 4.1   Jonathan Edwards (1703–58), widely considered the greatest American Puritan theologian. Eighteenth-century engraving. © Corbis

others. To understand the emergence of the modern American separation of church and state, it is necessary to consider the origins and outcomes of the American Revolution of 1776 (4.1.7).

Before this, however, we need to consider a development in eighteenth-century Europe, which both mirrored political and institutional changes taking place at that time, reflecting both the weakening power of the papacy and the growing power of nation states – the suppression of the Society of Jesus.

4.1.6.   The Suppression of the Jesuits, 1759–73

The Society of Jesus – widely known as the "Jesuits" – founded by Ignatius Loyola and others in August 1534, had become one of the most influential and powerful religious orders of the Catholic church (3.4.4). It was especially active in missionary work in Asia and Latin America, and was widely regarded as one of the most significant outcomes of the Catholic Reformation of the later sixteenth century.

Its power and influence, however, created hostility and opposition. Loyola, a former soldier, realized the importance of organization and discipline. His vision for the order envisaged a tightly centralized organization, which stressed total obedience to the pope and their religious superiors. As a result, they did not see themselves as being accountable to European nation-states or colonial powers.

Tensions began to rise in the Latin American colonies of Spain and Portugal (2.5.7), when the Jesuits intervened to protect the rights of Native Americans against the economically and socially exploitative agendas of the colonial powers. Where Spain and Portugal proposed to treat Native Americans as little more than slave labor, the Jesuits established local Native American city-states, known as *Reducciones* in Spanish, and *Reduções* in Portuguese. Modeled on religious ideals, these city-states provided a buffer against economic exploitation.

Some of the most important Native American societies were established in the Spanish territory of Paraguay, under Antonio Ruiz de Montoya (1585–1652). Under a system known as the *encomienda* (from the Spanish verb *encomendar*, "to entrust") the Spanish Crown allocated colonists a number of natives for whom they were to take responsibility, ensuring they were protected. In return, the colonists were allowed to demand labor from these natives. In effect, if not intention, this amounted to a mandate for slavery. The Jesuits subverted this, by establishing what were in effect "safe havens" for Native Americans, protecting them from exploitation.

Unsurprisingly, hostility towards the Jesuits on the part of the colonial powers of Portugal and Spain began to rise in the late seventeenth and early eighteenth centuries, reflecting concern about the social and economic impact of the Jesuits in their colonies. This hostility took three main forms.

1. Politically, it was alleged that the Jesuits had intentions to subvert legitimate national governments. Their allegiance to the Pope, rather than to any national agencies or authorities, led to them being viewed with intense suspicion. In January 1759 the Portuguese court announced that an assassination attempt on Joseph I (1714–77) had been uncovered and foiled. Rumors soon emerged that this plot had been hatched by the Jesuits. The Marquis of Pombal, Sebastião Carvalho (1699–1782), organized a press campaign against the Jesuits, which was widely followed across western Europe. It was only a matter of time before this criticism led to political action. The Jesuits were expelled from Portugal in 1758 and the order suppressed the following year. Spain expelled the Jesuits from the Spanish mainland and its colonies in 1766.

2. Theologically, it was argued that the Jesuits were committed to a theology which was of questionable integrity, and which had dubious outcomes. These arguments were especially influential in France. The movement known as "Jansenism" developed within France, developing a theology of grace which it regarded as faithful to the ideas of Augustine of Hippo. This movement was condemned as heretical in 1713. The Jansenists then launched a major theological assault on the Jesuits, who they believed to have engineered their condemnation. Public sympathy for the Jansenists grew. The Jansenist magistrate Abbé Germain Louis de Chauvelin (1685–1762) played a critically important role in persuading the *parlement* of Paris to examine the doctrine and the constitutions of the Jesuits, which eventually led to the suppression of the order in France and its colonies in 1764.

3. Ideologically, it was argued that the Jesuits were committed to a theocratic view of authority, which posed a major threat to liberty and conscience. This was especially the case in France, where Voltaire (1694–1778) and Jean le Rond d'Alembert (1717–83) –

both leading representatives of the Enlightenment – criticized the Jesuits for their religious intolerance, especially in their dealings with the Jansenists.

Clement XIII, who was educated by the Jesuits, became pope in 1758, at a time at which the papacy was facing increasing pressure from European nation-states. The suppression of the Society of Jesus in leading Catholic nations began in that same year, possibly reflecting a perception that Clement was weak, and unable to offer serious resistance to such developments. Clement defended the Jesuits in 1765, arguing that the order had been misrepresented. However, he found himself facing growing demands for action on his part against the Society of Jesus. Following his death in 1769, he was succeeded by the Franciscan Santarcangelo di Romagna, who took the papal name Clement XIV. He had little sympathy for the Jesuits. It was now inevitable that the Society of Jesus would be dismantled. The brief papal decree dissolving the Jesuits (without actually endorsing any of the criticisms directed against them) was issued at Rome in July 1773.

The suppression of the Jesuits is widely regarded as reflecting a new assertiveness on the part of Catholic nation-states, rather than as representing genuine failings on the part of the Jesuits themselves. Politically, the anti-Jesuit campaign served to highlight the lack of real power and influence on the part of the papacy at this time. The suppression of the order led to a serious weakening of the Catholic missionary endeavor in the second half of the eighteenth century, especially in Spanish and Portuguese colonies.

Yet in the end, the suppression of the Society of Jesus could not be sustained. The French Revolution (4.1.8) and ensuing Napoleonic wars (4.2.1) created a new situation within Europe, eroding the power of the nations that had played such a significant role in demanding the society's suppression. Judging the situation accurately, Pius VII announced the restoration of the Society of Jesus in August, 1814. War-weary nations had little enthusiasm for opposing this. Although it would be some time before the Jesuits were able to return to anything remotely approaching their previous activities, this dark period in the order's history was now behind it.

4.1.7.   The American Revolution of 1776

The historical roots of the American Revolution are complex, making it difficult to identify any one factor as the ultimate cause of the rebellion against British rule. The burdens of taxation, the lack of any political representation, and the desire for freedom were unquestionably an integral part of the accumulation of grievances that drove many colonials to take up arms against the British Crown. The thirteen British Crown Colonies in America became increasingly disenchanted with high levels of taxation and direct rule from London. The high levels of taxation were a direct result of a hugely costly war in the region during the period 1756–63, in which the British army and navy had managed to put an end to French influence. The British government sought to recover much of the cost of the war from the American colonies.

Yet religious issues also played their part. The "Great Awakening" (4.1.5) is seen by many scholars as having created a strong sense of religious values that were hostile to British Crown rule. The growing sense that all people were created equal by God, and that religious faith was a social leveler, helped create a cultural context that was receptive to a Christian republicanism, similar to that found in Calvin's Geneva in the late sixteenth century.

There was also a strong sense of injustice over the privileged status of the Church of England in the American colonies. The Church of England had become established by law in the southern states of Virginia, Maryland, the Carolinas, and Georgia, and even in four counties of New York State. Although dissent was permitted, the situation rankled Baptists, Congregationalists, and Presbyterians. Opposition began to grow.

In the early 1770s, Congregationalist ministers in New England regularly preached on the theme of religious and political freedom, linking both with resisting English tyranny. Throughout Puritan Massachusetts, pamphlets appeared offering a religious justification for the use of armed force against an oppressor, and urging young men to join militias. The rhetoric and theology were not entirely unlike those found earlier in the prelude to the English Civil War.

So was the American Revolution a war of religion, like the English Civil War? Most scholars believe it was not, and prefer to speak of it as a war of independence – a defensive revolution against tyrannical oppression. Religious concerns were certainly involved, above all a desire to ensure religious freedom, and eliminate the privileges of the established church. Yet it would not be true to say that these concerns dominated the agenda of those driving the revolution.

The patriots came from a wide variety of religious backgrounds, only some of which were driven by the anger of New England Congregationalists against the religious privileges of the Anglican establishment. George Washington (1732–99), commander-in-chief of the colonial armies in the American Revolution (1775–83), and subsequently the first president of the United States of America (1789–97), was somewhat unorthodox religiously, possibly being best described as a Deist – someone who believed in a generic notion of divinity, rather than the distinctively Christian conception of God.

For many, the American Revolution was a defining moment of religious purification, in which the excesses and privileges of the established church could be eliminated. Yet there was no question of eliminating Anglicanism, still less Anglicans. Following the revolution, the "Protestant Episcopal Church" was reconstituted in 1789 at Philadelphia as the successor to the Church of England in the American colonies. No Protestant denomination was designated as the "established church" in its place. The religious diversity of the newly established United States of America was such that any decision along these lines would have led to intense in-fighting. An alternative solution was therefore proposed.

In 1786, Thomas Jefferson's *Virginia Statute for Religious Freedom* set out the principle of the separation of church and state, and ended any legal oversight or enforcement of religious belief. The Constitution of the United States of America, adopted on September 17, 1787, by the Constitutional Convention in Philadelphia, makes no reference to God, or to Christianity. Where Jefferson's "Declaration of Independence" famously invoked a "Creator" in setting out its vision of human rights, the constitution avoided any such references.

The First Amendment to the Constitution, adopted on December 15, 1791, ended the formal establishment of religion. This amendment was initially aimed at limiting the power of the federal government to create or maintain its own religious establishment. The First Amendment did not, however, extend to individual states, allowing state and local governments to continue to uphold local forms of establishment, and to regulate or restrict religious liberties. For example, some of the New England states, such as Connecticut and Massachusetts, continued to have formal Congregationalist establishments into the nineteenth century.

The First Amendment is framed in terms that made its subsequent application problematic: "Congress shall make no law respecting an establishment of religion, or prohibiting the free exercise thereof." The new American constitution, thus amended, opened the way to a radical reshaping of the nation's religious landscape, sweeping away established structures, and creating new structures without parallel at that time. Some might argue that the constitutional separation of church and state was an attempt to marginalize religion in public life. This would, however, seem to be a mistaken perception.

For many at the time, such as the Baptist minister Isaac Backus (1724–1806), this separation amounted to a virtual guarantee that America would be a Christian nation, whose churches would be free from political interference and manipulation. As Backus argued, when "church and state are separate, the effects are happy, and they do not at all interfere with each other: but where they have been confounded together, no tongue nor pen can fully describe the mischiefs that have ensued." Backus saw the "wall of separation between church and state" as ensuring freedom of religious belief and practice for all, and privilege for none. The abolition of a religious establishment merely created a level playing field, on which the best forms of Christianity would be free to compete with, and ultimately overcome, its weaker and less authentic rivals.

There is no doubt that the success of the American Revolution was discussed intently in the salons of late eighteenth-century Paris, where discontent over an out-of-touch monarchy was also widespread. The most fundamental perception was simple: the existing political order could be changed, if enough people combined together to make this happen. The public mood in France began to change. France had become involved in the American War of Independence, which had won the government much popular acclaim but had virtually bankrupted the nation. The government had to raise money to clear its debts. And taxation was the only option. And it turned out to be a hugely unpopular option, which stoked the fires of open revolt.

4.1.8.   The French Revolution of 1789

Although the origins of the French Revolution lie in growing social unrest and intellectual agitation against the French monarchy, the trigger for revolt was financial. Food shortages and poor harvests saw the price of bread soar, causing widespread deprivation among the peasantry and working classes. French participation in the American revolutionary war had saddled the nation with massive debts, which urgently needed to be resolved.

The French king Louis XVI (1754–93), realizing that the situation was desperate, and that the measures needed to resolve it would require broad support, reluctantly summoned the Estates General in 1789 to reform the taxation system. This was the first time the body had been summoned since 1614. The Estates General refused to endorse the king's demands, and confronted Louis with a series of demands for social and financial reform that he was unwilling to accept. The "Third Estate" – the assembly of commoners – openly demanded radical change, and proclaimed themselves as representatives of the people. Although some concessions were made, they were not enough. Angered by the lack of serious reforms, protesters took to the streets of Paris. On July 14, 1789, a mob stormed the Bastille – a fortress used to house political prisoners. The fall of the Bastille became an icon of a revolution that captured the imagination of the French public.

The initial goals of the French Revolution appear to have been to achieve some form of social democracy, and a fairer distribution of national wealth. There was considerable popular resentment against wealthy landowners and the church, both of which were seen as bastions of privilege which needed to be reformed. At this stage, there appears to have been little overt hostility towards Christianity as a set of ideas; rather, criticism was directed against the institution of the French Catholic church, often with the support of disillusioned clergy.

To begin with, there was little sign of any anti-Christian agenda on the part of the revolutionary leadership. To eliminate any influence from Rome, Catholic clergy were now required to sign the Civil Constitution, pledging obedience to the republic. While this was a form of secularization, it can also be seen as a reassertion of the independence of the French church from Rome, asserted by Francis I after his defeat of papal forces in Italy in the early sixteenth century.

Clergy now became employees of the state, elected by their parish or bishopric. All priests and bishops had to swear an oath of obedience to the new order or face dismissal, deportation, or death. This caused considerable difficulty for pope Pius VI. After eight months, he ruled that the new French constitution was illegal, and that clergy should not sign it. The French church split into two factions, those who would sign (the "abjurors") and those who would not (the "non-jurors").

Yet as the revolution developed, more explicitly anti-religious views began to dominate. Voltaire and his circle argued that every positive religion – including Judaism, the various Islamic sects, and Christian denominations – had corrupted a pure, rational concept of God, known to every person through nature and reason. The reformation of religion might well focus on the French Catholic church, but it extended far beyond this. A new state religion was thus required, grounded in the worship of the Supreme Being.

A still more radical view, however, was rapidly gaining support. It claimed that the oppression of the French people by both the court and the church could be put down to a belief in God, including the "Supreme Being" acknowledged by Deist writers, such as Voltaire. A genuine revolution would therefore necessitate overthrowing this fundamental belief altogether, rather than attempting to reform it. Atheism was the Promethean liberator, which alone could guarantee the initial success and subsequent triumph of the revolution. Any notion of a transcendent God – whether deriving from Christianity or the "Religion of Nature" – was to be eliminated, and replaced with a secular alternative.

Over the period 1790–5, a series of developments shifted France from a constitutional monarchy in which the Catholic church had a continuing role to an implicitly atheist republic in which the only gods acknowledged were the ideals of the revolution, and those who supported them. Violence against priests and religious orders became common. A series of measures were passed into law, designed to eliminate any Christian religious or cultural footprint in French society. For example, the town of St. Tropez, named after a Christian who was martyred during the time of the Roman emperor Nero, was renamed "Héraclée" in 1793.

The anti-religious "Festival of Reason" was inaugurated on November 10, 1793. Churches across France were declared to be "Temples of Reason." The most important ceremony of this festival took place at Notre Dame in Paris, in which the cathedral's altar was replaced with one dedicated to liberty, and the inscription "To Philosophy" carved over the cathedral's main doors. The culmination of the ceremony was the enthronement of a "Goddess of Reason" on the cathedral's altar.

Yet the "Cult of Reason" proved to be short-lived. On May 7, 1794, this was abandoned, being replaced by the more restrained Deist "Cult of the Supreme Being." Robespierre was anxious that the program of dechristianization was causing growing resentment, and fueling counter-revolutionary sentiment. God required reinstatement – at least, in some modest form. The campaign against Christian symbolism and influence continued. But God was allowed back into the public domain.

Within a decade, the fledgling French Republic found itself overtaken by events, as Napoleon Bonaparte entered Paris, and seized power (4.2.1). A new constitution was proclaimed on December 15, 1799, declaring the end of the revolutionary era: "Citizens, the Revolution is established upon the principles which began it: it is over." The restoration of Catholicism soon followed.

Yet the French Revolution had changed the face of Christian Europe. Its after-effects would linger for many years. In the next section, we shall consider the revolutionary situation that resulted in many parts of Europe from this turning point in modern history. Yet a revolution of a somewhat different nature was taking place in England around the same time – the abolition of slavery.

4.1.9.   England: William Wilberforce and the Abolition of Slavery

The slave trade was an integral part of the British economy in the eighteenth century. Traders plied a triangular route between English ports, such as Bristol and Liverpool, and west Africa, where slaves were purchased from local tribal leaders in exchange for manufactured goods. The ships then headed across the Atlantic Ocean on the "middle passage" to American and Caribbean ports on islands such as Jamaica, Trinidad, and the Leeward Islands in a journey lasting up to eight weeks. The slaves were then sold, and the ships took on cargoes such as cotton, tobacco, and sugar, before returning to England. All of these were produced by slave labor on plantations.

Yet the practice was arousing increasing opposition on humanitarian and religious grounds. John Newton (1725–1807) was the captain of a slave ship who experienced a religious conversion in 1748, which led him to realize the inhumanity of his actions as a slave trader. He left his life as a slave-ship captain, and went on to be ordained as a minister of the Church of England, serving in the village of Olney. In 1764, he published his "Authentic Narrative" detailing his experiences while commanding a slave vessel, which aroused public concern about the morality of the slave trade.

In 1779, Newton published, in collaboration with William Cowper (1731–1800), the *Olney Hymns*. Many of these continue to be used today. Yet perhaps the most poignant of these take the form of theological critiques of the slave trade, above all its fundamental assumption of the racial inferiority of Africans to Europeans. This is perhaps stated most clearly in the hymn "The Negro's Complaint":

> Still in thought as free as ever,
>   What are England's rights, I ask,
> Me from my delights to sever,
>   Me to torture, me to task?
> Fleecy locks and black complexion
>   Cannot forfeit nature's claim;
> Skins may differ, but affection
>   Dwells in white and black the same.

Amid growing public concern about the slave trade, the University of Cambridge announced an essay competition in 1785 with the title: "Is it right to make men slaves against their will?" The prize was won by Thomas Clarkson (1760–1846), who later described how he had "a direct revelation from God ordering me to devote my life to abolishing the trade."

In 1787 Clarkson formed the Society for the Abolition of the Slave Trade, having published a detailed account of the inhumanity of the trade the previous year. Josiah Wedgwood, the owner of a pottery, joined the committee, and invited one of his craftsmen to design a seal for correspondence in support of abolition. The resulting design depicted a kneeling African in chains, lifting his hands imploringly, asking: "Am I Not a Man and a Brother?" It was a powerful image, which was widely adopted in London society.

Although some opposed slavery on the basis of secular considerations, such as the natural rights of humanity, the growing criticism of the slave trade was primarily religious in nature. Religious opposition to the trade came from two main quarters, both outside, or on the margins of, the established Church of England: initially, the Religious Society of Friends (better known as the Quakers), and subsequently the evangelical Anglican group known as the "Clapham Sect," which gathered around Henry Venn, rector of Clapham Church in London.

Prominent among the latter was William Wilberforce (1759–1833), the Member of Parliament for Hull, who had had a religious conversion experience in 1784. As a result of his conversion and conversations with other members of the Clapham Sect, Wilberforce had developed a commitment to the abolition of the slave trade on religious grounds. God, he argued, "has made from one blood every nation of men" (Acts 17:26). How then could people be treated as mere possessions? Or one race be deemed inferior to another? Needing a political sponsor to promote anti-slavery legislation in parliament, Clarkson approached Wilberforce.

It was a good choice. Wilberforce was a close friend and colleague of William Pitt, the prime minister. Wilberforce entered the parliamentary debate on May 12, 1789, with a long, closely reasoned speech of three-and-a-half hours, describing the impact of the trade on Africa and the appalling conditions of the "middle passage." Abolition, he argued, would

Figure 4.2   William Wilberforce (1759–1833), English philanthropist who pressed for the abolition of slavery. Engraving. Photo: IAM/akg-images

not merely end an immoral activity. It would lead to an improvement in the conditions of slaves already in the West Indies.

He was supported by other religious leaders who were hostile to the trade, including the former slave-trader John Newton, and the great Methodist statesman and preacher, John Wesley. Wesley's last letter, dated February 24, 1791, urged Wilberforce to maintain his parliamentary campaign against the trade.

In the end, fierce opposition from commercial interests within parliament defeated Wilberforce's attempts to end the slave trade. Wilberforce's advocation of principle over profit was seen by some as politically naive; England's economy, it was argued, depended on the trade. The outbreak of war with France distracted parliament from the slave question, as national concern mounted about a possible military threat from France, and the risk of a revolution in England. Yet Wilberforce and his allies persisted, gaining allies in parliament and securing increasing public support. In 1807, parliament passed legislation to end the slave trade. It was a triumph for Wilberforce and his circle. Yet parliament did not abolish slavery itself; simply the trade in slaves.

Wilberforce continued his campaign. In an 1823 *Appeal* for the slaves of the West Indies, Wilberforce appealed to "the express authority of Scripture" to challenge the social basis of slavery. Christianity, Wilberforce argued, insisted that "the lower classes, instead of being an inferior order in the creation, are even the preferable objects of the love of the Almighty."

It was not until shortly after Wilberforce's death in 1833 that parliament finally abolished slavery throughout the British Empire.

Although Wilberforce's challenge to slavery began in the eighteenth century, it only achieved its goals in the nineteenth. In view of the remarkable significance of this later period, we shall consider some of the major developments in western Christianity to take place during what the historian Eric Hobsbawm called "the long nineteenth century" – that is, the period between the French Revolution of 1789, and the outbreak of the Great War in 1914.

4.2.   An Age of Revolution: The Long Nineteenth Century in Europe

The French Revolution (4.1.8) was an important event in its own right. Yet many would argue that its aftermath was even more important. As European monarchies began to intervene in French affairs following the revolution, French revolutionary armies were raised through mass mobilization. The tide quickly turned; nations which had intervened in French affairs found themselves being invaded. The French revolutionary wars destabilized much of western Europe, creating political uncertainty. French armies occupied parts of Switzerland, Germany, and Italy, even reaching Rome in 1798 and deposing Pope Pius VI. The pope sought exile in France, where he died in 1799.

Yet infighting within the leadership of the French Revolution in the late 1790s led to a weakening of the movement, making its overthrow possible. A charismatic new leader emerged within France, precipitating still further political and religious upheaval across Europe.

4.2.1.   The Napoleonic Wars and the Congress of Vienna

On November 9, 1799, Napoleon Bonaparte – then a hugely popular and charismatic general in the French revolutionary army – seized power in France. On December 2, 1804, Bonaparte crowned himself emperor, breaking with the republicanism of the revolution. Yet the French revolutionary wars continued, as Napoleon sought to extend French influence southwards in the Iberian Peninsula, and eastwards into Poland and Russia. Kings, princes, and monarchs were deposed, and replaced with institutions based on due process of law, as set out in the Napoleonic Code. The metric system – kilograms and kilometers – replaced traditional units of weight and length. Only Great Britain seemed immune to Napoleon, in that its navy prevented any attempted invasion, while at the same time keeping its imperial trade routes operational, preventing economic meltdown.

Napoleon succeeded in establishing, however briefly, a more or less unified rule over much of western Europe, sweeping away the remaining medieval and feudal laws and replacing them with a unified consistent code of national law. France's status as a nation-state was a key factor in its ability to dominate feudal neighbors in Italy and Germany, who lacked the centralized structures needed to respond effectively to the French military challenge.

Figure 4.3   Napoleon Bonaparte, emperor of France, 1769–1821, by François Gerard (1770–1837), detail. The Art Archive/Musée du Château de Versailles (MV5321)/Gianni Dagli Orti

Nevertheless, France had overextended itself in the wars of the 1790s and 1810s, and simply could not sustain its new empire. Napoleon was forced to withdraw from Moscow in 1812, and was defeated at the battle of Waterloo in 1815. He abdicated as emperor, and was exiled to the island of St. Helena. The Congress of Vienna (1814–15) met to redraw the national boundaries of Europe. The primary object of the congress was to prevent any nation achieving such power that it could achieve total dominance. This objective involved the redefining of national boundaries, and the identification of "spheres of influence" of the leading European powers. However, this new Europe would differ significantly from the old, with major implications for the future of Christianity.

The most obvious change was the weakening of the power and influence of autocratic rulers. Where monarchs were restored, they found that they could no longer expect passive acquiescence from their subjects. The period of Napoleonic rule had created a culture based on merit and achievement. The forms of absolutism and feudalism that existed before the French Revolution were much more difficult to sustain after the end of the Napoleonic wars. Populations were more likely to resist monarchs than before.

The Napoleonic wars exhausted France, which ceased to be the dominant power in western Europe after its defeat. Spain and Portugal were both weakened, and found it increasingly difficult to maintain control over their South American colonies, many of which went on to develop credible independence movements inspired by the Venezuelan military and political leader Simón Bolívar (1783–1830). By the end of the war, Great Britain was firmly established as the dominant power in Europe, its naval power being supplemented by the economic potential of its growing empire and the industrial revolution.

In 1814, Louis XVIII returned to claim the throne of France, and reestablished Catholicism as the nation's religion. The situation of Catholicism within France was never easy, and real tensions between church and state continued unabated throughout most of the nineteenth century. Nevertheless, the church was able to regain at least some of its lost influence, prestige, and clergy. The period 1815–48 witnessed a series of popular revivals (usually referred to as "le Réveil") in French-speaking Europe.

Yet the impact of the French Revolution and its aftermath extended far beyond Catholicism in France. Although missions had established a significant Catholic presence in regions such as South America, Japan, and India, Catholicism remained a largely European religion at this stage, bounded by the new nation of Belgium in the northwest, Spain in the southwest, Austria in the northeast, and Italy in the southeast. Most of the one hundred million European Catholics were to be found in the Habsburg Empire, Italy, and France – all of which had been profoundly affected by the revolutionary and Napoleonic wars. Pius VII, pope from 1800 to 1823, was faced with a crisis. The status of the Catholic church in the "New Europe" needed to be clarified as a matter of urgency.

The Congregation for Extraordinary Ecclesiastical Affairs was established in 1814, with the objective of rebuilding Catholicism throughout Europe. The papal Secretary of State, Cardinal Ercole Consalvi (1757–1824), was given the responsibility of negotiating concordats with a series of states during the Congress of Vienna (1815). Consalvi had already negotiated a concordat with Napoleon in 1801, which restored some of the rights of Catholicism within France. Consalvi persuaded the Congress of Vienna to restore the papal states – territories in northern Italy under papal control, which had been annexed by French revolutionary armies in the 1790s.

After the trauma of the French Revolution, Catholicism began to regain at least something of the confidence it had known in earlier periods. The rise of Romanticism had a powerful effect on the reawakening of interest in Catholicism, particularly in Germany and France. François-René de Chateaubriand's *Genius of Christianity* (1802) did much to develop this new interest in the Christian faith, which can be seen reflected in many aspects of nineteenth-century culture. Other writers who drew on Romanticism in their defense of Catholicism included Alessandro Manzoni (1785–1873) in Italy and Friedrich von Stolberg (1750–1819) in Germany. Rationalism was seen by some as having led to the catastrophes of the past, such as the violence and excesses of the French Revolution. There was a new sympathy for the view that Christianity was a major source of artistic inspiration and cultural excellence.

Yet the impact of the Napoleonic wars would be felt in other Christian churches. A good example of the new pressures facing Christianity can be seen in the forced merger of Lutheran and Reformed churches in Prussia in the aftermath of the Council of Vienna. Napoleon's defeat of Prussia at the battles of Jena and Auerstedt in October 1806 brought home the need for institutional reform. Prussia's feudal system of government and military leadership had proved incapable of responding to the challenge of Napoleon. King William III of Prussia set out a series of reforms, designed to streamline and modernize his government. This had significant implications for Prussian Protestantism.

Since the seventeenth century, Prussia had been predominantly Protestant, with two major denominations – Lutheran and Reformed (3.5.1). In 1808, William III proposed a union of the two denominations within his realm. This proposal was implemented after the final defeat of Napoleon, when the Prussian Ministry of Religious, Educational, and Medical Affairs was established to administer the religious affairs of the region. Although individual Lutheran and Reformed congregations were free to retain their original identity, many joined the new union, which came to be known as the Evangelical Church in Prussia. William III increasingly imposed religious centralization on the Prussian churches, leading many Lutherans to believe that their concerns were being marginalized. In the late 1830s, many Prussian Lutherans emigrated to North America and Australia, where they could retain their original liturgical practices without state interference. The origins of the Missouri Synod lie in this development.

As we shall see, the nineteenth century would be a tempestuous time for Christianity in Europe. Yet it is important to note how developments in eastern Europe around this same time led to the consolidation of Christianity, rather than its marginalization. This is especially clear in the events which took place in southeastern Europe, as the Ottoman grip on power in the region began to wane.

4.2.2.   Orthodox Resurgence: The Greek War of Independence

The Ottoman Empire continued to be a significant force in southeastern Europe in the eighteenth century. The conclusive defeat of Ottoman armies by the Habsburgs in the 1690s had put an end to any possibility of Turkish expansion in Europe. Yet the resulting peace treaty left many parts of southeastern Europe under Ottoman control. The growing influence of Russia – an Orthodox nation – in the region was consolidated by its defeat of Ottoman armies in the Russo-Turkish War of 1768–74. Russia's victory over the Ottoman forces increased its territory, and gave it influence over Christian nations within the Ottoman Empire – including Serbia and Greece, both of which were traditionally Orthodox nations.

Resentment against the Ottoman Empire within both regions was rising, partly due to perceived religious discrimination against non-Muslims, who were required to pay a poll tax (*jizyah*). A Serbian revolt against Ottoman rule in 1788 was supported by the Austrians. However, the Austrian withdrawal from Serbia in 1791 led to the Ottomans returning, and resuming control of the region. Following a massacre of Serbian nobles in 1804, a popular uprising took place, encouraged by the Russian Empire. France supported the Ottoman Empire, fearing the growing power of Russia, as did Austria, which believed that the liberation movement of the oppressed Slavic peoples would quickly spread to Austrian territory. Yet the popular uprising gained momentum. In 1806, Belgrade was besieged. Following its capitulation to the revolutionaries, it was proclaimed the capital city of an independent Serbia.

Hopes of Greek nationalists now began to soar. Secret nationalist societies were formed in Greece, with the objective of securing liberation from Ottoman rule. Western European intellectuals promoted the idea of Greek independence. Many – such as the British poet Lord Byron (1788–1824) – were influenced by "philohellenism," a movement which saw the resurgence of Greece as a modern nation-state as linked with the recovery of its classic cultural status. The insurgency began in March 1821, although rivalry between its leaders limited its efficacy. Lord Byron traveled to Greece to join the rebellion, offering financial support to the fledgling Greek navy. In the end, the revolt failed. Ottoman reinforcements from Egypt were able to suppress the insurrection in southern Greece. By July 1827, the revolt had stalled.

However, the revolt was now of interest to the Great Powers. Russia, Great Britain, and France all sent naval task forces to the region. After what appears to have been a misunderstanding, most of the Ottoman navy was sunk at Navarino in October 1827. Now deprived of any means of transporting reinforcements or munitions, the Ottoman army began to lose ground. In the end, they withdrew from Central Greece. A series of conferences brokered by Russia, Great Britain, and France created the new state of Greece during the 1830s.

As noted earlier, the Ottoman period gave rise to religious tensions throughout the Balkans. The religion of the Ottoman Empire was Sunni Islam; that of the occupied regions of Europe was generally Orthodox Christianity. It was inevitable that any wars of independence would have religious components. The Greek War of Independence signaled the return of Orthodoxy as the official religion of the nation. Nationalist movements developed close links with the church, which was seen by many as having preserved the Greek language and culture during the long period of Turkish occupation. Whereas the French Revolution of 1789 identified Catholicism as an enemy, the Greek revolution of 1821 saw Orthodoxy as an ally.

4.2.3. Atheism and an Ideology of Revolution: Feuerbach and Marx

Perhaps one of the most revolutionary developments of the first half of the nineteenth century was not the formation of new political units or the shaping of social attitudes towards religion in Europe, but the emergence of a critique of religion that undermined its credibility. The European churches gained their social influence partly because they were seen as the bearers of a divinely given and divinely authorized message. But what if this message were simply an invention, shaped either by human needs or by its social context? In early nineteenth-century Germany, a school of thought emerged which argued that religion was not a response to divine revelation, but was in essence a matter of psychology or sociology.

The political and social background to this development needs explanation. The war between revolutionary France and the absolutist German princes and monarchs of 1792 raised new hopes of radical social reform within Germany. Liberal politicians such as Karl Theodor Welcker (1790–1869) pressed home popular demands for press freedom and other democratic rights. In 1817, some five hundred students celebrated the three-hundredth anniversary of the Reformation by marching to the Wartburg to demand constitutional changes and a united fatherland. Demands for political reform, often driven by a strongly nationalist agenda, became widespread.

In an uprising of June 1844, weavers in Silesia demanded that their "starvation wages" should be increased. They were bluntly told "to eat grass," and their revolt was put down harshly by the Prussian army. In 1847, widespread crop failures led to severe food shortages. Unemployment rose, and hunger riots by desperate workers demanding food were suppressed by the army. There were renewed demands for constitutional government, a bill of rights, and national unification. By April 1849, however, it was clear that any hope of a revolution had faded.

The Protestant churches of Germany were widely – though not entirely fairly – seen as reactionary social forces, preventing radical social change. Failure to neutralize their social and political power led to the development of an alternative strategy – the subversion of the ideas on which they were based.

Ludwig Feuerbach (1804–72), in his influential *Essence of Christianity* (1841), declared that God was an invention – something that human beings created as a means of expressing or satisfying their deepest desires and cravings. Far from being a transcendent reality, God was merely the "projection" or "objectification" of human feelings and emotions. Feuerbach's radical "critique of religion," based loosely on G. W. F. Hegel's philosophy of religion, argued that Christianity was merely a human psychological construction. "What religion once understood to be objective is now recognized to be subjective. What formerly was taken to be God, and worshipped as such, is now recognized to be something human." People created God after their own longings.

Feuerbach's approaches were attractive to many reforming intellectuals, partly because they were seen as a means of undermining the authority of the churches, and thus neutralizing the threat they posed to radical social change. Yet Feuerbach himself seemed reluctant to become involved in political action. In the end, the political aspects of his ideas would be developed in a far more radical manner by the political philosopher Karl Marx (1818–83). For Marx, ideas arise from – and reflect – a social and economic foundation. Ideas – including religious ideas – are thus ultimately an expression of their socioeconomic environment.

Marx agreed with Feuerbach's analysis of the origins of the religious notion of God, yet argued he had failed to show how the human desire to invent God is the result of the social situation of humanity. Religion, Marx argued, arose on account of the sorrow and injustice which resulted from political and economic alienation – for example, as a result of the "division of labor," which alienated workers from their products.

The roots of religion, according to Marx, lie in forces and influences within the material world. Religion has no real independent existence, but is merely an epiphenomenon, a symptom of something more real and substantial that lies underneath it – namely, the material world. "The religious world is but the reflex of the real world." Thus Marx argues that "religion is just the imaginary sun which seems to man to revolve around him, until he realizes that he himself is the centre of his own revolution." In other words, God is simply a projection of human concerns. Human beings "look for a superhuman being in the fantasy reality of heaven, and find nothing their but their own reflection."

Figure 4.4   Karl Marx (1818–83), German founder of international communism, photograph. The Art Archive/Karl Marx Museum Trier/Gianni Dagli Orti

Since religion is the product of social and economic alienation, Marx argued that radical social change would abolish the ultimate cause of religion, and hence bring about its irreversible decline. Those wishing to eliminate religion should thus focus their attention on securing revolutionary political action, which would permanently eliminate the factors that led to religious belief in the first place. "The struggle against religion is therefore indirectly a struggle against *the world* of which religion is the spiritual fragrance."

Feuerbach, Marx argued, failed to take this social dimension of the individual seriously, tending to see individuals as being detached from social structures. If social conditions determine the world of ideas, it follows that changing those conditions will have a critical effect upon the resulting ideologies. It is this insight which underlies Marx's often quoted comment on Feuerbach: "the philosophers have only interpreted the world, in various ways; the point, however, is to change it."

Religion thus eases the pain of the real world by creating a dream world – a "fantasy of a supernatural world where all sorrows cease." Feuerbach had already argued that religion was a consoling illusion; Marx now argues that the abolition of a social condition which condemns people to live by illusions will remove the causes of religious belief in the first place. This underlies what is probably Marx's most famous phrase about the nature of religion, which is found in his *Contribution to the Critique of Hegel's Philosophy of Law* (1843–4): "Religion is the sigh of the oppressed creature, the heart of a heartless world, . . . the *opium* of the people."

Marx's notion of religion as the "opium of the people" resonated throughout the politically alienated intellectuals of Europe, and would play a major role in shaping the Russian Revolution under Lenin during the early twentieth century. Yet further challenges to the intellectual foundations of Christianity were emerging around this time, including new theories about the origins of humanity which seemed to call into question the reliability of both biblical texts and Christian theology. We must now turn to consider the important Darwinian debates of the later nineteenth century.

4.2.4.   Human Origins: Darwin's *Origin of Species* (1859)

The publication of Charles Darwin's *Origin of Species* is rightly regarded as a landmark for both the natural sciences and Christian belief in Victorian Britain and beyond. On December 27, 1831, the sailing ship *Beagle* set out from the southern English port of Plymouth on a voyage that lasted almost five years. The ship's naturalist was Charles Darwin (1809–82). During the voyage, Darwin noted some aspects of the plant and animal life of South America which seemed to him to require explanation, yet which were not satisfactorily accounted for by existing theories.

One popular account of the origin of species, known to Darwin, found wide support within the religious establishment of the early nineteenth century. William Paley (1743–1805), archdeacon of Carlisle, argued that God had created everything more or less as we now see it, in all its intricacy. Paley accepted the viewpoint of his age – namely, that God had constructed (Paley prefers the word "contrived") the world in its finished form, as we now know it. The idea of any kind of development seemed impossible to him.

Paley argued that the present organization of the world, both physical and biological, could be seen as a compelling witness to the wisdom of a creator god. Paley's *Natural Theology* (1802) had a profound influence on popular English religious thought in the first half of the nineteenth century, and is known to have been read by Darwin. Paley was deeply impressed by Newton's discovery of the regularity of nature, which allowed the universe to be thought of as a complex mechanism, operating according to regular and understandable principles. Nature consists of a series of biological structures which are to be thought of as being "contrived" – that is, constructed with a clear purpose in mind. Paley used his famous analogy of the watch on a heath to emphasize that contrivance necessarily presupposed a designer and constructor. "Every indication of contrivance, every manifestation of design, which existed in the watch, exists in the works of nature."

Darwin's reflections on his voyage on the *Beagle* led him to propose an alternative theory. Darwin's approach, as set out in the *Origin of Species* (1859) and the *Descent of Man* (1871), held that all species – including humanity – resulted from a long and complex process of biological evolution. The religious implications of this will be clear. Traditional Christian thought regarded humanity as being set apart from the rest of nature, created as the height of God's creation, and alone endowed with the "image of God." Darwin's theory suggested that human nature emerged gradually, over a long period of time, and that no fundamental biological distinction could be drawn between human beings and animals in terms of their origins and development.

Traditional Christian theology regarded humanity as the height of God's creation, distinguished from the remainder of the created order by being created in the image of God. On this traditional reading of things, humanity is to be located within the created order as a whole, yet stands above it on account of its unique relationship to God, articulated in the notion of the *imago Dei*. Yet Darwin's *Origin of Species* posed an implicit, and *The Descent of Man* an explicit, challenge to this view. Humanity had emerged, over a vast period of time, from within the natural order.

If there was one aspect of his own theory of evolution which left Charles Darwin feeling unsettled, it was its implications for the status and identity of the human race. Darwin rejected any idea that evolution demonstrated an "innate and inevitable tendency towards perfection." The inevitable conclusion must therefore be that human beings cannot in any sense be said to be either the "goal" or the "apex" of evolution. It was not an easy conclusion for Darwin, or for his age, to accept.

The traditional Christian understandings of the notion of "creation" prevalent within popular religious culture – seen, for example, in Paley's *Natural Theology* – attributed the creation of the world, including humanity, to direct, special divine action. Darwin, however, found this notion of special creation problematic on several grounds. What of vestigial or rudimentary organs? And what of the uneven geographical distribution of species? Darwin argued that the origin of species is to be attributed to an extended natural process of variation and selection, in which no divine intervention is required or presupposed.

So did this mean that Darwin regarded God as redundant? Or non-existent? Darwin himself did not say so, and his religious interpreters of the later nineteenth century certainly did not think so. Indeed, some theologians took the view that Darwin had actually rescued Paley's approach, by placing it on a firmer intellectual foundation through rectifying a faulty and ultimately fatal premise.

Charles Kingsley (1819–75), canon of Westminster Abbey, was certainly one to take this viewpoint. In his 1871 lecture "On the Natural Theology of the Future," Kingsley singled out Darwin's work on orchids as "a most valuable addition to natural theology." Insisting that the word "creation" implies process as much as event, Kingsley went on to argue that Darwin's theory clarified the mechanism of creation. "We knew of old that God was so wise that he could make all things; but, behold, he is so much wiser than even that, that he can make all things make themselves." Where Paley thought in terms of a static creation, Kingsley argued that Darwin now made it possible to see creation as a dynamic process, directed by divine providence. This, Kingsley declared, was a much more noble and satisfying understanding of the process by which God brought all things into being – whether directly, or indirectly.

Yet while Darwin's theory of evolution did not lead to the elimination of God, it highlighted a particular difficulty for Christian theology: how could the goodness of God be maintained, in the light of the wastefulness of the evolutionary process? Surely there was a more efficient, more humane way of achieving these goals? Darwin himself felt the force of this point. Paley's argument emphasized the wisdom of God in creation. But what, Darwin wondered, of God's goodness? How could the brutality, pain, and sheer waste of

Figure 4.5   Engraving of Charles Robert Darwin (1809–82), British naturalist, in his old age. Science Photo Library

nature be reconciled with the idea of a benevolent God? In his "Sketch of 1842," Darwin found himself pondering how such things as "creeping parasites" and other creatures that lay their eggs in the bowels or flesh of other animals can be justified within Paley's scheme. How could God's goodness be reconciled with such less pleasant aspects of the created order?

There are indeed several important passages in Darwin's writings that can be interpreted to mean that Darwin ceased to believe in an orthodox Christian conception of God on account of his views on evolution. The problem is that there are other passages which variously point to Darwin maintaining a religious belief, or to his losing his faith for reasons quite other than evolutionary concerns. However, a note of caution must be injected: on the basis of the published evidence at our disposal, it is clear that Darwin himself was far from consistent in the matter of his religious views. It would therefore be extremely unwise to draw any confident conclusions on these issues.

There can be no doubt that Darwin abandoned what we might call "conventional Christian beliefs" at some point in the 1840s, although the dating of this must remain elusive. Yet there is a substantial theoretical gap between "abandoning orthodox Christian faith" and "becoming an atheist." Christianity involves a highly specific conception of God; it is perfectly possible to believe in a god other than that of Christianity, or to believe in God and reject certain other aspects of the Christian faith. Indeed, the "Victorian crisis of faith" – within which Darwin was both spectator and participant – can be understood as a shift away from the specifics of Christianity towards a more generic concept of God, largely determined by the ethical values of the day.

This "Victorian crisis of faith" is of such interest that it deserves more detailed discussion in its own right.

4.2.5.   The Victorian Crisis of Faith

It is generally accepted that religious belief in England and many European nations went through a period of decline and uncertainty during the long nineteenth century, particularly towards the end of this period. In this section, we shall consider developments within England. Although these can be paralleled from the narrative of other European societies at this time, England's status as an economic, military, and cultural power gave these developments particular significance.

At the beginning of the nineteenth century, there was little sign of any emerging crisis of faith. William Paley's *Natural Theology* (1802), which we noted in the previous section, affirmed the widespread view of the fundamental harmony of the natural sciences and Christian faith. This view was reaffirmed in the opening years of Queen Victoria's reign through the publication of the celebrated "Bridgewater Treatises" (1833–6), which emphasized how the beauty and regularity of the natural world confirmed the existence and wisdom of a creator God.

There was little public appetite for radical change, religious or political. Although the extremism of the French Revolution (4.1.8) was warmly welcomed by some young radicals of the 1790s and early 1800s, such enthusiasm soon dissolved. The poet William Wordsworth (1770–1850) illustrates both an initial enthusiasm at the abolition of a corrupt order, along with a growing unease about the violence and bloodshed it created. Atheism gained few supporters in England on account of the revolution; most English people seem to have seen anti-religious views as socially destabilizing and irresponsible.

Yet deeper forces were at work in English culture, creating a context within which a new and more distant attitude to faith would emerge. One was the Industrial Revolution, which developed sooner and more rapidly in England than in many other nations. While rural churches were often deeply embedded in the life of rural communities, the migration of rural populations to cities led to a disconnection between the working class and the church. Urban churches often failed to connect with burgeoning communities of industrial workers. This development is better understood as a growing alienation between sections of the English population and the institutional churches, rather than a growing distrust of Christian ideas and values. Nevertheless, these two are clearly connected.

A second development was the rise of biblical criticism, which became increasingly important in the second half of the nineteenth century. The edited collection *Essays and Reviews* (1860) caused a scandal on account of its critical attitude towards the Bible on the part of its seven liberal Anglican authors. The most controversial of the essays was Benjamin Jowett's "On the Interpretation of Scripture," which argued that the Bible ought to be read "like any other book." The impact of this collection of essays was perhaps greater than it might otherwise have been, as it was published a year after Darwin's *Origin of*

Species had opened up a debate about the reliability of the Bible's account of human origins.

Yet perhaps the most celebrated exponent of biblical criticism was John William Colenso (1814–83), a colonial bishop of the Church of England. Colenso was one of an increasing number of writers to raise doubts about the factual reliability of the Old Testament. Especially in his *The Pentateuch and the Book of Joshua Critically Examined* (1862), Colenso questioned the accuracy of the narratives of the historical books of the Old Testament. He disputed whether Moses had written the Pentateuch (the first five works of the Old Testament), and argued that its spiritual value did not imply its historical accuracy. "Though imparting to us, as I fully believe it does, revelations of the Divine Will and Character, it cannot be regarded as historically true." These views from the pen of a colonial bishop caused a scandal in Victorian England, in that they were seen to challenge the basic idea that the Bible could be trusted.

A third area of tension concerned the growing popular influence of science, which was increasingly coming to be seen as a cultural authority which was independent and critical of religion. The Darwinian debates (4.2.4) added significantly to these discussions. For many later Victorians, science was about the future, and religion was about the past. This perception was intensified by the publication of works arguing for the permanent "warfare" of science and faith, such as John William Draper's *History of the Conflict between Religion and Science* (1874) and Andrew Dickson White's *History of the Warfare of Science with Theology in Christendom* (1896).

Victorian Christianity responded to these developments in a number of manners. The "Oxford Movement," which emerged during the 1830s, was critical of German New Testament scholarship, and developed a program for the renewal of the "high church" movement within the Church of England. Some advocated disengagement from these cultural trends, anticipating some of the themes that were later associated with American Protestant Fundamentalism during the 1920s. Yet the dominant response was to attempt to reach a religious accommodation with these cultural developments. The willingness of the Victorian churches to come to terms with biological and geological science, social science, archaeology, comparative religion, and biblical scholarship can be seen partly as a pragmatic response to the changing cultural situation. To resist these changes, many senior churchmen believed, would only lead to the increasing cultural marginalization and isolation of organized religion within English society.

4.2.6. The Risorgimento: Italian Reunification and the Pope

The French Revolution (4.1.8) and the Napoleonic wars (4.2.1) caused severe difficulties for the papacy. Pius VI was evicted from Rome by revolutionary armies, and spent the last six months of his life exiled in France. The Papal States – a substantial area of territory, including most of the modern Italian regions of Lazio, Marche, Romagna, and Umbria – were invaded, and turned into French provinces. The Congress of Vienna more or less returned Italy to the situation it had known before the wars. The Papal States were restored, as was the pre-Napoleonic patchwork of regional governments, often ruled by external powers. For example, the city of Venice and the region around it (known as "the Veneto") were ruled by Austria from 1797 to 1866.

One of the outcomes of the Napoleonic wars was an upsurge in nationalism throughout many parts of Europe. Spain adopted a new liberal constitution in 1812, and was followed by Portugal in 1822. These developments were seen as moving away from the older system of absolute monarchical rule towards a more democratic approach to government. Many in Italy believed that the nation could be liberated from Austrian rule and reunited, with a new liberal constitution. A revolt in Piedmont in 1821 failed to achieve these objectives.

The Catholic church became involved in this movement when demands for autonomy emerged at Viterbo in 1836, in various parts of the Papal States in 1840, at Ravenna in 1843, and at Rimini in 1845. Papal resistance to such demands led to popular reaction against the Catholic church. In the Papal States, the papal flag was replaced with the *tricolore* – the green, white, and red flag used by insurgents in the Piedmont revolt of 1821. Gregory XVI, pope from 1831 to 1846, was alarmed at this display of nationalist fervor, and asked for Austrian help in suppressing the revolt. It was the first of many moves which pitted the papacy against the rising tide of nationalism.

Gregory's successor, Pius IX, was initially seen and welcomed by many as a reformer. He was elected pope in 1846 by a group of cardinals who were sympathetic to the demands for political liberalization that were becoming widespread throughout Europe, including Italy. Pius's early years as pope suggested he was indeed liberal in his outlook. He established a new constitution for Rome, and released political prisoners within the Papal States. Progressive forces throughout Europe believed that he would help bring about a new political order, especially within Italy. Among those who believed he was an ally for reform and national reconstruction at that time were Giuseppe Garibaldi (1807–82) and Giuseppe Mazzini (1805–72), leading figures in the movement now known as the "Risorgimento" (Italian: "resurgence" or "renewal").

Yet Pius IX became alienated from the reformers, for reasons that are not fully understood. Neither Garibaldi nor Mazzini were "revolutionaries"; their objective was the political reunification of Italy, and the elimination of foreign influence. Karl Marx dismissed their political goals as just another "middle-class republic." Yet Pius IX clearly regarded these nationalist objectives as a threat, both to the political existence of the Papal States and to the wider issue of papal authority in the region.

The turning point was the declaration of the Roman Republic in February 1849. As unrest spread in Rome in November 1848, Pius IX fled to the papal stronghold of Gaeta, fearing for his safety. In his absence, popular assemblies met and declared a new republic. Pius IX threatened excommunication for those involved in such political activities. However, the political developments in Rome unleashed a wave of hostility towards the church. Republican leaders appropriated land owned by the church, and distributed it to the poor. Pius IX appealed for foreign intervention to restore the situation. On July 3, French armies entered Rome, and restored the pope. They would remain there until July 1870. Pius IX had won this battle. But he had lost much popular support.

The Risorgimento continued, eventually leading to the formation of a single Italian kingdom in 1861. Although Garibaldi and his circle wanted to form an Italian republic, they were too heavily dependent on support from Victor Emmanuel II (1820–78), king of Sardinia, whose military resources were instrumental to the success of the campaign for unification. Victor Emmanuel's defeat of papal forces in 1860 led to his excommunication by the pope.

The pope's situation was made much more difficult through the outbreak of the Franco-Prussian War (July 19, 1870–May 10, 1871). France was now obliged to defend itself against the threat of German invasion, and consequently withdrew its troops from Rome. On September 20, 1870, the armies of Victor Emmanuel II captured Rome and annexed it. By the time of his death in 1878, Victor Emmanuel had taken up residence in a former papal palace in Rome, which was proclaimed the capital city of the new kingdom of Italy. He refused Pius IX's subsequent offer to annul his excommunication. The new kingdom of Italy guaranteed religious freedom to all, but gave no special privileges to the Catholic church.

The political events of this period consolidated the perception within Italy that the papacy was hostile to any forms of political liberalism or nationalism, and opposed to democratic ideals. Although the new Italian government took no action against the pope, and permitted him to receive ambassadors, Pius IX was in effect confined to the territory of the Vatican for the remainder of his life. Papal properties elsewhere in Rome – such as the Quirinal Palace, which became the residence of the Italian king – were confiscated.

Pius IX's sense of isolation in the midst of a nationalist and liberal context did much to convince him of the need for the Catholic church to redefine its position and reassert its authority in the face of what was seen as an increasingly hostile culture. The most important papal response to this new situation was the convening of the First Vatican Council of 1869, to which we now turn.

4.2.7.   The First Vatican Council: Papal Infallibility

The reemergence of the pope as a major figure within Catholicism during the nineteenth century can be attributed, at least in part, to the aftermath of the Napoleonic wars. In the decades prior to the French Revolution, the pope seems to have been largely ignored by the Catholic faithful, who regarded him as isolated and distant. However, Napoleon's dismissive treatment of the pope caused him to regain his prestige in the eyes of both the faithful and some European governments. Even in France, the heartland of movements which advocated nationally governed churches, there was a new respect for the pope, however grudging.

The scene was set for the reemergence of the papacy as a leading institution within Catholicism and beyond. The movement which advocated increased papal authority was known as "ultramontanism" – a word deriving from a Latin root meaning "beyond the mountains" (i.e., the Alps). The issue at stake was the extent to which the pope had authority "beyond the Alps" – that is to say, beyond Italy into Europe itself. Paradoxically, such agitation for increased papal authority in northern Europe came at a time when the pope's position in Italy was severely weakened by the Risorgimento (4.2.6).

The rise of revolutionary movements in France, Italy, and Germany during the late 1840s led to increased concern over the political stability of Catholic countries, and particularly the position of the pope himself. Faced with the prospect of steadily decreasing political power, culminating in his unhappy eviction from many of his former possessions as a result of the Risorgimento, Pius IX concentrated on establishing his spiritual authority within the church.

The most significant aspect of this program is widely agreed to be the opening of the First Vatican Council in 1869. The council was called to strengthen the church against nationalists, liberals, and materialists, who had challenged some leading themes of the Catholic faith, and deprived the church of control of schools and property in various parts of Europe, including Italy. Despite the political uncertainty in Italy at this time, nearly 750 of about 1000 eligible bishops and heads of religious orders traveled to Rome to attend the council. The council issued two major documents: *Dei Filius* ("The Son of God"), which reasserted the harmony between reason and faith, and the supremacy of the latter; and *Pastor Aeternus* ("Eternal Pastor"), which set out the doctrine of papal infallibility.

Political events caused the council some difficulties. The council was convened on June 29, 1868, and assembled in the Vatican at Rome on December 8, 1869. At this stage, French troops were still present in Rome, to protect the pope from insurrection and personal attack. When the Franco-Prussian War broke out in July 1869, these troops were recalled to France, leaving Rome and the pope defenseless against nationalist armies. At this stage, the bishops had returned home for the summer, with the intention of returning later in the year to complete the council's discussions. However, the sudden deterioration of the security situation within Rome threw those plans into chaos. On October 20, 1870, one month after the fall of Rome to Victor Emmanuel, Pope Pius IX suspended the council indefinitely. It had only finished part of its agenda. The remainder would never be completed.

Nevertheless, two major pieces of legislation were passed. *Dei Filius* reaffirmed fundamental Catholic doctrines in the light of the challenges of the age. Given the rise of rationalism, which rejected the notion of divine revelation partly through a belief in the supreme authority of reason, the council reaffirmed the rationality of faith on the one hand, and the inability of reason to penetrate to deeper spiritual realities on the other. "Even though faith is above reason, there can never be any real disagreement between faith and reason, since it is the same God who reveals the mysteries and infuses faith, and who has endowed the human mind with the light of reason."

Yet most historians regard the most important decision taken at the council to have been its formulation of the dogma of papal infallibility. This development can be seen as marking a decisive confrontation between liberal Catholics on the one hand, and ultramontanists on the other. In an age of unrest and instability, there was a need for continuity and clarity. The issue which brought this controversy into sharp focus was the location of supreme authority within the church. Was supreme authority invested in the great councils of the church, or in the papacy itself?

In the end, the outcome was a decisive victory for the ultramontanists. This was given formal expression in the famous dogma of papal infallibility, promulgated on July 13, 1870. *Pastor Aeternus* affirmed that the pope has "full and supreme power of jurisdiction over the whole Church," implying that this included both Orthodox and Protestant churches which regarded themselves as lying beyond the pope's authority. It then went on to declare that when the pope "speaks *ex cathedra*, that is, when, in the exercise of his office as shepherd and teacher of all Christians, in virtue of his supreme apostolic authority, he defines a doctrine concerning faith or morals to be held by the whole Church," he possesses that "infallibility which the divine Redeemer willed his Church to enjoy in defining doctrine concerning faith or morals."

This notion of papal infallibility had much support – but not total support – within the Catholic church. The topic had not initially been proposed for discussion at the council; it emerged during debate in 1870. Ultramontanism was politically controversial, and tended to be regarded as something of an embarrassment by socially liberal Catholics, and as a threat by nations with large Catholic populations, which were located close to Italy.

One of those nations was Germany. Otto von Bismarck (1815–98) was appointed Chancellor of Prussia in 1864. He embarked on a policy of German unification, which was pursued with increasing vigor after the end of the Franco-Prussian War in 1871. Bismarck regarded the dogma as an insult to German Protestants, and a potential threat to the emerging authority of the German state. Bismarck moved to check the power of Catholicism in Germany, in a development known as the "culture war" (German: *Kulturkampf*) during the 1870s. We shall consider this development in more detail.

4.2.8.   German Culture Wars: Bismarck and Catholicism

The Congress of Vienna had left Germany as a patchwork of small states, none of which were capable of exercising influence at a continental level (4.2.1). The idea of German unification had been a key theme in the revolutions of 1848–9, but never came to anything. However, as Austria began to become more powerful in the 1850s, the Prussian politician Otto von Bismarck (1815–98) began to agitate for the unification of Germany. He was convinced that only a united Germany would be able to stand up to the four Great Powers then dominating European affairs – Great Britain, France, Austria, and Russia.

A turning point was reached when Wilhelm I became king of Prussia in 1861. Wilhelm appointed Bismarck as both his president and foreign minister. Bismarck launched a war against Austria in 1866, in which a highly efficient Prussian army defeated its Austrian enemy. After annexing former Austrian territories, Prussia emerged as the dominant political and economic force in Germany. Realizing the threat this posed, France declared war on Prussia in July 1870. Seeing France as the aggressor, other German states rallied to Prussia's support. The Prussian victory of 1871 set the scene for the reunification of Germany, with Wilhelm I as its emperor (German: *Kaiser*), and Bismarck as its chancellor.

Bismarck, however, now had other enemies to fight. In 1871, he launched an assault on the Catholic church in Prussia. Bismarck did not attempt to interfere with Catholicism in more southern German states, such as Bavaria, where it was much more deeply embedded. Bismarck's motivations in attacking Catholicism were complex, and partly reflected a need to gain support from more liberal politicians and intellectuals. These had been enraged by the decision of the First Vatican Council concerning papal infallibility (4.2.7), which was seen as a highly authoritarian development. Catholicism was portrayed as a reactionary

Figure 4.6   Otto Von Bismarck, chancellor of Germany, 1870–90, in May 1875. © AF archive/Alamy

movement, totally out of place in a modern nation-state such as Germany. Pius IX was widely criticized in German liberal circles, and Bismarck – a Protestant Pietist – seems to have seen the suppression of Catholicism as a potential vote-winner.

In a series of repressive measures, introduced over the period 1871–5, Bismarck aimed to reduce the influence of Catholicism in Prussia. In 1873, the state took over responsibility for the training and appointment of clergy, leading to the closure of nearly half of the seminaries in Prussia by 1878. A law of 1875 abolished Catholic religious orders, removed all state subsidies to the Catholic church, and eliminated all religious safeguards from the Prussian constitution. The Catholic church decided to resist these laws. By 1876, all the Prussian bishops were either in prison or in exile. About one-third of all Prussian Catholic parishes were without a priest. Yet German Catholicism did not give up its opposition. Few Catholics broke ranks. An official state Catholic church, which refused to recognize the decisions of the First Vatican Council, attracted only small numbers.

In the end, this policy of religious repression proved impossible to sustain. The death of Pius IX in 1878 removed one of the chief causes of criticism of Catholicism. Although Catholics had been the object of discriminatory measures, they were not stripped of their rights to vote. Intense political agitation led to the formation of a Catholic Central Party, which became so powerful politically that Bismarck found that he was unable to govern without its tacit support. Protestants began to believe that legislation that was meant to be anti-Catholic was in danger of becoming more generally anti-Christian. Popular support for Bismarck's campaign ebbed. Aware of the implications of the conflict for the growing industrial might of Germany, Bismarck now shifted his hostility towards the socialists, who he portrayed as the enemy of future German progress.

Bismarck's authoritarian measures against Catholicism in Germany may have failed; nevertheless, they provided a template for other German chancellors who wished to suppress religious activity and influence. The strategies developed to neutralize both Protestantism and Catholicism by Adolf Hitler during the Third Reich can be seen as having their roots in Bismarck's campaign. The same approach was transferred from an authoritarian to a totalitarian context.

4.2.9.   Theological Revisionism: The Challenge of Modernism

One of the concerns to preoccupy the bishops assembled at the First Vatican Council (4.2.7) was the rise of modernism, which was portrayed as a serious threat to the wellbeing of the church. So what was this movement, and why did it raise such anxieties?

Modernism is best understood as a synthesis or amalgam of a number of ideas, all of which are linked with the rise of the Enlightenment in western Europe. The term "modernist" was originally used to refer to a school of Catholic theologians during the nineteenth century, which adopted a critical attitude to traditional Christian doctrines, especially those relating to the identity and significance of Jesus of Nazareth. Catholic concern about this approach led a condemnation of September 26, 1835, aimed at the approach of certain priests and professors in German universities, who were reinterpreting traditional Catholic doctrines using the philosophy of Descartes, Kant, and Hegel. The movement fostered a positive attitude towards radical biblical criticism, and stressed the ethical, rather than the more theological, dimensions of faith. In many ways, modernism may be seen as an attempt by writers within the Catholic church to come to terms with the outlook of the Enlightenment, which it had, until that point, largely ignored.

"Modernism" is, however, a loose term, and should not be understood to imply the existence of a distinctive school of thought, committed to certain common methods or indebted to common teachers. It is certainly true that most modernist writers were concerned to integrate Christian thought with the spirit of the Enlightenment, especially the new understandings of history and the natural sciences which were then gaining the ascendancy. Yet some later modernists drew inspiration from writers such as Maurice Blondel (1861–1949), who argued that the supernatural was intrinsic to human existence, or Henri Bergson (1859–1941), who stressed the importance of intuition over intellect. Yet there is not sufficient common ground between French, English, and American modernists, nor between Roman Catholic and Protestant modernism, to allow us to use the term "modernism" in the sense of a rigorous and well-defined school. It is best seen as referring to a set of attitudes, shaped by the intellectual culture of the Enlightenment.

Alfred Loisy (1857–1940) and George Tyrrell (1861–1909) were two of the most influential Catholic modernist writers. During the 1890s, Loisy established himself as a critic

of traditional views of the biblical accounts of creation, and argued that a real development of doctrine could be discerned within Scripture. His most significant publication,
The Gospel and the Church, appeared in 1902, by which time his views had been severely
criticized by the Catholic church hierarchy. This important work was a direct response
to the views of the liberal Protestant Adolf von Harnack, set out two years earlier in
What Is Christianity? Harnack's controversial views on the origins and nature of Christianity rested on the assertion that Christianity had only a loose connection with Jesus
of Nazareth.

Loisy rejected Harnack's suggestion that there was a radical discontinuity between
Jesus and the church; however, he made significant concessions to Harnack's liberal Protestant account of Christian origins, including an acceptance of the role and validity of
biblical criticism in interpreting the gospels. Three features of the work merit closer
attention.

1. *The Gospel and the Church* recognized a genuine place for biblical criticism in Catholic
    biblical scholarship and theological reflection. Loisy's critics saw this as a concession
    to the rationalist spirit of the age.
2. Loisy called into question whether the institutional church was really to be regarded
    as God's intention for the world. The most famous sentence of *The Gospel and the
    Church* makes this point succinctly: "Jesus proclaimed the Kingdom, and what actually
    came was the Church."
3. The work suggests that Christian doctrine has developed over time, rather than being
    delivered to the apostles as a fixed and permanent package. This viewpoint had already
    been advocated, though with some caution, by John Henry Newman (1801–90). It was,
    however, seen as a concession to evolutionist ways of thinking, and hence as being
    inconsistent with received Catholic tradition.

As a result of these concerns, the work was placed upon the list of prohibited books by the
Roman Catholic authorities in 1903.

The British Jesuit writer George Tyrrell followed Loisy in his radical criticism of traditional Catholic dogma. In common with Loisy, he criticized Harnack's account of Christian
origins in *Christianity at the Crossroads* (1909), dismissing Harnack's historical reconstruction of Jesus as "the reflection of a Liberal Protestant face, seen at the bottom of a deep
well." The book also included a defense of Loisy's work, arguing that the official Roman
Catholic hostility to the book and its author has created a general impression that it is a
defense of Liberal Protestant against Roman Catholic positions, and that "Modernism is
simply a protestantizing and rationalizing movement."

In part, this perception reflects the growing influence of modernism within the mainstream Protestant denominations. In England, the Churchmen's Union was founded in
1898 for the advancement of liberal religious thought; in 1928, it altered its name to the
Modern Churchmen's Union. Among those especially associated with this group may be
noted Hastings Rashdall (1858–1924), whose *Idea of Atonement in Christian Theology*
(1919) illustrates the general tenor of English modernism. Drawing somewhat uncritically

upon the earlier writings of liberal Protestant thinkers, Rashdall argued that the theory of the atonement associated with the medieval writer Peter Abelard was more acceptable to modern thought forms than traditional theories which made an appeal to the notion of a substitutionary sacrifice. This strongly moral or exemplarist theory of the atonement, which interpreted Christ's death virtually exclusively as a demonstration of the love of God, made a considerable impact upon English, and especially Anglican, thought in the 1920s and 1930s.

The rise of modernism in the United States followed a similar pattern. The growth of liberal Protestantism in the late nineteenth and early twentieth centuries was widely perceived as a direct challenge to more conservative evangelical standpoints. Newman Smyth's *Passing Protestantism and Coming Catholicism* (1908) argued that Roman Catholic modernism could serve as a mentor to American Protestantism in several ways, not least in its critique of dogma and its historical understanding of the development of doctrine. The situation became increasingly polarized through the rise of fundamentalism in response to modernist attitudes.

Although criticisms were made of some aspects of Catholic modernism by Pope Leo X in 1893, the fullest condemnations were made by his successor, Pius X, in September 1907. In the encyclical *Pascendi dominici gregis* ("the feeding of the Lord's flock"), Pius declared that the Catholic church now faced a threat from enemies within, as much as its critics outside the church. Modernism, whether it originated from laity or priests, was the "most pernicious of all the adversaries of the Church."

Pius's campaign to eliminate modernism from Catholic educational institutions, and positions of authority and influence within the church, came to an end with his death in 1914. The election of Benedict XV in September 1914 brought an end to any systematic drive against modernism. While Benedict strongly reaffirmed the substance of earlier condemnations of modernism, he was restrained in their implementation. By that time, the influence of the group had dwindled. In any case, the Catholic church now had other issues on its mind. The outbreak of the Great War refocused the attention of the church on more fundamental matters.

As the analysis presented here suggested, the church in Europe was in a somewhat defensive mood at the end of the long nineteenth century. But what of Christianity in America? How did it fare during this period?

4.3.   The Long Nineteenth Century in America

By the middle of the twentieth century, the United States of America was firmly established as one of the world's foremost Christian nations. Yet this development could not have been predicted in the aftermath of the American Revolution of 1776 (4.1.7). As America began to establish its constitutional identity, the place of religion in the nation's political establishment was carefully circumscribed. In this section, we shall consider the changing fortunes of Christianity in the United States in the period between the revolution and the outbreak of the Great War. We begin by considering one of the most distinctive themes in American public life – the constitutional separation of church and state.

4.3.1. Church and State: The Wall of Separation

The process of shaping the Constitution of the United States of America took more than a decade. There was widespread agreement that any constitution should avoid the European model of giving preference or privilege to any Christian denomination. There would be no "established" church, although a number of individual states initially retained a form of establishment in which multiple denominations received government support.

Three distinct opinions emerged in the aftermath of the American Revolution. Traditionalists, such as Patrick Henry (1736–99), argued that state support of religion was essential to maintain social order. In 1784, Henry submitted a bill to the Virginia legislature that would impose a tax to support churches, while allowing each citizen to determine which specific church their taxes should support. Rationalists such as Thomas Jefferson (1743–1826) and James Madison (1751–1836) argued that the separation of church and state was essential to guarantee liberty of conscience. A third group, consisting mainly of Baptists, Presbyterians, and Methodists, believed that Christian churches would be corrupted if they were given positions of political power or social privilege, and argued for the churches to be protected from the corrupting influence of government.

The second of these positions soon achieved political dominance. Jefferson and Madison believed that the separation of the religious and civil realms was the best way to ensure domestic peace and to avoid the oppression and injustice that could arise from religious establishment. They had no desire for the new American republic to be damaged by wars of religion like those that had caused such damage in Europe in the seventeenth century.

In 1779, Jefferson drafted a "Bill to Establish Religious Freedom," which he submitted to the Virginia legislature, arguing for freedom of religion, including the right not to support any religion. The government should not, he argued, compel anyone to support a religion in which they did not believe. There should be no religious test for anyone intending to hold public office. Magistrates should stay clear of religious controversies, only becoming involved in such disputes when they were a threat to the public good. Jefferson's bill was not passed the first time round when it was debated in 1779.

When it came up again for debate in 1786, however, it passed by a vote of sixty to twenty-seven. How is this change in opinion to be explained? It seems clear that Madison played a significant role in swinging opinion behind the bill, and coordinating support for it during the debate. Jefferson himself was abroad at the time of the vote.

The Constitution of the United States was finally adopted on September 17, 1787, by the Constitutional Convention in Philadelphia, Pennsylvania, and was subsequently ratified by conventions in eleven states. The constitution itself famously omits any reference to Christianity. The First Amendment, however, passed in September 1789, is widely regarded as being of fundamental importance to any understanding of the place of Christianity in American public life.

> Congress shall make no law respecting an establishment of religion, or prohibiting the free exercise thereof; or abridging the freedom of speech, or of the press; or the right of the people peaceably to assemble, and to petition the Government for a redress of grievances.

The amendment made two statements concerning the public role of Christianity in the United States. First, there was to be no legislative "establishment of religion." This could be interpreted as prohibiting any specific church group from becoming the "established religion" of the United States, without implying that the government was prohibited from bringing religious language, symbols, beliefs, or values into the public arena. A more radical interpretation of this "establishment clause" holds that it means that the government of the United States is prohibited from preferring religion to anti-religion, so that the judiciary is neutral, not simply in settling disputes between religious groups, but in settling disputes between religion and its critics.

The first two presidents of the United States – George Washington (president from 1789–97) and John Adams (president from 1797–1801) – are generally regarded as having been positive about the role of religion in public life, whatever their private religious views may have been. The third and fourth presidents – Thomas Jefferson (president from 1801–9) and James Madison (president from 1809–17) – were more emphatic about the separation of church and state, using the image of a "wall of separation" between church and state.

This striking phrase seems to have first been used by the Puritan writer Roger Williams (1603–83) in 1644. Williams spoke of a "wall of separation between the garden of the church and the wilderness of the world." In using this phrase, Williams was setting out an understanding of the church which was common amongst separatist Puritans: the world was a wilderness, but the church was a garden. To avoid the wilderness encroaching on the garden and overwhelming it, the garden had to be enclosed – an important image, reflecting the biblical idea of paradise as a "closed garden." For Williams, it was axiomatic that the state and church must be separate – for the good of the church.

Jefferson picked up on this image, and developed it for his own somewhat different ends in 1802. A group of Baptists from the town of Danbury in Connecticut wrote to Jefferson shortly after his election as president, expressing their concern that their religious liberty was not sufficiently protected by their state legislature. A religious majority, they suggested, might easily win the magistrate over to their cause, with damaging consequences for religious minorities. Jefferson responded by emphatically asserting the separation of church and state, in terms that seem to go beyond the constitutional amendment.

> I contemplate with sovereign reverence that act of the whole American people which declared that their "legislature" should "make no law respecting an establishment of religion, or prohibiting the free exercise thereof," thus building a *wall of separation* between Church and State. Adhering to this expression of the supreme will of the nation in behalf of the *rights of conscience*, I shall see with sincere satisfaction in the progress of those sentiments which tend to man all his natural rights, convinced he has no natural right in opposition to his social duties.

Determining the boundaries between the church and state would remain a significant theme of American religious life until the present day, and we shall return to this theme in the following chapter (5.3.2).

4.3.2. The Second Great Awakening and American Revivalism

Between 1800 and the eve of the Civil War, the population of the United States expanded from about five to thirty million. This growth in population was accompanied by territorial expansion, particularly the purchase of the state of Louisiana from France in 1803. Some believed that this expansion would lead to a loosening of the nation's original Christian moorings, as children sought to establish their independence from their parents, and communities to create new identities far removed from those of the original colonies. Yet there is abundant evidence that many sought to cope with the radical social and political change of the times by rediscovering their religious roots, and the secure sense of social location and personal identity that this entailed.

Protestant church attendance rose by a factor of ten over the period 1800–60, comfortably outstripping population growth. Twice as many Protestants went to church at the end of this period than at its beginning. Why? If any factor may be identified as responsible for this development, it is the "Second Great Awakening" (1800–30) and the new patterns of religious revivalism that this brought about. Such religious revivals not only became the defining mark of American religion but also played a central role in the nation's developing identity, independence, and democratic principles. Although the subject of criticism at the time, revivalism became deeply enmeshed within the American Protestant consciousness.

The first such revival broke out in rural Kentucky in 1801, taking the form of large camp meetings. The most famous of these was the "Cane Ridge" meeting, which lasted a week, and was attended by at least 10 000 individuals. These set a precedent for a wave of revivalist meetings throughout the frontier territories, making an appeal primarily to common folk, emphasizing the emotional rather than the intellectual appeal of faith. The outcome was the transformation of antebellum America, leading to the emergence of the Protestant "Bible Belt."

In many ways, this second Great Awakening changed the American religious landscape. The three Christian traditions with the strongest presence in Colonial America were Anglicanism, Congregationalism, and Presbyterianism. These groups were left relatively untouched by the Second Awakening, which led to a massive and disproportionate growth on the part of Baptists and Methodists. An equally important change concerned the conversion of slaves. The Second Great Awakening saw the first significant conversions of slaves, who generally joined the Baptists and Methodists, who were much more open to welcoming such conversions than Anglicans. They were also much more successful than Anglicanism in reaching a broader membership, perhaps because of the emotional appeal of revivalism, which contrasted with the somewhat more cerebral catechetical approach of Anglican churches.

Charles Grandison Finney (1792–1875) was one of the pivotal figures of the Second Awakening. Following his conversion in 1821, Finney abandoned his career as a lawyer, and became a Presbyterian minister. However, he distanced himself from some aspects of the older New England Calvinism, which he regarded as in the first place unbiblical and, in the second, an obstacle to effective evangelism. Finney's emphasis fell on the need for people to respond to the proclamation of the gospel, and on the skills that were thus required of the preacher to persuade them to do so. Finney clearly regarded it as perfectly acceptable – perhaps even as necessary – to use every technique of persuasion available in preaching for conversion.

Finney introduced many of the standard features of revivalist preaching, which rapidly became part of a largely unquestioned tradition. One such feature was the "anxious seat," a bench reserved for those who, as a result of the preacher's message, were "anxious" for their soul's safety, and wanted counsel and prayer. Yet the most familiar of all Finney's innovations was the "altar call" – the invitation to come forward in response to the invitation to receive the gospel. The technique was picked up by the later evangelist Dwight L. Moody (1837–99), and thus passed into virtually all of nineteenth- and twentieth-century revivalist preaching, from Billy Sunday (1862–1936) through to Billy Graham (5.2.3).

Finney's attentiveness to controlling and directing the revival process marked a significant shift from the days of the First Great Awakening. The Puritans Jonathan Edwards and George Whitfield had no place for an "altar call," or other such techniques. For them, revival was a matter of God's grace, lying beyond human control or influence. For Finney, revival "is not a miracle or dependent on a miracle"; rather, it is the "result of the right use of the constituted means." Although it would be unfair to accuse Finney of reducing revival to a set of techniques, both organizational and rhetorical, those elements are certainly present in his thought.

The impact of Finney and those who developed his approach to ministry was immense. The French political thinker Alexis de Tocqueville (1805–59) visited America in 1831, and recorded his impressions of the nation. The first thing that struck him on his arrival, he remarked, was "the religious atmosphere of the country." De Tocqueville was astonished at the number of American denominations, and their mutual toleration for each other. In particular, he noted the puzzling success of Catholicism, which seemed to flourish without any obvious state support. "America is the most democratic country in the world, and it is at the same time (according to reports worthy of belief) the country in which the Roman Catholic religion makes most progress."

Revivalism unquestionably shaped the American religious landscape. The emergence of the "Holiness Movement" is often seen as a response to the ideas and values of revivalism. Unlike forms of Protestantism that emphasized the defense of doctrinal orthodoxy, the Holiness movement was much more oriented towards morality and the spiritual life. It tended to raise ethics to the status that later fundamentalists have accorded doctrine. This emphasis upon "holy living" came to be linked with support for the abolition of slavery in the antebellum period. Oberlin College, Ohio – where Finney later served as professor of theology – became a stronghold of abolitionism, even advocating "civil disobedience" in the face of the fugitive slave laws.

The "Holiness" tradition's emphasis on issues of Christian living was not limited to an attempt to end slavery. Oberlin College became the center of some serious attempts to erase racial and gender barriers within both the antebellum church and society at large. Its pioneering moves towards coeducation led to its graduating some of the most vigorous and radical feminists of the era. Antoinette Brown (1825–1921), the first woman to be ordained in an American church, was a graduate of Oberlin. At her ordination in 1853, Wesleyan Methodist minister Luther Lee preached on "Woman's Right to Preach the Gospel."

After the Civil War ended in 1865, revivalism began to develop in new directions. Revivalist rhetoric was supplemented by the emergence of a popular American hymnody. Whereas the Puritans strongly disapproved of the singing of non-biblical texts in church, the Wesleyan revival movement in England had recognized the importance of hymns, both as a means of Christian education, and as a powerful way of praising God. After the end of the Civil War, as America moved towards becoming an industrial nation, the Protestant churches were able to remain in touch with the nation's soul through the use of music.

Dwight L. Moody, the greatest revivalist preacher of the second half of the nineteenth century, teamed up with musician Ira D. Sankey (1840–1908), after their meeting at a revivalist campaign in Indianapolis in 1870. Moody and Sankey proved a formidable combination in the public advocation of faith at a time of great social change, and were responsible for some of the best-known hymns of the late nineteenth century. Using popular songs as his model, Sankey developed the verse-chorus-verse-chorus model, which became characteristic of the revivalist meetings of the period.

One of the contributing factors to the rapidly changing American religious and cultural landscape was increasing immigration from Europe, a matter that deserves further discussion.

4.3.3.   European Immigration and Religious Diversification

Puritans were not the only religious minority to flee intolerance and insecurity in seventeenth-century England. In early 1634, a group of Catholic refugees settled in the Chesapeake Bay area. Maryland – named after Henrietta Maria (1609–66), the French Catholic wife of the English monarch Charles I – became the first Catholic colony in America. Although Maryland was criticized as being a Catholic enclave in the New World, it soon established its credentials as a place of religious toleration.

Yet the habits and prejudices of Protestantism were deeply ingrained in most of the original American colonies. When the British government extended full civil and religious freedom to Catholics in the colony of Quebec in 1774, American Protestants reacted with indignation, seeing this as legitimizing tyranny in the region. Yet the first amendment to the constitution prevented prejudice against Catholicism becoming government policy at national level. Despite its overwhelmingly Protestant legacy, the United States of America determined that it would not legislate nationally against Catholicism in any form.

Yet it must be noted that the First Amendment did not place restrictions on individual states legislating on matters of religion. States retained the right to place restrictions on religious liberty for certain groups, occasionally including Catholics. For example, North Carolina did not amend its constitution to allow Catholics to hold public office until 1835. One of the reasons for the growth of Catholic parochial schools was that the public school system in many states was seen to be too heavily biased towards Protestantism.

The "Louisiana purchase" (1803) changed the religious profile of the United States significantly. This former French colony – originally part of "La Nouvelle France" – was strongly Catholic, with settled cultural traditions reflecting this religious heritage. The subsequent incorporation of parts of Florida and Mexico into the Union in the first half of the nineteenth century increased the Catholic presence considerably, in that both these new acquisitions had been evangelized by the Spanish in previous centuries.

A fresh wave of immigration from European nations in the nineteenth century led to further changes in the nation's religious profile. Now that America was firmly established as an icon of religious freedom, Catholics chose to migrate there to escape political instability and economic deprivation in Europe. Large numbers of Irish and Italian Catholics arrived at cities such as Boston, New York, and Philadelphia. German refugees, fleeing Bismarck's repressive policies against Catholicism in the 1870s, tended to settle in the upper Midwest, in cities such as St. Louis and Cincinnati. Strong ethnic loyalties led to Catholic émigrés retaining the social and religious habits of Europe, and thus not integrating within American culture. This rapid rise of Catholicism in cities that had hitherto been staunchly Protestant led to social and religious tension. By 1850, Catholicism was the largest single Christian denomination in the United States.

The case of late nineteenth-century Boston illustrates this trend well. In 1800, Boston was a powerful symbol of the American Yankee Protestant heritage, at the heart of the largely Puritan Commonwealth of Massachusetts. Yet mass immigration from Catholic Ireland from 1840 onwards changed everything. In 1885, three Protestants were arrested by the police for preaching on the Common, sparking off protests that revealed the deep levels of insecurity within their community – above all, the sense of having become aliens and strangers in what was once their heartland.

Many Protestants were alarmed at the new religious directions their nation seemed to be taking. In 1834, Lyman Beecher published his *Plea for the West*, which portrayed the pope collaborating with Catholic European monarchs in a plot to take over the Mississippi Valley. Tensions rose, leading to the burning of a convent in Charlestown in 1834. These were given credibility as Catholic emigration to America began to surge in the second half of the nineteenth century. It is estimated that the Catholic population of the United States increased threefold in the second half of the nineteenth century. "Nativism" became a significant ideology, rallying those already settled in America against the newcomers, who they believed threatened to undermine their religious and political freedoms. Catholicism was regularly and aggressively portrayed as "the other" or "the threat," fundamentally at odds with the libertarian and republican principles of the United States. Rhetoric shaped perception; and perception became reality.

The identification of Catholicism as an enemy was pervasive within American Protestantism in the late nineteenth century. One delegate to the Evangelical Alliance meeting in New York in 1873 summed up this conviction in a memorable phrase: "The most formidable foe of living Christianity among us is not Deism or Atheism, or any form of infidelity, but the nominally Christian Church of Rome." At one level, American Protestantism was defined by anti-Catholicism. It would be a long time before America felt able to elect a Catholic president. The election of John Fitzgerald Kennedy (1917–63) as the thirty-fifth president of the United States in 1960 was widely regarded as marking a significant upgrading of the status of Catholicism in American public life.

4.3.4.   The Emergence of the "Bible Belt"

The original heartlands of Protestantism were in the greater New England area, especially Massachusetts (3.5.2; 4.1.5). It was here that Congregationalism and Presbyterianism took root, quickly becoming the most significant and dynamic forms of Protestant self-expression in the region. The southern colonies tended to be dominated by a socially conservative Episcopalianism (as Anglicanism came to be known after the Revolution of 1776), which lent tacit support to the hierarchical social structures that dominated their plantations and social life throughout much of the eighteenth century. The plantation aristocracy enjoyed their hunting, shooting, dueling, dancing, drinking, and gambling, and tolerated Anglicanism precisely because it tolerated them.

Religious commitment in the southern states was low; only one in ten southerners attended church in 1776. Yet the great era of Protestant expansion and consolidation that opened up in the nineteenth century focused on the Midwest and South, not the original Northeast – the territories now widely referred to as the "Bible Belt." How is this development to be explained?

The simple answer is that some of the forms of Protestant Christianity present in this region deliberately chose to adapt themselves to the realities of southern culture. This task of adaptation and modification by evangelical Baptists and Methodists took over two generations, and laid the foundations of the "Bible Belt." Ministers such as Stith Mead (1767–1834) and Freeborn Garrettson (1752–1827) were able to build bridges to different cultural groups – young people, slaves, women, and, perhaps most difficult of all, white males – to defuse initial anxiety and hostility against evangelicals.

Over the period 1770–1830, egalitarian forms of evangelicalism established deep roots in southern culture, despite the tensions this created with middle-aged white gentry. Episcopalianism remained the religion of the Protestant elite. Yet more populist forms of Christianity had established a deep hold on the population as a whole.

This process of adaptation to southern culture created a form of Protestantism which was markedly different from the forms found in the Northeast. This divergence was more than purely denominational (in 1830, the Northeast was dominated by Presbyterians and Congregationalists, the South by Baptists and Methodists). The Christianity of the Bible Belt made its appeal primarily to individuals, focusing on the transformation of their personal lives rather than of society as a whole. These characteristics appear to have persisted in the religious individualism of contemporary southern religious approaches to the reading of the Bible, and the understanding of the nature of salvation.

Yet the term "Bible Belt" reflects something deeper than denominational or theological distinctives. Those observers of southern religion in the late nineteenth and early twentieth centuries who coined the phrase used it primarily to denote the remarkable religious homogeneity of the region. Once the hiatus of the Civil War had passed, allowing the South to regain religious and social stability, it became clear that southern religion had crystallized into predominantly conservative forms of Protestantism, relatively unaffected by the social and intellectual challenges that Protestantism faced in the North, especially in urban centers.

The religious group which best illustrates the distinctive forms of Protestantism that emerged in this region is the Southern Baptist Convention, founded in Augusta, Georgia, in May 1845. Up to that point, Baptist congregations in the area had operated without feeling the need for any national or religional structure, and never thought of themselves as belonging to a "denomination." Yet there was a growing recognition that such a centralized denomination would be more efficient and more powerful, capable of achieving greater influence.

Anxious not to compromise the autonomy of local Baptist congregations, the convention adopted a model of church governance which was essentially Congregationalist: the decision of a local church in a matter of doctrine, discipline, or church order could not be overturned by any superior body, since there was no body which has authority over the local church.

Yet the upsurge in religious interest in the South was not limited to white Americans. Black Protestantism was already a significant force in the antebellum era, even though restrictions were placed upon it – for example, worship had to be supervised by whites. In Columbus, Mississippi, 80 percent of the antebellum Baptist church membership before was black. In Georgia at this time, about 35 to 40 percent of Baptist church members were black. The end of the Civil War brought about emancipation, and with it new possibilities for Protestantism.

With the ending of the Civil War, black Protestant churches underwent new growth – this time, under black leadership, unrestricted by white supervisors. Baptist churches quickly became established as core institutions of new-found black freedom, developing their own styles of worship and preaching. The legacy of the past meant that such congregations were not well-educated, so that preachers often seemed more concerned with heightening their congregation's sense of God's love and presence rather than educating them in the fundamentals of faith. Many inequities remained in the South, where blacks found themselves largely excluded from the traditional predominantly white denominations. Yet the foundation was being laid for significant future developments.

4.3.5.   The Civil War: Slavery and Suffering

We have already hinted at the importance of the Civil War for religion in America, and we must now turn to consider this in more detail. By 1860, the United States consisted of thirty-six states, having expanded considerably since the original thirteen states of 1766. The election of the Republican candidate Abraham Lincoln as president in 1860 triggered the immediate secession of seven southern states, later followed by four others. These were known as the "Confederate States." Although the full reasons for this decision to leave the Union are disputed, it is clear that the issue of slavery was a major issue.

The Republican Party was opposed to the expansion of slavery. Southern states were heavily dependent on slaves to maintain their economy, which was primarily based on cotton and tobacco plantations. There was widespread support within the northern intellectual elite for the abolition of slavery. Although Lincoln did not make any commitment to abolitionism in his presidential campaign, he clearly assumed that limiting slavery would lead to its eventual extinction.

At the start of the Civil War, Lincoln's publicly stated objective was to save the Union, not to free the slaves. Yet Lincoln gradually came to see the abolition of slavery as a divinely appointed task for the Union, giving its struggle a sense of divine dignity and purpose. This theme is best seen in Julia Ward Howe's *Battle Hymn of the Republic* (1862), which used strongly biblical imagery to lend religious authority to the battle against the slave states:

> Mine eyes have seen the glory of the coming of the Lord:
> He is trampling out the vintage where the grapes of wrath are stored;
> He hath loosed the fateful lightning of His terrible swift sword:
> His truth is marching on.

The first shots of the Civil War were fired when Confederate forces laid siege to Fort Sumter in Charleston Harbor on April 12, 1861, and ended when General Robert E. Lee surrendered his Army of Northern Virginia at the Appomattox Court House on April 9, 1865. A Union victory was inevitable, given the industrial superiority of the northern states, and the effectiveness of their naval blockade of the South, which prevented the Confederate states from exporting cotton or tobacco. The casualty figures on both sides were staggering by the standards of the time. It is thought that the war led to nearly 1 100 000 casualties and claimed more than 620 000 lives.

What was the role of religion in precipitating this devastating war? The American Civil War cannot conceivably be regarded as a "war of religion." Nevertheless, it is clear that religion was an important factor in shaping the antebellum culture in both northern and southern states. As noted earlier, the Second Great Awakening (1800–30) had a deep impact on much of American society. Yet this renewed interest in matters of faith had significantly different outcomes in the northern and southern states. Northerners appealed to the spirit of the Bible in opposing slavery, whereas southerners appealed to the letter of the Bible in defending slavery. In the North, believers appear to have developed a deeper desire to eradicate society of its problems and evils – including slavery – partly through a new awareness of the capacity of religion to transform individuals. In the emerging "Bible Belt" of the South, however, the revival tended to express itself in individual piety – a renewed personal faith, which did not necessarily extend to any vision for the transformation of society.

As noted earlier, the war created unprecedented casualties and provoked scenes of distress and mourning throughout the nation. A new interest in spiritualism flourished, as anguished families sought to reestablish contact with relatives who had died on the field of battle. A new genre of religious literature emerged in the United States in the aftermath of the Civil War – the so-called "consolation literature."

One of the most influential examples of this "consolation literature" was written by Elizabeth Stuart Phelps (1844–1911). *The Gates Ajar* (1868) tells of Mary Cabot, a New England woman who was trying to come to terms with the death of her brother, Roy, in

Figure 4.7   View of federal soldiers relaxing by the guns of an unidentified captured fort, Atlanta, Georgia, 1864. George Barnard/Buyenlarge/Getty Images

the Civil War. Mary longed for a restoration of her relationship with Roy. She initially sought help from her Calvinist pastor but is thoroughly dissatisfied with the consolation he offered her – "glittering generalities, cold commonplace, vagueness, unreality, a God and a future at which I sat and shivered."

Dissatisfied with this professional religious response to her concerns, Mary turns instead to her aunt, Winifred Forceythe. Heaven, she is quite clear, is fundamentally an extension of the present, characterized by restored human relationships, even when these were destroyed by the carnage of war. "I expect to have my beautiful home, and my husband, and [my daughter] Faith, as I had them here; with many differences, and great ones, but *mine* just the same."

Aunt Winifred went on to portray heaven in terms of an intensification of the beauties of nature ("glorified lilies of the valley, heavenly tea bud roses, and spiritual harebells") and of human culture ("whole planets turned into works of art"). Heaven, it turns out, is like an extended nineteenth-century family, in which little children are busy "devouring heavenly gingersnaps" and playing rosewood pianos, while the adults listen to learned discourses from glorified philosophers and the symphonies of Beethoven.

Phelps's account of what she believed to lie beyond the gates of Heaven clearly captivated her readers, if the sales of the book are anything to go by. *The Gates Ajar* can be seen to mirror a deepening disquiet within an increasingly sophisticated North American culture concerning religious beliefs in general, and the traditional Protestant view of the afterlife, which seemed – at least, to this public – to be cold, impersonal, and unattractive. The materialist vision of heaven she offered in its place retained many aspects of the traditional Christian doctrine, while subtly altering it at critical junctures – not least, in stressing the continuity of individuals, relationships, and environments between this life and the next.

Yet while Phelps wrote for white Protestants whose religious certainties had been shattered by the Civil War, other Christian groups were experiencing similar traumas, and developing ways of dealing with them. The immense hardships and deprivations faced by the African slave population of the southern states in the period before the American Civil War and in its immediate aftermath gave rise to a different kind of "consolation literature." One of the world's most valued art forms arose out of this deep encounter with pain, suffering, and poverty – the "Negro spiritual."

These spiritual songs offered hope and reassurance in the face of poverty, oppression, and suffering. They set out in simple words the impact of the hope of Heaven in what often seemed to be a hopeless world. One of the most famous is "Steal Away to Jesus":

> Steal away, steal away, steal away to Jesus,
> Steal away, steal away home,
> I ain't got long to stay here.

Yet if traditional Protestantism seemed to lack emotional and spiritual warmth, other forms of Christianity were more than willing to make up for this. Revivalism continued to offer bright and breezy approaches to faith, which appealed to many. Yet a new form of Christianity was in the process of emerging within the United States – Pentecostalism. In view of the enormous importance of this religious movement in the later twentieth century and beyond, we shall consider it further.

4.3.6. Pentecostalism: The American Origins of a Global Faith

Many of the Christian denominations making up American society had their origins in Europe – such as Presbyterianism, Episcopalianism, and Methodism. Yet the religious entrepreneurialism of the United States led to the emergence of numerous new denominations and visions of faith, originating within America itself. Most of these had Christian roots, wherever their subsequent development might lead them. Joseph Smith (1805–44) founded Mormonism in the 1820s in New York State as a form of Christian primitivism. Mary Baker Eddy (1821–1910) founded Christian Science in Massachusetts in 1879. The Jehovah's Witnesses emerged from the Bible Student Movement, founded in the late 1870s in Pennsylvania by Charles Taze Russell (1852–1916). Yet perhaps the most significant form of Christianity to emerge within the United States is Pentecostalism.

The first phase of the emergence of Pentecostalism took place on the first day of the twentieth century – January 1, 1901 – at Bethel Bible College, in Topeka, Kansas. The institution had been founded in the holiness tradition the previous October by Charles Parham (1873–1929), a former pastor in the Methodist Episcopal Church. Parham asked his students to investigate the New Testament evidence for the continued activity of the Holy Spirit in the Christian life.

It was seen as an empty, pointless question by many. The theological wisdom of the day took the form of "cessationism," widely taught by the Protestant theological establishment. This view held that the active gifts of the Holy Spirit, such as "speaking in tongues," belonged to the age of the New Testament itself, and were no longer available or operational. The New Testament was thus read from within a "cessationist" interpretative framework, which had already determined that such spiritual phenomena were things of the past. Parham was not so sure. Within his own holiness tradition, reports were circulating of what seemed to be charismatic phenomena. He asked his students for their views.

The students reported that a straightforward reading of the biblical texts suggested that such charismatic gifts were still a possibility. Impressed by the clarity of this response, Parham and his students began a prayer vigil on December 31, 1900, in the hope that the gift might be renewed. At 11 o'clock the following evening, on the first day of the twentieth century, one of the students – Agnes Ozman (1870–1937) – reported having such an experience. A few days later others, including Parham himself, followed suit.

Parham and his students began to tell others about this apparent recovery of the "gift of tongues." One of those who heard Parham speak in 1905 was the African-American preacher William J. Seymour (1870–1922), who was forced by the southern segregationist policies of that period to listen to his lectures through a half-opened door. Sadly, Parham – noted for his white supremacist views – did nothing to break down this racial wall of separation. Inspired, Seymour went on to open the "Apostolic Faith Mission" in a dilapidated church, then used only for storage, at 312 Azusa Street, Los Angeles in April 1906.

Over the next two years, a major revival broke out at Azusa Street, characterized by "speaking in tongues." The term "Pentecostalism" began to be applied to the movement, taking its name from the "Day of Pentecost" – the occasion, according to the New Testament, when the phenomenon was first experienced by the early Christian disciples (Acts 2:1–4). Significantly, at a time of ruthless racial segregation in American culture, brought about by the notorious Jim Crow segregation laws, the Azusa Street mission pointedly ignored racial issues. A black pastor led a diverse ministry team comprised of white people, black people, and Hispanics.

Primarily (though not exclusively) from this California base, Pentecostalism spread rapidly in America, appealing particularly to the socially marginalized, especially through Seymour's important concept of an ecstatic egalitarian ecclesiology. Unusually, it seemed to appeal to and be embraced by both white and African-American Christian groupings. It was regarded as eccentric, even dangerous, by American culture at large, as local newspaper headlines in Los Angeles during April 1906 made clear: "New Sect of Fanatics is Breaking Loose;" "Wild Scene Last Night on Azusa Street."

Charles Parham had no time for the racial inclusiveness proclaimed and practiced by Seymour and Azusa Street. In an abortive and counterproductive move, Parham attempted to take control of the Azusa phenomenon, being particularly disturbed by its commitment to interracial fellowship. Among other things, Parham later went on to teach that the white Anglo-Saxon Protestants were the privileged descendants of the lost tribes of Israel, and spoke in glowing terms of the Ku Klux Klan. He was never reconciled with Seymour, and eventually died in disgrace.

Yet Pentecostalism rapidly transcended its American roots, and became a global faith. We shall consider this further later in this work.

4.4.   An Age of Mission

As we noted in an earlier chapter, Catholic maritime powers in western Europe opened up new trade routes to Africa and India, as well as the newly discovered Americas in the 1490s and early 1500, leading to Catholicism gaining a presence in these regions through the work of Portuguese and Spanish missionaries (2.5.7). This missionary work was coordinated at national level – for example, through French missionaries and the Parisian mission society, Société des Missions Etrangères de Paris (French: "Paris Society for Foreign Missions"), which played an important role in missionary work in Indo-China.

It was not until the seventeenth century that a central ecclesiastical authority, the Roman *Congregatio de propaganda fide* (Latin: "Congregation for the Spreading of the Faith"), was established by Pope Gregory XV in 1622. In 1627, Pope Urban VIII established a training college for missionaries at Rome. This represented a new approach to missionary work which both strengthened its religious character, and also encouraged the scientific and linguistic education of missionaries, preparing the way for the creation of an indigenous clergy in the Americas, Africa, and Asia.

So why did these developments take place? One important reason was a growing realization that the expansion of Christianity needed to be coordinated centrally by religious authorities, rather than be allowed to be shaped by national churches with their own agendas. Concerns were rising in senior church circles that certain Catholic nations seemed more interested in promoting their own economic interests overseas than in spreading the Catholic faith. Yet there was another reason of no small importance: the realization that Protestantism was expanding its missionary endeavors, posing a significant threat to the global dominance of Catholicism.

Protestantism was slow to develop an interest in mission. The dominant agenda of the sixteenth and seventeenth centuries focused primarily on defending Protestant communities against encroachment from their enemies, whether Protestant or Catholic. Catholicism, in marked contrast, had made significant inroads in many parts of South America, Africa, and Asia around this time, due to the great voyages of discovery of the Portuguese and Spanish navigators.

Yet Protestantism's interest in mission was merely delayed, rather than denied. By the beginning of the long nineteenth century, Protestant missionary societies were actively promoting missions throughout the world. Protestantism was spread through a complex amalgam of trading links, colonial activity, and intentional outreach. Great Britain would play an especially important role in missionary work, as it began to become a global power, establishing colonies throughout the world.

The rise of Protestant maritime powers, such as Holland and England, led to growing confidence among Protestant missionary agencies, and a loss of confidence within their

Catholic counterparts during the eighteenth century. The papal suppression of the Society of Jesus (1773) had a significant negative impact on Catholic missionary work, especially in Asia and South America, leading to the loss of some 3000 missionaries (4.1.6). The Catholic church was seriously weakened by both the French Revolution (4.1.8) and the Napoleonic wars (4.2.1), and found itself distracted from missionary work. However, by the second half of the nineteenth century, Catholicism had recovered much of its earlier confidence, and was once more able to focus on mission.

The history of Christian missions in general, and Protestant missions in particular, has only recently been given the scholarly attention that it deserves. Before about 1990, studies of missions were largely written by retired missionaries, with their own axes to grind and causes to promote. Secular scholarship often relegated missionary work to an aspect of imperial history, often deploying what can now be seen to be caricatures of missionary work to reinforce their attitudes to western imperial history. On this view, missionaries were little more than imperial collaborators, who might aim to heal and teach their inferiors, but were primarily committed to the extension of imperial agendas.

Those caricatures are now receding into the past, as a new wave of scholarly studies has exposed a much more complex picture of missionary agendas, intentions, and concerns. Wherever possible, these insights are included in the analysis presented in this chapter. We begin by considering the impulses which led to the great Protestant missionary expansion of the late eighteenth century.

4.4.1.   The Origins of Protestant Missions

Three factors were of decisive importance in creating a new enthusiasm for missionary work within some parts of Protestant Europe during the late eighteenth century.

1. A shift in patterns of biblical interpretation, which led to the "Great Commission" (Matthew 28: 17–20) being interpreted as entrusted to every generation of believers, and not simply to the apostles.
2. The expansion of Protestant sea-power, leading to the establishment of European colonies in Asia, Africa, and Latin America. Great Britain was widely acknowledged as the supreme naval power of the late eighteenth and nineteenth centuries, which coincided with this significant period in overseas missionary work.
3. The development of the "voluntary society" as an evangelistic agency, bypassing the inertia of the churches. One of the most significant tensions in the history of Christian missions arose between churches and missionary societies, for reasons we shall consider later.

Each of these points merits further discussion.

Theological attitudes towards mission began to change decisively in the eighteenth century. Reformed and Lutheran theologians of the late sixteenth and early seventeenth centuries, such as Theodore Beza and Johann Gerhard, argued that the "great commission" came to an end with the close of the apostolic age. The reversal of this theological judgment was partly catalyzed by the voyages of exploration of the eighteenth century, which opened up the vast southern oceans. There was a growing realization that the world was larger than had been realized, and that there was a corresponding need for a Christian witness to these newly discovered lands. For example, William Carey (1761–1834), later to be one of the most important British missionaries to India, began to conceive the idea of a missionary calling after reading Captain Cook's account of his voyages in the South Seas over the period 1768–71. Theology and geography conspired to create a new vision for the place of missions in Christian life.

Alongside this, however, was an additional consideration – that undertaking missionary work presumed to force God's hands in the conversion of peoples. When William Carey suggested in 1792 that Baptist ministers should discuss "the duty of Christians to attempt the spread of the Gospel among heathen nations," he received a cool reception. As Carey later recalled, an older minister dismissed the suggestion as impertinent. "When God pleases to convert the heathen, He will do it without your aid or mine."

The expansion of Protestant sea-power led to the establishment of colonies by Protestant European nations, which allowed the model of evangelism determined by Confessionalized churches to come into operation. A colony was a region under the authority of the state; therefore, the state church was able to exercise a pastoral and evangelistic mission within this region. It is thus no accident that the first major Lutheran mission was located in India, as a direct result of a Danish Crown Colony being created at Serampore. The establishment of Dutch colonies in Indonesia (then known as the "East Indies") led to the establishment of Reformed churches in that region. However, Britain was by far the most active colonial power, with the result that English-speaking forms of Protestantism became widely established through imperial expansion, especially in the Indian Subcontinent, the Caribbean, and Australasia.

Furthermore, the rise of the "voluntary society" led to a new model for evangelism emerging, which eventually displaced older models in America and Great Britain – but not, it must be emphasized, in Germany and other European nations. Traditional models of evangelism focused on a Protestant state or denomination, thus making the enterprise dependent on an official bureaucracy.

In the second half of the eighteenth century, missionary leadership thus passed into the hands of entrepreneurial individuals, who created dedicated missionary societies which focused specifically on the objective of overseas mission. These consisted of highly motivated individuals who arranged their own fundraising, created support groups, and identified and recruited missionaries. Churches were seen as having institutional agendas which failed to engage with the missionary imperative. Such matters were best left to dedicated individuals, rather than being defeated by ecclesiastical bureaucracies.

The origins of the London Mission Society illustrate this trend well. News of William Carey's missionary work in India generated much interest in England in 1794, particularly among those working for the abolition of slavery. John Collet Ryland (1723–92), a Baptist minister, began to gather together a group of interested persons, both lay and ordained, who met in Baker's Coffee House in London to plan how they might develop inter-denominational missionary work. The number of supporters grew, and funds were raised. A ship was purchased, missionaries recruited, and a potentially significant mission undertaken (not entirely successfully) to the "the islands of the South Sea."

Reports of the voyages of Captain James Cook (1728–79) during the eighteenth century, including the discovery of Australia, led to a renewed interest in evangelizing this hitherto unknown region. The first major missionary expedition to the region was launched in August 1796, when thirty missionaries set sail for Tahiti. Although this mission faced considerable difficulties – not least of which related to the very different sexual attitudes then prevalent in England and Tahiti – it can be seen as marking the beginning of a sustained effort to establish Christianity in the region.

The geographical nature of the region made one of the most reliable means of evangelization – the establishment of mission stations – impossible. The populations of the islands were generally too small to justify the building and maintenance of such settlements. The most successful strategy to be adopted was the use of missionary vessels, which allowed European missionaries to direct and oversee the operations of native evangelists, pastors, and teachers in the region.

The most significant Christian missions in the region were located in Australia and New Zealand, which eventually came to serve as the base for most missionary work in the region. Christianity came to Australia in 1788. The circumstances of its arrival were not entirely happy. The fleet which arrived in New South Wales was transporting convicts to the penal settlements which were being established in the region. At the last moment, the social reformer William Wilberforce (1759–1833), later associated with the abolition of the slave trade (4.1.9), persuaded the British naval authorities to allow a chaplain to sail with the fleet. With the dramatic increase in immigration to the region from Britain in the following century, the various forms of British Christianity became established in the region. The formation of the "Bush Brotherhoods" in 1897 laid the basis for the evangelization of the interior of the continent.

Other missionary societies focused on different regions of the world. The Baptist Missionary Society (founded 1792, and initially known as "The Particular Baptist Society for the Propagation of the Gospel among the Heathen") and the Church Missionary Society (founded 1799, and originally known as "The Church Missionary Society for Africa and the East") developed a particular focus on specific regions of Africa. The Baptist Missionary Society focused on the Congo basin, and the Church Missionary Society on west and east Africa.

Yet the work of missionary societies was only one way in which Christianity in general – and Protestantism in particular – was spread across the world. The close links between European nation-states and their national churches inevitably meant that the expansion of colonial influence was accompanied by at least some degree of Christian influence. This institutional approach to mission, however, tended to be seen in terms of the planting of churches, rather than the conversion of souls.

The classic example of this merging of colonial and ecclesiastical concerns is seen in British colonial expansion in Africa, the Americas, and Asia, to which we now turn.

4.4.2. Missions and Colonialism: The Case of Anglicanism

It has long been recognized that there is a link between missionary work and the rise of colonialism. The presence of Catholic missions in Latin America, for example, was directly linked to Spanish and Portuguese commercial, military, and political interests in this area. To explore the link between colonialism and mission, we shall consider one specific example, which illustrates the issues particularly well: the colonial policies of Great Britain, and the development of colonial churches.

The rise of Great Britain as a naval and colonial power in the eighteenth century created a link between the expansion of British national interests and the establishment of colonial outposts of the national English established church, the Church of England. It is impossible to tell the story of Anglicanism without reference to the rise of the British Empire.

The process of colonization, especially in the eighteenth century, was often proceeded by the establishment of Anglican chaplaincies in new colonial outposts, whose primary function was the pastoral care of the British community of expatriates. Institutional approaches to mission often took the form of an intentional chaplaincy role for expatriates, leading to an accidental missionary role to native populations.

The way in which British colonies developed their own distinct implementations of an "Anglican" vision has been the subject of increased scholarly attention in recent years. There are no persuasive grounds for suggesting that successive British governments saw any particular reason to promote or encourage the emergence of Anglicanism in its colonies up to about 1780. Indeed, the entire colonial enterprise seems to have been secondary to entrepreneurial concerns. Colonial expansion was primarily conceived in commercial terms, as enhancing Britain's position as a trading nation. Wary of creating religious strife, the colonial authorities tended to avoid imposing English religious ideas and practices on indigenous populations. With some local exceptions, the colonial authorities tended to regard Anglicanism primarily as offering a chaplaincy to the resident British population, rather than as the preferred religious option to be imposed upon the local population.

Two distinct phases of the process of Anglicanization of Crown Colonies can be discerned. Between 1780 and 1830, the Crown actively sought to consolidate the links between church and state in its colonies, especially in British North America. The replication of English ecclesiastical structures was seen as a means of consolidating the stability and maintaining the distinct British cultural identity of colonies. The creation of bishoprics in Nova Scotia (1787) and Quebec (1791) can be seen as reflecting this principle, which was implemented initially in Britain's North American colonies in the late eighteenth century, and subsequently in the colonies of the Caribbean in the 1810s and 1820s. Although the Church of England was involved in this process, it was primarily driven by the colonial agendas of this period.

The election of a Whig government in 1830 ushered in a second phase in the Anglicanization of the colonies. No longer was the British government concerned to replicate the English ecclesiastical system, which privileged the Church of England, throughout its dominions. From now on it would be the church, rather than the state, which took upon itself the responsibility for extending Anglicanism overseas. Two leading English Anglican missionary societies – the Church Missionary Society (founded in 1799) and the Society for the Propagation of the Gospel in Foreign Parts (founded in 1701) – both of which had experience of recruiting both missionaries and chaplains for British colonial settlers – now played an increasingly important role in selecting clergy and bishops for the colonies. The Colonial Bishoprics' Fund, established in 1841, was a voluntary organization composed of clergy and prominent politicians which provided money for the creation of eleven bishoprics in the 1840s. When it became clear that many overseas positions were being filled by evangelicals, senior High Churchmen established St. Augustine's, Canterbury in 1848 as a means of countering this development.

Both the Church Missionary Society and Society for the Propagation of the Gospel played a significant entrepreneurial role in providing missionaries for outreach to indigenous populations and chaplains to British settlers, the former primarily in east Africa, and the latter in southern Africa. Both contributed significantly to the shaping of Anglican identity in these regions. Yet their visions for Anglicanism were quite distinct: the Church Missionary Society was evangelical in its outlook, and the Society for the Propagation of the Gospel became increasingly High Church during the 1850s. As a result, quite distinct forms of Anglicanism emerged in these regions, their divergences further catalyzed by later events, such as the East African Revival of the 1930s. East Africa was primarily evangelical in its outlook; South Africa was primarily Anglo-Catholic. In South America, the evangelical South American Mission Society (founded in 1844 as the Patagonian Mission) played a significant role in shaping the forms of Anglicanism in the region.

The link between Anglicanism and the colonial policies of Great Britain in the eighteenth and nineteenth centuries raises the broader question of whether missionaries were complicit in a colonial agenda. Until recently, it was common to argue that Protestant missions created a "state of colonialism" which was the precursor to the advent of a colonial state. On this view, the colonization of a region began with the assertion of the superiority of the values and ideas of the missionaries, which created a state of cultural subservience that was open to colonialist exploitation. On this view, the missionaries prepared the way for western imperial rule by undermining native confidence in their own ideas, values, and civilizations.

Yet this view has now been challenged by scholarship. It is now known that missionaries often attempted to subvert the "colonial mentality" that regarded native peoples in depersonalizing terms, often seeing them as little more than economic commodities. Perhaps the most interesting example of this is provided by the Bremen Mission in the German west African colony of Togo in the closing years of the nineteenth century. Franz Michael Zahn (1833–1900) energetically defended the right of the indigenous population to use their own language against the opposing views of the colonial authorities, and sought, on the basis of his theological convictions, to reaffirm the basic humanity of the colonized peoples.

The work of the London Mission Society among the Khoi people of southern Africa is particularly important in undermining the "mission as colonialism" approach. Far from propounding colonialism, they provided the Khoi with an ideology of resistance against their Afrikaner masters. Furthermore, Protestant missionaries worked actively in many parts of the world which never came under imperial rule – indeed, in some cases often working to subvert any such possibility.

It is now widely agreed that Protestant missionary undertakings were far from the imperialist adventures that older research suggested they were, whether by accident or design. The political realities of the age were such that it was inevitable that British, German, Dutch, and Danish missionary enterprises would become entangled with the dynamics of empire. Yet this does not mean that Protestant missionaries colluded or collaborated in the enterprise of empire. While exceptions can easily be identified, missionaries were rarely cultural imperialists.

4.4.3.   Christian Missions to Asia

Christianity is traditionally believed to have been established in India during the first century, in the form of the "Mar Thoma" church – a group of Christians who traced their origins to St. Thomas the Apostle. According to this ancient tradition, Thomas first set foot in India at Cranganore near Cochin, at that time a major sea port on the Malabar Coast with important trade connections with Palestine and its neighbors. The later voyages of the Portuguese navigator Vasco da Gama (c. 1460–1524) led to the opening up of the coastal regions of the subcontinent to Catholic missionaries, with Goa as their center of operations.

Catholic missionary work in Asia was based on techniques originally developed by Alessandro Valignano (1539–1606), which involved adapting or accommodating the fundamental themes of Christianity to Asian cultures. This required a good knowledge of the native language, a knowledge of and respect for Asian culture, and a willingness to train indigenous clergy. This approach involved drawing a distinction between "civil" and "religious" traditions, and ensuring that the former were respected and retained. As a result, Christian communities became established in large Chinese cities such as Nanjing, Shanghai, Hangzhou, and Beijing. A secondary strategy was also deployed in Asian cultures – the notion of mission "from above," in which missionaries aimed to convert the educated Confucian elite and imperial civil servants, rather than the population at large. The earlier work of Matteo Ricci (1552–1610) was seen as an excellent application of such an approach.

This strategy of cultural accommodation, which included the creation of a Chinese liturgy at a time when only Latin was recognized as the official language of worship, ended through the "Chinese Rites controversy." In 1704, a debate broke out over whether traditional Chinese ancestor worship was to be respected by missionaries. Was this a "civil" or "religious" issue? In the end, it was decided that this was a religious practice, which Catholicism could not respect.

In contrast, Protestant missions were relatively slow to establish themselves in this region; indeed, evangelism was often seen as subsidiary to commerce, and occasionally as an impediment to it. The first Anglican clergy in India, for example, were ships' chaplains, appointed by the English East India Company to provide pastoral care and spiritual support for the crews of their ships, so that they might carry out their commercial tasks more efficiently.

The first major Protestant mission to India was based at the Danish Crown Colony of Tranquebar on the Coromandel Coast, south of Madras. Lutheran orthodoxy remained hostile to missionary activity, for reasons noted earlier in this chapter (4.4.1); Pietists, however, were strongly in favor of evangelism. Among the German Lutheran Pietist missionaries of note in this undertaking were Bartholomäus Ziegenbalg (who directed the mission from its founding in 1706 to 1719) and Christian Frederick Schwartz (director from 1750 to 1787). The Lutheran faculty of theology at Wittenberg – Luther's old university – were outraged at such a development, and tried, unsuccessfully, to have it closed down.

In the event, this mission bore some fruit. A Lutheran community of many thousands arose in and around the cities of the region, such as Tranquebar itself, Tanjore, Tiruchirapalli, and Tirunelveli. Danish Pietism went into decline around the year 1800, partly due to the growing influence of rationalism, and much of the work in the region was taken over by a British agency – the Church Missionary Society. Around 1840, the Dresden-Leipzig Mission sent missionaries to the region, leading to many Tamil Christians reverting to Lutheranism.

However, the growing political power of Britain in the region inevitably favored the activities of British missionaries, even though the East India Company did not want their commercial work to be disrupted by such activity. English Baptists began work in Bengal in 1793, settling in the Danish colonial town of Serampore, upriver from Calcutta, beyond the authority of the East India Company.

The founding of Serampore College in 1818 was a landmark. It was presented to its supporters back in England as an institution that would train Indians to replace Europeans completely as missionaries, and so create a truly indigenous church. While there may be a degree of aspirational inflation implicit in this claim, designed to encourage existing donors and secure new ones, the objective was of considerable strategic importance, in view of the growing suspicions about the missionaries' relationship with the British colonial authorities.

Although British missionary societies and individuals were able to operate in India without any major opposition from other European agencies from about 1775, they received no active support from the British authorities. The East India Company, for example, was opposed to their activities, on the grounds that they might create ill-will among native Indians, and thus threaten the trade upon which it depended. However, the Charter Act (passed by the British parliament on July 13, 1813) revised the conditions under which the company was permitted to operate. From now on, British missionaries were given protected status, and a limited degree of freedom to carry out evangelistic work on the Indian Subcontinent. It was inevitable that their privileged status meant that they would be seen as agents of British rule and values. The Serampore program opened the way to the introduction of indigenized forms of Protestant churches.

Yet Britain was by no means the only western nation with missionary involvement in the Indian Subcontinent. The first major American missionary undertaking had its origins at Williams College, Williamstown, Maryland in 1810, where a group of students had been studying the history of the East India Company, and believed they were called to serve as missionaries in the region. This led the General Association of Congregational Ministers of Massachusetts to form the American Board of Commissioners for Foreign Missions in 1810, and send a group – including some of the original Williams College students – to Calcutta.

The issue of the relation of Protestantism to Indian culture remained important throughout the nineteenth century. It seemed to many that Protestantism was alien to India, insensitive to its cultural values and norms. The "Sepoy Mutiny" of 1857 is often seen as much as a revolt against alleged attempts to westernize Indian culture as a rebellion against colonial rule. Christians and Christian institutions were targeted, precisely because they were seen as the instruments or outcomes of western culture.

A similar situation arose in China. One of the many effects of the Opium War of the 1840s was to open the "Middle Kingdom" up to western missionaries. China had been isolated from the west until the nineteenth century, when growing interest in commerce opened up the region to western missionaries, predominantly from America and Britain. Hampered by a lack of knowledge of the written or spoken language, these missionaries labored under immense difficulties. Of these, James Hudson Taylor (1832–1905) may be singled out for special comment.

Hudson Taylor was initially a missionary with the Chinese Evangelization Society. Dissatisfaction with this organization led him to found the China Inland Mission in 1865. This mission was unusual in several aspects, not least its willingness to accept single women as missionaries and its interdenominational character. Hudson Taylor showed an awareness of the cultural barriers facing Christian missionaries in China, and did what he could to remove them – for example, he required his missionaries to wear Chinese, rather than western, dress. The China Inland Mission stood virtually alone among missionary societies at this time, in that it recognized the need for its missionaries to be taught Mandarin in schools especially established for this purpose. Other missionary societies merely provided their workers with language manuals and advice from native speakers.

The western powers gained major footholds in China as a consequence of the Opium War (1839–42). Under the Treaty of Nanjing (1842), China was forced to make major concessions to Britain, including the granting of "extraterritoriality" (that is, exemption from Chinese laws) to British nationals. This proved to be the first of a number of "unequal treaties" imposed upon China by western powers, which led to growing western influence in the region. During the period 1861–94, the "Self-Strengthening Movement," championed by Qing dynasty scholars and officials such as Li Hongzhang (1823–1901) and Zuo Zongtang (1812–85), attempted to achieve a confluence of western technology with traditional Chinese culture. Western missionaries were generally welcomed, not least on account of their perceived potential as educationalists.

However, China's defeat by Japan in the disastrous Sino-Japanese War of 1895 led to new tensions. A new conservative elite gave support to the anti-foreign and anti-Christian movement of secret societies which came to be known as "the Boxers." In 1900, Boxer bands were active throughout north China. Christianity was seen as something western, and hence un-Chinese. Foreign Christian missionaries were particularly at risk, as were any buildings associated with Christianity. Chinese Christians were massacred in many areas. Such was the scale of the action that foreign concessions in Beijing and Tianjin were besieged in June 1900, eventually provoking an armed intervention by the western powers.

At this point, the Qing court formally took command of the Boxer forces, and led a coordinated yet ultimately unsuccessful program of resistance to the western relief army. The Peace Protocol imposed upon the Qing court on September 7 marked a final humiliation for the dynasty. It did nothing, however, to advance the cause of Christianity, which was clearly identified as a western import. Many believed that Christianity was now a lost cause in the "Middle Kingdom."

4.4.4.   Christian Missions to Africa

As we noted earlier (1.4.6), Christianity became established in the Roman colonies of North Africa during the first centuries of the Christian era in the areas now known as Algeria, Tunisia, and Libya. A particularly strong Christian presence developed in Egypt, with the city of Alexandria emerging as a leading center of Christian thought and life. Augustine of Hippo, one of the most significant Christian leaders and writers of all time, was based in this region.

Much of this Christian presence in Africa was swept away through the Arab invasions of the seventh century (2.1.3). Coptic Christianity survived in Egypt, although as a minority faith. The situation began to change gradually during the later sixteenth century. Portuguese settlers occupied previously uninhabited islands off the west African coast, such as the Cape Verde Islands, establishing Catholicism in doing so. However, such offshore settlements had little impact on the mainland of Africa itself.

Christian missionary involvement in Africa really began seriously in the nineteenth century, and came to be increasingly linked with the presence of colonial powers in the region – such as Great Britain, Germany, France, and Italy. Catholic missionary work in Africa was generally carried out by religious orders, some of which had been founded for the specific purpose of evangelization in this region. For example, the Italian Comboni Missionaries were active in Sudan; the German Pallottines in Cameroon; the Missionary Benedictines in Tanzania; and the Missionary Oblates of Mary Immaculate and Austrian Trappists in South Africa. Some female religious orders became involved in missionary work, including the Sisters of Saint-Joseph of Cluny, founded in 1807 by Marie-Anne Javouhey (1779–1851).

Yet Catholic missionary work was not limited to religious orders. Charles Lavigerie (1825–92), the French colonial Bishop of Algeria, founded the "White Fathers," a society of African missionaries who worked among the Berbers and the peoples of the Niger, the Zambezi, and the great lakes of East Africa.

The coming of Protestantism to sub-Saharan Africa is to be dated from the late eighteenth century, and is closely linked with the great evangelical awakening in England at this time. Many were appalled at the slave trade, in which British merchants bought slaves from local tribal leaders in Africa, before exporting them to the plantations of the American colonies. The conversion of John Newton (1725–1807), a former slave-ship captain, to evangelical Protestantism created a growing awareness of the problems (4.1.9). Newton celebrated his conversion with one of the world's best-known hymns – "Amazing Grace" – which told of his own spiritual transformation. Yet this same writer also wrote hymns such as "The Negro's Complaint," which spoke of the dignity conferred on all people by God, which slavery could not diminish, still less abolish.

Evangelical Protestants responded to this new concern for Africa in two ways: first, working for the abolition of slavery, a project especially associated with William Wilberforce and his circle; second, by bringing the gospel to this region of the world. These were powerful visions, which caught the imagination of many in the 1790s, though it was not until August 1833 – a month after Wilberforce's death – that the British Parliament passed the Slavery Abolition Act, abolishing slavery, and giving all slaves in the British Empire their freedom.

Missionary work in the 1790s led to the establishment of small Christian communities among native tribes, particularly the Khoi. Gradually, surrounding tribes began to convert to Christianity. Here, as in many other situations, the motivation for conversion varied considerably. Some conversions clearly reflect a deep spiritual experience; others reflect a conviction of the truth of the Christian gospel; other conversions may reflect a belief that Christianity would make the benefits of western civilization more widely available to African culture. This is particularly clear in the case of the Ganda tribe of east Africa, where the decision to convert to Christianity (rather than Islam) seems to have been partly influenced by the superiority of British technology, and the suggestion that such conversion might lead to this technology becoming more widely available to them.

The dominant feature of sub-Saharan Africa in the nineteenth century is the growing presence of colonial powers in the region, some of which had Protestant state churches. Belgium, Britain, France, and Germany all established colonies in this region during the period. The forms of Christianity dominant in these European nations varied considerably, with the result that a considerable diversity of churches became established in Africa. Anglicanism, Catholicism, and Lutheranism were all well established by the end of the century; in South Africa, the Dutch Reformed church had a particularly strong influence among European settlers. This created a disturbing perception in some quarters that Protestantism was merely the religious component of colonial power, a western import to the region which would not survive any subsequent western withdrawal.

Perhaps the most celebrated colonial evangelist was David Livingstone (1813–73). Livingstone was convinced of the importance of commerce in relation to the Christianization of Africa. In 1838, he offered his services to the London Missionary Society, declaring his intention to go to Africa "to make an open path for commerce and Christianity." Exploiting the British government's interest in replacing the banned slave trade with more legitimate forms of commerce, Livingstone obtained government backing for an expedition to explore the Zambezi River as a potential gateway to the interior. He believed that the interior would be capable of commercial exploitation, such as the growing of cotton, then greatly in demand by the cotton mills of Lancashire.

Although the expedition turned out to be a commercial failure, it opened up the interior of the continent of Africa to missionary activity. Livingstone himself became a role model for many younger British Protestants. He gave a series of addresses at Cambridge University which led to the founding of the Universities' Mission to Central Africa in 1860.

Whereas the London missionary societies thought of the missionary enterprise primarily in sending white evangelists to Africa, the Protestant Episcopal Church of the United States believed that the best strategy was to send Afro-Americans to the region. At least 115 black American missionaries are known to have been present and active in Africa during the period 1875–99. Following the establishment of the west African republic of Liberia (1847) as a refuge for former slaves, black Protestant missionaries and church-builders went to the region, seeing their work partly as evangelism, and partly as nation-building. This

generated some friction with white missionaries in this area; nevertheless, it was an important staging post on the road to the indigenization of mission.

Yet the rise of Protestantism caused tensions to arise within traditional African societies.
An excellent example of this can be seen in the case of marriage customs. Western Protestantism was strongly monogamist; African culture had long recognized the merits of
polygamy. Increasingly, the European Christian insistence upon a man having only one
wife was seen as a western import, having no place in traditional African society. The
United African Methodist Church, an indigenous church which recognized polygamy,
traces its origins back to a meeting of the Methodist Church in Lagos, Nigeria, in 1917,
when a large group of leading lay people were debarred from the church on account of
polygamy. They responded by forming their own Methodist church, which adopted native
African values frowned on by the European missionaries.

The Berlin "Congo Conference" (1884–5) marked a significant turning point in the
European colonial presence in Africa. Rising tensions between the European powers – espe-
cially Germany and Belgium – led to an agreement to allocate different regions of Africa
to a "sphere of influence" of the European colonial powers, primarily France and Great
Britain. This led to an increase in the confessionalization of mission, with nations such as
Belgium, France, Italy, and Portugal lending support to Catholic missions, and Great
Britain to Protestant missions.

By the year 1900, Christianity had been firmly established in many parts of sub-Saharan
Africa. The confluence of colonization, civilization, and missionary work was perhaps most
obvious in the establishment of educational and health-care institutions. But major questions began to emerge. Was its presence in the region simply a consequence of western
colonial authority, so that it would disappear, along with other expressions of colonialism,
at some unknown date in the future? Similarly, the forms of Christianity established in the
region bore the unmistakable hallmarks of their predominantly European origins. Thus
the services and structures of the "Church of the Province of South Africa" – one of two
Anglican organizations in the region – looked remarkably like those of parts of British
Anglicanism. How would such obvious importations or transplants survive in such a
different cultural context? And what would happen when the British had to go home?
Could these planted churches hope to survive without their colonial patrons? We shall
return to these questions later (5.4.4).

4.4.5. Christian Missions to Native Americans

While the predominant model of Christian mission in the late eighteenth and nineteenth
centuries involved missionaries working abroad, a quite different model emerged in North
America, as Christian settlers encountered Native American cultures. Missionary work
began in New England as early as the seventeenth century, as Puritan settlers made contact
with local tribes. It is generally agreed that this colonial missionary outreach to Native
Americans failed. Nevertheless, it remains of considerable historical interest.

The Puritan missionary John Eliot (1604–90) became interested in the culture and
language of the Native Americans who lived around Roxbury, one of the first towns
founded in the Massachusetts Bay Colony in 1630, and learned Natic (as this regional

variant of Algonquian is known) to preach to them. He was able to attract support for his missionary work in the region, eventually managing to gain parliamentary approval in 1649 for the establishment of the Society for the Propagation of the Gospel in New England. His translation and production of the Bible into Natic took place over the period 1661–3, using a professional printer, Marmaduke Johnson, sent over from England in 1660 on a three-year contract.

Eliot believed that Native Americans who converted to Christianity should be gathered together into towns of "Praying Indians" where they could be supervised and nurtured in Christian knowledge. By 1674, there were fourteen such towns of "Praying Indians," with a total population of four thousand. Yet "King Philip's War" (1675–8) – a conflict between colonists and Native Americans – put the "Praying Indians" in an impossible position. They were disowned by their own tribes, and suspected of retaining tribal loyalties by the colonials. In the end, the tribes in eastern Massachusetts and Connecticut were broken up, and the survivors were forced to move west of the Connecticut River.

Catholic missionary work among Native Americans in North America tended to be concentrated in the region known as "La Nouvelle France" ("New France"), an area colonized by France during the period beginning with the exploration of the Saint Lawrence River by Jacques Cartier in 1534. This colonial region was at its greatest in 1712, extending from Newfoundland to the Rocky Mountains and from the Hudson Bay to the Gulf of Mexico. It consisted of five colonies: Canada, Acadia, Hudson Bay, Newfoundland, and Louisiana. Catholic missionaries working in these areas encountered Native American peoples such as the Montagnais, Huron, and Iroquois, whose settlement areas, languages, and cultures were studied by Jesuit missionaries, such as Jean de Brébeuf (1593–1649), who was martyred by the Iroquois in 1649, Jacques Marquette (1637–75), and Jean-Baptiste de la Brosse (1724–82), who produced a dictionary of the Abenaki language in 1760.

In the eighteenth century, Protestant mission work in colonial America shifted into a higher gear, as the revivals of the Great Awakening (4.1.5) kindled interest in spreading the gospel among Native Americans. Various groups were involved in this enterprise, including European émigrés influenced by the revivals in Germany and England (4.1.4). Unusually, Moravian settlers were prepared to live among, and even marry, Native Americans, much to the concern of the British colonial authorities. This special relationship with Native Americans proved to be of particular importance evangelistically.

A quite different form of engagement emerged in the early nineteenth century, in response to the religious changes of that era. The revivalism that developed in Kansas during the Second Great Awakening led to growing interest in evangelization of the native tribes of the area, with Baptists and Methodists – the two denominations most affected by the Awakening – undertaking major missionary enterprises.

One of the most significant and effective forms of missionary work was education. Baptist workers set up a training school near Topeka, which became a major center for evangelism in the 1850s. Medical missions also played an important role. Jotham Meeker (1804–55) combined his professional expertise as a printer with a somewhat amateur interest in medicine, using both as a way of establishing contact and trust with the Shawnees, Stockbridges, and Ottawas during the 1830s and 1840s.

The motivation of these Protestant missionaries to evangelize Native Americans was complex. Virtually all of the missionaries I studied in preparing this section believed deeply and passionately that the coming of the gospel would enlighten and liberate the peoples among whom they were ministering. Yet other motivations can be discerned, paralleling rather than contradicting their primary concern. One such motivation was a desire to preserve the identity and interests of such peoples in the face of rapid social change. At times, this led to serious misjudgments. The Baptist missionary Isaac McCoy (1784–1846), for example, came to the conclusion that "reservations" held the key to the safeguarding of the cultural identity of such peoples. He proposed that Kansas, Nebraska, and Oklahoma should become Native American states, to be free from white influence.

The case of the Canadian Baptist missionary Silas T. Rand (1810–89) highlights the importance of missionaries for the study of historical anthropology. Rand originally had aspirations to serve on foreign mission fields. However, his missionary interests were redirected in 1846, while ministering in Prince Edward Island, when he encountered the Micmac language.

Rand believed that Christianity would deliver the Micmac from the predations and depravations of white culture, and came to love and respect both the Micmac language and its folklore. He was determined to preserve both, acting as their advocate in land rights disputes, and publishing both the original texts and translations of their oral traditions. As in so many other cases, scholarly knowledge of the traditions, customs, and languages of America's first peoples were preserved and transmitted by the missionaries, many of whom developed a deep respect for the cultures within which they were working.

Similarly, the preservation of the Hawaiian language was due to American missionaries in the 1820s, who insisted on learning the native language in order to explain the gospel – only to come to see the preservation of this language as an important issue in itself. Hiram Bingham (1789–1869) even refused to teach the islanders English, believing that this would destroy their linguistic – and hence their cultural – identity.

A similar pattern can be seen in the ministry of Asher Wright (1803–75), a missionary to the Seneca people at Buffalo Creek, New York State. After graduating from Andover Seminary, Wright joined the Buffalo Creek mission, spending forty-four years working with the Seneca. His missionary work was not especially successful; however, his commitment to the people and knowledge of their language and customs led to the preservation of their distinctive features. Wright's ministry is one of many examples that raise questions about the "colonial" stereotype of missionaries, until recently widely encountered in accounts of Protestant missions to Native Americans during the nineteenth century.

4.4.6.   The Edinburgh World Missionary Conference, 1910

It is widely agreed that the high point of the era of modern Protestant missions was the World Missionary Conference, held in the Scottish capital city of Edinburgh in 1910. While this conference represented a landmark in missionary thinking, it is important to locate it within a broader context. Many of the achievements in mission thinking and organization that are often attributed to the Edinburgh conference are better seen as the outcome of similar gatherings dating as far back as 1854, and extending into the 1930s. Nevertheless,

Figure 4.8   World Missionary Conference, Assembly Hall, New College, University of Edinburgh, 1910. World Council of Churches Archives D5486-00

the Edinburgh conference was of iconic significance, comparable in some ways to an ecumenical council.

The most significant feature of the conference was that it was organized by missionary societies, rather than by churches. This conference focused on developing strategies for the future of missionary thinking and action, being led and resourced by practitioners. This contrasted sharply with the Ecumenical Missionary Conference, held in New York in 1900, which had been attended mainly by church leaders, and was judged to have achieved little in the way of active proposals for the future. The Edinburgh conference's organizers were all laymen – most notably, the American Methodist John Mott (1865–1955), one of the most active advocates of missionary work, whose *Evangelization of the World in This Generation* (1905) created a surge of enthusiasm and optimism for the missionary enterprise, especially within the United States.

Yet with the benefit of hindsight, the conference can now be seen to have reinforced existing Protestant paradigms of mission, when redirection and review was increasingly necessary. The world was changing; new strategies and approaches were clearly needed. The approach to mission at the conference was shaped by the dominant assumption that there was a reasonably homogeneous Christian world, primarily in Europe and North America, which was fully evangelized. Evangelism would remain the business of the "Home Church" – in other words, the spiritually and numerically robust churches of the west.

While recognizing the emergence of a "Native Church" in parts of the world, this was seen as needing continued direction from the west. There was little awareness of the importance of the indigenization of mission, using local people to engage local cultural realities. Mission territories were ranked in terms of their perceived significance. The world was, in effect, divided into "Christendom" and "Heathendom," with the former having missionary obligations to the latter. Japan, China, and India came first in the order of missionary priorities, followed by the Dutch East Indies and the Islamic world, with sub-Saharan Africa being seen as of the least importance.

This disregard for Africa is widely seen as one of the conference's most important failings. Out of around 1200 delegates attending the conference, there was only one African. Other criticisms made of the conference include its assumption that Latin America and the Caribbean were to be considered part of "Christendom," and its tendency to evaluate missionary impact not in terms of conversion statistics but of a more general influence on national education, politics, culture, and social policy, resulting from the success of missionary schools.

One of the most interesting outcomes of the conference was its reflections on how evangelism was to be linked to the growing science of "comparative religion," pioneered by academics such as Max Müller (1823–1900), professor of comparative philology at Oxford University from 1868–75. The report on "The Christian Message in Relation to Non-Christian Traditions" at the Edinburgh conference is widely seen as representing the high water mark of a "fulfillment" model for understanding the relation of Christianity to other faiths. The Spirit of God, it was argued, was at work in other religious traditions, preparing the way for their fulfillment in Christ. Rather than seeing other religions as degradations or denials of the truth, they were to be seen as important milestones along the road to the Christian faith.

These ideas developed in British India during the second half of the nineteenth century, as increasing numbers of British theologians became familiar with Hinduism at first hand. The "fulfillment hypothesis" was especially associated with J. N. Farquhar (1861–1929), who saw other faiths as pointing towards their fulfillment in Christianity. These ideas gained increasing popularity in the 1890s, resonating with a shift in both cultural and theological mood. In an editorial of 1908, the *Madras Christian College Magazine*, citing some words of Jesus of Nazareth from the Sermon on the Mount (Matthew 5:17), set out the leading principle of what was increasingly becoming the new missionary orthodoxy. "All that there is of truth and inspiration in other religions must find its fulfillment in Jesus Christ."

The approach endorsed by the Edinburgh conference echoes these themes, arguing that all or most religions were animated to some degree by the Spirit of God, who prepared the way for God's full revelation in Christ. This, it was argued, was better expressed in terms of a gradual process of absorbing other religions into the Christian faith, rather than aiming at confrontation with them. Yet many delegates were uneasy about this approach, arguing that such a "fulfillment" model failed to do justice to the obvious contradictions between Christianity and other religions – especially Islam.

The great era of Protestant missions came to an end in 1914, with the outbreak of the Great War (now referred to as the "First World War"). Many of the tentative patterns of collaboration between missionaries across national and denominational boundaries were overwhelmed by a tidal wave of nationalism unleashed by the war, and the economic and political uncertainties that ensued.

Sources of Quotations

p. 219: Thomas Paine, *Age of Reason*, II, 21.
p. 256: Thomas Jefferson, Letter to Messrs. Nehemiah Dodge and Others, January 1, 1802.

For Further Reading

Bradley, James E., and Dale K. Van Kley. *Religion and Politics in Enlightenment Europe.* Notre Dame, IN: University of Notre Dame Press, 2001.

Brooke, John, and Ian McLean, eds. *Heterodoxy in Early Modern Science and Religion.* Oxford: Oxford University Press, 2006.

Burleigh, Michael. *Earthly Powers: The Clash of Religion and Politics in Europe from the French Revolution to the Great War.* New York: HarperCollins, 2005.

Byrne, James M. *Religion and the Enlightenment: From Descartes to Kant.* Louisville, KY: Westminster John Knox Press, 1997.

Carey, Hilary M. *God's Empire: Religion and Colonialism in the British World, c. 1801–1908.* Cambridge: Cambridge University Press, 2011.

Diehl, Huston. *Staging Reform, Reforming the Stage: Protestantism and Popular Theater in Early Modern England.* Ithaca, NY: Cornell University Press, 1997.

Dolan, Jay P. *In Search of an American Catholicism: A History of Religion and Culture in Tension.* Oxford: Oxford University Press, 2004.

Draper, Jonathan A. *The Eye of the Storm: Bishop John William Colenso and the Crisis of Biblical Inspiration.* London: T&T Clark, 2003.

Foster, Stephen. *The Long Argument: English Puritanism and the Shaping of New England Culture, 1570–1700.* Chapel Hill: University of North Carolina Press, 1991.

Heyrman, Christine Leigh. *Southern Cross: The Beginnings of the Bible Belt.* Chapel Hill: University of North Carolina Press, 1997.

Hindmarsh, Bruce D. *The Evangelical Conversion Narrative: Spiritual Autobiography in Early Modern England.* Oxford: Oxford University Press, 2005.

Holmes, David L. *The Faiths of the Founding Fathers.* Oxford: Oxford University Press, 2006.

Lambert, Frank. *"Pedlar in Divinity": George Whitefield and the Transatlantic Revivals, 1737–1770.* Princeton, NJ: Princeton University Press, 2003.

Ledger-Lomas, Michael. "'Glimpses of the Great Conflict': English Congregationalists and the European Crisis of Faith, circa 1840–1875." *Journal of British Studies* 46 (2007): 826–60.

Lee, Joseph Tse-Hei. *The Bible and the Gun: Christianity in South China, 1860–1900.* New York: Routledge, 2003.

Malek, Roman, and Peter Hofrichter. *Jingjiao: The Church of the East in China and Central Asia.* Sankt Augustin: Institut Monumenta Serica, 2006.

Miller, Randall M., Harry S. Stout, and Charles Reagan Wilson, eds. *Religion and the American Civil War.* New York: Oxford University Press, 1998.

Mörner, Magnus. *The Expulsion of the Jesuits from Latin America.* New York: Knopf, 1965.

Neill, Stephen. *A History of Christianity in India, 1707–1858.* Cambridge: Cambridge University Press, 2002.

Noll, Mark A. *The Old Religion in a New World: The History of North American Christianity.* Grand Rapids, MI: Eerdmans, 2002.

O'Connell, Michael. *The Idolatrous Eye: Iconoclasm and Theater in Early Modern England.* New York: Oxford University Press, 2000.

Orr, D. Alan. *Treason and the State: Law, Politics, and Ideology in the English Civil War.* Cambridge: Cambridge University Press, 2002.

Porter, Andrew N. *Religion Versus Empire? British Protestant Missionaries and Overseas Expansion, 1700–1914.* Manchester: Manchester University Press, 2004.

Putney, Clifford. *Muscular Christianity: Manhood and Sports in Protestant America, 1880–1920.* Cambridge, MA: Harvard University Press, 2001.

Quataert, Donald. *The Ottoman Empire, 1700–1922.* Cambridge: Cambridge University Press, 2005.

Reinders, Eric. *Borrowed Gods and Foreign Bodies: Christian Missionaries Imagine Chinese Religion.* Berkeley: University of California Press, 2004.

Ross, Ronald J. *The Failure of Bismarck's Kulturkampf: Catholicism and State Power in Imperial Germany, 1871–1887.* Washington, DC: Catholic University of America Press, 1998.

Shevzov, Vera. *Russian Orthodoxy on the Eve of Revolution.* Oxford: Oxford University Press, 2004.

Stanley, Brian, ed. *Christian Missions and the Enlightenment.* Grand Rapids, MI: Eerdmans, 2001.

Stanley, Brian. *The World Missionary Conference, Edinburgh 1910.* Grand Rapids, MI: Eerdmans, 2009.

Van Kley, Dale K. *The Jansenists and the Expulsion of the Jesuits from France, 1757–1765.* New Haven, CT: Yale University Press, 1975.

Van Kley, Dale K. *The Religious Origins of the French Revolution: From Calvin to the Civil Constitution, 1560–1791.* New Haven, CT: Yale University Press, 1996.

Waldron, Jeremy. *God, Locke, and Equality: Christian Foundations of John Locke's Political Thought.* Cambridge: Cambridge University Press, 2002.

5

The Twentieth Century, 1914 to the Present

The assassination by a Serbian nationalist on June 28, 1914, of Archduke Franz Ferdinand of Austria, the heir to the throne of Austro-Hungary, sparked off an international conflict of unparalleled destructiveness. The European Great Powers were linked together by treaty obligations which virtually guaranteed that a declaration of war by one would lead to a Europe-wide conflict. On the one hand were Great Britain, France, and Russia; on the other, Germany, Austro-Hungary, and Italy.

The conflict began on July 28, 1914, with an Austro-Hungarian invasion of Serbia, followed shortly afterwards by a German invasion of Belgium, Luxembourg, and France. Since most of the combatants were colonial powers, the conflict quickly became global. After initially taking a position of neutrality, the United States entered the conflict on the side of Great Britain and France in April 1917. It was not an easy decision. The United States had many immigrant communities, representing both sides of the conflict.

It is thought that the total number of military and civilian casualties was in the order of thirty-five million. The unparalleled size of the theater of conflict and the damage it inflicted were reflected in the name given to it in English-speaking lands: the "Great War."

5.1. Setting the Context: Post-War Turbulence

The Great War had a massive impact on Christianity globally. Christianity was still a predominantly western phenomenon in 1914. At one level, the war fractured relationships between nations and churches. There would be no equivalent of the Edinburgh Missionary Conference of 1910 (4.4.6) for some time, partly due to the severity of the economic situation after the war, and partly on account of the strained relationships between national bodies – such as mission agencies and churches. It would be a long time, for example,

Christian History: An Introduction, First Edition. Alister E. McGrath.
© 2013 John Wiley & Sons, Ltd. Published 2013 by John Wiley & Sons, Ltd.

Figure 5.1   A convoy of horses and wagons pass by the ruins of St. Martin's Church and the Cloth Hall of Ypres during the Great War. © Hulton-Deutsch Collection/Corbis

before German and British Christians were able to restore any kind of meaningful working relationship between them.

Yet the war also finally put an end to the notion of "Christendom." This idea had been largely discredited following the fragmentation of Europe in the aftermath of the French Revolution (4.1.8). It had now received a mortal wound, from which it never recovered. European Christian nations had regularly fought one another in the past – but never with such ferocity.

The situation of Russia was of particular importance. Russia soon found herself overwhelmed by German technological superiority, and was forced to sue for peace. This caused existing internal tensions to reach breaking point, and is widely agreed to have been a trigger for the Russian Revolution – unquestionably one of the most important developments in the twentieth century for the fortunes of Christianity in Europe and far beyond.

Yet the Great War was not a religious war, in any sense of the term. It did not arise over religious issues, nor did religious beliefs or agendas play any significant role in its prosecution. It was a war between "nation-states," based primarily on nationalist objectives and agendas. A complex network of alliances and counterbalances had developed between the various European powers since the Franco-Prussian War, intended to neutralize the capacity of any Great Power to achieve continental dominance. In the end, the mechanism that was intended to prevent a conflict locked the Great Powers into a delicate state of equilibrium which, once disturbed, had the potential to escalate uncontrollably into total war.

Any account of the history of Christianity in the twentieth century must give due weight to the instability and disillusionment that arose in the aftermath of the Great War. Yet our concern initially lies with two events that took place during the Great War, which shaped the course of the twentieth century.

5.1.1.   The Armenian Genocide of 1915

The twentieth century opened with a catastrophe which traumatized Christians in the eastern Mediterranean region, and which was an ominous portent of things to come later that century. The ailing Ottoman Empire found itself caught up in the Great War, and began to fragment following a series of rebellions against Ottoman rule in the Middle East and beyond (4.2.2). The Ottoman Empire was a predominantly Islamic region, which was home to a significant number of non-Islamic peoples, including Armenian Christians. The Armenian people had adopted the Christian faith in 301, and regarded themselves as the oldest Christian nation in the region. In 1915, a series of massacres and forced deportations claimed the lives of between 1 million and 1.5 million Armenians – an event now referred to as the "Armenian Genocide."

The events of 1915 did not come entirely as a bolt from the blue. There had been a series of massacres of Armenian Christians in many Turkish cities during the period 1895–7, in which about 200 000 people are thought to have died. While the massacres of April 1915 were directed against non-Islamic religious minorities in general, rather than against Christians in particular, the people most severely affected were the Armenians. These events took place deep within the Ottoman Empire, under wartime conditions which made communication and intervention virtually impossible. Nothing could be done to stop the killings.

A month later, the governments of France, Great Britain, and Russia issued a declaration denouncing the massacres as "crimes against humanity and civilization," for which the entire Turkish government would be held responsible. The draft peace treaty with Turkey known as the "Treaty of Sèvres" (August 10, 1920) contained a specific provision by which the Turkish government undertook to hand over to the Allied powers the persons responsible for the massacres committed during the war on Turkish territory. However, the Treaty of Sèvres was not formally ratified and never came into force. It was replaced by the Treaty of Lausanne (July 24, 1923), which did not contain any provisions respecting the punishment of war crimes. Instead, it set out a "Declaration of Amnesty" for all offenses committed by Turkish agents between August 1, 1914, and November 20, 1922 – including the Armenian Genocide. No action was taken against Turkey, leading many – such as Adolf Hitler – to conclude that the international community was prepared to tolerate such acts of genocide, especially when they took place in the "fog of war."

The impact of this genocide upon world Christianity has been mixed. Regionally, it was seen as a catastrophe. Christians in the Middle East were stunned and numbed by the events. Many of them lived as religious minorities under Islamic rule, and feared that this massacre might lead to a more general repression of Christians by other Islamic powers in the region. Many drew the conclusion that dispersion was the only way of ensuring their safety. As a result, the largest Armenian communities today are to be found in the United States, where they found sanctuary.

In the dark days of 1915, some Armenians had looked to Russia for help. Was not this great nation a bastion of Orthodox Christianity? Might not its great resources be brought to bear on their desperate situation? Yet in 1917, events took a turn which few could have predicted. The Russian Revolution overthrew the czarist state, and ushered in an altogether new state ideology. No longer was Russia an Orthodox nation. If anything, she would be a nation committed to the elimination of religion from its territory – and, if possible, far beyond.

5.1.2.　The Russian Revolution of 1917

As we noted earlier (4.2.3), the political philosopher Karl Marx had argued that the origins of religion – Christianity included – lay in social and economic alienation. People turned to religion for consolation, in that they could not bear the weight of sorrow and pain caused by their poverty and alienation from their rights. In his famous words, religion is the "opium of the people" – a narcotic, which soothes the pains of life under capitalism, and disinclines people to take action to bring about radical social and political change.

For Marx, religion would die out if radical social change was effected. Eliminate capitalism, through a communist revolution, and the pain it created would disappear – and with it, any need for the comfort of religion. Religion, Marx argued, owed both its origins and its continued appeal to its power to comfort and soothe in the face of the ills of capitalism. Religion thus offered an indirect support to capitalism, in that it diminished the human will to rebel against its iniquities, and bring about the socioeconomic transformation that alone would change the world.

Marx's ideas never achieved significant influence in the heartlands of capitalism – in western European nations, such as Germany or Great Britain, or in the United States of America. They may have attracted attention from some academics and social critics; yet they failed to gain acceptance from and influence among those with power. The Russian Revolution of 1917 changed the situation radically and irreversibly. Suddenly, Marx's ideas were being taken seriously and put into practice by a state. For Vladimir Ilyich Lenin (1870–1924), religion was a tool of oppression, cynically used against the peasants by the Russian ruling classes. The Soviet Union now became the first state to have as its ideological objective the elimination of religion.

The Russian Revolution of 1917 took place in two stages. An initial uprising against the czarist regime took place early in 1917 in St. Petersburg, then the capital of Russia. This "February Revolution" (which actually took place in March 1917, according to the western calendar) took place against the background of massive Russian losses in the Great War, and increasing disillusionment with the policies of the czar. In the chaos of the situation, members of the Duma – the Russian imperial parliament – seized power, and declared themselves to be the provisional government of the nation. The czar and his family were

Figure 5.2   The Russian Revolution, October 1917. Vladimir Ilyich Lenin (1870–1924) addressing the crowd in Red Square, Moscow. Universal History Archive/Getty Images

placed under house arrest. At this stage, the intentions of the revolutionaries were to bring about a liberal democracy within the collapsed Russian Empire.

Yet a more radical group, led by Lenin and informed by Marx's ideas, was in the process of consolidating its influence. The Bolshevik (from the Russian word for "majority") faction seized its opportunity in the "October Revolution" (which actually took place in November 1917), establishing a workers' state. Civil war broke out, in which the Bolshevik "Red Army" fought the "White Army" of foreign troops and internal opponents of the Bolsheviks. By 1924, the czar had been executed and opposition to the Bolsheviks eliminated.

Lenin always regarded the intellectual, cultural, and physical elimination of religion as central to his socialist revolution, and had identified atheism as an essential element of his ideology long before the Bolshevik Revolution of October 1917. In laying down how the revolutionary cause was to be advanced within Russia, he wrote, "Our propaganda necessarily includes the propaganda of atheism." In an attempt to win the people from Christianity through argument, Lenin suggested it would be necessary "to translate and widely disseminate the literature of the eighteenth-century French Enlighteners and atheists."

Yet a problem soon became apparent. Marx's theories predicted that religion would vanish with the socialist revolution, in that its causes would be eliminated. With the revolutionary abolition of socioeconomic alienation, there was no need for any spiritual narcotic to dull the pain of life. There should be no reason for religious belief to continue to exist. Yet it soon became clear that religion was obstinately persisting. The outcome of this observation was inevitable: it would be necessary to enforce what the theory predicted would happen spontaneously. A barrage of repressive measures, from banners to bullets, from pamphlets to prison camps, was unleashed against the religionists of the Soviet Union.

Initially, attention was directed towards the religious group that was dominant in Russia itself – Orthodoxy. On January 23, 1918, Lenin issued a decree depriving the church of any right to own property, to teach religion in private or state schools, or to any group of minors. In a Soviet variant of Henry VIII's suppression of the English monasteries, Lenin proposed the confiscation of the wealth of churches and monasteries, and the execution of any who opposed it.

The Bolshevik Revolution of 1917 gave Lenin the opportunity to implement his political and religious objectives. When religious belief conspicuously and obstinately failed to disappear as a result of social and political change, he eventually put in place measures designed to eradicate it through the "protracted use of violence."

A key player in this atheist crusade was the League of Militant Atheists, a semi-official coalition of various political forces which operated within the Soviet Union from 1925 to 1947. With the slogan, "The Struggle against Religion is a Struggle for Socialism," the group set out to destroy the credibility of religion through social, cultural, and intellectual manipulation. Its carefully orchestrated campaigns involved using newspapers, journals, lectures, and films to persuade Soviet citizens that religious beliefs and practices were irrational and destructive. Good Soviet citizens, they declared, ought to embrace a scientific, atheistic worldview.

Churches were closed or destroyed, often by dynamiting; priests imprisoned, exiled, or executed. On the eve of the Second World War there were only 6376 clergy remaining in the Russian Orthodox church, compared with the prerevolutionary figure of 66 140. February 17, 1938, saw the execution of fifty-five priests. In 1917, there were 39 530 churches in Russia; by 1940, only 950 remained functional.

Stalin's suppression of religion, however, extended to other faiths, in line with his general ideological commitment to the forcible elimination of religion. Attacks on Jews were endemic throughout the period of the Soviet Union. Stalin was especially fearful of a secessionist Islamic movement gaining momentum in the southeastern republics of the Soviet Union, and forcibly suppressed Islam throughout the region.

The long-term impact of the Russian Revolution on the history of Christianity was considerable. Christianity was initially suppressed throughout the Russian Empire (now the Soviet Union). After Soviet military gains in the Second World War, eastern Europe came under its sphere of influence, leading to the imposition of often repressive measures against Christian churches and believers. We shall consider this development in a later section of this work (5.2.1).

5.1.3.   Post-War Disillusionment: The Theology of Crisis

The end of the Great War created considerable disillusionment. Had the vast cost of the war, both in terms of material and human lives, been worth it? The impact of the First World War upon European culture cannot be overstated. The years 1918–22 saw remarkable alterations in western European self-consciousness. Oswald Spengler's *Decline of the*

West (1918) spoke ominously of the death of western culture. Spengler argued that democracy is the form of government found in declining civilizations. What was needed, he argued, was strong leadership, if the west was to emerge from this dark and dangerous period. Such ideas also found support from the writings of J. B. Bury (1861–1927), who poured scorn upon the idea of continuous development of human culture, civilization, and ideas in his *Idea of Progress*, published in 1920.

The immediate post-war years were widely perceived as witnessing the final collapse of the cultural heritage of the nineteenth century, with shock-waves which were felt in every sphere of intellectual and creative activity. The Russian Revolution seemed to many to confirm the fragility of western culture, and raise questions about the future of democracies in Europe. In an unrelated development, much of western Europe suffered a flu pandemic, which was probably spread so rapidly on account of the Great War, with its mass movements of armies, especially aboard ships. It is also likely that widespread malnourishment made people weaker, and less able to recover. It is now thought that between fifty million and one hundred million people died from the pandemic worldwide.

It is very difficult to summarize the situation in which western Christianity found itself following the trauma of the Great War. Some believed that the situation before the war could be restored, leading to international Christian collaboration resuming. Others were more sanguine. It would take a long time to heal wounds and recover from the ruptured relationships caused by international conflict. Others believed that the conflict had exposed deep inadequacies in existing assumptions about the nature of the church and human nature, which would have to be addressed before progress could be made.

These questions were felt with particular force in Germany during the 1920s, as a defeated nation struggled to make sense of what had happened to it. The German churches and the theological establishment had backed Kaiser Wilhelm in his aggressive war policies. Adolf von Harnack and other leading German theologians had given their support publicly to the Kaiser in August 1914. After the war, German theology found itself with a burden of guilt concerning its earlier and somewhat uncritical advocacy of militarism.

One of the most important outcomes of this was the "theology of crisis," particularly associated with the Swiss Protestant theologian Karl Barth (1886–1968). Barth, who had studied theology in Germany, found himself disillusioned with the dominant approach to theology he found within Liberal Protestantism. This approach to theology – often dubbed "Culture-Protestantism" – took its leads from cultural trends. Barth saw the Great War as having destroyed the credibility of such an approach. How could a theology which was grounded in contemporary cultural norms ever presume to criticize such cultural norms?

Barth's approach to theology, which began to develop while he was the Reformed pastor in the Swiss village of Safenwil in the aftermath of the Great War, placed an emphasis upon God's discontinuity with culture. There was, he declared, a chasm – a "glacial crevasse" – between God and human culture, which could only be bridged from God's side. Human culture could never become the basis of an authentic knowledge of God.

Picking up on a phrase from the Danish philosopher Søren Kierkegaard (1813–55), Barth argued that there was an "infinite qualitative distinction" between God and human beings. Like an Old Testament prophet, Barth emphasized God's total holiness and remoteness from humanity in general, and from human culture in particular. God "stands over

Figure 5.3   Portrait of the theologian Karl Barth (1886–1968) in Basel. Photograph, 1956. Imagno/ Getty Images

and against humanity and everything human in an infinite qualitative distinction and is never, ever identical with anything which we name, experience, conceive or worship as God."

Barth adopted a strongly iconoclastic approach to theology, rejecting any attempt to anchor God in the natural world on the one hand, or human culture on the other. God is known only as God chooses to be known – in other words, in God's act of self-revelation in Jesus Christ. Others followed Barth in developing such an approach to theology, including the German Protestant theologian Friedrich Gogarten (1887–1967), who delivered a lecture on "the crisis of our culture" in 1920, emphasizing that the crisis of European civilization at that time was to be seen as an "annihilating and creative act of God," which made clear the absolute distinction between God and the world. Theology was poised between an age which had ended, and an unknown new age which had yet to arrive. It was like living in an "empty room."

The Swiss theologian Emil Brunner (1889–1966) was also a representative of this approach to theology. Unlike Barth and Gogarten, Brunner spoke English well, and traveled to the United States in the late 1920s. There, his message of a "theology of crisis" found a sympathetic audience. Few doubted that western theology was going through some kind of crisis. Indeed, American Christianity was facing a major dispute of its own, now known as the "fundamentalist controversy."

5.1.4.   America: The Fundamentalist Controversy

Fundamentalism arose as a religious reaction within American conservative Christianity to the development of a secular culture during the 1920s. The aftermath of the Great War in American culture was seen by many as marking a departure from America's traditional Christian (and especially Protestant) moorings. In part, this was a response to the greater mass production of consumer goods – especially autos – and a drive towards consumerism and a credit economy, which many regarded as encouraging materialism. Divorce rates soared. To many religious Americans, the nation seemed to have embraced new secular values, and moved away from older values of self-denial and the Protestant work ethic to a form of self-indulgence and materialism. The rise of fundamentalism is deeply rooted in these broader cultural developments.

Despite the wide use of the term to refer to religious movements within Islam and Judaism, the term originally and properly designates a movement within Protestant Christianity in the United States. By a series of historical accidents, the term "fundamentalist" derived its name from a series of twelve books which appeared from a small American publishing house in the 1910s. The series was unremarkably entitled *The Fundamentals*, and was intended to be an exploration of the "basics of faith" from a conservative Protestant perspective.

To begin with, the term "fundamentalism" did not have the overtones of obscurantism, anti-intellectualism, and political extremism that many now associate with it. It was seen as a movement on the fringes of American mainline Protestantism that believed that culture was moving in anti-Christian directions, and wanted to try and safeguard the Christian heritage. Fundamentalists initially saw themselves simply as returning to biblical orthodoxy. This point was recognized at the time by Kirsopp Lake (1872–1946), a leading British modernist writer who specialized in the field of New Testament and early Christian studies. In his *Religion of Yesterday and Tomorrow* (1926), which advocated a form of religion based on individual human perceptions and experience, rather than revelation, Lake described fundamentalism as "the partial and uneducated survival of a theology which was once universally held by all Christians."

Yet polemical associations were not slow to develop. The modernist context in which the fundamentalist movement came to birth had a significant influence in shaping the movement's response to the challenges facing it. Fundamentalism rapidly became a reactive movement, defined by what it opposed as much as what it affirmed. "Fundamentalism is orthodoxy in confrontation with modernity" (James Davison Hunter). A siege mentality became characteristic of the movement. Fundamentalist counter-communities saw themselves (to evoke the pioneer spirit) as circles of wagons, defending their distinctive beliefs against an unbelieving and increasingly secular culture.

Aspects of fundamentalist teachings may indeed be discerned in the writings of classic Reformed Orthodoxy, or in those of the Old Princeton School, such as Charles Hodge (1797–1878) and Benjamin B. Warfield (1851–1921). Yet the fundamental characteristic of fundamentalism came to be oppositionalism – that is to say, it was a movement that believed it was under threat from cultural developments, and reacted aggressively and defiantly to that perceived threat. It is the ferocity, as much as the substance, of fundamentalism that has shaped American perceptions of its identity and character.

The negative consequences of this polarization can be seen especially from the painful history of the Presbyterian church in the United States during the 1920s. In 1922, an ill-tempered controversy broke out over whether traditional doctrines should be modified in the light of modern scientific and cultural knowledge. The conservatives seemed to be winning ground. In response, Henry Emerson Fosdick (1878–1969) preached a polemical sermon in May 1922 entitled "Shall the Fundamentalists Win?" Fosdick rejected core beliefs of fundamentalism, arguing that belief in the virgin birth was unnecessary; that belief in the inerrancy of Scripture was untenable; and that the doctrine of the Second Coming was absurd. One hundred and thirty thousand copies of the sermon, rewritten by a skilled public relations expert and funded by the oil magnate John D. Rockefeller Jr. (1839–1937), were circulated. A vigorous riposte soon followed from the conservative side. Clarence Edward Macartney (1879–1957) entitled his reply "Shall Unbelief Win?"

The situation rapidly polarized. There seemed to be no middle ground, making toleration impossible. There could be no compromise or way out of the situation. Presbyterians were forced to decide whether they were, to use the categories of the protagonists, "unbelieving liberals" or "reactionary fundamentalists." The church was shattered. There were other options, and saner voices; yet the highly politicized climate of opinion made it impossible for them to gain a hearing. "Oppositionalism" led to the issue being perceived in highly simplistic terms within conservative Presbyterian circles: either an unbelieving culture would win, or victory would go to the gospel. There were no alternatives.

Conservatives soon discovered that there seemed to be little they could do to stop the influence of modernist thinkers such as Fosdick growing within their denominations. The slide into modernism seemed inexorable. The result was a growing demand within fundamentalist circles for separation from allegedly corrupt denominations. If it proved impossible to reform denominations from within, the only course open was to break away from the denomination, and form a new yet doctrinally pure church body. Such a separatist approach can be traced back to the dawn of American Protestantism. Roger Williams (c. 1604–84), founder of Rhode Island, was one of the leading proponents of a pure separatist church, arguing that Christian believers were under an obligation to separate from apostate churches and from a secular state.

The fundamentalist war against modernity led to a closed, cautious, and defensive attitude on the part of fundamentalists towards what they regarded as a secular culture and largely apostate churches. Separatism seemed the only way ahead. If culture and mainline denominations could not be converted or reformed, there was no option but to become a voice in the wilderness.

One of the main enemies identified by fundamentalism was Darwinism (4.2.4). Although several of the essays in *The Fundamentals* were supportive of evolution as a scientific theory, radical opposition to Darwin's theory of evolution became a litmus test of fundamentalist orthodoxy. Although some scholars suggest that this opposition arose primarily because Darwinism seemed to pose a threat to traditional methods of biblical interpretation, it is more helpful to see this as a reaction against what was seen as a defining characteristic of secular culture at this time.

This opposition to Darwin's theory of evolution led many fundamentalists to agitate for its exclusion from the curriculum of public schools. This led to the famous Scopes "monkey" trial of 1925. John T. Scopes (1900–70), a young high school science teacher, was prosecuted for disobeying a recently adopted statute which prohibited the teaching of evolution in Tennessee's public schools. The American Civil Liberties Union moved in to support

Scopes, while William Jennings Bryan (1860–1925) served as prosecution counsel on behalf of the World Christian Fundamentals Association. It proved to be a public relations disaster for fundamentalism.

Bryan, who had billed the trial as a "duel to the death" between Christianity and atheism, was totally wrong footed by the celebrated agnostic attorney Clarence Darrow, who called Bryan to the stand as a witness for the defense, and interrogated him concerning his views on evolution. Bryan was forced to admit that he had no knowledge of geology, comparative religions, or ancient civilizations. In the end, Bryan succeeded in winning the trial in the courtroom. Scopes was fined $100. The State Supreme Court reversed the verdict against Scopes on a technicality, allowing Scopes to walk free. Bryan died five days after the trial.

But a perhaps somewhat more important trial was taking place in the nation's news-papers, in which Bryan was declared to be unthinking, uneducated, and reactionary. Fundamentalism might make sense in a rural Tennessee backwater, but had no place in sophisticated urban America. In particular, the journalist and literary critic H. L. Mencken successfully portrayed fundamentalists as intolerant, backward, and ignorant, standing outside mainstream American culture.

From that moment onward, fundamentalism became as much a cultural stereotype as a religious movement. It could not hope to win support among the educated and cultural elites within mainline Protestantism. The damage inflicted would never be undone. It was only with the emergence of a new form of evangelicalism after the Second World War that momentum and credibility were regained (5.2.3).

5.1.5.   Mexico: The Cristero War

Mexico was a former Spanish colony which established its independence in the early nine-teenth century. However, a war with the United States lost it much territory in the 1850s (now mainly included in the states of California, New Mexico, and Texas). In 1857, a new constitution was established, acknowledging that Catholicism was the chief religion of the nation, but refusing to allow it any privileges. Growing anti-clericalism was reflected in a secular constitution, which stripped the church of much of its property, and limited its social role.

Following the long and despotic presidency of Portino Diaz (president from 1876 until 1911), a revolution established a new constitution in 1917. This secularist constitution imposed secular education on the schools, outlawed monastic orders, prohibited public worship outside church buildings, placed severe limits on the right of religious organiza-tions to hold property, and denied priests or nuns the right to wear clerical attire, to vote, to trial by jury, or to criticize government officials or comment on public affairs in religious periodicals. These anti-Catholic measures were not popular, and were initially only imple-mented to a limited extent.

In 1924, however, the atheist Plutarco Elías Calles (1877–1945) assumed the presidency. In June 1926 he signed the decree officially known as "The Law for Reforming the Penal Code." This strongly anti-Catholic decree provoked hostility in many parts of Mexico. It became illegal to wear religious items, or say "Adiós" in public. (The Spanish word "Adiós" literally means "to God," in much the same way as the French "Adieu.") After a series of attempts to defeat the measures by economic boycotts, the resistance movement – now known as Cristeros (from the Spanish watchword *Cristo Rey* – "Christ the King") – declared a revolt. On January 1, 1927, an armed insurrection against the government began.

Initially, the revolt failed to achieve much success. Its irregular forces had little training, and poor weaponry. They were no match against the regular Mexican army. By June 1928, the Cristeros had some 50 000 men under arms. Yet neither side managed to achieve a breakthrough, despite a revolt within the Mexican army early in 1929. The Mexican army might have been demoralized, but the Cristeros lacked effective leadership. They also lacked the support of most of the Mexican bishops, who disliked their fanatical Catholicism as much as they disliked Calles's fanatical atheism. One of Graham Greene's earliest novels – *The Power and the Glory* (1940) – is about a priest on the run during the Cristero War.

In the end, the conflict was resolved through the good offices of the American ambassador to Mexico, Dwight Whitney Morrow (1873–1931), a strongly pragmatic diplomat who established enough common ground between the government and church to allow a peace deal. On June 21, 1929, a set of "arrangements" were agreed, with the government making small concessions to the Catholic church. In practice, the main development was that the government would not insist on implementing its anti-Catholic measures, while leaving them on the statute book.

One significant outcome of the Cristero conflict was the mass emigration of Catholics from Mexico to the southern United States where they would be able to worship in total freedom. A surge of refugees seeking religious asylum in California and Texas significantly changed the religious demography of these regions.

In Mexico itself, the church was faced with the problem of reconstructing its human resources base. There had been a radical depletion of priests during the period of conflict. Priests had been imprisoned, exiled, executed, or assassinated. In 1926, Mexico had 4500 Catholic priests. A decade later, it had fewer than four hundred. Calles's influence lingered until the early 1930s, and can be seen in the intensification of the anti-religious education provision in the Constitution of 1934. Calles's fanatical anti-Catholicism was not continued by later governments after the Second World War, which successively distanced themselves from his excesses.

5.1.6.   The Psychological Critique of Religion: Sigmund Freud

In an earlier section, we noted the importance of Karl Marx and Charles Darwin for religious belief in general, and Christianity in particular. Marx offered a reductionist account of religion (4.2.3); Darwin was seen to challenge some of its fundamental themes (4.2.4). Although Sigmund Freud (1856–1939) had developed his psychological theories of the origin of religion before the Great War, their impact was felt mainly in the post-war period, especially in North America.

Freud first introduced psychoanalysis into the United States during his visit to Clark University, Worcester, Massachusetts, in 1909, and was pleasantly surprised by the enthusiastic American reaction to his ideas. His seeds had fallen into fertile soil. In 1910, the Psychopathological Association was established in Washington, DC. It was soon followed by the New York Psychoanalytic Society in 1911 and the American Psychoanalytic Associa-

Figure 5.4   Sigmund Freud, neurologist and founder of psychoanalysis (1856–1939), at his desk in London, c. 1938/9. Photo: akg-images

tion in Baltimore in 1914. In 1917, the Johns Hopkins Medical School began offering courses in psychoanalysis.

Freud's critique of religion achieved considerable cultural traction during the period between the two world wars, making consideration of its basic themes important for this work. Freud argued that religion could be accounted for psychoanalytically. Religion is a human creation, the result of an obsession with ritual and veneration of a father figure. Freud's strongly reductionist account of the "psychogenesis of religion" is now criticized for lacking rigorous empirical evidential foundations. Yet at the time, it was taken with great seriousness. *Totem and Taboo* (1913) considered how religion has its origins in society in general; *The Future of an Illusion* (1927) dealt with the psychological origins (Freud often uses the term "psychogenesis" here) of religion in the individual. For Freud, religious ideas are "illusions, fulfillments of the oldest, strongest and most urgent wishes of mankind." Similar ideas were developed in a later work, *Moses and Monotheism* (1939), published at the end of his life.

To understand Freud at this point, we need to examine his theory of repression. These views were first set out in *The Interpretation of Dreams* (1900), a book which was generally ignored by the critics and the general reading public. Freud's thesis here is that dreams are wish-fulfillments – disguised expressions of wishes that are repressed by the consciousness (the ego), and are thus displaced into the unconsciousness. In *The Psychopathology of Everyday Life* (1904), Freud argued that these repressed wishes intrude into everyday life at a number of points. Certain neurotic symptoms, dreams, or even small slips of the tongue or pen – so-called "Freudian slips" – reveal unconscious processes.

The task of the psychotherapist is to expose these repressions which have such a negative effect on life. Psychoanalysis (a term coined by Freud) aims to lay bare the unconscious and untreated traumatic experiences, by assisting the patient to raise them up into consciousness. Through persistent questioning, the analyst can identify repressed traumas which are having so negative an effect upon the patient, and enable the patient to deal with them by bringing them into the open.

As we noted earlier, Freud's views on the origin of religion need to be considered in two stages: first, its origins in the development of human history in general, and second, its origins in the case of the individual person. We may begin by dealing with his account of the psychogenesis of religion in the human species in general, as it is presented in *Totem and Taboo*.

Developing his earlier observation that religious rites are similar to the obsessive actions of his neurotic patients, Freud declared that religion was basically a distorted form of an obsessional neurosis. His studies of obsessional patients (such as the "Wolf Man") led him to argue that such disorders were the consequence of unresolved developmental issues, such as the association of "guilt" and "being unclean" which he associated with the "anal" phase in childhood development. He suggested that aspects of religious behavior (such as the ritual cleansing ceremonies of Judaism) could arise through similar obsessions.

Freud argued that the key elements in all religions included the veneration of a father figure and a concern for proper rituals. Freud traces the origins of religion to the Oedipal complex. At some point in the history of the human race, Freud argues (without substantiation), the father figure had exclusive sexual rights over females in his tribe. The sons, unhappy at this state of affairs, overthrew the father figure, and killed him. Thereafter, they are haunted by the secret of parricide, and its associated sense of guilt. Religion, according to Freud, has its origins in this prehistorical parricidal event, and for this reason has guilt as a major motivating factor. This guilt requires purging or expiation, for which various rituals were devised.

The emphasis within Christianity upon the death of Christ and the veneration of the risen Christ seemed to Freud to be a superb illustration of this general principle. "Christianity, having arisen out of a father-religion, became a son-religion. It has not escaped the fate of having to get rid of the father." The "totem meal," Freud argued, had its direct counterpart in the Christian celebration of communion.

Freud's account of the social origins of religion is not taken with great seriousness, and is often seen as representative of the highly optimistic and somewhat simplistic theories which emerged in the aftermath of the general acceptance of the Darwinian theory of evolution (4.2.4). His more significant account of the psychological origins of religion in the individual once more appeals to the idea of veneration of a "father figure." Freud suggests that the origins of this veneration lie in childhood. When going through its Oedipal phase, Freud argues, the child has to deal with anxiety over the possibility of being punished by the father. The child's response to this threat is to venerate the father, identify with him, and to project what it knows of the father's will in the form of the superego.

Freud explored the origins of this projection of an ideal father figure in *The Future of an Illusion*. Religion represents the perpetuation of a piece of infantile behavior in adult life. Religion is simply an immature response to the awareness of helplessness, by going back to one's childhood experiences of paternal care: "my father will protect me; he is in control." Belief in a personal God is thus little more than an infantile delusion, the projection of an idealized father figure. For Freud, humanity now had the knowledge and insight to move beyond this primitive superstition, and develop more rational and scientific understandings of the world, and of the place of humanity within that world.

Although Freud's critique of religion received much attention in America during the period between the world wars, it is arguable that one of his more significant achievements was creating a culture in which psychotherapy became socially acceptable. Counseling became part of a therapeutic culture, perhaps encouraging the notion that one of the chief functions of religion itself was making believers feel better about themselves. Although such approaches to religion (such as Mary Baker Eddy's "Christian Science") were already widespread within American Protestantism, Freud's approach was seen by many as superior, on account of its apparent scientific basis.

Freud's optimistic approach offered hope to unhappy Americans in a way that the medical and clerical professions could not. His approach proposed that psychological contentment could be achieved by the individual, without any need to change society as a whole. In many ways, Freud's approach led to the counselor displacing the priest as the mediator of salvation. The continuing importance of counseling in the pastoral programs of many American churches today is an indirect witness to the importance of Freud in shaping at least some aspects of religious expectations within the nation, and goes some way towards exploring the continuing American Christian fascination with the relation of faith and psychology.

5.1.7. The German Church Crisis of the 1930s

Germany was economically weakened and nationally humiliated by its defeat in the Great War. Where the economies of other nations gradually began to recover in the 1920s, Germany remained locked into political and economic stagnation. Things were made worse by the reparations Germany was required to pay her former enemies, and the emergence of rampant inflation within the German economy. In the immediate post-war period, revolutionary socialism – inspired to some extent by the Russian Revolution – became influential, both as a critic of capitalism and religion. The militant secularist Adolph Hoffmann (1858–1930), appointed Prussian Minister for Education and Public Worship in November 1918, unsuccessfully attempted to ban prayer and religious instruction from state schools, confiscate church property, and abolish theology from the academic curriculum of universities.

Although parliamentary democracy had been established in Germany following the ending of the monarchy, the Weimar Republic failed to live up to public expectations and hopes. In March 1920, the first attempt by right-wing nationalists to overthrow the government took place, setting a pattern of instability that would continue into the 1930s. An attempt to seize power by Adolf Hitler and the National Socialists in November 1923 – the famous "Beer Hall Putsch" – failed ignominiously.

Things went seriously wrong in 1929. The German economy was already slowing down early that year. The Wall Street Crash of October 1929 marked the beginning of a worldwide slump of unprecedented severity, which proved fatal for the political stability of the Weimar Republic. A chain of events was unleashed which led to the political triumph of Hitler's

National Socialist German Workers' Party, widely known as the "Nazis." Adolf Hitler was installed as the German Chancellor in 1933.

Under Hitler, the German churches would face considerable challenges. National Socialism was not in any sense a Christian philosophy. Its origins are still poorly understood; however, it is clear that it reflects long-standing nationalist beliefs concerning Germanic culture, especially the role of a pan-Germanic alliance in dominating central Europe. Hitler's program demanded control over most aspects of German life, including the German churches. Unlike Stalin, however, Hitler believed that it might be possible to secure the compliance of the churches without the use of force and oppressive measures.

His success in doing so probably surprised him. Fear of the radical socialist agenda of the elimination of religion from society led many German Christians to respond positively to Hitler's Nazi program, which was relatively easily presented in terms of the renewal of German culture. This had particular resonance with the movement within German Protestantism often referred to as "Culture Protestantism," which proposed a close link between religion and culture (5.1.3).

Nazi rule was at first welcomed by many German churchmen, partly because it offered a bulwark against the ominous state atheism sponsored within the Soviet Union, and partly because it seemed to offer a new cultural role for religion. The "German Christian" movement developed, adopting a positive response to Hitler's program for national reconstruction and unity.

Yet the unity of the German Christians did not last long. Division arose from September 1933, partly over the so-called "Aryan clause" that demanded that no Jew should hold office in the church. The strongly anti-Jewish rhetoric of the Nazi Party divided those who saw supporting Hitler as a temporary and pragmatic accommodation to German political realities, and those who wanted to reconstruct Christianity totally.

The crisis point came at a rally in the Sports Palace in Berlin on November 13, 1933. Reinhold Krause (1893–1980), a schoolteacher who had risen to prominence within Nazi circles in Berlin, demanded a radical Nazification of Christianity, including the rejection of the Old Testament as a Jewish book, and the adoption of a more "heroic" interpretation of Jesus as someone who protested against the corruptions of Judaism. It was a turning point. German Christians were now fragmented and divided, unable to agree among themselves about how to respond to the shifting political situation.

The general failure of the German churches to make a significant impact on Hitler's rise to power, and his gradual move towards reaffirmation of German imperial claims, raised serious questions concerning the moral credentials of Christianity, which troubled thoughtful Christians. One of Nazism's more thoughtful critics was the Catholic philosopher and theologian Dietrich von Hildebrand (1889–1977), who argued that the Nazis gained credibility through the relativism of the German culture of the period. The only way to resist the movement was through a vigorous reassertion of objective moral values, such as those of Christianity. A form of Christianity which failed to resist cultural trends, or which lent them active support, would thus be powerless to resist Nazism – or similar movements in the future.

One issue of major continuing concern is the way in which mainline churches and their theologians showed an uncomfortable tendency to accept, endorse, and incorporate the latest cultural trends, without subjecting them to penetrating examination. German academic culture was, however, receptive towards Hitler's ideas. The noted philosopher Martin Heidegger (1889–1976) gave Hitler enthusiastic support in his rectoral address at the University of Heidelberg in May 1933. A number of prominent Christian theologians – including Paul Althaus (1888–1966), Emanuel Hirsch (1888–1972), and Gerhard Kittel (1888–1948) – gave explicit support to National Socialism, particularly in its earlier period.

Some scholars have argued that Martin Luther's "doctrine of the two kingdoms" (3.3.2) was implicated in the rise of Nazism. This doctrine proposes a radical separation between church and state, while nevertheless allowing the state an influence in the life of the church. While there is probably some truth in this, its importance is perhaps too easily overstated. One of the major concerns for many Christians in Germany in the 1930s was the fear of a socialist revolution, which was widely expected to enforce atheism as its public philosophy, as it had in the Soviet Union.

The real problem was that Christians in Germany had a long tradition of being law-abiding, regarding this as their Christian obligation. When the Nazis seized power in 1933, they set in place a legal framework to impose totalitarian rule. Laws established for an essentially democratic purpose were subverted to other ends. The traditional Protestant notion that law was somehow grounded in objective realities of the world or in social consensus proved incapable of responding to the arbitrary enforcement of power by the Third Reich.

One response was to propose a return to natural law, insisting that there was a higher authority than human legislative assemblies. In 1936, Heinrich Rommen (1897–1967) published a short work entitled "The Eternal Return of Natural Law." Rommen, a professional lawyer who had been imprisoned briefly by the Nazis for his work with a Roman Catholic social action group, pointed out that Germany's modern dictators were "masters of legality," able to use the legal and judicial systems to pursue their own political agendas. Germany's legal professionals, he argued, were so used to thinking about law in purely positivist terms that they were left intellectually defenseless in the face of the National Socialist threat. In this dire situation, one needed to appeal to a higher authority than the state – that is, God. Natural law offered precisely the intellectual lifeline that was so badly needed.

Karl Barth (5.1.3) and Dietrich Bonhoeffer developed another approach – a radical theological critique of any political system which placed anything other than God at the center of an individual or nation's life. Leaders of the "Confessing Church" – a movement within the German Protestant churches which rejected any compromises with Nazism – met at Barmen in late May 1934, and issued the document often known as the "Barmen Declaration." This declared that the church could not adjust its ideas in the light of "prevailing ideological and political convictions." It had to remain faithful to its Christian roots, as witnessed in the person of Jesus Christ, and the text of the Bible.

Yet such protests proved ineffective against the rhetorical and political power of a totalitarian state. Where Otto von Bismarck relied on authoritarian approaches in his failed attempt to suppress Catholicism in Germany in the nineteenth century (4.2.8), Hitler relied on totalitarian approaches – above all, the naked used of power and force – in his somewhat more successful suppression of Christianity.

The anti-Jewish attitudes and policies of Adolf Hitler were ultimately expressed in the Holocaust, a program of extermination which played a major role in shaping relations between Christianity and Judaism in the period after the Second World War. Although others judged to be enemies of the state by the Nazis were sent to the gas chambers in the Second World War, by far the greatest number were Jews, who had fallen foul of the institutionalized anti-Semitism of the Third Reich. Hitler had learned from the Armenian Genocide that actions committed in a situation of total war did not attract international attention, and appears to have assumed that his own program of genocide would not attract international condemnation.

The Holocaust had a strong impact on Jewish–Christian relations after the Second World War, raising difficult questions about Christian complicity in Hitler's wartime policies and projects. It was also an important factor leading to the creation of the state of Israel in May 1948.

5.1.8.   The Spanish Civil War (1936–9)

Throughout the early modern period, Spain had remained a Catholic nation. Although the Peninsular War led to social and political instability throughout the Iberian Peninsula, Spain emerged from the conflict relatively intact. Yet the instability experienced by many European nations during the nineteenth century affected Spain. Following the forced abdication of the Spanish monarch in 1873, a republic was declared. This was not long-lived, and the monarchy was restored shortly afterwards. It was, however, not popular, and republicanism emerged as an important political movement after the First World War. Although Spain had not been involved in this war, its impact on the Spanish economy was significant.

Post-war Spain remained unstable. A military coup in 1923 toppled a civilian government. Following the end of the coup and the abdication of the king, elections in June 1931 led to a republican government, dominated by socialists and radicals. Anticlerical measures were included in the constitution drawn up by the Second Spanish Republic, including the partial disestablishment of the Catholic church, and the prohibition of members of religious orders from teaching in schools. Tensions developed with monarchists, leading to violence in the streets of many Spanish cities. The Falangists – a political group similar in some ways to Italian fascists – were formed in 1933, and became increasingly active politically.

In January 1936, a "Popular Front" of republicans, secularists, and communists won a sizeable majority in national elections. Rumors began to emerge of a further possible military coup, to be led by General Francisco Franco (1892–1975), who had already been involved in the suppression of a local revolution in the Asturias. The military coup was launched from Spanish Morocco in July 1936, and quickly established control over the southern and western regions of Spain.

The Civil War quickly became an international affair, with Germany and the Soviet Union seeing this as a "proxy war" in which military technology and tactics could be tried. The most notorious incident of this kind was the bombing of the Basque village of Guernica in April 1937, depicted in a famous painting by Pablo Picasso, which resulted from the German air force's Condor Legion developing new bombing techniques. The Republicans were supported by the Soviet Union, the "International Brigades" of left-wing volunteers, and Mexico; the Nationalists were supported by Germany, Italy, and neighboring Portugal.

Although religious issues were not seen by many as being of primary importance, the Republicans were strongly opposed to religion in general, particularly Catholicism, playing any role in national life. While both sides were guilty of atrocities, recent historians have concluded that the events leading up to the Civil War and the war itself represented the most extensive and violent persecution of Catholicism in western history, in some ways being even more intense than that of the French Revolution.

During the 1934 uprising in the Asturias, churches and other religious buildings were burned, and Catholic clergy and laity murdered. The Nationalists now found it easy to represent themselves as defenders of "Christian civilization" against communism and anarchy. Virtually all the Nationalist groups had strong Catholic connections and convictions. The victory of the Nationalists in the Civil War in 1939 brought an end to state hostility towards Catholicism, while setting the scene for future developments.

Yet perhaps it is more important to notice how attitudes towards Christianity during the Spanish Civil War fitted into a larger pattern. Partly in response to the success of the Russian Revolution of 1917, many European radicals of the immediate post-war era sought to advance revolutionary agendas throughout Europe, with limited success. Such revolutionary movements tended to regard established churches as their enemy, and develop programs designed to limit their influence and reduce their visibility in public life. Characteristically, such programs involved the secularization of education, the withdrawal of state funding from church institutions and programs, the removal of religious symbols from the public arena, and discriminatory measures against priests and members of religious orders.

Yet the Spanish Civil War is important to historians partly on account of its role as a training ground for the German army and air force. Strategies and innovations were developed that would be put to use in the opening phase of the Second World War. Although the impact of the Second World War was not as shocking as that of the First World War, it remained one of the most destructive and devastating conflicts of modern times, and created a post-war Europe that was increasingly hostile to Christianity, especially in its eastern regions.

5.2.   Shifts in Western Christianity since the Second World War

The Second World War began on September 1, 1939, with the German invasion of Poland, leading to declarations of war on Germany by France and Great Britain, both of whom had agreed to protect Polish neutrality. This new global conflict would have a profound effect on the world's economy and political order, leading directly to the slow break-up of the British Empire, and the rise of the United States and the Soviet Union as global superpowers.

The lingering impact of the Second World War would have a major impact on Christianity, in and beyond the west. As a full understanding of the atrocities committed against Jews and others in the Nazi extermination camps became public knowledge,

Jewish–Christian relations deteriorated significantly. Many Jews believed that Christians were complicit in the Holocaust, having failed to act to prevent it.

In this section, we shall consider how Christianity fared in the new world order which resulted in the aftermath of this sustained period of global warfare.

5.2.1. The New World Order: Christianity and the Cold War

On August 23, 1939, Nazi Germany and the Soviet Union signed a non-aggression pact, which included secret protocols dividing Romania, Poland, Lithuania, Latvia, Estonia, and Finland into German and Soviet spheres of influence. Germany was able to invade Poland without fear of Soviet intervention, in the knowledge that the Soviet Union would appropriate the eastern region of Poland in subsequent weeks. Yet as German victories mounted, Hitler began to plan for the invasion of the Soviet Union. The invasion began on June 22, 1941, under the codename "Operation Barbarossa." The Soviet Union now entered the war on the Allied side.

Slowly, the war shifted in the Allies' direction. A bridgehead was established in Normandy in June 1944, leading to a war on two fronts against Germany. Rapid industrialization in the 1930s allowed the Soviet Union to replenish its forces from factories safe beyond the Ural Mountains. By the spring of 1945, the Red Army was advancing westwards, sweeping resistance aside as it headed for Berlin. Soviet forces occupied much of eastern Europe. And it soon became clear that they had no intention of withdrawing. Political opposition to communist rule was neutralized by the formation of anti-fascist political fronts, in which communists were initially able to secure dominance, and subsequently establish communist states. Albania, Bulgaria, Czechoslovakia, Hungary, Romania, and Yugoslavia all became part of the Soviet sphere of influence, along with the eastern part of Germany.

The immediate impact of these developments for Christianity was predominantly negative. The state ideologies of the eastern bloc were atheistic and materialist (5.1.2), with the churches being seen as the antiquated remnants of an old world order that had no place in the future. Initially, relatively little attention was paid to the churches, as the state authorities were more concerned with eliminating armed insurrection and neutralizing political opposition to the new social order.

By 1947, however, anti-religious measures were enforced throughout the Soviet bloc. In Poland, Catholic social and charitable organizations were made illegal, Catholic schools were closed, and crosses were removed from classrooms and hospitals. Such measures were directed against religion in general, rather than Christianity in particular. In Bulgaria, for example, repressive measures were taken against both Orthodoxy and Islam.

The hostility of the Soviet Union and its satellite states to religion is evident throughout the decades immediately following the Second World War. Despite Josef Stalin's attempts to eliminate it, belief in God was still widespread in the Soviet Union when Stalin died in 1953, forcing the Communist Party to begin an aggressive program of indoctrination the following year, decreeing that "the teaching of school subjects (history, literature, natural sciences, physics, chemistry, etc.) should be saturated with atheism." Soviet school textbooks repeatedly asserted the malevolence of religion through slogans such as "Religion is a fanatic and perverse reflection of the world," or "Religion has become the medium for the spiritual enslavement of the masses."

From 1925 onwards, the League of Militant Atheists had urged the burning and dynamiting of huge numbers of Soviet churches, including some of great cultural importance. All were doomed to be swept out of the way as reminders of an earlier age of faith. This destruction of religious buildings and symbols continued after the war in the Soviet bloc. For example, the University Church of St. Paul in Leipzig, an architectural masterpiece completed in 1240, was blown up in May 1968 to avoid the awkwardness of having to tolerate symbols of the divine in the new "Karl Marx Platz" of this leading city of the German Democratic Republic.

Churches in the west were unable to have any significant influence on the repressive measures being taken against Christianity within the Soviet bloc. Many believed that it was only a matter of time before the "Cold War" erupted into open warfare, with the real possibility of the use of nuclear weapons. The most significant crisis points after the Second World War were the Berlin Blockade (1948–9), the Korean War (1950–3), the Hungarian Uprising (1956), and the Cuban Missile Crisis (1962). While no global conflict ever ensued, with or without nuclear weapons, the two decades after the end of the war were charged with anxiety and uncertainty.

Soviet geopolitical influence spread further in the late 1940s. The Chinese Communist Party was founded in Shanghai in 1921. From 1931 to 1934, the revolutionary leader Mao Zedong (1893–1976) led a revolution which established the Soviet Republic of China in the mountainous areas of Jiangxi. After a long revolutionary struggle, led primarily by Mao Zedong, the Chinese Communist Party assumed full control of mainland China by 1949, forcing its opponents to retreat to the offshore island of Taiwan.

The Soviet Union backed Mao Zedong, and exercised significant influence in securing his victory, and subsequently using Chinese military power as the basis for further expansion in southeastern Asia – initially in Korea, and subsequently in Vietnam. The Chinese repression of Tibetan Buddhism – a natural extension of the anti-religious views of the Chinese Communist Party – was widely condemned internationally.

Perhaps the most important religious development under Mao Zedong was the "Cultural Revolution." This oppressive period is generally regarded as beginning on May 16, 1966, with a directive issued by the Central Committee of the Communist Party of China, and ending with the arrest of Jian Qing and other members of the "Gang of Four" after Mao Zedong's death in 1976. Its repressive measures were designed to eliminate western influences and any lingering remnants of religious belief. Christianity thus found itself under a double burden, in that it was a religion which was considered to be western in origin. Its future seemed increasingly uncertain. Since it was virtually impossible to obtain reliable information from within China, many western observers believed that Christianity had been eliminated from the region. But as we shall see, it had not (5.4.3).

5.2.2.   The World Council of Churches: The New Ecumenism

As will be clear from the analysis presented in this book, Christianity has its fair share of internal divisions. The separation of the Latin-speaking west from the Greek-speaking east had been under way for some time before the "Great Schism" of 1054 made it official. The sixteenth-century Reformation led to the establishment of a group of Protestant churches – Anabaptist, Anglican, Lutheran, and Reformed – which disagreed with Rome and (perhaps more importantly) with each other. Protestantism turned out to be a movement with an inherent tendency to fragment. Today, it is estimated that there are at least 20 000 Protestant denominations in the world.

So could these differences be set aside, allowing the churches to reunite? Or at least achieve better working relationships? These aims underlie the ecumenical movement, which began to develop momentum after the Second World War. The term "ecumenical" comes from the Greek word *oikumenē*, meaning "the known inhabited world." Although informal efforts to achieve better relationship between the churches had been under way for some time, the events of the twentieth century gave a new impetus for ecumenism. In the aftermath of the Armenian Genocide (5.1.1), a synod of the Orthodox church issued an encyclical in 1920, calling for a "fellowship of churches" similar to the League of Nations.

Following the end of the Second World War, there were massive attempts to reconcile the warring parties in order to reconstruct Europe, and ensure it had a viable future. A parallel movement developed within the churches. Was not this a God-given moment in which Christian unity might be pursued and achieved? It was against this background that the World Council of Churches was created in the aftermath of the Second World War. The decision to headquarter the council in Geneva was based partly on the fact that this Swiss city was host to the pre-war League of Nations, and the post-war international organizations.

The first assembly of the World Council of Churches, held in August 1948 in Amsterdam, was seen as a beacon of hope for post-war Europe. Although the plans to inaugurate this organization went back to 1936, the Second World War both delayed this event, and highlighted its potential importance. The main Protestant churches in the west agreed to work together, and to keep working together. Although there were obvious tensions between liberal and progressive Christians and their more conservative counterparts, this potential difficulty was defused by some skilful footwork on the part of the conference organizers.

So what is the World Council of Churches? From the outset, it was clear that this was a Protestant body. Catholic and Orthodox churches might send observers; initially, however, full membership was limited to Protestant churches. Although the new body initially described itself as "a fellowship of churches which accept our Lord as God and Saviour," it became clear that clarification was needed. How did this body relate to others – such as denominational leadership structures? These questions were engaged at the second meeting of the World Council of Churches, held in Toronto in 1950, and further developed at later meetings.

According to its Toronto declaration, the purpose of the World Council of Churches is "to bring the churches into contact with one another and to promote discussion of questions of Church unity." Its initial intention was to transform the prevailing indifference to the need for ecumenical fellowship and unity, through theological dialogue and spiritual fellowship, into a deep and conscious conviction of the need for Christian unity.

The World Council of Churches has always made it clear that it is not some type of "megachurch," which exists over and above its constituent churches. The constitution of the body excludes any role which takes away authority from member churches. "The World Council shall not legislate for the churches." Neither the Assembly nor the Central Committee of the World Council of Churches were to possess any "constitutional authority whatever over its constituent churches." Ecclesiological pluralism was thus built into the structures and thinking of the World Council of Churches from its inception. This was "a fellowship of churches" which sought to encourage its member churches to work towards the goal of their visible unity. But there was no agenda to impose such a union on its members.

There was no doubt that this was seen as a welcome and necessary move, not least as the situation of the churches began to change in the west. In the 1970s and 1980s, a growing sense that western culture was becoming increasing secular and hostile to Christian faith led to many Christians wondering if they ought to suspend hostilities between Christian groupings, and concentrate upon the issue of survival. Furthermore, the expansion of Christianity into traditionally Islamic areas of the world, together with the growth of significant Islamic groups in the west through immigration, has led many Christians to predict that this will be the next major area of confrontation. Should not Christians unite in the face of such a possible threat? Might future survival depend on unity? As Benjamin Franklin famously quipped at the signing of the Declaration of Independence (July 4, 1776), "We must indeed all hang together, or, most assuredly, we shall all hang separately."

Yet the history of the World Council of Churches has not been entirely happy, and persuaded many that it had failed to live up to the high expectations of the new body in the immediate post-war period. The council found itself experiencing difficulty in holding its members together. The organization increasingly drifted towards a more liberal theological stance during the 1960s and 1970s, and alienated many of its natural conservative constituency. Its token demonstrations of support for armed liberation movements in Africa alarmed those who saw Christianity as espousing non-violent resistance to oppression, and looked to Martin Luther King (1929–68) as an example.

By about 1990, it became clear that there was diminishing enthusiasm within the mainstream churches for the form of "visible unity" that had become the hallmark of the thinking and policies of the World Council of Churches. With the passing of time, it became increasingly clear that this vision was somewhat unrealistic, and failed to take seriously the realities of church life. What most grass-roots Christians wanted was better working relationships with their fellow Christians of other denominations. They did not want their denomination to be swallowed up by someone else, or to take anyone else over. They wanted better relationships with other Christians at both the individual and institutional level. The rise of "bottom-up" grass-roots ecumenism has significantly reduced the role of "top-down" ecumenical efforts in the twenty-first century.

The World Council of Churches now plays a token and somewhat peripheral role in global Christianity. Yet the ecumenical vision which inspired it has not faded; it has simply changed direction, with the initiative shifting to individuals and voluntary organizations. By the end of the twentieth century, "bottom-up" ecumenism had come to play a more significant role in the life of the Christian churches than the official "top-down" approach of ecumenical institutions.

5.2.3.   Billy Graham and the "New Evangelicalism"

Earlier, we noted the importance of the fundamentalist controversies of the early twentieth century in the United States. A perception that American culture was becoming increasingly secularized and hostile towards faith led conservative American Protestants to disengage from mainstream culture, and form counter-cultural communities. The Puritan writer Roger Williams's 1644 reference to a "wall of separation between the garden of the church and the wilderness of the world" (4.3.1) was taken up by many in the 1930s, who saw their churches as outposts of theological orthodoxy, separated from the secular world by rigid criteria of membership (5.1.4).

As the Second World War came to an end, it became clear to some conservative Protestant observers that this strategy had been counterproductive. Two conservative Protestants spearheaded a new approach. William Franklin Graham Jr. (born 1918), better known as "Billy Graham," and Carl F. H. Henry (1913–2003) pioneered a sea-change in conservative attitudes within North America. Initially referred to as "neo-Evangelicalism," this movement quickly became mainstream, and came to be known simply as "evangelicalism."

The intellectual moorings of the movement were laid out by Henry in his *Uneasy Conscience of Modern Fundamentalism* (1947). Henry argued that fundamentalism was too other-worldly and anti-intellectual to gain a hearing among the educated public, and unwilling to concern itself with exploring how Christianity related to culture and social life in general. He proposed a reconnection with mainstream American culture. Within a decade, the movement had a new seminary and journal to advocate its aims. Fuller Theological Seminary was founded in Pasadena, California, in 1947 by radio evangelist Charles E. Fuller (1887–1968), broadcaster of the "Old Fashioned Revival Hour," in partnership with Harold John Ockenga (1905–85), pastor of Park Street Church in Boston, Massachusetts. It quickly became associated with the new vision of evangelicalism, and weathered controversy over its alignment with the movement.

Henry's early career as a journalist led to him being invited by Graham and L. Nelson Bell (1894–1973) to give editorial leadership to a new journal then being launched. As editor-in-chief of *Christianity Today* from 1956 until 1968, Henry established the profile, shared concerns, and credibility of evangelicalism, leading to such major global ventures as the 1966 World Conference on Evangelism, as well as a series of publications dedicated to the consolidation of the evangelical renaissance then emerging within North America and beyond.

Yet the figurehead of the new movement was the evangelist Billy Graham. By the early 1940s, Graham had established a growing reputation as an evangelist, and was being seen as the successor to Billy Sunday (1862–1935) – a former baseball player who had developed a nationwide evangelistic ministry in the earlier decades of the twentieth century.

Although Graham was initially associated with the fundamentalist wing of American Protestantism, he gradually became alienated by its rigidity. Graham found that the nega-

Figure 5.5   American evangelist Dr. Billy Graham addressing the congregation at Earl's Court, London, at the beginning of his thirty-two-day Greater London Crusade, June 1966. Fox Photos/ Getty Images

tive cultural attitudes of fundamentalism increasingly got in the way of his evangelistic ministry. In 1956, the popular fundamentalist magazine *Christian Life* published an article entitled "Is Evangelical Theology Changing?" It argued that the old guard based itself on the biblical verse "ye should earnestly contend for the faith" (Jude 3), whereas the new generation preferred to base itself on "ye must be born again" (John 3:7). A heated controversy resulted. Three months later, the same journal published an interview with Graham, in which he declared that he was "sick and fed up" with such controversies. For Graham, the ill-judged strategy of "oppositionalism" had become a barrier to the preaching of the gospel.

The growing alienation of Graham from fundamentalism became clear when he accepted an invitation in 1955 to hold a crusade in New York City. The invitation came from a coalition of Christian churches, many of which were not fundamentalist. By the time the crusade opened to massive publicity in the spring of 1957, fundamentalism seemed to be something of the past. *Christianity Today* and the Graham crusades became the icons of the new vision for evangelicalism, which displaced the old.

In North America, evangelicalism is to be understood as a post-fundamentalist phenomenon. This contrasts with the European scene, where evangelicalism generally arose as a movement within mainline Protestant churches. In America, the movement arose in reaction to the perceived deficiencies of fundamentalism. While it is unquestionably true that evangelicalism picked up and developed many insights deriving directly from other movements – above all, the Reformation, Puritanism, and Wesleyanism – the fact remains that the impetus to retrieve these great evangelical traditions came from a conviction that fundamentalism had failed at the cultural, scholarly, and spiritual levels.

As a result of such developments, evangelicalism began to emerge as a movement of major public importance in the United States in the 1950s. The full public recognition in America of the new importance and public visibility of evangelicalism is generally thought to date from the early 1970s. The crisis of confidence within American liberal Christianity in the 1960s was widely interpreted to signal the need for the emergence of a new and more publicly credible form of Christian belief. In 1976, the influential *Newsweek* magazine declared that the United States of America was living in the "Year of the Evangelical," with a born-again Christian (Jimmy Carter) as its president.

These developments had their parallels outside the United States. In England, the Anglican evangelical John Stott (1921–2011) developed a ministry which reflected many of the themes of American evangelicalism from his London base church at All Souls, Langham Place. Stott championed the idea of evangelical reconnection with the mainline of the Church of England at a conference at Keele in 1967, which is widely regarded as marking the end of evangelical isolationism within England's established church.

This new willingness on the part of evangelicalism to engage with social, cultural, and political issues proved to be of major significance to American political life in the 1980s and beyond. Evangelicals began to become actively involved in political campaigning and advocation, generally for the Republican Party. Although the origins of the "Religious Right" are complex, one significant factor was the transformation of evangelical attitudes towards politics in the 1960s.

Yet as American religious involvement in cultural issues began to increase in the post-war period, a quite different pattern began to emerge in western Europe. For many historians, the 1960s saw trends developed that led to the emergence of a post-Christian Europe.

5.2.4.   The 1960s: The Origins of a Post-Christian Europe

In 1900, five of the world's ten most populous Christian countries were in western Europe: Britain, Germany, France, Spain, and Italy. Three others – Russia, Poland, and Ukraine – lay in eastern Europe. Europe was the heartland and focus of the Christian faith, rivaled only by North America. Today, the situation has changed radically. In 2005, only one western European nation remained on the list of most populous Christian countries.

Every western European nation has become secularized, as indicated by four key indicators.

1. Church attendance has fallen radically. Church attendance is, in most cases, under 10 percent of the population in western Europe.
2. National and religional policy-making does not regularly make reference to the church.
3. Schools, hospitals, and social welfare are largely in the hands of the state, and are not controlled by the churches.
4. The cultural knowledge of the basic themes of the Christian faith has become more tenuous, especially among young people.

Western Europe is now the most secular region in the world. So how did this happen? How did a region of the world which was instrumental in missionary work throughout much of the world from about 1600 to 1900 become a post-Christian society? This question is often framed in the light of religious renewal and revival in most parts of the world. Why is western Europe the exception?

This question is important. Many sociologists of the 1960s argued that de-Christianization was an inevitable consequence of modernity, and regarded the European fortunes of religion as normative. Other situations, such as that found in the United States, showing quite different patterns of religious commitments, were treated as deviations from this norm, reflecting exceptional circumstances.

It is significant that many of the advocates of the "secularization thesis" of the 1960s were western European sociologists, who regarded the developments they then observed in their own region as having global significance. European secularism was a sign of the future, a trailblazer which led where other cultures would follow. Two European sociologists made particularly significant contributions underlying the "secularization" thesis earlier in the twentieth century. Max Weber (1864–1920) argued that what he termed "rationalization" – the increasing cultural dominance of a scientific mindset – could only destroy the "magical garden" of pre-modern worldviews, such as religion. Weber had misgivings about this development, arguing that it trapped people within an "iron cage" of rationality. Emile Durkheim (1858–1917) argued that religion was fundamentally a metaphor of social order, which would be articulated and safeguarded by other, more rational, means.

Yet the passing of time has suggested that Europe is the conspicuous exception to a persistently religious world, rather than the harbinger of a new secular world order. Europe now tends to be treated as the exception, in that the global trend is towards a sustained or increased religiosity, especially in public life. The American sociologist Peter Berger, who actively championed the secularization thesis in the 1960s, has now abandoned it, regarding the thesis as inconsistent with cultural developments in recent decades.

Some scholars locate the origins of secularization in the advent of modernity. On this approach, the onset of the process generally referred to as "modernization" fundamentally altered the place and nature of religious beliefs, practices, and organizations in such a way that their relevance to the lives of nation-states, social groups, and individuals was significantly reduced. Urbanization and industrialization are often cited as social trends that reinforce this tendency towards secularist outlooks. As industrialization, urbanization, and rationalization increase, it is argued, religiosity must correspondingly decrease. It was during the 1960s, it is often argued, that these trends began to make themselves felt.

The 1960s marked a period of transition, in which the settled assumptions of the western past were called into question with unprecedented vigor. An impatience with the ways and ideas of the past were linked with the belief that a new beginning lay just around the corner. Everything was to be swept aside, so that a total reconstruction could take place. Europe witnessed a surge in interest in Marxism in the early 1960s. The student riots in Paris of May 1968 were hailed as the harbinger of a shake-up at least as great as that which had swept away an earlier *ancien régime* in 1789. "The existing moral order was the enemy," commented the editor of *Libération*, the left-leaning newspaper. Similar student protests at Columbia University in New York, together with widespread discontent with the Vietnam War, hinted at a global shift in values.

It was at this time that the "Death of God" movement soared to prominence in the United States, suggesting to some that American culture was entering a period of secularization, like its European counterpart. Books such as Paul van Buren's *Secular Meaning of the Gospel* (1963) and Thomas J. J. Altizer's *Gospel of Christian Atheism* (1966) generated headlines in the secular press. God was announced to be dead, and that was the end of the matter. Society was entering a new phase. In the event, such prophecies of the death of God in American culture proved premature. Yet in Europe, the process of secularization was much more deeply embedded in culture.

So why did this development take place in western Europe? No satisfactory answers have yet been given. Some sociologists have argued that Protestantism's distinctive "desacralization" or "disenchantment" of nature and society encouraged the emergence of the natural sciences, secularism, and atheism. Peter Berger suggested that Protestantism caused "an immense shrinkage in the scope of the sacred in reality." Protestants, he argued, did not see themselves as living in a world that was "ongoingly penetrated by sacred beings and forces." Instead, they understood that world to be "polarized between a radically transcendent divinity and a radically 'fallen' humanity" that was devoid of any sacred qualities or connections.

In contrast, Berger argued, Catholicism had contained secularizing forces through its deeply symbolic understanding of the natural world, and humanity's place within it. Without realizing what it was doing, Protestantism, for Berger, opened the floodgates of the forces that would shape modernity, and ultimately cause Protestantism such grief in its European heartlands.

Although the "secularization" thesis is now regarded with suspicion, it was widely held during the 1960s. This led many churches to ask deep questions about their future in what they believed would be an increasingly secular world. The most significant attempt to engage this question was the Second Vatican Council, in which Catholicism sought to confront such cultural trends, and forge robust and realistic strategies to meet them. We shall consider this landmark council in what follows.

5.2.5. The Second Vatican Council: Reform and Revitalization

The Catholic church was well aware of the radical social and cultural changes that seemed to be sweeping through western culture in the post-war period, especially in western Europe. There was a clear need for theological reconstruction and reformulation, in order to be able to translate the Catholic faith into terms that connected with the new cultural situation. Yet Pius XII, who was pope from 1939 until his death in 1959, did not believe that there was any pressing need to engage these issues. There was no mood for reform within the papal establishment.

The death of Pius XII led to the election of a new pope, John XXIII, in October 1958. Elected at age seventy-eight, John XXIII was expected to be an "interim pope." It was to be a transitional papacy, without any suggestion of major changes. Less than three months later, John XXIII took the church's establishment by surprise, when he announced he would

Figure 5.6   A session of the Second Vatican Council at St. Peter's Basilica, Rome. David Lees/Time Life Pictures/Getty Images

be convening an ecumenical council to formulate the church's responses to the realities of the post-war world. The general mood within the church was that there was a need for a few "house-keeping measures" within the church. The announcement of a reforming council was unexpected. The Italian word used to refer to this process of reform and renewal was *aggiornamento* – "a bringing up to date." In many ways, this would be the watchword of the council. John XXIII spoke frequently of the need to "open the windows of the Church to let in some fresh air." He expressed the hope that it would be the beginning of a new Pentecost for the church.

The council began its deliberations within the Vatican under John XXIII on October 11, 1962, and closed under Paul VI on December 8, 1965. More than 2000 bishops and other senior Catholic figures attended, representing the substantial geographical expansion of Catholicism since the previous council, which met briefly in Rome from 1869–70 (4.2.7). The death of John XXIII on June 3, 1963, did not derail the council; his successor, Paul VI, immediately declared his intention to continue his predecessor's project.

What were the achievements of the council? In what way did the idea of *aggiornamento* work out in practice? The council took place against a backdrop of resurgence of confidence within Catholicism in response to developments such as the election of a Catholic – John F. Kennedy – as president of the United States. Perhaps this sense of confidence contributed to the council's bold declarations about the role of the church in the world, urging all Catholics to dialog with developments in the world around them. Catholicism would not be like American fundamentalism in the 1920s and 1930s. It would not retreat into a ghetto, but would engage with the world. In many ways, this spirit of positive, constructive, and confident engagement with the world remains one of the most striking characteristics of the council.

Its decisions, however, must also be given due weight. The council reaffirmed the collegiality of bishops, without calling into question the authority or status of the pope, emphasizing their important role in governing and guiding the church. A new emphasis was placed on the role of the laity, encouraging them to become engaged with their social and political context. The Catholic church's attitude to other churches became more relaxed and positive, acknowledging that they were indeed Christian bodies, while noting that they were separated from the Catholic church.

This new generosity towards other Christians was matched by a commitment to positive and respectful engagement with other faith traditions. Of particular importance was the council's recognition that the Catholic church had been complicit in creating prejudicial attitudes towards Jews, particularly in suggesting that they had been responsible for the death of Christ. This was an important gesture of conciliation towards the world's Jews, especially in the aftermath of the Holocaust.

The council also engaged one of the leading points of contention between Protestantism and Catholicism – the status of the Bible. Protestants were suspicious of the Catholic emphasis on tradition, so clearly stated at the Council of Trent (3.4.5). Trent seemed to suggest that the Bible and unwritten tradition were two equally significant sources of revelation. Protestants were unable to accept that tradition was an independent source of revelation. Yet just as importantly, Protestants regarded the reading of the Bible by both clergy and laity as an integral part of the Christian life, and found it difficult to understand why the Bible seemed to be given such a low profile in Catholic preaching and devotion.

The council changed such perceptions through its declaration *Dei Verbum* (Latin: "The Word of God"), which made clear the importance of biblical scholarship for the life of the church. Both the church and individual Christian believers needed to be guided and nourished by reading the Bible in the light of biblical scholarship. The council called upon those "officially engaged in the ministry of the Word" to "immerse themselves in the Scriptures by constant sacred reading and diligent study."

Yet some would say that the council's most important decision was its first. The decree *Sacrosanctum Concilium* (Latin: "this most holy Council") was approved on December 4, 1963, by a landslide majority. The vote was 2147 in favor, and four against. This reforming decree laid the foundations of liturgical renewal. One of its most important decisions was laying the foundations for the liturgy being translated into the vernacular. This significant development was linked with a growing willingness to authorize vernacular translations of the Bible.

The Second Vatican Council's limited approval for the use of the vernacular in the liturgy was reflected in growing Catholic interest in vernacular biblical translations. The most important of these was the Jerusalem Bible, which grew out of the work initiated by the *École Biblique* (French: "Biblical School") in Jerusalem. A group of scholars had been working on this project since 1946, aiming to produce a new annotated French translation of the Bible, which would be more sensitive to the nuances of the text than previous Catholic translations. The Jerusalem Bible was published in French in 1956 and subsequently appeared in English in 1966. One of its most distinguished advisers for the English edition was J. R. R. Tolkien, who contributed particularly to the translation of the book of Jonah.

The Jerusalem Bible's translation caused some concern to many Catholics, in that it seemed to erode the biblical foundations for some traditional beliefs and practices. For example, consider the words of the angel Gabriel to Mary, as recorded in Luke 1:28. The Catholic Douay-Rheims translation of the Bible, which dates from the late sixteenth century, renders these words as follows: "Hail, full of grace, the Lord is with thee: blessed art thou among women." The translation provided by the Jerusalem Bible is very different: "Rejoice, so highly favored! The Lord is with you." This omits the traditional rendering, "full of grace," and the final phrase "blessed art thou among women," which were both familiar to Catholics through recitation of the *Hail Mary*.

The radical decisions taken by the council were met with suspicion in many more conservative parts of the Catholic world, such as Ireland. Observing this resistance, many concluded that the "spirit of the council" could not be implemented until an older generation of bishops that was fixed in its ways and locked into older habits of thought and action had given way to a new generation. Yet there was little doubt that the Second Vatican Council represented a landmark in Catholic life and thought, signaling a new way of engaging the world.

5.2.6.   Reconnecting with Culture: The Rise of Apologetics

Many western Christians during the twentieth century regarded their faith as being increasingly called into question by developments within their cultures. The height of the social impact of the Christian churches in western Europe is generally thought to have been reached just before the First World War. After that, they began to lose something of that influence, through an extended period of erosion. Yet the challenges that were emerging to Christianity in the west did not simply concern its social role and status. Increasingly difficult questions were being raised about its intellectual credentials. Was belief in God intellectually meaningful in the modern world?

These intellectual challenges to faith came from a number of directions. The forms of biblical criticism that had emerged in the nineteenth century seemed to call into question the historical reliability of the New Testament. Darwin's theory of evolution called into question some traditional Christian narratives of creation, raising doubts about the status of humanity within the natural domain (4.2.4). The "critiques of religion" developed by Ludwig Feuerbach, Karl Marx, and Sigmund Freud raised questions about the social and psychological origins of the idea of God (4.2.3; 5.1.6). And finally, modern science seemed to eliminate the conceptual space once occupied by God.

So how was Christianity to respond to these concerns? The twentieth century saw a new injection of intellectual energy into the discipline of apologetics – the engagement of contemporary cultural concerns about the rationality and morality of Christian belief. The discipline has a long history, tending to emerge as significant when Christianity encountered intellectual hostility. For example, Justin Martyr, one of the early church's most important apologists, wrote in the context of intense antagonism and suspicion towards Christianity in second-century Rome.

To illustrate the new importance of apologetics in western Christianity at this time, we shall focus on the situation in England, and consider three of its leading apologists of the twentieth century. All were lay Christians, outside the leadership structures of the Christian churches.

G. K. Chesterton (1874–1936) was a journalist and novelist, who countered the skepticism of the Edwardian age (1901–10) with a well-framed and well-phrased restatement of the fundamentals of the Christian faith. His early works – such as *Heretics* (1905) and *Orthodoxy* (1908) – set out both to challenge some of the settled intellectual assumptions of his day, such as those of the playwright George Bernard Shaw, and reassert the reasonableness of their Christian alternatives. His *Everlasting Man* (1925) is widely regarded as being one of his best apologetic works, and achieved considerable influence.

Dorothy L. Sayers (1893–1957) rose to fame during the 1920s as a novelist, noted chiefly for her murder mysteries involving Lord Peter Wimsey. Yet she became a vigorous defender of Christian doctrine, both against those within the Christian churches who regarded it as obsolete, and those outside the churches who considered it unintelligible. Agreeing with both groups that morality was of compelling importance, Sayers argued that morals ultimately rested on a set of beliefs, which had to be formulated in the form of doctrines.

Although initially an atheist, C. S. Lewis (1898–1963) converted to Christianity at some point around 1931–2. Lewis was a Fellow of Magdalen College, Oxford, whose primary teaching responsibility lay in the field of English literature. Yet Lewis gradually developed a secondary role – that of a Christian apologist, capable of explaining the basic ideas of the Christian faith in an engaging and stimulating way to a lay audience. His first work to adopt this approach was *The Problem of Pain* (1941), which offered a way of looking at pain and suffering that Lewis believed minimized the difficulties they posed for faith.

As a result of the success of this work, Lewis was invited to speak on the British Broadcasting Corporation's Home Service. Britain was then in the depths of the Second World War, and the BBC had hopes that Lewis would provide encouragement to the nation. Lewis developed these talks into the book *Mere Christianity* (1952), which is often identified in popular surveys as the most influential religious book of the twentieth century. Why? Lewis's Oxford colleague Austin Farrer argued that his remarkable influence lay in the fact that he affirmed both the rational integrity and imaginative appeal of faith. "We think we

Figure 5.7 The British literary scholar, novelist, and Christian apologist C. S. Lewis (1898–1963). Private Collection/The Bridgeman Art Library

are listening to an argument; in fact, we are presented with a vision, and it is the vision that carries conviction."

While offering a defense of the reasonableness of faith, Lewis emphasized the ability of faith to connect with the deepest human intuitions about life, and captivate the human imagination. It is an important point, which British churches need to take to heart as they reflect on how best to reconnect the Christian faith with their wider culture.

Yet all three of these apologists have one important shared insight – that one of the best ways of commending Christian faith was through works of fiction or drama. Chesterton's "Father Brown" series, Sayers's radio plays such as "The Man Born to Be King," and Lewis's "Chronicles of Narnia" all adopted an approach to apologetics that engaged the imagination, not just the mind. In a skeptical age, they realized, it was not enough simply to show that Christianity made sense; it had to be shown to be imaginatively compelling.

Yet many believed that these approaches were rendered irrelevant by the massive cultural shifts of the 1960s, when a new wave of restlessness swept through western culture. The sales of Lewis's works declined following his death in 1963, reflecting a general perception that his approach to Christianity belonged to the past. We shall consider these radical developments of the 1960s in what follows.

5.3.   The Sixties and Beyond: Western Christianity in an Age of Transition

The 1960s saw radical changes in social attitudes throughout the western world. For some, this led to the questioning of Christianity's ideas; for others, to its social role; for some, to both. It was clearly an age in which Christianity would undergo change and development. Yet it was far from clear what forms these would take. The theories of secularization dominant in the 1960s suggested that increasingly industrialized societies – such as the United States – would undergo some form of secularization. Yet the situation turned out to be somewhat more complex, as the prominent role of the churches in the civil rights movement and the emergence of the American "religious right" make clear.

5.3.1.   Christianity and the American Civil Rights Movement

The American Civil War (4.3.5) led to a number of tensions within the Union, in which the former southern "slave" states developed state and local laws which allowed them to maintain racial segregation along antebellum lines. The so-called "Jim Crow laws," enacted between 1876 and 1965, mandated policies of racial segregation similar to those in force in South Africa in the 1950s and 1960s, under the name of *apartheid* ("separateness"). These laws laid the foundation for racial segregation in all public facilities in the southern states of the former Confederacy.

It is widely agreed that, despite the importance of individual activists and campaigners, the key to the success of the civil rights movement was the black churches of the southern states. These represented the most significant social and political force to emerge from the former slave communities. Although these were socially marginalized in the southern states during the period between the two world wars, these churches were the only institutions with the finances, structure, and mass membership needed to bring about a mass mobilization of African-Americans with the power to change society.

The strongly religious tone of the rhetoric of the civil rights movement partly reflects the failure of American Liberalism to achieve any success in civil rights legislation and policy at the height of its power during the 1930s. In the end, the ideology of political liberalism became subordinated to the religious vision and worldview which characterized many of the grass-roots within the movement. The struggle for civil rights was widely understood to be a religious struggle, echoing the great themes of the Old Testament narratives of the liberation of Israel from its bondage in Egypt. For this reason, mass political meetings of the civil rights campaign often mimicked the structure and tone of church services, partly because they were seen as a natural extension of the religious and social visions, deeply rooted in the history of the black South.

The event which triggered the civil rights movement was the Montgomery Bus Boycott of 1955. In December 1955, a black woman – Rosa Parks (1913–2005) – was arrested under the Jim Crows laws for refusing to give up her seat on a public bus in the city of Montgomery in the state of Alabama to a white man. Opposition to this arrest, and the discriminatory attitudes towards black people which lay behind it, was led by the black Baptist pastor Martin Luther King (1929–68). The resulting Montgomery Bus Boycott lasted for more than a year, and generated national publicity. A United States District Court ruling in 1956 finally ended racial segregation on all Montgomery public buses.

Encouraged by this development, King sought to mobilize opinion to end segregation on buses throughout the South. After a series of meetings early in 1957, King launched the Southern Christian Leadership Conference, specifically with the aim of harnessing the social capital of black churches to challenge existing laws on segregation. It was a controversial move, as many pastors and church leaders – both black and white – believed that the churches should concentrate their attention on the spiritual and pastoral needs of their congregations, rather than become engaged in political action.

Yet despite this tendency to political quietism, the churches became increasingly involved in non-violent protests. A successful campaign in Birmingham, Alabama, was followed by a massive march on Washington in August 1963. The Kennedy administration, spurred to activity largely by the media coverage of police over-reaction against demonstrators in Birmingham, began to roll back southern legislation, ending much – though not all – of the racial discrimination in the South.

The civil rights movement is notable for bringing about two developments, which marked the re-entry of the churches into the political process in the United States. First, King's program of social action was clearly seen to be based on a theological vision of transformation and renewal, rather than the agenda of a specific political party. King chose to align himself with neither Republican nor Democrat, but operated outside the political establishment.

His speech "I have a Dream" (August 28, 1963), which is widely hailed as a rhetorical masterpiece, is deeply rooted in the Old Testament vision of justice and freedom, providing a theological defense for acting for change. Prophetic themes from Isaiah 40 are woven into the fabric of the speech, articulating both hope and vision.

Second, King's success made it clear that churches could become involved in political debates and direct action without compromising their principles. The civil rights campaign made it religiously acceptable for churches and individual Christian leaders to become politically engaged.

This second lesson was developed further by a very different Christian political group – the "Religious Right."

5.3.2.   The Rise of the American "Religious Right"

Conservative Protestants in the United States in the early 1960s generally tended to be politically disinterested and inactive. Politics was seen as something that was best left to politicians. Jerry Falwell (1933–2007), a conservative Southern Baptist pastor, was critical of more liberal Baptists for becoming involved in the civil rights conflict of the 1960s. Like most American conservative religious leaders of that age, he saw his role as limited to ministering to the spiritual and pastoral needs of his people. This can be interpreted as a lingering after-effect of the fundamentalism of the 1920s, which encouraged believers to disengage from the world around them (5.1.4).

Falwell's change of heart illustrates well the sea-change that swept through conservative American Protestant churches, in response to developments of the age. Three pivotal court decisions were handed down in 1962–3. *Engel v. Vitale*, 1962, ruled that a prayer used in the New York school system was unconstitutional. The text of the prayer was: "Almighty God, we acknowledge our dependence upon thee, and we beg Thy blessings upon us, our parents, our teachers and our Country." In *Murray v. Curlett* (1963) and *Abington Township School District v. Schempp* (1963), the Supreme Court ruled that school prayers and Bible readings constituted violations of the Establishment Clause of the First Amendment. These were followed by other decisions which alarmed conservatives, including the legalization of first trimester abortion (*Roe v. Wade*, 1973), and the sanctioning of government involvement in private Christian academies (*Lemon v. Kurtzman*, 1971).

Murray v. Curlett (1963) was of iconic significance, in that the case was brought by Madalyn Murray O'Hair (1919–95), known for her communist and atheist sympathies. O'Hair was founder of the organization American Atheists, and served as its president from 1963 to 1986. At this time, American suspicion of communism was at its height, partly due to the Cuban Missile Crisis, which some feared might lead to nuclear war. O'Hair had earlier attempted to defect to the Soviet Union, but had been refused entry by the Soviet Embassy in Paris. She returned to the United States, and in 1960 brought an action against the Baltimore school district when her son was required to participate in Bible reading at school. By the time the case reached the Supreme Court, O'Hair's strident anti-religious views had persuaded many alarmed religious conservatives that this was the first phase of an attempt by atheists to eliminate religion from public life.

These decisions were thus widely regarded by religious conservatives as an attempt to secularize the United States, using the constitutional separation of church and state as a means of eliminating religion from the public school system, and possibly from public life in general. Falwell and others saw these developments as a wake-up call, and began to organize opposition. Activists such as Falwell himself, pastor Pat Robertson (born 1930), and constitutional lawyer Phyllis McAlpin Stewart Schlafly (born 1924), set out to defend traditional Christian values in all areas of life, often reinforcing these values with an appeal to a simpler small-town America of the past, whose values they suggested were being eroded by secularists with anti-American agendas.

There are clear convergences with Protestant fundamentalism in the 1920s (5.1.4), in that both fundamentalism and the Religious Right felt under threat from rapid cultural change that was moving America in a secular direction. Yet there was a fundamental difference between the two movements. Fundamentalism chose to withdraw from mainstream culture, and snipe from the sidelines. The Religious Right chose to engage mainstream culture, and change it from within. By the late 1970s, it was clear that this strategy was having considerable success. Evangelicalism had become a significant political force.

Although the "Religious Right" drew support primarily from evangelical Christians (5.2.3), who became increasingly active and articulate, the movement attracted politically conservative Catholics, Jews, Mormons, and occasionally even secularists. Yet the movement divided evangelicals. Many retained the older evangelical distrust of politics, and believed that the political activism encouraged by Falwell and Robertson would ultimately damage spiritual values and the reputation of the churches. Though sympathetic to the aims of the movement, some argued that it was more important to concentrate on pastoral and spiritual matters than to win elections.

The election of Jimmy Carter (born 1924) as president in 1976 brought home the rising political power of evangelicalism. Although Carter, a Democrat, had little sympathy for the values of the Religious Right, his religious values appealed to conservative Christians. Yet it was clear that the Religious Right's preference would be for a Republican president, who took religion seriously.

The 1980 presidential campaign of Ronald Reagan (1911–2004) is widely seen as marking a public realization that religion was no longer a matter of private conviction, but about a battle for public values. Although Reagan was not a religious person (the contrast with Carter is significant), he realized the importance of religion as a political issue. At a National Affairs Briefing organized by the Religious Roundtable during the presidential campaign in 1980, Reagan made a quip to the gathering of conservative Christian leaders that became a game-changer: "I know you can't endorse me, but I endorse you."

One of the issues that remains central to the campaign of the Religious Right against secular tendencies in American politics concerns the interpretation of the First Amendment to the Constitution (4.3.1). Secularists argued that this provided a "wall of separation" between church and state, and between religion and public life. Any state endorsement or support of religious activity or belief is thus to be deemed unconstitutional. The Religious Right argue that the First Amendment was intended only to prevent any specific religious group from achieving establishment status – such as that of the Church of England in some of the colonial states – and was never intended to exclude religion from public life.

5.3.3. The Erosion of Denominationalism in the United States

The religious landscape of the United States has been substantially shaped by the structures and habits of thought of its European origins. The Protestant denomination is essentially a European phenomenon, reflecting the shifting patterns of church life and controversy in western Europe from the sixteenth to the eighteenth century. Patterns of religious affiliation and belonging reflecting the general situation of western Europe, and often the very specific conditions of religious life in England, were exported to Africa, America, Asia, and Australia by both settlers and missionaries. As a result, the emerging church life of four great continents has been shaped, to a greater or lesser extent, by the historical contingencies of western Europe.

The Protestant denomination initially seemed to thrive in the United States, possibly reflecting ecclesial loyalties on the part of immigrants arising from their European roots. In his *Social Sources of Denominationalism* (1929), the prominent American theologian H. Richard Niebuhr (1894–1962) argued that denominations were a distinguishing mark of American religious life. They were rooted in historical differences of social class, wealth, national origin, and race – and hence were integral to the complex tapestry of American cultural identity.

The next decades seemed to confirm Niebuhr's view. Throughout the 1950s, the growth of the traditional Protestant denomination surged in the United States. Congregationalists, Episcopalians, Methodists, and Presbyterians reported net annual membership gains. Each denomination vigorously defended its sovereignty and vested interests. In 1956, a survey showed that 80 percent of Episcopalians believed that it was wrong to hold worship service with other Christian groups. A year earlier, a Gallup poll shows that 96 percent of the adult population of the United States belonged to the same denomination as their parents. Their churchgoing habits had not changed over a generation.

Yet by 1990, many of these denominations were in decline. By this time, the mainline denominations had lost between one fifth and one third of their 1965 memberships, at a time when the population growth of the United States had surged. A real numerical decline thus converted into a significant reduction in the proportion of America's population associating with these denominations.

Christian denominations in America are one of the very few institutional expressions of early modern European culture still in existence. But why, many Americans are increasingly asking, should modern America's religious life be made dependent upon a European model – especially when that model was now seen as having failed back in its homelands? Both individual churches and Christians in America are showing an increasing reluctance to define themselves denominationally. Many churches have named themselves after their localities, skillfully dropping any reference to their denomination. The same issues can be seen in the titles of seminaries. The institution now known as "Denver Seminary" was formerly "Denver Conservative Baptist Seminary"; "Virginia Theological Seminary" was formerly "the Protestant Episcopal Theological Seminary in Virginia." These changes suggest that the inclusion of denominational identities is no longer viewed as a positive in marketing terms.

Niebuhr's argument reflected his perception that Protestant denominations reflected historical memories of a European origin, perceptions of social location within a stratified society, and issues of personal identity. Yet in the 1990s, some strongly entrepreneurial Protestants found themselves more and more frustrated by the institutional inertia of traditional denominational structures. They regarded these as unresponsive bureaucracies, uninterested in local initiatives or innovations.

Frustration with denominational structures is not, of course, anything particularly new. The great New York preacher Harry Emerson Fosdick (1878–1969), who played such an important role in the great fundamentalist controversies of the 1920s (5.1.4), once made the astonishing revelation that he had once considered leaving "the historic Christian organizations" in order to start his own "independent movement." Fosdick was dismissive of those who demanded ecclesiastical loyalty, holding that his only loyalty was to Christ. Yet despite his frustrations, he never set up his own church, even though his personal reputation was such that its future would have been secure.

Yet since the 1990s, American Protestantism has been increasingly characterized by the growth of market-shaped or market-driven congregations, led by strongly entrepreneurial individuals. Their sense of theological vision, coupled with a "can do" mentality that was nourished and inspired by the Protestant work ethic, eventually drove them to achieve their goals outside the structures of traditional denominations, especially in the aftermath of the theological and cultural turmoil of the 1960s. Like Martin Luther, they did not particularly want to work outside their mother churches – but the needs and realities of the new cultural situation seemed to provide them with no alternatives. The outcome was a surge of new initiatives, meeting needs which were held to be largely ignored by mainline denominations, and setting new patterns for how churches work, develop, and organize themselves.

The theological basis for this development was laid during the opening decades of the history of Protestantism. In his *Institutes of the Christian Religion* (1559), John Calvin had argued that a true Christian church was not defined by its institutional history or connections, but by the proper exercise of preaching and sacramental administration. In the late twentieth-century American context, this was interpreted to mean that new churches and denominations could be founded, provided they were based on good preaching and the proper administration of the sacraments. Enterprising individuals, often fired up by a vision for a specific form of ministry, could start their own congregations, or even their own denominations.

The outcome of this was inevitable – the emergence of a consumerist mentality, through which Protestants felt able to pick and choose the local church that suited their needs, beliefs, or aspirations. And if they didn't find one that was just right, they would establish their own. Catholic critics of Protestantism often point to its innate fissiparous tendencies, which they suggests indicates a lack of concern for the fundamental unity of the church.

While this congregational inflationism is unquestionably problematic, it has two fundamental strengths, both of which are of decisive importance for the shaping of Protestantism in the United States and beyond.

1. It allowed Protestantism to deal with rapid social and cultural change, which often leads to churches being locked into the realities of a bygone age. Entrepreneurial pastors and preachers can easily recast a vision of the gospel, adapted to the new situation – in much the same way as older visions were adapted to their situations – and thus prevent Protestantism being trapped in a time warp. It enables Protestants to respond to perceived needs for specialist ministries to specific groups through the formation of voluntary societies, which often come to exercise a para-church role.

2. It enabled Protestant churches to deal with situations in which the denominational leadership is seen to be radically out of touch with its membership – typically, by pursuing theological agendas or cultural trends which are not accepted by the majority of their congregations. It does not matter whether these agendas are right-wing or left-wing, conservative or liberal. Protestantism empowers the congregation, firstly to protest against their leaders; secondly, to remove them; and thirdly, to form their own congregation elsewhere, *while still remaining a Christian church*. While some Protestant denominations attempt to shield themselves against such accountability to their membership, these fundamental rights remain, in principle, as part of the movement's core identity. A Protestant believer can leave one denomination and join another – while still remaining a Protestant.

A further point of importance here concerns the impact of C. S. Lewis's notion of "Mere Christianity." This way of thinking, set out by Lewis in his widely read book *Mere Christianity* (1952), undermines the importance of denominational identity by arguing that the various Christian churches are simply different implementations of an underlying consensual core Christianity. Lewis's *Mere Christianity* was, and remains, a manifesto for a form of Christianity that exults in essentials, regarding other matters as of secondary importance. Yet Lewis's notion of "Mere Christianity" was more than a rejection of denominational supremacy. It was also a subtle critique of the abuses of power and privilege that so easily arise in more institutionalized forms of Christianity. Lewis is generally critical of the clergy in his writings. As a lay Christian, he came to see himself as representing a form of Christianity that recognized the crucial role of the laity, allowing neither clergy nor ecclesiastical institutions any special privileges.

It is not unfair to suggest that the Protestant vision of the church unleashes a Darwinian process of competition and survival, gradually eliminating maladapted churches, and ensuring that what survives is well suited to the needs and opportunities of the day. We shall consider some of these developments later in this chapter.

Our attention now turns to developments in Europe, where the long papacy of John Paul II witnessed dramatic changes, and the forging of a new international role for the Catholic church.

5.3.4.   Faith Renewed: John Paul II and the Collapse of the Soviet Union

The situation in Europe after the Second World War was complex, and posed particular challenges for the Catholic church. The establishment of the "Soviet bloc" meant that many Catholic parts of eastern Europe unexpectedly found themselves under communist control (5.2.1), with severe restrictions being placed on the activities of churches and religious believers. In the west, the radical questioning of traditional structures of authority and beliefs in the 1960s created a cultural context that challenged many Catholic ideas.

The Second Vatican Council began to address some of the issues raised for Catholicism in the west, although its implementation led to some impatience developing, particularly in relation to the question of artificial contraception. Yet the influence of the Soviet Union and its eastern European satellite states arguably caused a much greater problem. There seemed little that the papacy could do to engage the situation. Influence was seen as resting on pragmatic factors – such as military force. On being criticized by Pope Pius XII, the Soviet leader Josef Stalin dismissed this intervention as inconsequential. "How many battalions has the Pope?"

Pope Paul VI died in August 1978. Like his predecessor, John XXIII, Paul VI was an Italian pope, who had worked hard to improve relations with other Christian churches, and to open the windows of the church to the world. It was unclear who his successor would be. Some favored Cardinal Giuseppe Siri (1906–89), the conservative archbishop of Genoa, whose criticisms of the Second Vatican Council suggested he would lead the church in a more conservative direction. In the event, the papal conclave elected the Italian Albino Luciani (1912–78), who took the name "John Paul I." It soon became clear that he would be a reforming pope, concerned to implement the decisions of the Second Vatican Council.

John Paul I died suddenly on the thirty-third day of his reign – September 29, 1978. His unexpected death prompted speculation that he had been assassinated, although this is not regarded as persuasive by historians. A papal conclave was convened once more. The car-

Figure 5.8 Pope John Paul II among a crowd of people, Vatican City, Rome, June 1, 1979.
© Vittoriano Rastelli/Corbis

dinals appear to have initially divided along traditionalist and reformist lines, with the former favoring Giuseppe Siri and the latter the archbishop of Florence, Giovanni Benelli (1921–82). Although Benelli came close to being elected, it was clear that neither of the leading contenders commanded sufficient support to be elected. A compromise candidate was therefore sought.

To the surprise of the outside world, the conclave elected Karol Józef Wojtyła (1920–2005), the Polish archbishop of Kraków. Wojtyła announced that he would be known as "John Paul II," which was interpreted both as a tribute to his predecessor and an indication that he would continue his reforming trajectory. John Paul II was only fifty-eight at the time of his election, making him one of the youngest popes in recent history.

Although the appointment created huge interest throughout the world, its impact was greatest in Wojtyła's native land. Poland lay within the Soviet bloc at the time of his election, and was one of the most devoutly Catholic countries in Europe. The communist authorities had proved unable to suppress Catholicism, and had instead concentrated their efforts on limiting its influence. The election of a Polish pope – the first non-Italian pope for nearly five hundred years – caused a surge of national pride, and gave a new significance to the nation's Catholic identity.

During a pastoral visit to Poland in June 1979 – the first of nine such visits to his homeland – John Paul II was overwhelmed by enthusiastic crowds. As the national mood changed, partly in response to Catholic resurgence, resistance against the communist authorities grew. In a landmark development, the trade union "Solidarity" was established in August 1980 at the Lenin Shipyard at Gdańsk under the leadership of Lech Wałęsa (born 1943). The imposition of martial law in December 1981 failed to repress the movement, even though its regional leaders were imprisoned.

The events in Poland served as triggers to comparable developments throughout the Soviet bloc. Central control began to weaken, especially during the period when Mikhail Sergeyevich Gorbachev (born 1931) served as General Secretary of the Communist Party of the Soviet Union. On being elected as general secretary in 1985, Gorbachev enacted his policies of *perestroika* (Russian: "restructuring") and *glasnost* (Russian: "openness"). Though intended to liberate the economy of the Soviet Union from an excessive bureaucracy, they ended up by significantly weakening the grip of the Communist Party over both the Soviet Union and its allies.

It became increasingly clear that religion was no longer being repressed. For example, in February 1988 a Red Army choir performed "Ave Maria" before John Paul II at the Vatican. In the same year, Mikhail Gorbachev both permitted and promoted the celebration of a millennium of the Christian faith in Russia and the Ukraine. Three years later, the Soviet Union ceased to exist. It was formally dissolved on December 25, 1991, with its fifteen component republics becoming independent sovereign states. Within a decade, Orthodoxy had reestablished itself as a major spiritual and political force within the new Russian Federation.

Mikhail Gorbachev remarked that the collapse of the Iron Curtain would have been impossible without John Paul II. This is correct, provided it is not understood to imply that the pope was the sole cause of the collapse. Many factors were involved, and many would argue that the resurgence of religion – catalyzed to no small extent by this charismatic pope – was one of the factors that destabilized the eastern bloc. John Paul II himself took a different view, suggesting that communism collapsed on account of its own inner contradictions. "It would be simplistic to say that Divine Providence caused the fall of Communism. In a certain sense Communism as a system fell by itself."

The reign of John Paul II saw major challenges developing for Catholicism, including a decline in the priesthood and church attendance in western nations, the growing numerical strength of evangelicals and Pentecostals in Latin America, Asia, and Africa, and debates over the decentralization of power to local parishes. Although initially regarded by some as a reformist, John Paul II's reign was chiefly notable for its reassertion of traditional papal attitudes, and a distinct cooling of relations between Catholics and other churches. Yet many would argue that the most significant event of his reign was the collapse of the Soviet Union, and the emergence of a new order in eastern Europe.

5.3.5.   Challenging the Establishment: Feminism and Liberation Theology

The rapid social changes following the Second World War led to challenges to many traditional Christian beliefs and practices. One of the most important is the emergence of "liberationist" movements, which sought to free groups from domination by cultural or political power groups. In this section, we shall note two such groups: feminism, originally known as "Women's Liberation," and Latin American liberation theology.

In the west, one of the most significant critiques of monotheistic religions emerged from the growing feminist movements, which argued that the fundamentally male notions of God embedded within Judaism, Christianity, and Islam were linked with their original patriarchal cultures. These were no longer defensible in cultures within which women asserted their own identity and authority.

Though there are clear historical precedents – such as the women's suffrage movement, which campaigned for the right to vote in the early twentieth century – feminism emerged during the late 1960s. Though some feminists focused their attention on specific political or social issues, others argued for the need to undermine sexual domination as the pervasive ideology of western culture, arguing that this ideology lay behind many of its political structures and cultural beliefs or practices.

More recently, the movement has become increasingly heterogeneous, partly through accepting a diversity of approaches on the part of women within different cultures and ethnic groupings. Thus the writings of black women in North America are increasingly coming to be referred to as "black womanism," recognizing that the notion of "women's experience" is not a universal notion, but is shaped by gender and class.

The impact of feminism on Christianity has been primarily in the west, and has led to two significant developments. First, the movement campaigned for a greater representation of women within the churches, especially among the clergy. This campaign complemented the activities of others, who argued for the ordination of women on biblical grounds, holding that the New Testament questioned all social, gender, and power relationships on the basis of the new order of the gospel. Some denominations had begun to ordain women before the Second World War. The Salvation Army, for example, had forty-one women officers and forty-nine men officers in 1878. Denominations which emphasized the importance of tradition (Catholicism and Orthodoxy) and churches which interpreted the New Testament as prohibiting women from exercising leadership have resisted such developments. We shall return to this issue later (5.3.7).

Second, the movement argued that traditional Christian language showed a bias towards male role models and language. A number of post-Christian feminists, including Mary Daly in her *Beyond God the Father* (1973) and Daphne Hampson in *Theology and Feminism* (1990), argued that Christianity, with its male symbols for God, its male savior figure, and its long history of male leaders and thinkers, is biased against women, and therefore incapable of being salvaged. Women, they urge, should leave its oppressive environment. Others, such as Carol Christ in *Laughter of Aphrodite* (1987) and Naomi Ruth Goldenberg in *Changing of the Gods* (1979), argue that women may find religious emancipation by recovering the ancient goddess religions (or inventing new ones), and abandoning traditional Christianity altogether.

Other feminists have reacted against such curt dismissals of Christianity, and argued for a more nuanced and informed reading of the Christian tradition. Feminist writers have stressed how women have been active in the shaping and development of the Christian tradition, from the New Testament onward, and have exercised significant leadership roles throughout Christian history. Indeed, many feminist writers have shown the need to reappraise the Christian past, giving honor and recognition to an army of faithful women, whose practice, defense, and proclamation of their faith had hitherto passed unnoticed by much of the Christian church and its (mainly male) historians.

The maleness of Christ has been a topic of particular discussion by feminist writers, who have noted how this has sometimes been used as the theological foundation for the belief that only the male human may adequately image God, or that only males provide appropriate role models or analogies for God. In response, feminist writers have argued that the maleness of Christ is a contingent aspect of his identity, on the same level as his being Jewish. It is a contingent element of his historical reality, not an essential aspect of his identity. Thus it cannot be allowed to become the basis of the domination of females by males, whether in the church or in society, any more than it legitimates the domination of Gentiles by Jews, or plumbers by carpenters.

The rise of liberation theology in Latin America during the 1960s is also of importance. One of the most dramatic developments to take place globally in the aftermath of the Second World War was the spread of Marxism. Although imposed by force in many parts of eastern Europe and central Asia, its ideas proved inspirational to many groups in Latin America, Africa, and Asia, who were disillusioned with the existing social order, and wanted to change it radically. Marxism offered a worldview which promised to transform society – and it was a worldview without God. It seemed to provide a way of throwing off colonialist and imperialist shackles, and finding liberation.

In Latin America, Marxism quickly gained the initiative, with Cuba functioning as a revolutionary template and base from 1965, after Fidel Castro overthrew the US-backed Cuban president Fulgencio Batista (1901–73) in a violent revolution of 1959, and declared Cuba a communist state in 1961. In Brazil, Marxism adapted to the local situation, with theorists such as Caio Prado (1907–90) enabling it to present its socioeconomic vision as the remedy for the nation's ills. Recognizing the importance of dealing with the social issues this reflected, some prominent Catholics in the region developed a "liberation theology" which sought to emphasize the transformative social vision of the gospel.

Liberation theology began to emerge in 1968, when the Catholic bishops of Latin America gathered for a congress at Medellín, Colombia. This meeting – often known as CELAM II, an abbreviation of the Spanish phrase "Consejo Episcopal Latinoamericano" (Latin-American Episcopal Council) – sent shock-waves throughout the region by acknowledging that the church had often sided with oppressive governments in the region, and declaring that in future it would be on the side of the poor.

This theme was picked up and developed by liberation theology. The church is oriented towards the poor and oppressed. "The poor are the authentic theological source for understanding Christian truth and practice" (Jon Sobrino). In the Latin American situation, the church is on the side of the poor: "God is clearly and unequivocally on the side of the poor" (José Miguéz Bonino). The fact that God is on the side of the poor leads to a further insight: the poor occupy a position of especial importance in the interpretation of the Christian faith. All Christian theology and mission must begin with the "view from below," with the sufferings and distress of the poor.

Whereas classical western theology regarded action as the result of reflection, liberation theology inverts the order: action comes first, followed by critical reflection. "Theology has to stop explaining the world, and start transforming it" (Bonino). True knowledge of God can never be disinterested or detached, but comes in and through commitment to the cause of the poor. There is a fundamental rejection of the Enlightenment view that commitment is a barrier to knowledge. Bonino's comment, noted above, reflects Karl Marx's criticism of Ludwig Feuerbach. Philosophers, Marx remarked, have only interpreted the world. "The important thing is to change it."

Liberation theologians have defended their use of Marxist ideas on two grounds. First, Marxism is seen as a "tool of social analysis" (Gustavo Gutiérrez), which allows insights to be gained concerning the present state of Latin American society, and the means by which the appalling situation of the poor may be remedied. Second, it provides a political program by which the present unjust social system may be dismantled, and a more equitable society created. Liberation theology is thus critical of capitalism and affirmative of socialism. God's preference for and commitment to the poor is a fundamental aspect of the gospel, not some bolt-on option arising from the Latin American situation or based purely in Marxist political theory.

Liberation theology was a significant response to the revolutionary fervor of many parts of Latin America in the 1960s and beyond. Since then, its appeal has dwindled, partly because it focused on distant goals, and partly on account of the rise of another religious option for the poor of Latin America – Pentecostalism, which we shall discuss later.

5.3.6. Responding to Cultural Change: New Forms of Churches

The 1960s was a period of social ferment and demands for change (5.2.4). In America, the media proclaimed the "death of God." In England, a bishop attracted huge media attention in 1963 when he published an article in a leading English Sunday newspaper with the provocative title: "Our Image of God must go." John Robinson, bishop of Southwark, used the article to promote his forthcoming book, entitled *Honest to God*. When the book appeared, it became a bestseller. The initial print run ordered by the publishers was a mere 8000 copies, of which 2000 were intended for export to the United States. The print run was sold out on the first day of publication. The demand for the book took everyone by surprise. It is estimated that the book sold 350 000 copies in England during its first seven months.

Many radical questions were asked at this time, both in England and America. Some began to doubt whether the traditional Protestant denominations were capable of coping with new developments in American society. Yet American Protestantism rose to the challenge, and developed new approaches to church life and ministry which resonated with the cultural mood. New ways of "being church" emerged, adapted to the needs of specific groups of people. In what follows, we shall consider some representative examples.

The Calvary Chapel fellowship of churches, presently consisting of a network of about 1000 congregations, traces its roots back to 1965, when Chuck Smith (born 1927) began to pastor a church of that name in Costa Mesa, California. The congregation grew quickly, reaching 2000 by 1967. As it attracted attention, other congregations began to align themselves with its approach. Calvary Chapel made it clear that it did not wish to be seen as a "denomination" but rather as a "fellowship of churches." Where traditional denominations established churches in areas using a corporatist model of "branches" or "offices" of the central organization, Calvary Chapel's approach is more of a franchise, which avoids the financial and organizational overheads of traditional denominations. Any congregation prepared to accept the "Calvary Chapel Distinctives" can become a member of this fellowship, and identify itself as belonging to this network of churches.

A similar model is used by the Vineyard Movement, which currently has over 1500 affiliated churches. This originated in Anaheim, California, and is particularly associated with the ministry of John Wimber (1934–97). The Vineyard Movement grew out of Calvary Chapel network, the break arising partly on account of Wimber's concern that Calvary did not give sufficient attention to the role of spiritual gifts. The charismatic movement was becoming a significant presence in California in the 1970s, and Wimber had been involved in its development, teaching a controversial course on "signs and wonders" at Fuller Theological Seminary. Once more, the Vineyard Movement does not regard itself as a denomination, but as an association or fellowship. It has no centralized structures or authority figures.

Yet the impact of such movements goes beyond the reshaping of denominational options and structures, and the provision of new and less centralized models of the church. Developments such as these within Protestantism have led to new and informal worship styles, an explosion in "worship songs," a new concern for the dynamics of worship, and an increasing dislike of the traditionalism of formal liturgical worship, especially when this involves the cumbersome use of hymn books or service books – particularly where these are seen as culturally alienating to "seekers" from within secular American culture.

This is perhaps seen most clearly in the emergence of the Willow Creek network, which traces its origins back to 1981. Founded in South Barrington, just outside Chicago, Willow Creek Community Church aimed to present the Christian faith without the baggage of Protestant ecclesiastical tradition – such as clerical robes, hard pews, collection plates, and old-fashioned hymns. "Seeker-sensitive" worship would take place in an environment in which "unchurched" individuals could feel at home, while nevertheless learning about the Christian faith. Founding pastor Bill Hybels (born 1952) wanted Willow Creek to be "a safe place where seekers can hear the very dangerous, life changing message of Jesus Christ."

Its success led to many other churches wanting to use its methods. Once more, any suggestion that this was a new "denomination" was avoided. Individual congregations could associate themselves with Willow Creek; there would, however, be no centralized structures. Willow Creek – like Calvary Chapel and the Vineyard – has given rise to a global network of churches, who look to it for guidance.

The phenomenon of the "community church" allows entrepreneurs to develop their gifts in ways that would be impossible within the confining and restricting structures of most traditional denominations. These churches are strongly sensitive to the needs of their local communities, possessing a local grounding and knowledge which informs their strategies and agendas.

Perhaps the most celebrated recent example of a "community church" was established at Saddleback Valley, in Orange County, California, in 1980 by Rick Warren (born 1954) and his wife Kay, who had just graduated from Southwestern Baptist Theological Seminary in Texas. It aimed to reach out to those who did not traditionally attend church, in a way that was seeker-sensitive on the one hand, and theologically conservative on the other. The vision was to establish "a place where the hurting, the depressed, the frustrated, and the confused can find love, acceptance, help, hope, forgiveness, guidance, and encouragement." Warren's best-sellers *The Purpose Driven Church* (1995) and *The Purpose Driven Life* (2002) have had a significant impact on the reshaping of Protestant attitudes to creating community, evangelism, pastoral care, and outreach – all unimpeded by any cumbersome and expensive denominational apparatus.

The term "mega-church" has increasingly come to be used to refer to large churches, with attendances of over 4000, which are able to sustain extensive pastoral, social, and preaching ministries, often based at large church campuses. These large churches are often able to offer a much wider range of services to their members than traditional churches, which in turn becomes a further stimulus to growth.

So is this the future? Many suggest that a major transformation of the religious life of the United States is under way, in which the mega-churches are, in effect, becoming the new dioceses, with large numbers of orbiting planets. They are more responsive to social changes, easier to manage, and cheaper to run than traditional denominations. Just as the great medieval monasteries planted smaller monasteries ("daughter houses") in outlying regions, resourced by the mother house until they were deemed strong enough to be self-sufficient, so the mega-churches are in the process of spreading. The future of Protestant denominations in America may well be deeply shaped by this major new trend.

And what of other western nations? Throughout western Europe, churches have made accommodations to shifts in culture. The American model of establishing new denominations is often avoided as impractical or culturally unacceptable. Instead, many existing denominations have developed ministries to specific social groupings, often using familiar existing church buildings for new purposes.

In Finland, the "Tuomasmessu" (Finnish: "Thomas Mass") has evolved as a traditional Lutheran worship service, which is particularly adapted to the needs and concerns of those who are in doubt, or challenged by sin. The structure and focus of the service reflects the gospel account of a dinner celebration in the house of a Pharisee, with Jesus, a prostitute, and village people present. One of the most striking features of the service is its integration of modern spirituality and ancient traditions. The service was founded at the Agricola Church in Helsinki in the spring of 1988, and is now widely used throughout Finland.

In Great Britain, the "Alpha Course" has developed as a means of outreach and ministry. The Alpha Course was founded at Holy Trinity, Brompton in London in 1978, and has now become an international phenomenon, used widely by many denominations across the globe. It takes the form of a ten-week program which introduces some of the fundamentals of the Christian faith in a generally relaxed environment, in which inquirers are invited to ask any questions they may have. The group of people who assemble for the course rapidly become a community, sharing in the experience of encountering Christianity and each other at the same time. The sharing of meals is an important element in this community-building dimension to the program, which brings together the dual themes of "believing" and "belonging."

5.3.7. The Equality Agenda: The Protestant Debate over Women's Ordination

The churches have always faced issues of inclusiveness, particularly in relation to issues of membership and leadership. Hints of this can be seen in the New Testament, where tensions clearly emerged over the status of various groups within the early Christian communities. Was Christianity a form of Judaism, so that Gentiles could only be admitted if they were to be circumcised, and follow strict Jewish food laws? Or was Christianity a new religious movement, which welcomed Jews without endorsing either circumcision or food laws? And what about the status of women within these communities? Or slaves? Or homosexuals?

As we noted earlier, early Christianity came to the settled view that all were one "in Christ" – whether Jew or Gentile, whether male or female, whether master or slave (1.1.6). Differences of race, gender, or social position were declared to place no obstacles between all believers sharing the same common faith. This may have largely settled the issue of the membership of Christian communities. But it did not resolve the issue of who was to lead them. The term "ordination" is generally used to refer to the process by which someone is formally admitted to a position of leadership within churches, despite the wide use of terms to refer to such leadership roles – such as priest, pastor, and minister.

Three main arguments were widely held to inhibit or prevent women from leading Christian communities.

1. The New Testament appears to limit leadership roles to males. At one point, Paul declares that he "does not permit women to be teachers" (1 Timothy 2:12), and argues that they should be "silent" in churches (1 Corinthians 14:34).
2. The tradition of the church is to have male leaders; to do otherwise is to break with this tradition.
3. Christ was male, and gathered around him male apostles. This makes it clear that those who act as Christ's representatives through ministry and leadership must also be male.

Although there are some notable exceptions, most Christian churches – Catholic, Orthodox, and Protestant – had an exclusively male leadership throughout most of their histories. One of the most notable exceptions to this role was Catherine Booth (1829–90), who with her husband, William Booth, founded the Christian Revival Association in 1865 and the Salvation Army in 1878. The Booths regarded the active participation of women in ministry to be both theologically defensible, and vital to Christian ministry.

Catherine had already preached publicly in her early life, and published a pamphlet in defense of this view, entitled *Female Ministry; or, Woman's Right to Preach the Gospel* (1861). Following her husband's illness, Catherine took on an increasingly heavy preaching responsibility. She eventually became one of the most famous female preachers in England. Her final sermon was delivered to an audience of 50 000 people.

Yet it would still be some time before the mainline Protestant denominations felt able to accept such a development. The massive social changes of the twentieth century, however, saw women propelled into positions of secular ministry and leadership, and did much to undermine traditional hostility towards women in leadership roles in western society. During the Great War, women took on many roles traditionally assigned to men, due to the vast numbers of males who had been conscripted for military service on the battlefields of France.

Pressure to review questions of leadership began to emerge again in the 1960s, as a new cultural mood emerged throughout much of western culture, which was more open to questioning and challenging the past. Catholicism and Orthodoxy, which both regarded tradition as being of defining importance in this matter, did not initiate discussion on the extension of leadership to women. Yet Protestant denominations in North American and Europe came to believe that the time was right for a review of both the cultural situation within which Christian ministry was embedded, and the theological arguments relating to the ordination of women.

Although it seems that a significant motivation for re-opening the question of women's ordination within Protestant denominations was based on cultural shifts in the west that now made this socially acceptable, this was supplemented by a number of arguments which sought to explain why Christians in the past had affirmed a male-only leadership, and why the time was now right to review this. The main arguments against the ordination of women were met as follows.

1. The New Testament is not quite as specific on the question of women's ordination as had previously been thought. Paul's injunctions are local and personal, and are not to be taken as universally binding. Furthermore, the New Testament already depicts women in ministry roles within the circles of Jesus of Nazareth, and within early Christian communities.
2. Tradition is something that is living, and capable of growth and adaptation. It does not mean the uncritical repetition of past conventions or behavioral norms.
3. While Christ was indeed male, his mission was partly to break down older religious views, including the nature of leadership. Christ's circle included many women, many of whom were sent out in a pastoral or apostolic role.

Alongside these, further arguments began to come into play. The first of these was theological. Ordination was about the discernment of God-given gifts, and a communal authorization to use these within the Christian churches. Did not women have such gifts? And should not these be recognized and used in public ministry? The second was political. The issue of women's ministry was an equality issue. Both male and female ought to be allowed to carry out the same roles.

Although such arguments are seen as contentious and unpersuasive by some, they have had a decisive impact on western Protestant denominations since the 1970s. The Anglican Communion is a case in point. In 1975, the General Synod of the Anglican Church of Canada passed legislation allowing for women priests. A year later, the General Convention of the Episcopal Church authorized the ordination of women both to the priesthood and the episcopate. The Church of England agreed to the ordination of woman priests in 1992, and began ordaining them in 1994. Many Anglican provinces held that, given that women had now been admitted to the priesthood, there was no fundamental theological objection to their becoming bishops.

This development has caused dissension within some denominations. It has also raised further questions about equality of opportunity, including the issue of the ordination of homosexuals. In the non-western world, pressure for the ordination of women appears to be significantly less, perhaps reflecting the influence of cultural contexts which are not accustomed to women in leadership roles.

So what of Christianity outside the west? How has this developed in the twentieth century? As we shall see, massive growth outside the west, especially in Africa and Asia, has led to the center of gravity of Christianity moving decisively from the western world to the developing nations, with major implications for the future of Christianity.

5.4.   The Shift from the West: The New Christianity

As will be clear from this volume, the history of Christianity until about 1600 tends to focus on developments in Europe. This is unhelpful in a number of ways, not least in that it tends to suggest that Christianity is essentially a European religion. This is clearly not true. It is a faith which originated in the Middle East, which adapted itself remarkably well to the European context – so well that many naturally assume that it originated in, and has come to be defined by, this context. Yet Europe is ultimately only one of a number of contexts in which Christianity has settled and developed. Others must be noted, especially in North Africa and parts of the Middle East.

The great European missionary ventures of the early modern period, initially on the part of the Catholic church, and subsequently by Protestants, vastly extended the geographical range of the Christian faith. Yet in most cases, the forms of Christianity planted in European colonies bore a marked resemblance to their homeland. It was as if European church practices, architecture, and traditions were parachuted into alien territory. As we noted earlier, most missionaries were far from being complicit in colonialism. Yet there was always a temptation for missionaries in Latin America and Africa to rely on what had been tried and tested in a European context.

The First World War ended what is widely regarded as the great missionary phase of western Christianity, driven by a conviction that the twentieth century would be a "Christian Century." A series of triumphalistic congresses in the late nineteenth century had confidently proclaimed the inevitability of the conversion of the world within the next generation. The First International Convention of the Student Volunteer Movement met in Cleveland in 1891, and adopted as its motto the slogan "the evangelization of the world in this generation." It was the largest student conference assembled in its time, and was carried along by an ebullient confidence that did not evaporate until after the First World War.

Yet this missionary enterprise was largely sustained by western churches, who sent missionaries into regions they regarded as unchurched. The post-war period saw a reduction in commitment to missionary work, partly for economic reasons, and partly due to concerns about the international situation. Perhaps to the surprise of the western missionary societies, Christianity began to spread without them, as more indigenous forms of Christianity took root in parts of the world that had hitherto had little contact with the Christian faith.

The numerical center of Christianity as a whole, including Protestantism, shifted decisively away from the west between 1900 and 2000. Christianity is already predominantly a religion of the global south. Population growth in these areas, when set alongside the evangelistic and missionary successes of the twentieth century, mean that an increasing proportion of increasingly large populations are now Christian. For example: in 1900, the population of Africa was ten million people, of which 9 percent were Christian; in 2005, the population was more than four hundred million, of which 46 percent are Christian.

The styles of Christianity developing in Asia, Latin America, and Africa are noticeably different from those found in the United States, and even more different from those found in western Europe. The Protestantism of the global south tends to be more charismatic or Pentecostal, generally with traditional moral values, and little time for the modernist modes of reading the Bible that have dominated the west until recently. This means that the Protestant denominations of the global south tend to have more in common with each other, than with their equivalents in America or Europe. African Lutherans tend to have more in common with African Methodists than with American Lutherans, despite the denominational link. This is especially evident in the case of Anglicanism, in which the totally different social mores and theological presuppositions of African and American Anglicans is causing serious, possibly irreconcilable, tensions within the denomination.

In this final section, we shall look at the massive expansion of Christianity beyond the western world in the twentieth century. It is perhaps one of the most fascinating periods in Christian history, raising important questions for historians, cultural theorists, and theologians. Yet perhaps it is appropriate first to explore how Christianity has fared in its original homeland, the Middle East, in the twentieth century.

5.4.1.   The Middle East: The Decline of Arab Christianity

Although it rapidly expanded into other parts of the Mediterranean world, Christianity originated in Palestine. The city of Jerusalem was the base for a bishopric until Islamic conquests of the seventh century led to a decline in its importance within the Christian world (2.1.3). Many pilgrimage sites relating to the life of Jesus of Nazareth are located in this region. So how has Christianity fared in this region in recent decades? The simple answer is that it has faced serious difficulties in this region, and is generally regarded as being in decline.

Until the beginning of the twentieth century, Christianity had established an uneasy but nevertheless workable relationship with Islam, the dominant religious force in the region. The Ottoman Empire gave a significant degree of religious freedom to non-Islamic faiths, especially Judaism and Christianity. By the early nineteenth century, the Ottoman Empire extended throughout the Middle East and deep into Persia. Christians were active participants in the renaissance of the Arab language and letters (often referred to as the "Nahda"). Christian scholars such as the Lebanese Marronites Butros al-Bustani (1819–83) and Nasif al-Yaziji (1800–71) played a leading role in this development, seeing it as a counterweight against sectarian tensions within the regions, which often led to communal violence.

The Great War led to the defeat of the Ottoman forces throughout the Middle East, and substantial changes throughout the Arab world. The Balfour Declaration of 1917, which gave British support to the establishment of a Jewish state in Palestine, created widespread discontent throughout the Arab world, which flared into open warfare with the establishment of the State of Israel in 1948. Although these developments were not in themselves necessarily damaging for Christianity in the region, they led to increasingly politicized forms of Islam emerging, some of which portrayed Christianity as the last vestiges of the Crusades in an Islamic region.

The Coptic Christians of Egypt, who represent the largest Christian community in the Middle East, suffered loss in numbers following the revolution of 1952, which brought Gamal Abdel Nasser (1918–70) to power. Increasing anxiety about their safety and future led many Copts to emigrate to Australia, western Europe, or the United States. Subsequent western-led interventions in the region – such as the occupation of Iraq in the 2000s – were easily portrayed by Islamic fundamentalists as Christian encroachment on Islamic lands. Christian demographics in many parts of the Arab world – including Iraq – are in decline, leading many to wonder what the long-term future of Christianity might be within the region that originally gave it birth.

Yet if Christianity is experiencing difficulty in its original homeland, it is expanding considerably in other parts of the world, changing as it adapts to new cultural contexts. We turn our attention now to an Asian nation which has, in the course of a single century, become a majority Christian nation: Korea.

5.4.2.   Korea: The Surprising Transformation of a Nation

At the beginning of the twentieth century, the only predominantly Christian nation in Asia was the Philippines – a strongly Catholic country, with a small Protestant minority. By the end of the twentieth century, Korea has established itself as a largely Christian nation, with Protestantism – especially Presbyterianism – being by far the largest Christian group. Yet in 1901, only a tiny proportion of the Korean population – perhaps 1 percent – was Christian. So how did a country with virtually no Christian presence come to be, in effect, a majority Christian nation?

The answer is complex. Christianity was known to some Koreans as early as the eighteenth century, when diplomatic links with China and Japan led to contacts with Catholic missionaries in the region. In 1603, Yi Gwang-jeong, a Korean diplomat, returned from Beijing with several books by the Jesuit missionary to China, Matteo Ricci. Although the Catholic church faced persecution locally in the early nineteenth century on account of its foreign origins, it nevertheless made significant inroads. In part, this was because the church used Hangul, the phonemic Korean alphabet, rather than following the aristocratic habit of using Chinese characters. The Catholic church became the first Korean organization to use Hangul, and used this script for Christian literature printed for use in Korea. Its greater popular appeal is thought to have helped secure a following for Christianity outside the traditional Korean aristocracy.

Although Catholicism was thus established in Korea by the 1880s, it was a very small community. Many scholars suggest that the serious growth of Christianity in Korea is to be traced back to two American Protestant missionaries around 1884: the Methodist Henry Appenzeller (1858–1902), and the Presbyterian Horace Underwood (1859–1916).

Both actively promoted education as a means of embedding Christianity in Korean society. Some form of Pentecostal revival appears to have developed around 1907, and been significant in bringing about conversions among the native population.

Elsewhere in Asia, Christianity was easily depicted by its critics as the lackey of western imperialism. Yet Christianity came to be perceived as an ally, rather than an enemy, by Koreans in the twentieth century. In Korea the major enemy of the twentieth century was not the west, but Japan. Korea was annexed by Japan in 1910, and remained under Japanese rule until the end of the Second World War. Unusually, Christianity came to be seen as being on the side of Korean nationalism, especially in the face of Japanese oppression.

Throughout the Japanese occupation, Christians played an active role in the Korean independence movement out of all proportion to their numbers. Of the 123 people tried for insurgence by the Japanese in the 1911 popular revolt against Japanese rule, ninety-eight were Christians. At this time, Christians made up just over 1 percent of the Korean population. The significance of this point could hardly be overlooked.

Korea underwent partition into a communist north and democratic south following the Korean War, which broke out on June 25, 1950. The heavy involvement of missionary agencies in the relief programs which followed the ending of the war created a powerful stimulus to the development of Christianity, which was catalyzed still further by the Korean churches' programs of social action during the 1960s.

Korea has been affected by the global expansion of Pentecostalism since the Second World War. The movement developed in ways that adapted to local environments, with leadership rapidly passing from American to indigenous pastors. In 1952, the American Assemblies of God sent Abner Chesnut to Korea as their first missionary. The Korean Assemblies of God was organized in 1953, and opened its first Bible school during the following year. Paul Yonggi Cho – who went on to become the founder of Yoido Full Gospel Church – was one of its first students. The form of Pentecostalism that Cho developed was clearly influenced by Presbyterianism (the dominant form of Christianity in the Korea at that time), and by worship traditions originating from the revivalist and holiness traditions. Yet it is unquestionably Korean, having adapted to its local context rather than retained the forms of those who planted it.

Today, Korea sends out Christian missionaries to nations throughout Asia, and increasingly to the large Korean diasporas of major western cities, from Sydney to Los Angeles, from Melbourne to New York. These are now closely linked with a network of churches, which increasingly serve as a focal point for community action, mutual support, and spiritual nourishment. In 1979, Korean churches sent ninety-three missionaries overseas. In 1990, that number had increased to 1645; in 2000, to 8103.

South Korea is now home to some of the world's largest Protestant churches, such as the Yoido Full Gospel Church, a Pentecostal church based in the Yoido district of Seoul. The church began in ex-army tents in the slums of Seoul in 1958, with an emphasis on the transformative impact of the gospel through the empowerment of the Holy Spirit in the face of the adverse social and economic conditions of the depressed post-Korean War economic situation. Today, the church has a membership of 700 000. Its main place of worship can hold 25 000 people, forcing it to hold multiple services on Sundays.

Figure 5.9   Crowd leaving Yoido Full Gospel Church, Seoul, Korea, after Sunday services. Hyungwon Kang/Time Life Pictures/Getty Images

5.4.3.   China: The Resurgence of Christianity in the Middle Kingdom

The years immediately before the Great War saw Christianity in crisis in much of China (4.4.3). As China's relationship with the Great Powers worsened in the first years of the twentieth century, Christianity increasingly became stigmatized as a western influence. Chinese nationalist movements came to see the rejection of Christianity as an integral aspect of their political programs.

These concerns had been raised in the past. Realizing the dangers posed by the perception that Christianity was culturally alien to China, Henry Venn (1796–1873), general secretary of the Church Missionary Society, and Rufus Anderson (1796–1880), foreign secretary of the American Board of Commissioners for Foreign Missions, both argued for Chinese churches that were based on self-governance, self-support, and self-propagation, without being dependent on the west for their finance or outreach.

These ideas were explored further at a Christian missionary conference in Shanghai in 1892, which concluded that the future wellbeing of the Chinese church depended on the indigenization of its leadership and modes of worship. The founding of the China Christian Independent Church in the years before the Great War reflects this concern for autonomy on the part of some Chinese Christians.

On rare occasions, Christians were allowed to evangelize; this liberal attitude, however, usually reflected deeper political agendas. For example, the Qing Dynasty saw Christianity as a force that could neutralize the threat of Buddhist Tibet, by weakening the influence of the Dalai Lama. In 1905, Tibetan Lamas responded to this threat by massacring the missionaries and native converts to Christianity.

Once the Great War had ended, Catholic and Protestant missionaries resumed their work in China. However, the occupation of China by Japan placed limitations on these efforts. More seriously, the 1949 communist revolution – like its European counterparts – was strongly anti-religious, regarding Christianity both as a western influence and the "opium of the people." Western missionaries realized the implications of this development, and began a slow and reluctant withdrawal from the People's Republic of China.

In the enforced absence of western missionaries, the Chinese churches were obliged to rely on their own resources. The idea of self-sufficient Chinese churches had been discussed for some time in missionary circles, partly due to growing frustration with the apparent inability of mission boards in London or New York to understand the complexities of the Chinese context. Many wondered why Chinese Christians should take their cues from overseas. Why not take ownership of the situation for themselves?

These ideas, already familiar to Chinese Christians from the 1890s, became acutely important following the communist revolution of 1949. Wishing to avoid any suggestion that Christianity was a tool of western imperialism, or an unwelcome western cultural import, Y. T. Wu (1893–1979), a Chinese Christian leader, initiated the Three-Self Patriotic Movement. This movement advocated the "Three Self" strategy of "self-governance, self-support, and self-propagation," as a means of eliminating foreign influences from the Chinese churches and reassuring the new communist government that the churches would be committed to the newly established People's Republic of China. Realizing that it could not eliminate Christianity, the revolutionary government sought to do the next best thing – to control it.

Yet the attempt to control Christianity during the 1950s and early 1960s gave way to a more radical attempt to eliminate religion altogether – especially religions that were seen as western – during the Great Cultural Revolution (1966–76). This movement aimed at eliminating foreign influence and remaining "bourgeois" influences within the People's Republic of China, and restoring Mao Zedong's prominence within the Chinese Communist Party. The campaign of the "four olds" (old customs, old culture, old habits, and old ideas), launched in August 1966, led to Red Guards destroying ancient buildings, records, and documents. Buildings with religious significance – whether ancient or modern – were demolished. Intellectuals were seen as a special threat on account of their learning, and were targeted by the Red Guards for special treatment.

The death of Mao Zedong on September 9, 1976, led to significant changes in China. The "Gang of Four" – seen as the instigators of the more violent and extreme elements of the Cultural Revolution – were arrested less than a month after Mao's death, causing rejoicing throughout much of China. This marked the end of a turbulent political era in the People's Republic of China, and opened the way to social, political, and economic reconstruction.

One of the most significant achievements of the Cultural Revolution was the severe weakening of China's traditional Buddhist religious heritage. Buddhism and Confucianism were denounced as threats to the revolution, and violently suppressed. Yet the violence of the Cultural Revolution created intense popular distrust of communism, both as a working political system and as an ideology capable of conferring meaning and value on life. In many ways, the Cultural Revolution created a vacuum of meaning within China. The evidence suggests that Christianity was able to fill this vacuum.

The decade of Cultural Revolution ended western influence in the People's Republic of China. For Chinese Christianity, this meant the breaking of links with western missionary organizations or denominational structures, and the emergence of forms of Christianity that were largely self-supporting and self-governing. Many churches chose to operate outside the state system. The underground "house church" movement did not seek government authorization for its pastors, and conducted services without government approval.

This state supervision of the religious affairs of the People's Republic of China has proved particularly difficult for the Catholic church, given the central role of the pope in relation to Catholic identity on the one hand, and the appointment of bishops on the other. The Chinese Patriotic Catholic Association was established in 1957 by the Religious Affairs Bureau of the People's Republic of China to ensure state control over Catholics within its borders. Although Catholics in Macau and Hong Kong were able to retain links with the Vatican, the People's Republic of China refused to allow the Catholic church to operate within its borders if it was subject to foreign interference, particularly in relation to its political agendas and the appointment of bishops.

Since 1990, Christianity has grown substantially in all its forms within China. The reasons for this development are not fully understood. The Chinese government appears to have taken a pragmatic attitude towards this development, especially in working to secure a better relationship with the Vatican. Although some are suggesting that China may become the nation with the most Christians in the next few decades, it is clearly unwise to speculate about what is such a poorly understood phenomenon.

5.4.4.   The Rise of Post-Colonial Christianity: African Initiated Churches

Many in the twentieth century regarded Christianity as a colonial religion, imposed on native populations by their European masters (4.4.4). When the Europeans returned home, it was believed, Christianity would be abandoned as a colonial trapping, with massive reversion to the traditional religions of the region. In fact, the removal of western power generally removed western constraints which had until then prevented the emergence of more culturally adapted forms of Christianity.

The withdrawal of colonial powers – such as Britain and France – from their former territories during the 1960s allowed their churches to develop theologies, ministries, and styles of worship which were adapted to their contexts, rather than being poor copies of those found in the homelands of the colonial powers. In most cases, the departure of the colonial power was followed by renewal, as the cultural restraints on indigenous variants of Christianity were finally removed. Political independence rapidly led to ecclesiastical independence, and the ending of cultural suppression of indigenous theologies and worship patterns. Although these patterns can be observed throughout the post-colonial world, they are probably best studied from the African context.

During the nineteenth century, Catholic and Protestant missionaries established churches throughout southern Africa (4.4.4). These were generally African implementations of European models, with little more than cosmetic adaptations to the local culture. Catholicism became the dominant form of Christianity in French and Belgian colonies, as did Anglicanism in British colonies.

With the departure of the colonial powers in the decades following the Second World War, African Christianity underwent significant changes. Leadership within the churches gradually devolved from Europeans to Africans, resulting in a growing adaptation of the colonial churches to local customs and traditions. Yet alongside this development, many indigenous churches began to emerge, without any historical connection with European denominations. These "African Initiated Churches" (AICs) are strongest and most numerous in Southern Africa, West Africa, the Congo Basin, and Central Kenya. Three major categories of AICs can be identified.

1. "Ethiopian" and "African" churches. AICs which do not claim to be prophetic nor to have special manifestations of the Holy Spirit have been referred to as "Ethiopian" or "Ethiopian-type" churches in Southern Africa and "African" churches in Nigeria. These churches are generally earlier in origin than the other two types, and arose primarily as a political and administrative reaction to European mission-founded churches. For this reason "Ethiopian" or "African" churches are very similar to the historical Protestant churches from which they emerged. For example, they usually practice infant baptism, read set liturgies, wear European clerical vestments (often black), and use forms of worship that are less enthusiastic or emotional than other AICs.

2. "Prophet-Healing" and "Spiritual" churches. These churches tend to have their historical and theological roots in the Pentecostalist movement, emphasizing the working of the power of the Spirit in the church. This is the largest grouping of AICs, which includes a wide variety of some of the biggest churches in Africa. It includes the Kimbanguist movement and the African Apostolic Church in Central Africa, the Aladura and Harrist churches in West Africa, and the Zion Christian Church and the *Amanazaretha* in Southern Africa. The theology of these churches tends to be more precisely formulated than in European mission-founded churches, and the differences in belief systems, liturgy, and prophetic healing practices are often considerable. The most obvious distinguishing feature of these churches throughout most of Africa is the almost universal use of uniforms for members, often white robes with bright sashes.

3. "New Pentecostal" churches. This group of churches of more recent origin (mostly after 1980) also emphasize the power and the gifts of the Holy Spirit. They are today probably the fastest growing expression of Christianity in Africa and have exploded on the African religious scene since about 1975 to such an extent that they are challenging many previously accepted assumptions about the character of African Protestantism. Examples of these are the Deeper Life Church in Nigeria, the Zimbabwe Assemblies of God Africa, and Grace Bible Church in South Africa. The difference between these churches and those of western Pentecostal origin has mainly to do with their forms of church government. In the case of the "new" churches, the leadership is entirely black and is essentially local and autonomous, with no organizational links with Pentecostal denominations outside Africa.

The history of Christianity in Africa in the later part of the twentieth century is often dominated by events in the Republic of South Africa. Rivalry between Britain and the Netherlands as colonial powers in this region led to two churches of European origin being established there: the Dutch Reformed Church, and the Church of the Province of South Africa. These churches tended to be politically disengaged, and did not initially challenge the policy of racial segregation known as *apartheid* (Afrikaans: "separateness"), enforced by the National Party governments of South Africa from 1948.

Resistance to the policy emerged primarily from the Church of the Province of South Africa. Following the Soweto Riots of 1976, Desmond Tutu (born 1931) became an increasingly vocal critic of the government. Tutu was bishop of Lesotho from 1976 until 1978, then bishop of Johannesburg. He quickly became the figurehead of the anti-apartheid movement, and was awarded the Nobel Prize for Peace in 1984, before becoming the first black archbishop of Cape Town in 1986. This gave him a high-profile platform from which he could challenge the government's policies with relative impunity.

Since then, the religious demography of South Africa has changed. The end of white minority rule led to a surge of popularity in African Initiated Churches. It is estimated that there are more than 10 000 such churches in the nation, with a membership of nearly thirteen million. Some nine hundred of these are in Soweto.

The expansion of Christianity in southern Africa has raised many questions, not least in relation to how the gospel interacts with African traditional religions. One of the most important themes in such traditional religion is the "cult of the ancestors," based on the belief that one's ancestors are an essential link in a hierarchical chain of powers stretching from this world to the spirit world. Deceased ancestors are integral to the traditional African social structure. While remaining part of the family, they are understood to be intermediaries with the spirit world. African Initiated Churches often criticize traditional religion on the one hand, while developing practices which can be seen as Christian "alternatives." Thus many such churches recognize the ministry of prophets who play a role similar to that of the *mganga* (Swahili: "doctors" or "healers") in the "cult of the ancestors."

5.4.5.   The Rise of Pentecostalism in Latin America

Latin America was colonized by Spain and Portugal during the sixteenth and seventeenth centuries (2.5.7), with the result that Catholicism became the established religion of the area. Immigration from Europe, particularly from Germany, led to small Protestant communities being founded in many parts of the continent during the nineteenth century. An Anglican church was established in Buenos Aires in 1821. Yet Protestants – referred to in this region using the Spanish term *evangélicos* – were generally seen as an elite minority, standing slightly outside the religious mainstream. They were never seen as a threat to the Catholic establishment, being content to retain their historic denominational beliefs and practices, usually imported from Europe, without attempting any form of outreach to the local population.

The rise of Pentecostalism in the region, which dates from the first decade of the twentieth century, has significantly altered its religious dynamics (4.3.6). A revival that broke out in a Methodist church at Valparaiso, Chile, in 1909 set the scene for a series of indigenous Pentecostal phenomena throughout the region, now generally referred to as the "Revival" (Spanish: *Avivamiento*). Although this was assisted, especially in the aftermath of the Second World War, by missionaries from Pentecostal denominations in the United States, Latin American Pentecostalism has retained its own distinctive identity.

Why has Pentecostalism expanded so rapidly in the region? Sociological studies suggest that the accelerated transformation of Pentecostalism in Latin America has a number of causes, including its openness to adaptation to resonate with local cultural beliefs and values, and political issues. Yet the determining issue often seems to be accessibility. Whereas nineteenth-century Protestant movements represented a religion of the written word, Pentecostalism is essentially an oral religion that makes virtually no educational demands of its followers.

The rise of Latin American Pentecostalism has transformed the religious dynamic of the region. In Brazil, Chile, Guatemala, and Nicaragua, Pentecostals now far outnumber all other Protestant groups, and on some projections may soon constitute the majority of the population. Pentecostals are also growing rapidly in areas adjacent to Latin America, such as the Caribbean, where Jamaica, Puerto Rico, and Haiti have seen large increases in Pentecostal congregations.

The greatest transformation of the Latin American religious landscape in the last fifty years – if not in the last five hundred years – is the transition from a monopolistic religious economy to a free-market one. Protestantism was a small yet significant presence in Latin America since the early nineteenth century – yet it did not flourish, even with the disestablishment of Catholicism as the official state religion throughout Latin America between the middle of the nineteenth century and the first quarter of the twentieth. Yet it was only with the development of Pentecostalism in the first decades of the twentieth century that the popular classes had a culturally appropriate alternative to Catholicism. The implications for Catholicism are obvious, and have been noted with concern by the bishops of the region.

The growing influence of Pentecostalism in Latin America was probably assisted by decades of division and strife between progressive and conservative wings of the Catholic church in the region, often associated with the rise of liberation theology in the 1960s and 1970s (5.3.5). Recent papal visits to the region – such as Benedict XVI's visit of May 2007 – have sought to reestablish unity within the Catholic church, and reconnect with the peoples of the region. This has involved a move away from political engagement and confrontation towards a more traditional emphasis upon spirituality and pastoral care.

A further significant response has been to develop contemporary worship styles within Catholicism which mimic the informality of evangelicalism and Pentecostalism, while retaining the basic structure and content of Catholic liturgy. Neo-charismatic elements within the Catholic church have shown that the needs and expectations of many who might otherwise be drawn to Pentecostalism can be met through Catholicism. The rise of Pentecostalism outside the church has thus proved a potent catalyst for the development of the charismatic movement within it. After four centuries of religious monopoly, the Catholic church has had to get used to competition. The indications are that it is rising to the challenge.

Yet the implications for classic forms of Protestantism in the region are no less significant. Having also enjoyed something of their own kind of religious monopoly for a century, these traditional Protestant denominations have found themselves confronted with an alternative model of ecclesiology and spirituality that has challenged some of their core presuppositions. The most important of these concern word-centered preaching and spirituality, and an essentially static conception of the denomination that creates no anticipation or expectation of church growth.

Latin American Protestantism has a long and distinguished record of social involvement with the poor and marginalized – but not of evangelizing them. One of the most significant outcomes of Pentecostal growth within such socioeconomic groups has been the challenge to this non-evangelistic conception of mission. Yet there are other challenges. The many charismatic groups in Latin America have opened up new opportunities for spiritual leadership on the part of women, challenging the male-dominated church culture of historical Protestantism in the region.

The unexpected rise of Pentecostalism in Latin America during the twentieth century raise some significant questions. One of them has to do with the future religious shape of the United States of America. Hispanics are already the largest ethnic minority in the United States, and are predicted to become the majority within the next fifty years. It has traditionally been assumed that this will lead to the United States becoming increasingly Catholic. Yet recent developments in Latin America call any such assumption into question. Latino Pentecostal congregations have sprung up in most American cities, with many experiencing significant growth. The religious future of the United States remains far more open than many realize.

5.4.6.   Virtual Christianity: The Internet and New Patterns of Faith

In an earlier section, we noted how the technology of printing transformed Christianity (2.5.1). Anyone who could read, and was wealthy enough to afford to buy books, could gain access to the religious ideas of religious reformers and conservatives, Catholics and Protestants, whether academic or popular. Anxious governments and churches tried to retain at least some control over this movement of ideas. Yet in the end, books were able to cross national borders, and change people's minds. Luther never visited England; yet his ideas were widely discussed in Cambridge University during the 1520s. Why? Because his books had reached England, thanks to the Hanseatic trade route.

It is widely believed that the creation of the Internet must now be ranked as a technological development whose transformative potential is at least equal to that of printing. And just as printing changed Christianity, so the Internet is having a deep impact on the shaping of popular Christianity in the twenty-first century.

The technical foundations on which the Internet would be based were established during the 1950s, as it became clear that the technology to allow computers to communicate with each other was in the process of emerging. The Internet began as a research project commissioned by the US Defense Department in the 1970s which would allow it to link its computers across different military bases. As the research progressed, the Internet expanded beyond the control of the US Defense Department, linking many major universities. Slowly, corporate organizations realized the value of Internet and adopted it as a means of communicating and developing their corporate culture and marketing. However, it was in the mid-1990s that the Internet became widely available as a means of allowing communication, with massive implications for the transformation of culture.

The Internet is a way of linking computers so that they can share information. Yet a critical stage in exploiting this capacity was the creation of World Wide Web by Sir Timothy Berners-Lee (born 1955), allowing web pages to be written and read using a simple universal language. The World Wide Web rapidly developed as a medium for people to interact with each other, and to gain and share information.

The widespread use of the web in global culture has had a significant impact on Christianity. Religious leaders have their own websites, blogs, and Twitter feeds. Without needing to leave their desks, anyone can now read — and in many cases, see and hear — the latest sermons by the pope or the archbishop of Canterbury, or the leader of a prominent mega-church.

The new technology allows anyone immediate access to Christian texts. In one sense, this development parallels the invention of printing; in other, however, it clearly goes beyond it. Many Protestant Christians, who would formerly carry printed copies of the Bible around with them, now access it — in multiple translations — through the Internet. Virtual libraries of "Christian classics" across the denominational spectrum are now accessible, usually without any need for a subscription. Bible-smuggling into China and other parts of the world has generally been supplanted by the ready availability of the Bible and other major Christian resources through dedicate websites. These are often sponsored by religious charities, so that they can be accessed without cost.

More importantly, the Internet has expanded the traditional notion of a "gathered community" at worship into an extended virtual community, which can participate in real time in the worship of a community by Internet streaming. Mega-churches are able to extend the reach of their physical congregations into living rooms across the world, allowing believers to share in their worship and hear their sermons. A pastor can address a global audience, without having to travel. Evangelicals were the first to appreciate the importance of the Internet, and use it as a tool for outreach and evangelism. But everyone else now seems to be catching up.

Yet there are clear concerns about the directions in which "virtual Christianity" is heading. Christianity is not a religion of solitariness, but of community. Some of those who left the cities in third-century Egypt to develop their spiritual life in the desert did so as hermits, living in isolation. Yet most formed communities, realizing that the ideals and values of the Christian faith were best actualized through interaction with others — in short, through fellowship, achieved by attending church.

The Internet has changed patterns of social relationships and interaction, allowing virtual interaction to take the place of physical encounter. Some Christian leaders are concerned about a weakening of the traditional Christian emphasis upon the church as a community which shapes character, transmits the Christian proclamation, and encourages the development of social identity. The phenomenon of the solitary web surfer has its Christian equivalent — the solitary worshipper, who observes but does not participate in church life.

It remains to see where the developments noted in this chapter will take Christianity in the future. But what is clear is that the world's most numerous faith is in the process of exploring new territory in its twenty-first century.

For Further Reading

Alberigo, Giuseppe, and Matthew Sherry. *A Brief History of Vatican II*. Maryknoll, NY: Orbis Books, 2006.

Anderson, Allan. *An Introduction to Pentecostalism*. Cambridge: Cambridge University Press, 2004.

Armour, Ian D. *A History of Eastern Europe 1740–1918*. London: Hodder Arnold, 2006.

Balmer, Randall. *Mine Eyes Have Seen the Glory: A Journey into the Evangelical Subculture in America*. New York: Oxford University Press, 2000.

Barry, John M. *The Great Influenza: The Epic Story of the Deadliest Plague in History*. New York: Penguin Books, 2005.

Berger, Peter L. *The Desecularization of the World: Resurgent Religion and World Politics*. Grand Rapids, MI: Eerdmans, 1999.

Boles, John B. *The Great Revival: Beginnings of the Bible Belt*. Lexington, KY: University Press of Kentucky, 1996.

Brooke, John Hedley. *Science and Religion: Some Historical Perspectives*. Cambridge: Cambridge University Press, 1991.

Bruce, Steve. *God Is Dead: Secularization in the West*. Oxford: Blackwell, 2002.

Carpenter, Joel. *Revive Us Again: The Reawakenings of American Fundamentalism*. New York: Oxford University Press, 1997.

Chesnut, J. Andrew. *Competitive Spirits: Latin America's New Religious Economy*. New York: Oxford University Press, 2003.

Coleman, Simon. *The Globalization of Charismatic Christianity: Spreading the Gospel of Prosperity*. Cambridge: Cambridge University Press, 2000.

Davis, Nathaniel. *A Long Walk to Church: A Contemporary History of Russian Orthodoxy*. Boulder, CO: Westview Press, 2003.

Dickinson, Anna. "Quantifying Religious Oppression: Russian Orthodox Church Closures and Repression of Priests 1917–41." *Religion, State & Society* 28 (2000): 327–35.

Dolan, Jay P. *In Search of an American Catholicism: A History of Religion and Culture in Tension*. Oxford: Oxford University Press, 2004.

Ellingson, Stephen. *The Megachurch and the Mainline: Remaking Religious Tradition in the Twenty-First Century*. Chicago: University of Chicago Press, 2007.

Ericksen, Robert P. *Theologians under Hitler: Gerhard Kittel, Paul Althaus, and Emanuel Hirsch*. New Haven, CT: Yale University Press, 1985.

Frey, Sylvia R., and Betty Wood. *Come Shouting to Zion: African American Protestantism in the American South and the British Caribbean to 1830*. Chapel Hill: University of North Carolina Press, 1998.

Friesen, J. Stanley. *Missionary Responses to Tribal Religions at Edinburgh, 1910*. New York: Peter Lang, 1996.

Froese, Paul. "Forced Secularization in Soviet Russia: Why an Atheistic Monopoly Failed." *Journal for the Scientific Study of Religion* 43 (2004): 35–50.

Frykenberg, Robert Eric. *Christianity in India: From Beginnings to the Present*. New York: Oxford University Press, 2010.

González, Justo L., and Ondina E. González. *Christianity in Latin America: A History*. Cambridge: Cambridge University Press, 2008.

Greeley, Andrew M. *The Catholic Revolution: New Wine, Old Wineskins, and the Second Vatican Council*. Berkeley: University of California Press, 2004.

Hart, Darryl G. *Defending the Faith: J. Gresham Machen and the Crisis of Conservative Protestantism in Modern America*. Baltimore, MD: John Hopkins University Press, 1994.

Harvey, Paul. *Redeeming the South: Religious Cultures and Racial Identities among Southern Baptists, 1865–1925*. Chapel Hill: University of North Carolina Press, 1997.

Hassan, Sana. *Christians Versus Muslims in Modern Egypt: The Century-Long Struggle for Coptic Equality*. Oxford: Oxford University Press, 2003.

Heyrman, Christine Leigh. *Southern Cross: The Beginnings of the Bible Belt*. Chapel Hill: University of North Carolina Press, 1997.

Hollenweger, Walter J. *Pentecostalism: Origins and Developments Worldwide*. Peabody, MA: Hendrickson Publishers, 1997.

Hudson, D. Dennis. *Protestant Origins in India: Tamil Evangelical Christians, 1706–1835*. Grand Rapids, MI: Eerdmans, 2000.

Isichei, Elizabeth. *A History of Christianity in Africa from Antiquity to the Present*. London: SPCK, 1995.

Jenkins, Philip. *The Next Christendom: The Coming of Global Christianity*. New York: Oxford University Press, 2002.

Johnson, Curtis D. *Islands of Holiness: Rural Religion in Upstate New York, 1790–1860*. Ithaca, NY: Cornell University Press, 1989.

Kaggwa, Robert. *Christianity in Africa*. Oxford: Wiley-Blackwell, 2011.

Kennedy, Paul. *The Rise and Fall of the Great Powers*. New York: Random House, 1988.

Knox, Zoe Katrina. *Russian Society and the Orthodox Church: Religion in Russia after Communism*. London: Routledge, 2005.

Lande, Aasulv. *Meiji Protestantism in History and Historiography: A Comparative Study of Japanese and Western Interpretation of Early Protestantism in Japan*. Frankfurt am Main: Peter Lang, 1989.

Lee, Joseph Tse-Hei. *The Bible and the Gun: Christianity in South China, 1860–1900*. New York: Routledge, 2003.

Lincoln, C. Eric, and Lawrence H. Mamiya. *The Black Church in the African-American Experience*. Durham, NC: Duke University Press, 1990.

Linden, Ian. *Global Catholicism: Diversity and Change since Vatican II*. New York: Columbia University Press, 2009.

Long, Michael G. *Billy Graham and the Beloved Community: America's Evangelist and the Dream of Martin Luther King, Jr*. New York: Palgrave Macmillan, 2006.

Longfield, Bradley J. *The Presbyterian Controversy: Fundamentalists, Modernists, and Moderates*. New York: Oxford University Press, 1993.

MacLean, Iain S. *Opting for Democracy?: Liberation Theology and the Struggle for Democracy in Brazil*. New York: Peter Lang, 1999.

Martin, David. *Tongues of Fire: The Explosion of Protestantism in Latin America*. Oxford: Blackwell, 1990.

McLeod, Hugh. *The Religious Crisis of the 1960s*. Oxford: Oxford University Press, 2007.

McLeod, Hugh, and Werner Ustorf, eds. *The Decline of Christendom in Western Europe, 1750–2000*. Cambridge: Cambridge University Press, 2004.

Miller, Donald E. *Reinventing American Protestantism: Christianity in the New Millennium*. Berkeley: University of California Press, 1997.

Moffett, Samuel H. *A History of Christianity in Asia*. 2 vols. Maryknoll, NY: Orbis Books, 1998.

Noll, Mark A. *The Old Religion in a New World: The History of North American Christianity*. Grand Rapids, MI: Eerdmans, 2002.

O'Malley, John W. *What Happened at Vatican II*. Cambridge, MA: Harvard University Press, 2008.

Payne, Stanley G. *Franco and Hitler: Spain, Germany, and World War II*. New Haven, CT: Yale University Press, 2008.

Pecora, Vincent P. *Secularization and Cultural Criticism: Religion, Nation, & Modernity*. Chicago: University of Chicago Press, 2006.

Peris, Daniel. *Storming the Heavens: The Soviet League of the Militant Godless*. Ithaca, NY: Cornell University Press, 1998.

Phan, Peter C., ed. *Christianities in Asia*. Oxford: Wiley-Blackwell, 2011.

Porter, Andrew N. *Religion Versus Empire? British Protestant Missionaries and Overseas Expansion, 1700–1914*. Manchester: Manchester University Press, 2004.

Reinders, Eric. *Borrowed Gods and Foreign Bodies: Christian Missionaries Imagine Chinese Religion*. Berkeley: University of California Press, 2004.

Roslof, Edward E. *Red Priests: Renovationism, Russian Orthodoxy, and Revolution, 1905–1946*. Bloomington: Indiana University Press, 2002.

Ruokanen, Miikka, and Paulos Huang, eds. *Christianity and Chinese Culture*. Grand Rapids, MI: Eerdmans, 2010.

Sanneh, Lamin O., and Joel A. Carpenter. *The Changing Face of Christianity: Africa, the West, and the World*. New York: Oxford University Press, 2005.

Snape, Michael F. *God and the British Soldier: Religion and the British Army in the First and Second World Wars*. New York: Routledge, 2005.

Stanley, Brian, ed. *Missions, Nationalism, and the End of Empire*. Grand Rapids, MI: Eerdmans, 2003.

Stoll, David. *Is Latin America Turning Protestant? The Politics of Evangelical Growth*. Berkeley: University of California Press, 1990.

Taylor, Charles. *A Secular Age*. Cambridge, MA: Harvard University Press, 2007.

Tusell, Javier. *Spain: From Dictatorship to Democracy. 1939 to the Present*. Oxford: Blackwell, 2007.

Wheeler, Michael. *The Old Enemies: Catholic and Protestant in Nineteenth-Century English Culture*. Cambridge: Cambridge University Press, 2006.

Xi, Lian. *Redeemed by Fire: The Rise of Popular Christianity in Modern China*. New Haven, CT: Yale University, 2010.

Where Next?

This short textbook has introduced you to some of the leading events, developments, and themes of Christian history. It has offered you a series of snapshots, short and snappy accounts of things that really deserve whole chapters or books in their own right. It is a sketch map of a vast landscape, which needs to be explored in much greater detail. Sadly, much that is of interest and importance has had to be omitted, due to pressures of space. So see this book as mapping the landscape, and helping you to begin a more thorough exploration of its details.

So where do you go next? It is hoped that the suggestions that follow may be helpful in giving you an idea of how you can take your studies further.

1. Explore the territory in more detail. If this little book is a sketch map, see it as preparing the way for a much more detailed map. By the time you've read this book, many of the features of the landscape of Christian history will be familiar to you. There are more detailed accounts of the overall development of this history that will fill in much more detail, building on the solid foundations laid by this introduction. The suggestions made in the sections "For Further Reading" at the end of each chapter will give you an idea of which books might help you go further in this way.

2. Examine an historical period in more detail. Many people find themselves drawn to a specific period in the history of Christianity – sometimes because it is simply so interesting, or because it seems to be relevant to issues under discussion today. Some examples of periods that many find particularly interesting include Christianity in England during the Tudor period, the Great Awakening in New England in the eighteenth century, and the formation of modern Europe following the Napoleonic wars. All of these are dealt with in this volume; all will prove richly rewarding for those

Christian History: An Introduction, First Edition. Alister E. McGrath.
© 2013 John Wiley & Sons, Ltd. Published 2013 by John Wiley & Sons, Ltd.

wanting to study them in more detail. Once more, the suggestions made in the "For Further Reading" sections will give you an idea of which books might help you in your studies.

3. Focus on a specific historical individual. Even a cursory reading of the history of Christianity makes clear that certain individuals stand out as being of considerable interest and importance. Obvious examples would include Augustine of Hippo, Martin Luther, John Calvin, Jonathan Edwards, C. S. Lewis, and Pope John Paul II. Many people find biographies compelling reading, partly because they mingle historical analysis with the exploration of a personal narrative.

4. Consider a specific aspect of Christian theology that you consider to be of particular importance, and explore its development over time, and how it affects the lives of individuals and the churches. There are plenty of themes for you to explore: Christology (how Christians have tried to make sense of the identity and significance of Jesus of Nazareth), ecclesiology (the doctrine of the church), the doctrine of justification, and the doctrine of the Trinity all repay study.

But wherever you decide to take your studies next, I hope that you will have found this introduction useful, and wish you well in whatever lies ahead.

A Glossary of Christian Terms

What follows is a brief discussion of a series of technical terms relating to the history of Christianity that you are likely to encounter in the course of reading. The following work is particularly recommended to those wishing to gain more detailed understanding of Christian terms:

Elizabeth A. Livingstone and F. L. Cross. *The Oxford Dictionary of the Christian Church*. 3rd edn. Oxford: Oxford University Press, 1997.

Adoptionism
The heretical view that Jesus was "adopted" as the Son of God at some point during his ministry (usually his baptism), as opposed to the orthodox teaching that Jesus was Son of God by nature from the moment of his conception.

Alexandrian School
An early Christian school of thought, especially associated with the city of Alexandria in Egypt, noted for its Christology (which placed emphasis upon the divinity of Christ) and its method of biblical interpretation (which employed allegorical methods of exegesis). A rival approach in both areas was associated with Antioch.

Anabaptism
A term derived from the Greek word for "re-baptizer," and used to refer to the radical wing of the sixteenth-century Reformation, based on thinkers such as Menno Simons or Balthasar Hubmaier.

Christian History: An Introduction, First Edition. Alister E. McGrath.
© 2013 John Wiley & Sons, Ltd. Published 2013 by John Wiley & Sons, Ltd.

Anthropomorphism
The tendency to ascribe human features (such as hands or arms) or other human characteristics to God.

Antiochene School
An early Christian school of thought, especially associated with the city of Antioch in modern-day Turkey, noted for its Christology (which placed emphasis upon the humanity of Christ) and its method of biblical interpretation (which employed literal methods of exegesis). A rival approach in both areas was associated with Alexandria.

Anti-Pelagian writings
The writings of Augustine relating to the Pelagian controversy, in which he defended his views on grace and justification. See "Pelagianism."

Apocalyptic
A type of writing or religious outlook in general which focuses on the last things and the end of the world, often taking the form of visions with complex symbolism. The book of Daniel (Old Testament) and Revelation (New Testament) are examples of this type of writing.

Apologetics
The area of Christian theology which focuses on the defense of the Christian faith, particularly through the rational justification of Christian belief and doctrines.

Apostolic era
The period of the Christian church, regarded as definitive by many, bounded by the resurrection of Jesus Christ (c. AD 35) and the death of the last apostle (c. AD 90?). The ideas and practices of this period were widely regarded as normative, at least in some sense or to some degree, in many church circles.

Arianism
A major early Christological heresy, which treated Jesus Christ as the supreme of God's creatures, and denied his divine status. The Arian controversy was of major importance in the development of Christology during the fourth century.

Atonement
An English term originally coined by William Tyndale to translate the Latin term *reconciliatio*, which has since come to have the developed meaning of "the work of Christ" or "the benefits of Christ gained for believers by his death and resurrection."

Bishop
The senior Christian pastor within a given geographical area, traditionally known as a "diocese." The term derives from the Greek word *episkopos* ("supervisor" or "one having oversight"), and refers to the bishop's duty of care to clergy and people in that region.

Calvinism

An ambiguous term, used with two quite distinct meanings. First, it refers to the religious ideas of religious bodies (such as the Reformed church) and individuals (such as Theodore Beza) who were profoundly influenced by John Calvin, or by documents written by him. Second, it refers to the religious ideas of John Calvin himself. Although the first sense is by far the more common, there is a growing recognition that the term is misleading.

Cappadocian Fathers

A term used to refer collectively to three major Greek-speaking writers of the early Christian period: Basil of Caesarea, Gregory of Nazianzen, and Gregory of Nyssa, all of whom date from the late fourth century. "Cappadocia" designates an area in Asia Minor (modern-day Turkey), in which these writers were based.

Catechism

A popular manual of Christian doctrine, usually in the form of question and answer, intended for religious instruction.

Catholic

An adjective which is used both to refer to the universality of the church in space and time, and also to a particular church body (sometime also known as the Roman Catholic church) which lays emphasis upon this point.

Chalcedonian definition

The formal declaration at the Council of Chalcedon that Jesus Christ was to be regarded as having two natures, one human and one divine.

Charisma, charismatic

A set of terms especially associated with the gifts of the Holy Spirit. In medieval theology, the term "charisma" is used to designate a spiritual gift, conferred upon individuals by the grace of God. Since the early twentieth century, the term "charismatic" has come to refer to styles of theology and worship which place particular emphasis upon the immediate presence and experience of the Holy Spirit.

Christology

The section of Christian theology dealing with the identity of Jesus Christ, particularly the question of the relation of his human and divine natures.

Conciliarism

An understanding of ecclesiastical or theological authority which places an emphasis on the role of ecumenical councils, rather than the absolute authority of the Pope.

Confession

Although the term refers primarily to the admission of sin, it acquired a rather different technical sense in the sixteenth century – that of a document which embodies the principles of faith of a Protestant church, such as the Lutheran Augsburg Confession (1530) embodies the ideas of early Lutheranism, and the Reformed First Helvetic Confession (1536).

Consubstantial
A Latin term, deriving from the Greek term *homoousios*, literally meaning "of the same substance." The term is used to affirm the full divinity of Jesus Christ, particularly in opposition to Arianism.

Creed
A formal definition or summary of the Christian faith, held in common by all Christians. The most important are those generally known as the "Apostles' Creed" and the "Nicene Creed."

Deism
A term used to refer to the views of a group of English writers, especially during the seventeenth century, the rationalism of which anticipated many of the ideas of the Enlightenment. The term is often used to refer to a view of God which recognizes the divine creatorship, yet which rejects the notion of a continuing divine involvement with the world.

Dialectical Theology
A term used to refer to the early views of the Swiss theologian Karl Barth (1886–1968), which emphasized the "dialectic" between God and humanity.

Diocese
A term derived from the Greek word *diokēsis* ("a province"), referring to the geographical district under the supervision of a bishop, normally divided into smaller units known as "parishes." The term "see" (from the Latin: *episcopalis sedes*, "the seat of the bishop") is sometimes used as an alternative term for "diocese."

Docetism
An early Christological heresy, deriving from the Greek verb *dokein* ("to appear") which treated Jesus Christ as a purely divine being who only had the "appearance" of being human.

Donatism
A movement, centering upon Roman North Africa in the fourth century, which developed a rigorist view of the church and sacraments.

Ebionitism
An early Christological heresy, which treated Jesus Christ as a purely human figure, although recognizing that he was endowed with particular charismatic gifts which distinguished him from other humans.

Ecclesiology
The section of Christian theology dealing with the theory of the church (Greek: *ekklēsia*).

Enlightenment, The
A term used since the nineteenth century to refer to the emphasis upon human reason and autonomy, characteristic of much of western European and North American thought during the eighteenth century.

Eschatology
The section of Christian theology dealing with the "final things" (Greek: *ta eschata*), especially the ideas of resurrection, hell, and eternal life.

Eucharist
The term used in the present volume to refer to the sacrament variously known as "the mass," "the Lord's Supper," and "holy communion."

Evangelical
A term initially used to refer to reforming movements, especially in Germany and Switzerland, in the 1510s and 1520s, but now used of the movement, especially in recent English-language Christianity, which places especial emphasis upon the supreme authority of Scripture and the atoning death of Christ.

Exegesis
The science of textual interpretation, usually referring specifically to the Bible. The term "biblical exegesis" basically means "the process of interpreting the Bible." The specific techniques employed in the exegesis of Scripture are usually referred to as "hermeneutics."

Exemplarism
A particular approach to understanding the significance of the death of Christ, which stresses the moral or religious example set to believers by Jesus Christ.

Fathers
An alternative way of referring to the "patristic writers" of the early church.

Feminism
A movement in western culture since the 1960s, which lays particular emphasis upon the importance of women's experience, and has directed criticism against the patriarchalism of Christianity.

Five Ways, The
A standard term for the five arguments for the existence of God associated with Thomas Aquinas.

Fourth Gospel
A term used to refer to the Gospel according to John. The term highlights the distinctive literary and theological character of this gospel, which sets it apart from the common structures of the first three gospels, usually known as the "Synoptic Gospels."

Fundamentalism

A form of American Protestant Christianity, which lays especial emphasis upon the authority of an inerrant Bible. Protestant Fundamentalism originated in the 1920s, and is best seen as a reaction against a drift towards a more secular American culture.

Hermeneutics

The principles underlying the interpretation, or exegesis, of a text, particularly of Scripture, especially in relation to its present-day application.

Hesychasm

A tradition, especially associated with the eastern church, which places considerable emphasis upon the idea of "inner quietness" (Greek: *hesychia*) as a means of achieving a vision of God. It is particularly associated with writers such as Simeon the New Theologian and Gregory Palamas.

Historical Jesus

A term used, especially during the nineteenth century, to refer to the historical person of Jesus of Nazareth, as opposed to the Christian interpretation of that person, especially as presented in the New Testament and the creeds.

Homoousion

A Greek term, literally meaning "of the same substance," which came to be used extensively during the fourth century to designate the mainline Christological belief that Jesus Christ was "of the same substance of God." The term was polemical, being directed against the Arian view that Christ was "of similar substance (*homoiousios*)" to God.

Humanism

In the strict sense of the word, an intellectual movement linked with the European Renaissance. At the heart of the movement lay, not (as the modern sense of the word might suggest) a set of secular or secularizing ideas, but a new interest in the cultural achievements of antiquity. These were seen as a major resource for the renewal of European culture and Christianity during the period of the Renaissance.

Incarnation

A term used to refer to the assumption of human nature by God, in the person of Jesus Christ.

Justification by faith, doctrine of

The section of Christian theology dealing with how the individual sinner is able to enter into fellowship with God. The doctrine was to prove to be of major significance at the time of the Reformation.

Liberal Protestantism

A movement, especially associated with nineteenth-century Germany, which stressed the continuity between religion and culture, flourishing between the time of F. D. E. Schleiermacher and Paul Tillich.

Liberation Theology

Although this term designates any theological movement laying emphasis upon the liberating impact of the gospel, the term has come to refer to a movement which developed in Latin America in the late 1960s, which stressed the role of political action and orientated itself towards the goal of political liberation from poverty and oppression.

Liturgy

The written text of public services, especially of the eucharist.

Logos

A Greek term meaning "word," which played a crucial role in the development of the Christology of the early church. Jesus Christ was recognized as the "word of God"; the question concerned the implications of this recognition, and especially the way in which the divine "logos" in Jesus Christ related to his human nature.

Lutheranism

The religious ideas associated with Martin Luther, particularly as expressed in the Lesser Catechism (1529) and the Augsburg Confession (1530).

Manicheism

A strongly fatalist position associated with the Manichees, to which Augustine of Hippo attached himself during his early period. A distinction is drawn between two different divinities, one of which is regarded as evil, and the other good. Evil is thus seen as the direct result of the influence of the evil god.

Modalism

A Trinitarian heresy, which treats the three persons of the Trinity as different "modes" of the Godhead. A typical modalist approach is to regard God as active as Father in creation, as Son in redemption, and as Spirit in sanctification.

Modernism

A movement that developed in the nineteenth century, particularly within the Catholic church, arguing for an accommodation of basic Christian ideas and modern thought, particularly biblical criticism, evolutionary theory, and a scientific understanding of nature.

Monophysitism

The doctrine that there is only one nature in Christ, which is divine (from the Greek words *monos*, "only one," and *physis*, "nature"). This view differed from the orthodox view, upheld by the Council of Chalcedon (451), that Christ had two natures, one divine and one human.

Neo-Orthodoxy

A term used to designate the general position of Karl Barth (1886–1968), especially the manner in which he drew upon the theological concerns of the period of Reformed Orthodoxy.

Ontological argument
A term used to refer to the type of argument for the existence of God especially associated with the scholastic theologian Anselm of Canterbury.

Orthodoxy
A term used in a number of senses, of which the following are the most important: Orthodoxy in the sense of "right belief," as opposed to heresy; Orthodoxy in the sense of the forms of Christianity which are dominant in Russia and Greece; Orthodoxy in the sense of a movement within Protestantism, especially in the late sixteenth and early seventeenth century, which laid emphasis upon need for doctrinal definition.

Patristic
An adjective used by some scholars to refer to the first centuries in the history of the church, following the writing of the New Testament (the "patristic period"), or thinkers writing during this period (the "patristic writers"). For many writers, the period thus designated seems to be c. 100–451 (in other words, the period between the completion of the last of the New Testament writings and the landmark Council of Chalcedon). The adjective "early Christian" is now widely used in preference to this older term.

Pelagianism
An understanding of how humans are able to merit their salvation which is diametrically opposed to that of Augustine of Hippo, placing considerable emphasis upon the role of human works and playing down the idea of divine grace.

Pietism
An approach to Christianity, especially associated with German writers in the seventeenth century, which places an emphasis upon the personal appropriation of faith, and the need for holiness in Christian living. The movement is perhaps best known within English-language world in the form of Methodism.

Postmodernism
A general cultural development, especially in North America, which resulted from the general collapse in confidence of the universal rational principles of the Enlightenment.

Praxis
A Greek term, literally meaning "action," adopted by Karl Marx to emphasize the importance of action in relation to thinking. This emphasis on Christian faith as "praxis" has had considerable impact within Latin American liberation theology.

Protestantism
A term used in the aftermath of the Diet of Speyer (1529) to designate those who "protested" against the practices and beliefs of the Roman Catholic church. Prior to 1529, such individuals and groups had referred to themselves as "evangelicals."

Quadriga
The Latin term used to refer to the "four-fold" interpretation of Scripture according to its literal, allegorical, tropological or moral, and anagogical senses.

Radical Reformation
A term used with increasing frequency to refer to the Anabaptist movement – in other words, the wing of the Reformation which went beyond what Luther and Zwingli envisaged, particularly in relation to the doctrine of the church.

Real Presence
A term used to refer to the belief that Jesus of Nazareth is present in the bread and wine of the eucharist. Christian theologians have interpreted the nature of this presence in different ways down the ages.

Reformed
A term used to refer to a tradition of theology which draws inspiration from the writings of John Calvin (1510–64) and his successors. The term is now generally used in preference to "Calvinist."

Sabellianism
An early trinitarian heresy, which treated the three persons of the Trinity as different historical manifestations of the one God. It is generally regarded as a form of modalism.

Sacrament
A church service or rite which was held to have been instituted by Jesus Christ himself. Although Roman Catholic theology and church practice recognize seven such sacraments (baptism, confirmation, eucharist, marriage, ordination, penance, and unction), Protestant theologians generally argue that only two (baptism and eucharist) were to be found in the New Testament itself.

Schism
A deliberate break with the unity of the church, condemned vigorously by influential writers of the early church, such as Cyprian and Augustine.

Scholasticism
A particular approach to Christian theology, associated especially with the Middle Ages, which lays emphasis upon the rational justification and systematic presentation of Christian theology.

Scripture Principle
The theory, especially associated with early Protestant theologians, that the practices and beliefs of the church should be grounded in Scripture, rather than customs inherited from the past. Nothing that could not be demonstrated to be grounded in Scripture could be

regarded as binding upon the believer. The phrase *sola scriptura*, "by Scripture alone," was often used to summarize this principle.

Soteriology
The section of Christian theology dealing with the doctrine of salvation (Greek: *sotēria*).

Synoptic Gospels
A term used to refer to the first three gospels (Matthew, Mark, and Luke). The term (derived from the Greek word *synopsis*, "summary") refers to the way in which the three gospels can be seen as providing similar "summaries" of the life, death, and resurrection of Jesus Christ.

Theodicy
A term coined by the German philosopher G. W. Leibnitz to refer to a theoretical justification of the goodness of God in the face of the presence of evil in the world.

Theotokos
Literally, "the bearer of God." A Greek term used to refer to Mary, the mother of Jesus Christ, with the intention of reinforcing the central insight of the doctrine of the incarnation – that is, that Jesus Christ is none other than God. The term was extensively used by writers of the eastern church, especially around the time of the Nestorian controversy, to articulate both the divinity of Christ and the reality of the incarnation.

Transubstantiation
The doctrine according to which the bread and the wine are transformed into the body and blood of Christ in the eucharist, while retaining their outward appearance.

Trinity
The distinctively Christian doctrine of God, which reflects the complexity of the Christian experience of God. The doctrine is usually summarized in maxims such as "three persons, one God."

Two Natures, doctrine of
A term generally used to refer to the doctrine of the two natures, human and divine, of Jesus Christ. Related terms include "Chalcedonian definition" and "hypostatic union."

Vulgate
The Latin translation of the Bible, largely deriving from Jerome, upon which medieval theology was largely based.

Zwinglianism
The term is used generally to refer to the thought of Huldrych Zwingli, but is often used to refer specifically to his views on the sacraments, especially on the "real presence" (which for Zwingli was more of a "real absence").

Index

Christian History: An Introduction, First Edition. Alister E. McGrath.
© 2013 John Wiley & Sons, Ltd. Published 2013 by John Wiley & Sons, Ltd.